W9-BJZ-552

Being Religious, American Style

BEING RELIGIOUS, AMERICAN STYLE

A History of Popular Religiosity in the United States

Charles H. Lippy

WITHDRAWN

THEODORE LOWNIK LIBRARY
BENEDICTINE UNIVERSITY
5700 COLLEGE ROAD
LISLE, IL 60532-0900

PRAEGER

Westport, Connecticut
London

200,973
L766b

The Library of Congress has cataloged the hardcover edition as follows:

Lippy, Charles H.
    Being religious, American style : a history of popular religiosity
in the United States / Charles H. Lippy.
        p.   cm.—(Contributions to the study of religion, ISSN
0196–7053 ; no. 37)
    Includes bibliographical references and index.
    ISBN 0–313–27895–4 (hc : alk. paper)
    1. United States—Religious life and customs—History. I. Title.
II. Series.
    BL2525.L56   1994
    200'.973—dc20   93–50545

British Library Cataloguing in Publication Data is available.

Copyright © 1994 by Charles H. Lippy

All rights reserved. No portion of this book may be
reproduced, by any process or technique, without the
express written consent of the publisher.

A hardcover edition of *Being Religious, American Style* is available from Greenwood Press,
an imprint of Greenwood Publishing Group, Inc. (Contributions to the Study of Religion,
number 37; ISBN 0–313–27895–4).

Library of Congress Catalog Card Number: 93–50545
ISBN: 0–275–94901–X (pbk.)

First published in 1994

Praeger Publishers, 88 Post Road West, Westport, CT 06881
An imprint of Greenwood Publishing Group, Inc.

Printed in the United States of America

The paper used in this book complies with the
Permanent Paper Standard issued by the National
Information Standards Organization (Z39.48–1984).

10 9 8 7 6 5 4 3 2 1

Contents

Preface

"We talked about everything that usually gets left out of courses in religious history." That comment came from a student enrolled in a graduate course on American popular religion that I had the privilege of teaching at Emory University in the spring of 1991. At the time I was on leave from Clemson University and carried a part-time appointment as visiting professor at Emory while doing the preliminary research for this book. The opportunity to engage in ongoing research with a group of graduate students who were likewise pursuing an interest in American popular religion sharpened my own thinking in ways too numerous to count.

The comment from that one student during our final seminar meeting has haunted me, for it reveals a great deal about the traditional approaches to telling the story of religion in American culture and also what drew me more and more into looking at what "usually gets left out." Over a decade ago, for four years the American Academy of Religion included a working group on American popular religion. Participation in that group first drew me into thinking about the dynamic of religion in the United States and how the usual way of examining works of great thinkers, scrutinizing identifiable movements and religious groups, and consigning the rest to the periphery always seemed to leave out ordinary men and women. While I wrote a few brief articles treating popular religion topics as a result, I did not then envision this book.

During this period, Peter Williams, my good friend and collaborator on the *Encyclopedia of the American Religious Experience*, published his *Popular Religion in America*, a book I have used frequently as a supplementary text in undergraduate courses. Williams focused primarily on popular extraecclesiastical movements that he saw arising in part as a symbolic response to social change resulting from modernization. This book is invaluable for anyone who would understand popular religion, although its focus differs from that of this study. Williams concentrates on movements that frequently, but not always, took on institutional form, whereas I look more at the ways ordinary folk go about the business of making sense of the world, regardless of connections to movements or institutions. Nevertheless, Williams' work spurred my own thinking in new directions. Then came the opportunity to prepare and edit for Greenwood Press a reference work on figures who have helped shape American popular religion in the twentieth century. The major challenge of that book was working with other scholars to select figures for inclusion. In the end I was struck more by the number omitted than by those included. More and more I became convinced that there was a need to take a deeper look at the ways ordinary folk in the history of the United States went about the business of being religious, of creating and sustaining personal religious beliefs, values, and practices.

At the same time, my teaching responsibilities were often taking me far afield from American religion. Yet the demands of teaching courses in the religions of Asia and other world religions in their own way continued to challenge the ways I thought about religion in the United States. Scholars who were specialists in non-Western religions, for example, much more readily acknowledged and appreciated the vibrancy of the religious life of ordinary folk as it existed alongside of but in tandem with formal religious traditions. There was a religiosity of the people, a popular religion if you will, that had its own story apart from the story of any established religious tradition or institution. In the summer of 1988, while participating in a Fulbright program in India, I gained fresh insight into what my colleagues in non-Western religions had long known about the religiosity of ordinary women and men and how that personal religiosity was related to and yet distinguished from the more formal religion advanced by traditions, institutions, and religious professionals. In retrospect I spent as much time rethinking my own understanding of the dynamics of American religion as I did pondering things Hindu while I was in India.

All of these forces propelled me to embark on an extended inquiry into popular religiosity in American culture. Yet when I began my reading, I quickly realized that there was no consensus among scholars about defining precisely what popular religion or popular religiosity encompassed. Therefore, the opening chapter of this book wrestles with matters of definition and description. Then I began to look from a historical perspective more closely at "everything that usually gets left out" of analyses of religion in the United States to try to understand the religiosity of Americans over the centuries. The more I read, the more inspiration I received from a statement of Mark Twain: "The gospel of Christ came filtered down to nineteenth-century Americans through stage plays and through the despised novel and

Christmas story, rather than from the drowsy pulpit."[1] There will not be much from the drowsy pulpit in the pages that follow, for I have little to do with religious institutions, traditions, or professionals such as preachers. Constantly before us will be ordinary men and women and the ways they go about making sense of the world they live in and giving meaning to their personal experience. That "making sense" and "giving meaning" I regard as the primary tasks of religion.

As my work progressed, the sources crying out for scrutiny became overwhelming, and it became necessary to place some limits on what would be included. I have chosen to limit my analysis to the area that now encompasses the United States, although I recognize the value in extending the inquiry to include other areas of North America. It is my intent, however, not to look only at the religiosity of male Euro-Americans, the base of many traditional interpretations of American religion. Rather, I have endeavored especially to include consideration of sources and ideas that reveal the dynamics of personal religiosity among women, African Americans, Native American Indians, and certain ethnic communities.

Along the way I benefited greatly from the studies of others. Throughout, the earlier work of Peter Williams looms in the background. For the colonial period, I am especially indebted to the writings of Jon Butler and David D. Hall. Nathan O. Hatch in several written works has called attention to the increasing importance of laity and the growing emphasis on private experience in the early national period. I trust that my intellectual debt to them and to many others is obvious in the attributions to their work in the notes, although the approach and interpretation taken here are my own.

I wish to express appreciation especially to Paul Courtright of the Department of Religion of Emory University who arranged for my visiting appointment there and also to Dana White of Emory's Institute for the Liberal Arts. Both were instrumental in organizing a faculty discussion group on American religion during the 1990–91 academic year and in making it possible for me to offer the graduate seminar on American popular religion. Every member of the seminar spurred me to think in new ways. I am most appreciative of their support, encouragement, and questions. I am grateful as well to Clemson University for sabbatical leave during 1990–91 so I could pursue the bulk of research for this study. In addition, I have learned much from extended conversations with colleagues. In addition to those mentioned, Patrick Allitt and E. Brooks Holifield of Emory University and Terry Todd of Columbia University have contributed immensely to helping me refine my thinking. Roger Rollin, my colleague at Clemson and a former president of both the American Culture Association and the Popular Culture Association in the South, graciously read the entire manuscript in draft form and offered many helpful suggestions for improving the final product. While this book was in progress, I began another editorial project, this one dealing with popular religious periodicals of the United States. My coeditor, Mark Fackler of Wheaton College, has proved a valued associate. Finally, I appreciate the support of Marilyn Brownstein, George Butler, and Peter Coveney of Greenwood Press, all of whose editorial counsel has been most helpful.

NOTE

1. Quoted in R. Laurence Moore, "Religion, Secularization, and the Shaping of the Culture Industry in Antebellum America," *American Quarterly* 41 (June 1989): 216.

3, 9-11, 18

Chapter 1

What Is Popular Religion?

Popular religion, folk religion, unofficial religion, invisible religion, common religion, religious populism—all of these terms point to a dimension of religious life that is elusive and difficult to describe. They suggest an aspect of being religious that is distinguished from formal religious belief systems and institutions, but still represents a vital part of being religious. Just what is this dimension and why is it so hard to define precisely? These questions provide the focus for the first part of this chapter.

A second concern centers on why students of Western religion have only recently become intrigued with this phenomenon. The first full-length study of one aspect of American popular religion is Louis Schneider and Sanford Dornbusch's *Popular Religion: Inspirational Books in America*, published in 1958.[1] Prior to that study, there is scant mention of popular religion in studies of religion in the United States or elsewhere in Western culture. Histories of Christianity, for example, discuss the development of Christian doctrine, growth of church structure, contributions of key individuals in shaping the tradition, and the like. But beyond description of Christian worship, one finds little appraisal of what ordinary Christians actually thought or did when they were being religious. The same holds true for other expressions of religion in Western culture. Why? And, by implication, why has the same not held true for examining religion in non-Western cultures?

While it is by no means the only answer, one response revolves around sources for the study of popular religion. Just where does one find materials to examine popular religion? How can one determine precisely what shapes the religious thinking of ordinary people? Is popular religion so individualistic that it is impossible to generalize about currents or trends, about modes of thinking, about ways of acting? That is, is popular religion so idiosyncratic that attempting to locate it is akin to the proverbial wild goose chase? These questions frame the third section of this chapter.

Let us assume for a moment that we can arrive at a working definition of popular religion, understand why relatively little attention has been paid to it until recently, and identify sources that will provide an entree into the popular religious mind. Other questions then remain. When did popular religion become a feature of American religious life? Is it something new? Have there been strains of popular religion present since the European invasions of the New World? Are there any unifying themes that might give coherence to this elusive phenomenon? To leap ahead in our discussion, we shall find that popular religion has been a constant in American religious life and that a cluster of motifs provides insight into its character and dynamism. Identifying such is the task of the final section of this chapter.

Students of "popular religion" are not of a single mind about what the phrase denotes. The word "popular" has as its base the Latin *populus*, meaning people. Hence popular religion, however defined, has to do with what ordinary people believe and practice and how they incorporate such into their own lives. Popular religion then is a part of what Philippe Ariès and others have called "private life," the basic daily life of common people and their efforts to carve a realm of meaning for themselves in ordinary existence.[2] To this extent popular religion suggests a differentiation between the religion of ordinary people and the religion of theologians, priests, and other religious professionals.[3] Simply put, the latter are primarily concerned with matters of right belief and practice, offering rational arguments to support them, providing guidance in their appropriation by the people at large, and transmitting them as part of a formal religious tradition to subsequent generations. Such matters may well not be part of the consciousness of ordinary people as they go about their daily routines or even as they are "being religious."

Schneider and Dornbusch, in the pioneering study already mentioned, see popular religion as a practical, technique-laden approach to being religious, one that emphasizes the function of religion in enabling ordinary people to deal with the problems they confront in daily life. It brings them inner happiness and emotional security. Popular religion for Schneider and Dornbusch is thus linked to sentiment or feeling more than to formal, reasoned doctrine and practice.[4] What emerges here is the sense that popular religion exists alongside formal religious belief and practice; it points to the ways in which individuals take religious belief, interpret it in practical terms, and put it to work to do something that will give order and meaning to their lives. Popular religion therefore is related to organized religion as we usually think of it, but not equated with it. A formal religious tradition provides a repository of beliefs from which individuals draw, but what particular beliefs make a difference in a person's life and how that person uses them remain an individual matter.

Peter Williams also highlights the links between popular religion and more formal religious traditions, seeing popular religion as having a peripheral relationship to organized religion. For Williams, popular religion is "extra-ecclesiastical symbolic activity . . . carried on outside the formal structures provided by most societies for such activity."[5] Williams connects popular religion with the vast social change resulting from the process of modernization. During times of social change, established ways of thinking and acting, entrenched ways of being religious, find their power to give coherence to life challenged by new social forces or new social conditions. In such situations, ordinary people reach out for alternative ways of making sense out of life.

Williams regards these alternatives as bearing a significant relation to organized religion and as movements involving groups of people, not just individuals per se. He identifies three characteristics of popular religious movements:

1. In terms of *social structure*, all these movements exist apart from or in tension with established religious groups with regular patterns of organization and leadership.

2. In terms of *sociology of knowledge*, the beliefs and lore of these movements are transmitted through channels other than the official seminaries or oral traditions of established religious communities, whether tribal or modernized.

3. In terms of *symbolism, expression*, and *behavior*, . . . [p]opular movements . . . generally look for signs of divine intervention of manifestation in the realm of everyday experience.[6]

One example must suffice. Williams suggests that popular religion manifests itself in practices such as erecting religious shrines in front yards or having religious processions on a particular saint's day that remain common in areas settled by Roman Catholic immigrants from Central and Eastern Europe in the later nineteenth century. They are practices of the people that supplement Roman Catholicism as a religious tradition, that are informally transmitted to successive generations by descendants of these immigrants rather than official structures of the church, and that initially served to ease the social dislocation felt by an immigrant people adjusting to a new cultural situation.

Others who highlight the connection between popular religion and the religion fostered by formal traditions see popular religion as a distortion of institutional religion rather than being in a symbiotic relationship with it. Luis Meldonado, for example, argues that the intuitive, imaginative, emotive, and theatrical character of much popular religious expression renders it an aberration of presumably "real" religion.[7] The seemingly marginal quality of popular religion has also received emphasis in the work of Jean Seguy.[8] This somewhat negative judgment, however, does not deny the power of popular religion. Indeed, Meldonado claims that popular religion reflects the need of ordinary people for more simple, more direct, and more practical access to the divine than the trappings of formal religion offers, a point to which we shall return.

The dimension of feeling and the concern to find ways to tap into spiritual power to meet immediate needs also mark Ernest Henau's understanding of popular religion.[9] But Henau claims that popular religion has a syncretistic character. That is, while popular religion may have direct connections to the belief system of a formal religious tradition, it may also blend such with beliefs and practices that come from other sources. Writing primarily about Christianity, Henau notes that this fusion may join non-Christian ("pagan") practices and habits with standard Christian doctrine in the way individuals construct private worlds of meaning.

Scholars have seriously debated the extent to which popular religion is a private matter and why. Sociologist Thomas Luckmann has argued that privatization of religion is a hallmark of the contemporary period.[10] Urbanization and industrialization are mainly responsible for this privatizing, according to Luckmann, since they created an increasingly diffuse and complex social order. As people are bombarded with a dazzling array of belief systems that all claim to endow human experience with meaning, they simply pick and choose from among them to create a viable, but intensely personal—if not idiosyncratic—meaning system that works for them. This highly personal focus renders religion "invisible," for how religion actually functions in the lives of real people cannot be confined to formal religious traditions or institutions.

Wade Clark Roof, another sociologist, has also noted the growing privatism of religious expression and a concomitant weakening of commitment to religious institutions.[11] Roof and his associate, William McKinney, set out to explain trends among mainline religious bodies in the United States such as the decrease in membership in mainline Christian groups and a corresponding increase in membership among groups once consigned to the periphery. But they are quick to note that the loss of one does not automatically mean a gain for the other. Rather, many who once maintained formal religious affiliation cease to do so, while others who had previously eschewed membership in a religious institution take on such commitment. Roof and McKinney suggest that this erosion in the old mainline represents a dropping out of organized religion that in turn signals the growing privatization of religion. It does not mean that people abandon religious belief, but that they develop personally tailored religious worldviews independent of religious institutions. As others have noted, such worldviews may be syncretistic, becoming more akin to what Luckmann called "invisible religion" as they are more and more consigned to the private sphere.

Is this invisible religion, this private religion, what is meant by popular religion? To the extent that it denotes how people actually make sense out of their human experience, how they find meaning in life, then invisible, private religion is surely akin to popular religion. Yet if religion is completely privatized, if all individuals have their own religion that is in no way shared with others, then religion has become so elusive, so invisible, so idiosyncratic that we cannot finally locate it in order to study what it is and how it works.

Other scholars see social class differentiation as basic to describing popular religion. Vittorio Lanternari insists that while popular religion and official or institutional religion are not popular opposites, each reflects different social strata within a culture.[12] Official religion tends to be the religion of an elite, of those who exercise effective power and therefore dominate a society. Thus Lanternari claims that the emergence of popular religion represents one way those in the lower social strata, those with little economic and political power, respond to the dominant classes. In other words, popular religion becomes a means of establishing a positive social identity for the oppressed. Paulo Suess has also emphasized the role of class in nurturing popular religion, particularly in societies in which monotheism has prevailed.[13] Monotheism, which undergirds much of Western religion, breeds a hierarchical social order according to Suess. Positing a single divine being as supreme over all has as its corollary a classist social structure in which the few exercise power over the many. Hence Suess sees a greater polarity between popular religion and official or institutional religion than does Lanternari.

But wedding popular religion to class structure requires limiting expressions of popular religion to identifiable movements. In turn such movements may develop structure, organization, and institutions of their own against those of the dominant social classes. From this vantage point, the privatization of religious expression could not result in popular religion since that process is independent of social class. Certainly there is a private sphere to the ordinary lives of those in the upper socioeconomic classes as well as among the lower socioeconomic classes. Also, as Max Weber, Ernst Troeltsch, and H. Richard Niebuhr have argued, religious movements that emerge initially among the lower socioeconomic classes often undergo a natural process of transformation as adherents gain in social standing or as groups endure over several generations.[14] That is, in time, movements of the underclasses may take on much of the character of movements formerly associated with the dominant classes. While there are notable exceptions to this "routinization," the gradual change makes it difficult to determine when these movements ceased being manifestations of popular religion.

Others have linked popular religion with folk culture or folk religion, with peasant cultures that are preliterate or less literate than complex societies. Anthropologist Robert Redfield has distinguished between the "great tradition" and the "little tradition" in peasant societies.[15] The "great tradition" encompasses the sacred texts long passed down among the elite through oral tradition and then in written form, the ministrations of a priestly class, and the like. In other words, the "great tradition" represents the more formal dimensions of religious life in preliterate cultures. But among the people there prevails a host of other stories and "texts," of rituals and activities, of ways of acting and ways of viewing the world that exist alongside this great tradition. Here among the common folk we find the locus of popular religion, again syncretistic and sometimes at odds with the orthodoxy perpetuated by the great tradition. More recently, Rosemary Radford Ruether finds the syncretism inherent in popular religion a product of less literate folk cultures. For example, she sees the renewed interest in the goddess among feminists in Western culture as a recovery of strains of popular religion that prevailed before patriarchy came to dominate Western religion.[16]

Those who designate popular religion as "folk religion" are especially drawn to its apparent roots in preliterate cultures. Gustav Mensching, for example, ties folk religion to a residue of magic from "primitive" cultures in which the ability to control or manipulate sacred power would lead to happiness, prosperity, and personal success for both individuals and societies.[17] Here folk or popular beliefs are common to a culture; there is not the sense of privatization that others have noted. Indeed Mensching believes there is a sameness to this universal or folk religion across cultures. Likewise, studies of the religiosity of Mexican Americans led Virgil Elizondo to emphasize that popular religion is that which is common to a people as a collective entity, not something private or individual.[18] For Elizondo, this commonality allows popular religion to provide a base for the collective identity of a people. So, too, Pieter Vrijhof argues that popular religion is a constant human phenomenon. It is religiosity in general that comes to the fore only because institutional differentiation in Western societies has made religion a discrete and separate component of culture.[19]

E. Wilbur Bock has also explored the connection between folk religion and official religion.[20] Bock argues that all societies both need and develop commonly held symbol systems. Some of these symbols come from the official or formal religious traditions in a culture; others come from a reservoir of folk beliefs. They mix together in such a way that individuals and subcommunities may draw on both to support commonly held values, but need not espouse the complete package of either to do so. Bock points to the way holiday celebrations in American culture demonstrate this mix. The celebration of Christmas, for example, draws on the myths surrounding Santa Claus, the exchanging of gifts, and the decoration of Christmas trees from the fund of folk belief and practice; it also draws on specifically Christian affirmation of the birth of Jesus. A similar process in the celebration of Easter combines the folk practice of coloring Easter eggs with the Christian belief in the resurrection of the Christ. What is important is that the process of mixing the folk and tradition-specific is common to human cultures.

Given this diverse understanding of what makes up popular religion, many reject the label as so vague as to be useless even as a descriptive category. Among these is Robert Towler, who prefers to speak of "common religion."[21] For him, "common religion may be described as those beliefs and practices of an overtly religious nature which are not under the domination of a prevailing religious institution."[22] Common religion, diffuse and unorganized, figures significantly in any society for Towler because official religion cannot provide all of what people want or need for giving meaning to what otherwise would remain perplexing. He sees this common religion as "a base-line of religiousness" that, although less conspicuous to observers than the religion nurtured by institutions, is a constant in human society.[23] What Towler labels common religion, however, differs little from what others mean by popular religion, the expression of a basic religiosity not capsuled neatly in the formal belief systems and sanctioned practices of a particular religious tradition.

More recently, sociologist Robert Wuthnow has written about "religious populism" in contemporary American culture.[24] Wuthnow is trying to account for the appeal alternative ways of being religious have for persons once part of mainstream formal religious traditions. He looks to the interplay of that cultural pluralism long prevalent in American culture and the emphasis on individual choice in matters of belief. The result is an ethos in which persons create value systems or belief systems that may reflect some mainstream values, but may also include alternative beliefs and values. Wuthnow recognizes that such religious populism has no need for internal consistency. Rather this popular religiosity is fluid, constantly changing as mass media flood the market with a barrage of new ideas. Yet this religious populism retains the same function that others give to popular religion, common religion, or folk religion: providing people with a way to make sense out of ordinary experience, to offer comfort and a secure identity in a world that seems to challenge meaningful existence.

It may well be easier to describe popular religion rather than define it because of the awkwardness in understanding just what "popular" denotes when applied to religion. But a larger problem may be understanding what "religion" denotes, for most of the discussion assumes that religion must reflect structured belief and an organized set of practices identified with a formal tradition or "official" religion. What constitutes religion are those doctrines and practices determined by religious professionals (theologians, philosophers, denominational officials, clergy) and the institutions they perpetuate (churches, synagogues, temples, synods, councils, and the like). In other words, a religious elite effectively determines what religion actually is.

Consequently what diverges from the systematic beliefs and practices sanctioned by religious authority becomes viewed as aberrant and in conflict with genuine religion. It represents a challenge to religion. Hence those who link popular religion to folk religion or who see popular religion as reflecting a residue from preliterate cultures frequently denigrate the legitimacy of what ordinary people actually believe and practice because they see belief and practice set by an elite as the norm. At the same time even those who eschew the designation of popular religion tacitly acknowledge its universality when they opt for alternative designations such as "common religion" or "unofficial religion." Although the content of this popular religion is not universally the same, in all societies there exists a perceivable difference between what religious authorities and sanctioned religious institutions promote and what ordinary people are actually thinking and doing.[25]

Sociologists have long recognized this dichotomy in debates over "functional" and "substantive" approaches to religion. Both approaches recognize that religion provides some sense of meaning in life, offering people a way to understand and interpret their experience as individuals and as part of a larger collectivity. Those preferring a substantive approach draw a narrow circle of what constitutes religion, insisting that authentic meaning derives from particular belief systems that relate to a power or force other than human (the supernatural, "God"). Advocates of a substantive understanding see such belief systems as both comprehensive and coherent, identified with a formal religious tradition and its institutions, and both guided and guarded by professionals like theologians and priests. Those who follow a substantive approach are concerned with "right" belief and "right" practice, with identifying and combatting wrong belief (heresy) and deviant behavior, with transmitting a pure tradition to succeeding generations.

Functionalists cast a wider net. They look at how ordinary people and even societies actually make sense out of what transpires in life, how they go about the business of endowing life with meaning. They recognize that people draw on beliefs and practices associated with "official" religions, but do not limit their appropriation of meaning to them. Scholars who ponder whether nationalism, sports, or an economic system such as Marxism may be "religions" consciously or unconsciously reflect this functionalist understanding, for they presume that some individuals may use such to erect a framework of meaning for life. But the net may be so widely cast as to encompass virtually anything and everything, leaving the word "religion" itself devoid of meaning. Yet functionalism retains the advantage of being "more likely to catch the ways in which ordinary people go about creating a universe of meaning."[26]

Functionalism is also better able to appreciate the syncretism that many see as a fundamental characteristic of popular religion. The blending of beliefs and practices from many sources to create a personal world of meaning concerns advocates of a substantive approach, for such fusion means the contamination of pure, authentic belief. But if fashioning such a mix is precisely what ordinary people do, counter functionalists, then we must take it seriously. From another perspective, syncretism defies normative standards fixed by institutions and traditions. If syncretism lies behind the working beliefs of ordinary people, then syncretism, not a system of beliefs and practices set by a religious elite, is the actual norm.

Given the confusion over definition, it is more useful to talk about popular religiosity than popular religion. I deliberately use the word "religiosity" rather than "piety." While piety may connote religiousness in general, it commonly refers to particular devotional practices or a particular style that a specific religious tradition advocates to signal dedication and commitment. Piety often carries a negative nuance; the one who practices piety gets portrayed as "holier than thou," a paragon of affective excess in matters of devotion. Religiosity is more open-ended. It takes in both beliefs and practices associated with official religion as well as those that come from other sources. It appreciates individual blends of belief and practice without claiming that any one mix is normative. Religiosity accepts what people actually think and do without a priori judgments as to whether a specific belief or practice is really religious or not. Religiosity highlights what people are about in creating and maintaining worldviews that permit them to give meaning to life. At no time do I intend for religiosity to point to the saccharine sentimentality too frequently identified with piety.

Writing on a different subject, the historical connections between Christianity and anti-Semitism, Gavin Langmuir distinguished between religion and religiosity.[27] He suggested that religion refers to a social phenomenon and religiosity to a personal one. That is, what we generally think of as a religious tradition, a religious institution, a denomination, or a system of doctrine make up a religion for they require a tacit consent among a group of people in order to operate. It is therefore a social matter. Religiosity is different. It may be highly personal, indeed even idiosyncratic. Yet it also bears a relation to the symbols, beliefs, and practices of a religion or even of more than one religion in the way persons appropriate such in sustaining their own worldviews.

While this understanding may seem to imply that personal religiosity or popular religion is sui generis to each individual (and hence beyond scholarly scrutiny), such is not necessarily the case. There may be considerable overlap among the beliefs and practices that individuals in a given culture adapt for their personal use. Edward Shils has suggested that every society has a "central zone" of symbols, values, and beliefs that govern that society; indeed, sharing such a common fund of symbols, values, and beliefs is what holds a society together.[28] Membership in society then is based on one's relation to this central zone. Of course, Shils saw this "central zone" as emanating from those persons and institutions that exercised power within a given society. Hence to some extent the origins of these symbols, values, and beliefs are the elite, and to that extent they would seem distant from the inchoate symbols, values, and beliefs that fuse together in popular religiosity. But there is considerable latitude here. To be part of a society, one need not accept the entire reservoir of shared symbols, values, and beliefs. There is much room for individual choice and for adding other symbols, values, and beliefs to those chosen. Even rejection of some symbols, values, and beliefs is a type of relation to the larger whole, moving one in varying degrees to what Shils calls the periphery of society.

What I understand by popular religiosity is precisely this sort of dynamic. There is a central zone of religious symbols, values, and beliefs—many of them provided by official, formal religious traditions—that comprises the totality of religion in a culture. But what is held in common may not receive systematic articulation or even rational justification by the religious elite of any one tradition, let alone by the ordinary people of a culture. As individuals draw on this central zone and on subsidiary zones, they erect for themselves worlds of meaning, they create identities for themselves, they engage in the age-old task of religion by finding a way to make sense out of their lives. Because these subsidiary zones also are related to the central zone, an individual's personal religiosity does not exist in a vacuum. "Popular religiosity" refers to this dynamic process of creating and maintaining personal worlds of meaning and the interconnectedness of the religiosity of a people within a given society. While there may be unique features to the religiosity of any one individual, it is thus possible to paint in broad strokes some features of popular religiosity among a people who share a central zone of symbols, values, and beliefs.[29]

What distinguishes popular religiosity from more readily describable manifestations of religion in any culture is its lack of order and organization.[30] For example, throughout this book, I shall argue that among Americans there has always flourished a lively sense of the supernatural and a conviction that the empirical world is the arena where supernatural powers of good and evil struggle to hold sway. The human quest for meaning in turn is largely an attempt to gain access to that realm of power and to use that power to benefit the individual. Such deployment of sacred power gives one a sense of control, of being able to chart one's own destiny. That control becomes the key to experiencing happiness and to seeing life as endowed with meaning. But virtually all of the formal religious traditions also posit a sense of the supernatural and offer some means of access to its power. What is the difference? Quite simply the difference is the order and organization that religious traditions impose. Whether it be in creeds that summarize acceptable belief or tomes of systematic theology that attempt to justify belief, traditions bring order and organization to ideas of the supernatural. At the same time, the process of ordering brands some beliefs as unacceptable ("heresy") and points out inconsistencies among apparently contradictory beliefs (e.g., free will versus determinism). The syncretism of popular religiosity and its lack of organization mean not only that individuals may espouse some ideas that the religious tradition with which they may personally identify would condemn, but that they may simultaneously espouse beliefs that would seem contradictory. In sum, popular religiosity lacks the drive for conceptual coherence that marks established religious traditions and institutions.

The business of bringing order and organization to belief to a large extent tames or domesticates the power of the supernatural, for the supernatural becomes contained within the doctrines and practices of the institution. Such is the import of the claim of early Christian writers that "there is no salvation outside of the church." As well, institutions and professionals who serve the tradition come to control access to the realm of the sacred, whether such is intended or not. Formal worship and sacraments, with trained professionals presiding, become fixed means of tapping into the now more delimited supernatural sphere. To be sure, no formal tradition eschews individual acts of piety and devotion, but most in some way seek to control them or at least organize them. Prayer is an obvious example. Virtually no tradition would prohibit individuals from praying or from seeing prayer as a personal means of access to the sacred. But there will be directives on how to pray, guidebooks to channel devotion, suggested exercises for personal piety. In addition to whatever assistance these may provide the individual, they reflect an effort to assure that personal piety remains within the boundaries of acceptable belief and behavior. The genius of popular religiosity is ignoring these boundaries.

The lack of formal order characteristic of popular religiosity does not mean a total absence of structure. The various media on which individuals draw in constructing personal worlds of meaning certainly have some structural dimensions. One might well argue, for example, that televangelism, one of the more significant sources of signals bolstering much popular religiosity in the later twentieth century, represents a kind of institutionalism of aspects of one style of being religious. Yet there is no "Church of Popular Religion," no systematic theology or theologians of popular religion, no creeds summarizing beliefs basic to popular religiosity. The emphasis on lack of coherent, comprehensive organization in popular religiosity is one way to highlight its individual character and its symbiotic relationship with those structures and institutions more readily classified as religious.

Many who write about popular religion regard its manifestation as a recent phenomenon, one that has emerged because of modernization and industrialization. Peter Williams, for example, subtitled his study of popular religious movements in America "Symbolic Change and the Modernization Process in Historical Perspective." While historians have debated what modernization denotes and when the "modern age" began, Williams sees popular religion as a product of a social process that stretches back only a few hundred years. Similarly, Thomas Luckmann offered a complementary position when he argued that religion becomes increasingly invisible as society becomes more complex. That is, popular religion accompanies the process of urbanization and industrialization that foster more complex social orders.

At the same time, those who insist that popular religion arises as a reaction to dominant, established official religious traditions are claiming that without the prior embodiment of religion in a specific tradition, there would be no popular religion. So, too, those who see folk religion or the religious practices of preliterate societies generating popular religion are suggesting that popular religion emerges as a later developmental stage in the history of religion. Indeed, Pieter Vrijhof argues that one can discern the presence of popular religion only when religion has become a differentiated sphere within society. Popular religion then appears as a supplement or alternative to a religious tradition. In the American context, Robert Wuthnow claimed that "religious populism" came to the fore only after World War II, largely as a result of the expanding role of mass media in American culture and their ability to present an array of alternative religious ideas to the public. Wade Clark Roof and William McKinney also focused on the post–World War II period in their claims about the increasing privatization of religion and hence the stronger presence of popular religion.

To some extent, all these scholars are taken by the structural differences between contemporary Western societies and earlier tribal cultures. It is a commonplace in religious studies that most tribal cultures lack a word for religion. The less complex organizational patterns of such societies meant that religion, politics, economics, family life, and a host of other arenas that make up society were so intertwined as to be indistinguishable. Hence because religion was not a separate sphere of personal or social life, there was no need to have a special word for it. Only as work became differentiated from worship, as rule became distinct from ritual, did religion become one component among many that comprised a culture and religious traditions take on a life of their own. Because religion as an organized, discrete phenomenon awaited the emergence of a more complex social structure, the assumption has prevailed that popular religion also required complex social order for its existence. This line of thinking works, however, only if one assumes that popular religion demands an established religious tradition as a counterfoil.

Much evidence suggests that popular religion is not exclusively a modern phenomenon and that linking popular religion to complex societies reflects a distinctly Western understanding of both religion and culture. Robert

Redfield's distinction between the "great tradition" and the "little tradition" in peasant society provides a useful tool to understand this point. Students of various Asian cultures have long been aware of strains of popular religiosity, a "little tradition" whose origins are so deep-rooted as to be lost. Within the Hindu tradition in India, for example, there remain today countless religious rituals that never appear in the sacred texts of the "great tradition."[31] Some are carried out primarily in the home rather than in the temple, some celebrated by women without the ministrations of temple priests, some enacted in particular villages or specific regions but not in all Hindu areas, some popularized by itinerant poet-singers. Even the archaeological remains of the Indus Valley civilization, the earliest known roots of parts of Hindu culture, suggest the parallel existence of a social religiosity and a popular religiosity. Among the remains are some carefully crafted seals and figurines that foreshadow the prominence of Siva and the discipline of yoga in the later "great tradition." But a larger number of artifacts, less artistically refined, portray an archetypal earth goddess figure. While the evidence is too fragmentary to allow a firm conclusion, the more artistically sophisticated materials may reflect something of an "official" religion of the Indus Valley culture, while the goddess figures may stem from popular religiosity.[32] For millions of ordinary Hindu folk today, this popular religiosity is as important as, if not more important than, taking an offering to a temple or receiving a blessing from a properly trained priest. The point, of course, is that in Hindu culture a vibrant popular religiosity has not been dependent on modernization, industrialization, or urbanization for its genesis or sustenance.

Another example comes from Chinese culture. Most who study Chinese religious life recognize as basic such phenomena as a sense of harmony and rhythm to the natural world (and seeing humanity as part of that realm), a lively interest in astrology and divination, and reverence for elders and ancestors. As well, numerous distinct religious traditions have flourished at various times in Chinese history. Among them are strains of Mahayana Buddhism and Daoism. Western scholars have frequently distinguished between "philosophical" Daoism and "religious" Daoism.[33] To the former they consign the great texts of the Daoist tradition such as the *Dao De Jing* and the ruminations of thinkers such as Zhuang-zi. Over the millennia the millions of Chinese who might be influenced by Daoism continued to rely on astrologers and diviners in their quest for happiness and immortality. They may have also called on the ministrations of Buddhist priests at critical junctures in life and faithfully carried out ancestral practices that became more associated with the formal Confucian tradition than with things Daoist. In essence, a popular religiosity prevailed for centuries in traditional China, revealing the syncretism that later scholars identified as characteristic of popular religion. Again, to borrow Redfield's categories, what students of Chinese culture have called philosophical Daoism represents the great tradition perpetuated by the elite, while religious Daoism reveals the popular religiosity associated with the little tradition. As in Hindu culture, this popular religiosity has a distinguished history independent of any connection with modernization, industrialization, and urbanization.

Other examples suggest that popular religiosity has been a constant feature of human life at every moment everywhere. Rereading the evidence leads to the conviction that if we put aside the assumption that a formal religious tradition determines norms and standards of what constitutes religion and religiosity, we will find as distinguished a history of popular religion in Western culture as in Asian societies. Biblical scholars, for example, point out that one issue confronting the leaders of the emerging Christian tradition in the first several centuries of the common era was how to plant orthodoxy among people who freely appropriated some Christian ideas and symbols, combined them with others, and created a religious style reflective of popular religion. In the New Testament, the admonition in 1 Timothy 6:20 to "avoid the godless chatter and contradictions of what is falsely called knowledge" reflects inroads of what later generations have called gnosticism, as well as the amalgamation of some gnostic teaching with Christian belief and practice on the part of ordinary people, the creation of a form of popular religiosity.[34] So, too, the injunction in 1 John 4:1 to "test the spirits" to see whether presumably Christian teachers affirm that "Jesus Christ has come in the flesh" (1 John 4:2) reveals the presence of those who, in a manifestation of popular religiosity, affirmed the significance of Jesus, but refused to acknowledge the divinity of Jesus.

Church historians have long recognized that the precise date of the birth of Jesus is unknown, but that fixing it on 25 December coopted the importance attached to winter solstice festivals among the people. The need to do so indicates that among ordinary people there was apparently little if any conflict in fusing "pagan" belief and practice with Christian affirmation in a popular religiosity. Numerous scholars have shown how the medieval fascination with relics of the saints, the concern of church leaders to quash heresy, the continuing affirmation of the power of witchcraft, and even such devotional practices as pilgrimages represent the way ordinary people adapted features of the formal Christian tradition, fused them with other beliefs and practices, and forged a popular religiosity that allowed them to find a sense of meaning in life.[35] The point should be obvious: popular religion and popular religiosity have always been part of the human quest for meaning in life in civilizations both East and West.

Why then have scholars ignored the presence of popular religion, particularly in analyzing Western religion? The most viable answer is that scholars of Western religion have allowed the dominant religious traditions and institutions to define what constitutes religion. Accordingly, they have viewed the whole primarily as refracted through the perspective of the elite. They have assumed that beliefs and practices advanced by religious professionals are the norms for people who identify with a particular tradition and that if beliefs and practices of ordinary folk do not mirror those promoted by the elite, they surely ought to. Examples of popular religion tend to be seen as aberrations from the norm or as movements peripheral to the mainstream, although some that endure over several generations gain greater acceptability.

Yet for generations the story of Western religion centered on religious institutions and materials emerging from them. For example, most histories of Christianity pore over creedal statements adopted by various church councils of the first five centuries of the common era to draw conclusions about the content and character of Christian belief. They examine surviving writings of the "church fathers" (although we now are aware of a significant body of material written by women) to chart the growth of Christianity as an institution. They look at tomes written by figures like St. Augustine to sketch the development of doctrine and theology. What ordinary people who identified themselves as Christians on their own terms were thinking and doing gets omitted.

For much of Western religious history, only a sketchy understanding of popular religiosity is possible. As the Christian church became an entrenched religious institution, it naturally sought to enforce conformity. Variants of official belief were classified as dangerous heresy, their adherents often forcibly eliminated, and most sources that would tell their story destroyed or suppressed. In many cases, what we know about popular religiosity comes from records kept by those who sought to wipe it out. While the details differ considerably, there is evidence to suggest that there were cognate processes at work in the other major Western religious traditions, more so in Islam than in Judaism.

A few historians have begun to explore the dimensions of popular religion in American life, but the task is just beginning. Peter Williams is the only one who has attempted an overview, though, as has been noted, he focuses more on movements than on personal religiosity. For the colonial period, we now have the work of David D. Hall and Jon Butler, which informs much of the next chapter.[36] But by and large, those who examine popular religiosity fix their vision on the later twentieth century. Why? Again there is a simple answer. To a large extent, the media explosion of the twentieth century generated such a quantity of materials pitched to a mass audience that it is impossible to ignore their impact on shaping popular consciousness in virtually every aspect of life, not just in the religious arena. These materials are different from those that have been the historian's stock-in-trade for generations. Generally scholars have concentrated on written materials and artifacts of "high culture" produced and/or preserved by an elite, just as they have allowed a religious elite to limit their vision of what constitutes religion. The twentieth century has witnessed not only a tremendous increase in written materials, but also the widespread accessibility of oral and visual materials thanks to radio, television, and film. The deluge of sources has made it impossible to ignore popular culture in general and popular religion in particular. As one commentator astutely observed, historians of Western religion "can no longer follow current developments adequately by examining documentation generated by officials."[37]

Fortunately, materials abound for the study of popular religiosity in American culture. But some cautions are in order. The most important concern the kinds of conclusions that we can responsibly offer, given the highly personal nature of much popular religion. Claiming that we can get inside the life experience of all ordinary people and neatly construct a profile of popular religiosity from the time of the European conquest to the present is too grand, if not impossible. We can, however, look at the signals being sent to ordinary people about what sorts of beliefs, values, and practices were available for them to mold into personal worldviews. Such signals come from many different sources, including formal religious traditions. They come from print materials, especially devotional literature, periodicals, novels, and the like that are targeted to a lay audience or the ubiquitous "general public." They are found in vernacular architecture, for how we design and use space reveals something of the values we hold. They are found in the music that people make part of their daily lives, not just the great hymns of a religious tradition (although there are vital signals communicated there), but also the songs of a culture that tell us what matters to people who compose them, hear them, and remember them.

For the colonial period, for example, we can examine surviving lists of inventory for booksellers to see what kinds of materials were most in demand, and there survive hundreds of wills and estate probate records that give clues about what kinds of books people retained in their libraries. But here one caution immediately arises. To a large extent the clientele of colonial booksellers came from the ranks of the elite; so, too, those of sufficient economic standing to leave estate records may also have been among the elite. Yet we also know much about the dissemination of information in the colonial period and the relatively high literacy rate among white Euro-Americans. While oral transmission was probably most vital, books were shared among friends and acquaintances to a much larger extent than is probably the case today. The greater dependence on conversation as a means of transmitting information and the sharing of written materials means that ideas circulated more widely among ordinary people than we might first assume.[38] As well, there are hundreds of surviving diaries, some kept by preachers and theologians, but many containing the ruminations of ordinary folk as they pondered meaning in life. From the colonial period, too, come the first religious periodicals designed for circulation among ordinary people.

By the mid-nineteenth century, publishers were producing novels in an inexpensive format for purchase by the masses. While few appear on read-ing lists for university courses in American literature, some were best-sellers of their day. Even if we had accurate figures of the number of copies sold, we could not ascertain total readership with any certainty. But we can assume that people purchased such literature and talked about it in casual conversation because it sent signals about beliefs and values that resonated with their own life experience. Then there were "devotional materials that began to issue from [denominational] presses, the magazines of missionary societies and other groups oriented to social reform, and the many news-papers and kindred publications published in the native languages of im-migrant peoples." All of them "helped to perpetuate the sense that individuals could construct a private religious world that complemented whatever formal religious groups offered."[39] All of them fostered popular religiosity.

The greatest abundance of materials comes from the twentieth century. The technological advances that have made radio, television, film, video cassette recorders, and compact discs part of daily life have vastly increased the barrage of signals coming to ordinary people about what is important in life and how to find happiness. Some may be explicitly religious. For example, religious professionals from Roman Catholic Bishop Fulton J. Sheen in the 1950s to independent Baptist Jerry Falwell in the 1980s have used the medium of television to entice people to define personal beliefs and values. One did not need to be a Catholic to draw from the beliefs and values articulated by Sheen four decades ago any more than one needs to be a Baptist to receive the signals sent by Falwell, blend them with others, and construct a realm of meaning that allows the individual to make sense out of life.

Add to these for the later twentieth century the spate of "self-help" books that line the shelves of bookstores and fill the racks in gocery stores and drug stores.[40] Some have even made best-seller lists. But the very designa-tion "self-help" takes us to one of the basic roles of religion in providing persons with a way to interpret their lives and endow their experience with meaning. The particular religious tradition—if any—with which a given author may identify matters not; nor does the formal religious affiliation of the reader. People are free to draw on the beliefs, values, and practices advanced in this literature, combine them with others, and construct a workable worldview.

In American culture there has long been a range of sources outside of formal religious institutions to which individuals might look for helpful signals in erecting a personal worldview. Consequently, popular religiosity is not merely a phenomenon of the modern or postmodern period, but a constant in American culture. In the pages that follow we shall see the many and diverse ways in which popular religiosity, that inchoate, unorganized, and highly syncretistic sense of the supernatural, has expressed itself in

American life. Much that comprises popular religiosity will have some relation to the formal religious institutions and traditions that have found a
home on American soil, but never be synonymous with or restricted to the
beliefs and practices of those institutions. My claim is simply that for the
vast majority of Americans, a sense of the supernatural so lively that it
cannot be contained in creed and doctrine permeates life. Hence we shall
also look at ways ordinary men and women have sought and continue to
seek direct personal access to the realm of the supernatural in order to use
its power to give them control over their lives and to endow their lives with
meaning.

For a nation with governmental structures shaped by persons heavily
influenced by the Age of Reason or the Enlightenment, this approach may
seem bold. It may also strike the religious elite as improbable, given the
volumes penned by theologians on the increasing secularization of American society and the wails of denominational officials bemoaning the erosion
of membership in the old mainline religious bodies. Yet as recently as 1986
a Gallup poll conducted for the Christian Broadcasting Network revealed
that 94 percent of those surveyed affirmed belief in God.[41] While poll takers
did not attempt to define what "God" denoted, it is safe to assume that
God refers at least to some supernatural entity, some force that is other
than human. The figure of 94 percent is also considerably higher than the
65 percent who claimed membership in an organized religious body in
1988 and much higher than the total reported by religious groups in their
own statistics.[42] But the 94-percent figure suggests that a sense of the supernatural is prevalent among the people called Americans, that it is fundamental to the "central zone" of beliefs and values that shape American
culture, and that it is basic to popular religiosity.

So, too, would the recent burst of popular interest in angels that seems
to have taken the intellectual and religious elite by surprise. In the summer
of 1993 news wire services noted that nearly forty books on angels were
available or due for release by publishers, some of them leading sellers
among religious titles. "And this is on top of the angel catalogs, calendars,
audio cassettes and an AngelWatch newsletter that are flooding the market."[43] Angels may be part of the complex doctrine of the major religious
traditions in the United States, those of Christianity, Judaism, and Islam,
but they are also part of the worldviews associated with the so-called New
Age movement and numerous manifestations of the occult. But for ordinary
folk, the half of the American public that purportedly believes that angels
are empirically real, it matters not whether angels can be pigeon-holed
within a tradition or a movement. They are simply part of a sacred realm
that underlies all of life. In a word, the interest in angels reflects the lively
sense of the supernatural that lies at the core of popular religiosity.

The chapters that follow trace that sense of the supernatural as it em-
powers ordinary people to erect and inhabit their own worlds of meaning.

As we shall see, affirming such will enable us to understand such apparently disparate phenomena as why early New England Puritans maintained an interest in astrology even as their preachers extolled the doctrine of election. It will allow us to understand why in the later nineteenth century when theologians feared the application of critical methods of analysis to scripture and the implications of evolutionary theory, ordinary people were devouring the novels of Elizabeth Stuart Phelps with their vision of a supernatural afterlife where all the exigencies of empirical reality would vanish. It will also give us insight into the appeal of self-help and New Age literature in our own time when science and technology seem to reign supreme.

Obviously, not every American believes in God, however defined, nor do all Americans believe the same things about God. But even rejection of beliefs, values, and practices that are part of the "central zone" of American symbolic identity affirms their power for the many. My claim is simply that at the heart of American popular religiosity there has always been a lively sense of the supernatural and that ordinary men and women for generations have sought access to the realm of the supernatural in order to find meaning and purpose in life. Sometimes they gain that access through religious traditions and institutions, but more often through fusing together an array of beliefs and practices to construct personal and very private worlds of meaning. If we would understand the dynamics of being religious, American style, we must explore the elusive phenomenon of popular religiosity.

NOTES

1. Louis Schneider and Sanford M. Dornbusch, *Popular Religion: Inspirational Books in America* (Chicago: University of Chicago Press, 1958).

2. See Philippe Ariès and Georges Duby, eds., *A History of Private Life*, 5 vols. (Cambridge, Mass.: Belknap Press of Harvard University, 1987–91).

3. Pieter Vrijhof emphasizes this distinction in "Official and Popular Religion in Twentieth-Century Western Christianity," in *Official and Popular Religion: Analysis of a Theme for Religious Studies*, edited by Pieter Vrijhof and Jacques Waardenburg (The Hague: Mouton, 1979), pp. 217–43.

4. Schneider and Dornbusch, pp. 12–42, 157.

5. Peter W. Williams, *Popular Religion in America: Symbolic Change and the Modernization Process in Historical Perspective* (Englewood Cliffs, N.J.: Prentice-Hall, 1980), p. 228.

6. Williams, pp. 17–18.

7. Luis Meldonado, "Popular Religion: Its Dimensions, Levels, and Types," in *Popular Religion*, edited by Norbert Greinacher and Norbert Mette (Edinburgh: T. and T. Clark, 1986), pp. 3–11.

8. Jean Seguy, "Images et 'religion populaire': Reflexions sur un colloque," *Archives de sciences sociales des religions* 44 (July–September 1977): 25–43.

9. Ernest Henau, "Popular Religiosity and Christian Faith," in Greinacher and Mette, pp. 71–81.

10. Thomas Luckmann, *The Invisible Religion* (New York: Macmillan, 1967).

11. Wade Clark Roof, "American Religion in Transition: A Review and Interpretation of Recent Trends," *Social Compass* 31 (1984): 273–89. Roof expands his arguments in the work coauthored with William McKinney, *American Mainline Religion: Its Changing Shape and Future* (New Brunswick, N.J.: Rutgers University Press, 1987).

12. Vittorio Lanternari, "La religion populaire: Perspective historique et anthropologique," *Archives de sciences sociales des religions* 53 (1982): 121–43.

13. Paulo Suess, "The Creative and Normative Role of Popular Religion in the Church," in Greinacher and Mette, pp. 122–31.

14. See Max Weber, "The Protestant Sects and the Spirit of Capitalism," in *From Max Weber: Essays in Sociology*, translated by Hans H. Gerth and C. Wright Mills (New York: Oxford University Press, 1946), pp. 302–22; Weber, *Sociology of Religion*, translated by Ephraim Fischoff (Boston: Beacon Press, 1963), pp. 95–117; Ernst Troeltsch, *The Social Teaching of the Christian Churches*, 2 vols., translated by Olive Wyon (New York: Macmillan, 1931), 1:328–54, 380–82; 2:688–703, 805–7, 993–1000; and H. Richard Niebuhr, *The Social Sources of Denominationalism* (New York: Henry Holt and Co., 1929), pp. 26–76.

15. Robert Redfield, *Peasant Society and Culture* (Chicago: University of Chicago Press, 1956).

16. Rosemary Radford Ruether, "Women-Church: Emerging Feminist Liturgical Communities," in Greinacher and Mette, pp. 52–59.

17. Gustav Mensching, "The Masses, Folk Belief, and Universal Religion," in *Religion, Culture, and Society*, edited by Louis Schneider (New York: Wiley, 1964), pp. 269–73.

18. Virgil Elizondo, "Popular Religion as Support of Identity: A Pastoral-Psychological Case-Study Based on the Mexican-American Experience in the USA," in Greinacher and Mette, pp. 36–43.

19. Vrijhof, pp. 217–43.

20. E. Wilbur Bock, "Symbols in Conflict: Official versus Folk Religion," *Journal for the Scientific Study of Religion* 5 (1966): 204–12.

21. Robert Towler, *Homo Religiosus: Sociological Problems in the Study of Religion* (New York: St. Martin's, 1974), especially pp. 128–62. Also see E.J.M.G. Roebroeck, "A Problem for Sociology: Contemporary Developments in the Roman Catholic Church," in Vrijhof and Waardenburg, pp. 166–99.

22. Towler, p. 148.

23. Towler, p. 152.

24. Robert Wuthnow, *Experimentation in American Religion: The New Mysticisms and Their Implications for the Churches* (Berkeley: University of California Press, 1978). See especially "The Appeal of Astrology," pp. 44–60, and "The Coming of Religious Populism," pp. 189–201. See also Wuthnow, *The Restructuring of American Religion: Society and Faith since World War II* (Princeton, N.J.: Princeton University Press, 1988), chap. 8.

25. Catherine L. Albanese, "The Study of American Popular Religion: Retrospect and Prospect," *Explor* 7 (Fall 1984): 9–15, claims that popular religion must include both the elite and the masses to avoid an "us" and "them" division. She suggests that popular religion encompasses only what is held as sacred by all the

people. I believe it impossible to find anything that would be held as sacred by all the people in exactly the same way at any time.

26. Charles H. Lippy, ed., *Twentieth-Century Shapers of American Popular Religion* (Westport, Conn.: Greenwood, 1989), p. xviii.

27. Gavin I. Langmuir, *History, Religion, and Antisemitism* (Berkeley: University of California Press, 1990).

28. Edward Shils, "Centre and Periphery," in *The Logic of Personal Knowledge: Essays Presented to Michael Polanyi on His Seventieth Birthday*, edited by Paul Ignotos et al. (London: Routledge and Kegan Paul, 1961), pp. 117–30.

29. For purposes of precision, I would prefer to use only the designation of "popular religiosity" to talk about the components of the religious worlds of ordinary people, but because of convenience and convention, I shall sometimes use "popular religion" and "popular religiosity" interchangeably. I never intend to imply that popular religion is a religion in the sense of being an official, formal tradition with a systematic structure of beliefs and practices nurtured by an elite corps of religious professionals.

30. Numerous conversations with Professor E. Brooks Holifield of Emory University helped me refine my sense of the lack of organization or the disorder that I believe characterizes popular religiosity. At one point, Holifield suggested that a more apt title for this analysis would be "Disorganized Religion in America."

31. On some of the more popular dimensions of the Hindu tradition and connections to the "great tradition," see John Stratton Hawley, *Krishna, the Butter Thief* (Princeton, N.J.: Princeton University Press, 1983); Frederique Apffel Marglin, *Wives of the God-King: The Rituals of the Devadasis of Puri* (New York: Oxford University Press, 1985); Wendy Doniger O'Flaherty, *Women, Androgynes, and Other Mythical Beasts* (Chicago: University of Chicago Press, 1980); V. Raghavan, *The Great Integrators: The Saint Singers of India* (Delhi: Ministry of Education and Broadcasting, 1966).

32. See Sir Mortimer Wheeler, *Civilizations of the Indus Valley and Beyond* (New York: McGraw-Hill, 1966), and *The Indus Civilization*, supplementary volume to the *Cambridge History of India* (Cambridge, England: Cambridge University Press, 1953).

33. This distinction is found in many basic textbooks such as David S. Noss and John B. Noss, *A History of the World's Religions*, 8th ed. (New York: Macmillan, 1990), chap. 9.

34. On gnostic adaptation of what became orthodox Christian belief, see Elaine Pagels, *The Gnostic Gospels* (New York: Random House, 1979).

35. See, for example, the essays in James Obelkevich, ed., *Religion and the People, 800–1700* (Chapel Hill: University of North Carolina Press, 1979).

36. See David D. Hall, *Worlds of Wonder, Days of Judgment: Popular Religious Belief in Early New England* (New York: Knopf, 1989); and Jon Butler, *Awash in a Sea of Faith: Christianizing the American People* (Cambridge, Mass.: Harvard University Press, 1990).

37. P. Staples, "Official and Popular Religion in an Ecumenical Perspective," in Vrijhof and Waardenburg, p. 286.

38. Richard D. Brown, *Knowledge Is Power: The Diffusion of Information in Early America, 1700–1865* (New York: Oxford University Press, 1989).

39. Lippy, p. xxi.

40. The best guide to earlier self-help literature is Elise Chase, *Healing Faith: An Annotated Bibliography of Christian Self-Help Books* (Westport, Conn.: Greenwood, 1985).

41. George Gallup, Jr., and Sarah Jones, *100 Questions and Answers: Religion in America* (Princeton, N.J.: Princeton University Press, 1989), pp. 4–5.

42. Gallup and Jones, pp. 70–71.

43. Richard Scheinin, "Do You Believe in Angels?" *Anderson* (S.C.) *Independent-Mail*, 27 June 1993, B1, B4. Knight-Ridder News Service carried Scheinin's article. See also Ken Garfield, "People Take Comfort in Wings of Angels," *Charlotte Observer*, 11 October 1992, A1, A10.

Chapter 2

Popular Religiosity in Early Colonial America

Locating the real dynamic of religion in private, personal experience, a hallmark of popular religiosity in the minds of most analysts, is by no means a recent occurrence. The centrality of individual religious experience, the syncretism that characterizes virtually all forms of popular religiosity, as well as the inchoate sense of the supernatural that undergirds much popular belief and practice have long been a part of American religion. We can, for example, see all these features in the religious life of those European immigrants, the Puritans, whose religious and political ways have left an enduring imprint on the culture of the United States. The Puritans who came to the New World, traditional ways of thinking go, were persons of the Book. Intent on shaping their lives according to scriptural precept, they pored over the pages of the Bible, endured lengthy expository sermons, and scrutinized every aspect of their lives to discern signs that God had elected them to salvation. Lurking in the background was the brand of Calvinism that had nurtured the Puritan movement in England, with its emphasis on divine sovereignty and the inscrutable will of God who chose some for salvation and some for damnation.[1]

We generally think of the Puritans as Christian folk par excellence, whose commitment to the path of purity carried over into the structures of society and government that they erected in the New England wilderness. Much of this perception of the Puritans and their religion emerges from the enormous body of sermons that found their way into print, sermons that often extolled the fine points of covenant thinking rooted in Calvinist ideology, that held up the lives of the pious as models for the faithful to imitate, that talked about the nature and purpose of government. It comes, too, from the tomes, letters, diaries, and papers of folk like Cotton Mather and John

Winthrop, Samuel Sewall and Michael Wigglesworth, and others so prominent in the Massachusetts Bay Colony that materials from their pens made
their way into library collections and archives to stimulate the thinking of
later generations. In such documents we glimpse inside the minds of many
who pondered the mysterious ways of God and struggled to determine
whether they themselves were among the elect of God even as they recorded
mundane affairs of daily life.

Christian the Puritans were, but perhaps not in the sense that that label
is commonly used. Historians have long known that church membership
figures, the barometer prized by twentieth-century statisticians and poll takers to measure religiosity, are not an accurate gauge of either religious belief
or practice for much of American history, especially for the colonial epoch.
Not only are such records fragmentary and often inaccurate, but church
membership carried much different meaning for New England Puritans
than it does today. For committed Puritans, church membership was not
treated lightly; it was a step taken with fear and trembling for it assumed
that candidates for membership could testify with certainty that they were
among those God predestined to salvation. To some, such certitude no
doubt reeked of presumption—better to remain outside the church covenant than to claim to know the mind of God. For others, formal membership may simply not have been a matter of importance; like millions of
Americans today, they regarded themselves as religious without having official affiliation with a religious institution.

If we look at the surviving records, the relatively low incidence of membership may create the impression that not only the Puritans of New England, but most Americans in the colonial period were not religious at all.
Jon Butler has estimated that after 1650 not more than one in three New
Englanders was a formal church member and concluded that this low figure
meant that it was inaccurate to regard even most New England Puritans
as genuine Christians.[2] It is a commonplace that even by the time of the
American War for Independence, probably not more than 10 percent of
the white population of the new nation were formally identified as church
members. Such figures, however, have little bearing on popular religiosity.
Church membership figures reflect official identification with a particular
religious body. They may not tell us much about the religious worldview
of ordinary people, about the beliefs and practices on which individuals
from all ranks of society drew to construct a framework of meaning for
their lives, about the reservoir of cultural signals and symbols that in varying degrees shaped the consciousness of the people. If we broaden our
scope to look at popular religiosity, we will find that men and women in
the colonial period, as today, had at their disposal not only specifically
Christian beliefs, values, and practices, but a host of others that in a myriad
of configurations comprised popular religiosity. Fundamental to that shared

central zone of beliefs, values, and practices was an abiding sense of the supernatural.

The Christian roots of that sense of the supernatural are found in the worldview captured in the Pauline literature of the New Testament that influenced so much of the Calvinist thinking buttressing Puritan and virtually all colonial religiosity. For St. Paul, the world humans inhabit is itself a realm of supernatural power, where opposing forces compete for control of human destiny. The Pauline injunctions regarding "principalities and powers," "rulers of this age," and "elemental spirits of the universe" all point to the invisible realm of evil supernatural power.[3] Humans needed to be constantly on the alert, for such powers could thwart the best of human intention, turn humanity away from God, and, if successful, transform humans into mere puppets. St. Paul saw affirmation of divine power revealed in Christ as an antidote to the control of such demonic supernatural powers, the only agency that could release humans from their influence and consequently enable them to submit their lives to the supernatural power of God. In the first century, popular appreciation of the need to understand and manipulate this spiritual realm spurred interest in such phenomena as astrology and in religions that promised adherents true knowledge of the secrets of the universe. Such knowledge would allow people to coerce the spiritual forces at work in the world to operate for their benefit rather than their detriment. St. Paul and early Christians inveighed against such efforts, regarding them as counter to divine providence. But New Testament writers' condemnation of such popular belief suggests how widespread it was, even in Christian circles.[4]

The world of seventeenth-century settlers in the English colonies was obviously vastly different than the world of the first century. But colonists still understood the world as a place where supernatural powers held sway and regarded such powers as potential allies or enemies in infusing life with meaning. As in the first century, so, too, in the seventeenth, accommodation to these prevailing powers encouraged popular interest in astrology, magic, and kindred phenomena that was part of the intellectual baggage colonists brought with them from Europe.[5] While many clergy and church leaders saw such dabbling with the occult as incompatible with Christian belief, the bulk of the population freely combined dimensions of the occult and aspects of specifically Christian teaching to create worlds of meaning that made sense out of their experience.

Historians David D. Hall and Jon Butler have demonstrated the extent to which magic, astrology, and other occult phenomena were part of the daily life of most ordinary people in New England (and very likely elsewhere in the English North American colonies) in the seventeenth century.[6] What is the evidence for such interest? What signals did it send to ordinary people as they constructed their own religious worldviews? How were they able to combine belief in an occult supernatural realm with Christianity in a popular religiosity? Butler calls particular attention to the surviving lists of books in personal libraries not just of New Englanders but also of colonists elsewhere and in the few fledgling town libraries from the late seventeenth and early eighteenth centuries.[7] While throughout the colonies religious titles are the most frequent, works dealing with astrology, alchemy, witchcraft, and other occult matters are not uncommon. Indeed John Winthrop, Jr., son of the first Massachusetts Bay governor, possessed one of the most extensive personal collections on alchemy.[8]

Historians have also long known that the best-selling nonreligious books in the colonial period were almanacs.[9] As Michael Hall has observed, "The New England almanacs, written by the Cambridge dynasty and intended for an educated public, must nevertheless have reached the least literate reading public in America as in Europe."[10] While there is no extant copy, an almanac was apparently the first book actually printed in British North America (1639), and almanacs accounted for about 80 percent of all secular literature printed in New England in the seventeenth century.[11] While explicitly religious content figured prominently in American almanacs published in the seventeenth century, material dealing with astronomical data and other calendrical phenomena became increasingly significant. English almanacs of the sixteenth and seventeenth centuries routinely devoted considerable attention to such matters. Ordinary folk who purchased or read almanacs more and more prized them for their astrological charts and guides to occult workings.[12] Michael Hall aptly noted: "Almanac writers in Massachusetts in the 1670s and 1680s were hard-pressed to distinguish between advances in astronomy and the organized fancy of astrology."[13] Simply put, "Astrology . . . was good for sales," and almanac compilers who sought to minimize such information found few buyers for their works.[14]

Rarely, however, do religious histories of colonial America mention almanacs, much less see them as vital to understanding colonial religiosity. Yet their popularity alone tells us much about the popular values and beliefs of the day, although we cannot determine the extent of readership of such works. Even if we could, we would be unable with any precision to say exactly how people used these almanacs or other books on the occult.[15] But their prevalence suggests that their content resonated with the lived experience of people from all ranks of life, that they captured dimensions of the worldviews of ordinary people. Hence Marion Stowell has asserted that the colonial almanac provides "the single most composite representation of the Puritan mind."[16]

What might colonists have found in almanacs and works on the occult that was helpful to them in making sense out of life? If intellectuals talked of natural law, what ordinary folk observed of nature was both orderliness and capriciousness. The orderly movement of the planets intrigued those who were advancing the science of astronomy, but it also sparked interest in astrology. Could not the location of planets and stars at the time of one's birth be omens of personality and destiny? Alongside the growing science of medicine, there prevailed notions that sickness resulted from supernatural powers bringing disorder to human life. Could not healing then be mediated by those who understood the powers that prevailed in the universe? Did not the stars govern parts of the body? Those who lived close to the soil well recognized their dependence on unseen forces to produce good crop yields. Was there a way to tip the scales for human benefit? Could the unseen forces of nature be harnessed for the welfare of humanity? The passion for almanacs requires that we give an affirmative answer. Hence it was not only the astrological charts in early American almanacs, but essays on health, medicine, and other topics pertinent to daily life that suggested a congruence between human experience in this life and the mysteries of the natural realm and the forces that prevailed there.[17] Simply put, the almanacs were popular guidebooks to a supernatural realm.[18] After all, even John Sherman, almanac publisher and pastor at Watertown, observed that the stars were "part of the Heavenly Host" whether or not one placed any value in astrology.[19]

The implications of this connection between explicit Christian belief and acceptance of a supernatural dimension in what scientists then as now saw as the natural world require closer scrutiny. For ordinary people who dabbled in astrology and alchemy, there was no disjunction between the occult and formal Christian doctrine. What ordinary folk heard from Puritan pulpits and read in sermons and tomes published by Puritan preachers may well have reinforced the popular perception that spiritual forces were operative everywhere. Simply put, belief in the power of the stars to guide human destiny was not incompatible with belief in divine providence. After all, there is a fine line between the fatalism associated with occult phenomena like astrology and the doctrine of predestination identified with formal Puritan ideology. Marion Stowell has called what prevailed the Puritan "double vision."[20] That is, the occult was part of the order created by God. Astrology, for example, might reveal signs from God, clues about God's mysterious workings in the universe, communications from God to ordinary people.[21] Acceptance of the occult was not denial of God's ultimate power. Rather, the occult became one way in which God worked in the world. But not only God. Like persons who shared the Pauline worldview in the first century, American colonists recognized that this vast supernatural realm also contained forces that could work against the best self-interests of humanity. Nowhere does this darker side of the supernatural realm come into clearer focus than in the colonial concern for witchcraft.

Usually writers of American religious history restrict discussion of witchcraft to the famous episodes at Salem Village (now Danvers), Massachusetts, that erupted in 1692.[22] But we err if we so limit our vision. There are two important matters that we will miss. The first is that acceptance of witch-craft, defined as the belief that spiritual forces could endow individuals with supernatural powers that in turn they could muster for good or for ill, was fundamental to the mind-set of Europeans, particularly the English, during the age of colonization and conquest. Scholars have written extensively on the European witch craze of the seventeenth century.[23] Assuming that some persons could and did possess supernatural capacities was part of the worldview of most who settled in the New World; it was not unique to Salem.

Focusing only on Salem also causes us to forget that there were differences between how witchcraft was perceived by church and political leaders and by ordinary folk. From the official point of view, witchcraft was usually construed as a form of spiritual possession; it did not have to be connected with presumed maleficent actions thought to harm others. In other words, witchcraft was more a manifestation of heresy than of evil conduct because it represented association with or allegiance to spiritual powers other than God. For this perspective, we need look no further than early colonial legislation that made witchcraft a capital offense. The Fundamental Orders of the Plymouth Colony adopted in 1636 made witchcraft illegal because it signified "solemn compaction or conversing with the Devil," not because it brought harm to others.[24] So, too, laws adopted in the Bay Colony and in Connecticut in the early 1640s emphasized the heretical character of witchcraft, not its presumably evil results.[25] The dimension of malefice came into play only when individuals were actually accused of being witches, most likely because of the difficulty in verifying whether one was in league with Satan if there were no public acts of an evil character that could serve as evidence.[26] Curiously, prior to Salem, accusations rarely mentioned the satanic dimension basic to the laws against witchcraft, but rather the use of occult power to do evil.[27] The point simply is that belief in the reality of witches and the practice of witchcraft were widespread among common people, not confined to the well-known atrocities at Salem.[28]

It seems unlikely that ordinary people automatically connected possession of seemingly supernatural qualities to evil power since they were convinced that the world was full of supernatural forces. Such possession was another dimension of popular religiosity, one that could have much positive benefit for those who had this power and for others as well. David D. Hall has reminded us that seventeenth-century Puritan New England was home to many who had reputations for fortune-telling, for being able to effect healing through use of herbal remedies and other occult means, and for evidencing other miraculous powers.[29] Acceptance of the reality of such extraordinary capabilities was also part of the popular worldview that colonists had imbibed in Europe before coming to the New World.[30] It is also a commonplace that colonists of all ranks and stations attributed to su-

pernatural intervention many phenomena for which a later age would find
natural causes—earthquakes, fires, sudden deaths, the birth of stillborn or
malformed infants, and the like. For those intrigued by such unusual occurrences, publishers produced a spate of "wonder books," collections of
accounts of strange events ascribed to supernatural forces that were pitched
to a popular audience.[31] While demand for such did not match that for
almanacs, these "wonder books" reinforced the popular perception that
there was much in the world that could be understood only as the result
of supernatural intervention.

Two matters are of particular import for understanding the role this
acceptance of the prevalence of the supernatural played in popular religiosity. The first is its function in enabling women and men to make sense
out of their own experience and that of those around them. The second is
the ways in which "official" religion, doctrine propounded by the clergy
and other persons in positions of formal leadership, wittingly or unwittingly reinforced popular belief. Again, David D. Hall points us in the right
direction in claiming that "prophecy and magic were alike in helping people
to become empowered, prophecy because it overturned the authority of
mediating clergy and magic because it gave access to the realm of occult
force."[32] On the one hand, acknowledging the presence of supernatural
powers, whether good or ill, enabled ordinary people to understand why
certain things happened to themselves and to others, things that did not fit
into a neat pattern. By having some sense of cause, such phenomena could
at least be understood. Understanding why something occurred—attributing it to the work of some supernatural force—does not mean one had to
accept everything as good or having some positive benefit. But one can
incorporate such matters into a meaningful worldview, basic religious activity. That itself, as Hall intimated, is a form of power. But it is a power
the people have, independent of formal religious institutions and religious
professionals such as clergy.

On the other hand, having access to such occult power, directly or even
indirectly through the knowledge and skills of others, can bring a feeling
of control over one's life, especially in a context where ambiguity prevails.
We need to be wary of constructing for colonial life a scenario dependent
on psychosocial insights of a later time. But there is little doubt that the
process of crafting a social and political order from scratch in the wilderness of the New World fostered much ambiguity. Other historians have
recounted the changing roles of the clergy, for example, during the colonial
epoch, and how unsettledness marked clerical self-definition then as now.[33]
The same holds true for those who emerged as political leaders. What legitimate power did they exert? How were church and state related? For
those outside the ranks of public power, ambiguity also prevailed. The
contingencies of colonial life alone promoted ambiguity. In such a context,
it simply made sense to turn to those who had access to a realm of superior

power in order to gain some control over one's life. The belief in the occult basic to popular religiosity granted just such control. It was practical to incorporate occult belief and practice into private religiosity.

At the same time, it is important to realize that institutional religion buttressed this popular religiosity, even in the clergy's railing against such things as witchcraft and magic. Two of the more well-known Puritan divines who addressed such matters in the seventeenth and early eighteenth centuries were Increase Mather and his son, Cotton Mather. Both Mathers tried to distinguish between what they regarded as extraordinary manifestations of God's power in the universe and presumed evidences of satanic power. Both preferred to speak of "wonders" of divine intervention in the natural order, of "illustrious providences," rather than of miracles or other occult phenomena, probably to mark a boundary between theologically acceptable affirmation of supernatural power and dangerous affirmation of satanic influence. Most seventeenth-century theological writers avoided use of the word "miracle" because of the Protestant conviction that genuine miracles had not existed since the close of the apostolic age.

Increase Mather's *Essay for the Recording of Illustrious Providences*, for example, is not only a compendium of wonder tales and stories akin to those in the popular "wonder books."[34] It also highlights the widespread use of amulets in healing and the use of homemade herbal remedies and other devices to provide protection from witches and evil spells. Mather devotes four chapters to a discussion of witches and other examples of supernatural possession. Mather also treats more traditional evidences of apparently supernatural forces, such as hurricanes, earthquakes, thunder, and lightning. Elsewhere he wrote about persons who possessed supernatural sight on specific days of the week and popular belief in "enchanted pins" that could be plunged up to two inches into the body without drawing blood.[35] Mather's intention in all this was twofold. First, he wanted to point out the danger he believed inherent in much popular practice. He condemned much as superstition to be rejected by true believers. But even in his condemnation he was affirming its reality in practical terms, for the primary reason for eschewing practices like placing horseshoes over entrance ways to thwart evil spirits was the satanic origin of the power represented. It was as if such practices actually bolstered diabolical power in the act of trying to fend it off. Throughout *Illustrious Providences* there is a keen sense of the constant presence and power of Satan and evil spirits controlled by Satan. Mather may wish to deny their ultimate efficacy, but in so doing he affirms their reality. Indeed, as Robert Middlekauff has argued, part of Mather's unstated agenda was actually to convince skeptics of the reality of witches and other occult phenomena.[36]

Second, Mather hoped to identify those occurrences that were authentic signs of God's power at work in the world. "There are Wonders in the Works of Creation as well as Providence," he wrote, "the reason whereof the most knowing amongst Mortals, are not able to comprehend."[37] He, like others who discussed similar topics, pointed to events like earthquakes, comets, and other "natural disasters" such as fires as manifestations of godly power, as signs of divine judgment calling people to repentance.[38] For him, such repentance included abandoning use of amulets, the practice of divination, and other aspects of popular religiosity. A closer look at Increase Mather's ongoing interest in comets gives greater appreciation of his views. Mather discussed his understanding of the significance of comets in several works in addition to *Illustrious Providences*, offering his most extended statement in *Kometographia*.[39] For him, comets were prophetic signs of divine intervention in human affairs and also examples of the mysterious supernatural power of God. On the one hand, comets signaled the nearness of the end of all things, the eschaton of Christian theology that would commence when Christ returned to the earth. On the other hand, they also had the power to cause a range of natural consequences such as earthquakes and floods that could adversely affect human welfare.[40] While the former represents an effort to bring belief in the supernatural within the bounds of official orthodoxy, the latter clearly sustains popular belief in the potentially malevolent influences of supernatural forces. At one point, Mather engaged in some speculation that surely reinforced popular acceptance of supernatural presence in comets, for he claimed that the sighting of a comet in 1682, when put in the context of planetary conjunctions, presaged the conversion of the Jews to Christianity and the downfall of Roman Catholicism by 1694.[41] As Michael Hall observed, "For all his Puritan objection to astrology, [Increase] Mather was never able to disentangle astronomy, astrology, and his understanding of a providential world."[42] Nor was such distinction made on the level of popular religiosity.

Cotton Mather addressed such supernatural wonders in many published sermons and treatises and in some that survive in unpublished manuscript form. Three years before the infamous Salem trials, he offered his *Memorable Providences, Relating to Witchcrafts and Possessions*.[43] There is a tinge of irony in Mather's title, for his aim was to demonstrate the evil character of what he described and to distinguish it from legitimate expressions of divine providence. Like his father five years earlier, Mather called attention to the popular use of charms and enchantments, particularly for effecting cures and warding off evil. All these he saw as temptations to be avoided, for they brought practitioners into association with the Devil. Such also formed the base of his treatment of the Salem episode in *The Wonders of the Invisible World*.[44] Indeed, the reality of the Devil dominates *Wonders of the Invisible World*.

In some ways, Cotton Mather's *Magnalia Christi Americana* may also be seen as an attempt to counter popular belief in occult phenomena.[45] Here too he recounted a series of wondrous acts, but acts of Christ, of divine providence. In Mather's opinion these gave ample evidence of God's goodness in providing a place for a holy people in New England and in protecting them from even greater ravages of satanic power than they had already encountered. As well, in the *Magnalia*, Mather sought to undermine popular reliance on almanacs. The almanac, he sneered, was "an engine to convey only silly impertinencies, or sinful superstitions, into almost every cottage in the wilderness."[46] Yet such did not keep him from issuing his own almanac in 1683.[47] Like his father before him, Cotton Mather saw in natural phenomena such as earthquakes and comets signs of supernatural intervention in nature. In one treatise, for example, he argued that a violent earthquake would precede Christ's return.[48] Yet he also harbored a private interest in astrology.[49] One of Mather's unpublished works is also to the point. About thirty years after the Salem hysteria, he drafted a medical treatise entitled *The Angel of Bethesda*.[50] The details of his medical counsel need not concern us. But Mather was moving toward a more scientific understanding of disease, abandoning earlier notions that sickness resulted either from demonic intervention in life or from divine punishment for human shortcomings. Yet he bemoaned the continued reliance of people on using charms and similar presumed remedies for disease, castigating them as blasphemy for they represented human efforts to manipulate God's power. Such manipulation of supernatural power is basic to magic and to much popular religiosity.

To understand the dynamics of popular religiosity, several features of the Mathers' inveighing against popular belief and practice merit mention. Neither Increase nor Cotton Mather would have mentioned matters such as the use of amulets and herbal remedies, the practice of divination, and fascination with other occult phenomena had they not been widespread. One need not condemn what does not exist. They perceived a threat to pure religion in popular practice of the day. Yet in singling out certain features of popular religiosity for criticism, the Mathers and others of their ilk gave them increased plausibility. The supernatural power they condemned in such "memorable providences" was real in the experience of ordinary people. For the Mathers, connecting this power with the Devil may have been sufficient reason to avoid it. But one must ponder whether the supernatural power of a God who punished sin through inflicting disease or who brought suffering through earthquakes and natural disasters appears that much different from other supernatural powers in its operation. For those not taken by the fine points of theological argument, the difference must have seemed minimal. Little wonder that people remained intrigued with magic, astrology, and other occult matters long after the hysteria occasioned by the Salem witch trials faded into the past.

Richard Weisman has argued that while both popular religiosity and the theology promoted by clergy had significant investment in the existence of a supernatural world, they represented rival systems for dealing with suffering.[51] He also suggests that the efforts of the Mathers and others to address popular fascination with supernatural power and channel it into acceptable affirmation of divine providence was an attempt to impose a theological rationale on popular belief. Weisman is on the right track, but his argument deserves expansion. In targeting suffering as the primary venue, Weisman is raising the age-old question of theodicy, how to account for seemingly undeserved pain, suffering, and anguish without paradoxically attributing them to a loving, benevolent Deity. Popular religiosity, with its keen sense of the supernatural, stretched well beyond issues of theodicy. Rather, affirmation of the supernatural power and acceptance of its expression through occult means stood as one way in which ordinary people made sense out of the world. In the Puritan worldview especially, with its roots in Pauline understanding, the relation between empirical reality and supernatural reality was plastic and ill-defined. Astrology, witchcraft, and the occult in general offered people a way to tap into that supernatural realm and at least understand its workings, if not establish a modicum of control over it.

Occult phenomena represent only one component of popular religiosity in seventeenth-century America. We need also to look at signals perpetuating a lively sense of the supernatural that people received from popular religious literature. Students of the history of literature have attempted to identify for the colonial period what we would call "best-sellers." Collections of sermons most frequently appear on such hypothetical lists, along with works promoting personal religious devotion that were more likely read and pondered by people on their own than cited in learned sermons by the clergy. Such devotional works offer another entree into popular religiosity, though again we must recall that in the seventeenth century there was less of a gap between the religious elite and ordinary people when it came to materials available for private use.[52] Such works were intended for use in household worship, and gender roles of the day assigned leadership of such devotions to the male head of the household. But these materials were available for personal, private use, and, despite prescribed gender roles, these materials were particularly important not only in nurturing women's religiosity but in informing the beliefs, values, and practices women instilled in their children.

On all lists of colonial popular best-sellers appears *The Practice of Piety: Directing a Christian How to Walk, That He May Please God* by Lewis Bayly, bishop of Bangor.[53] First published around 1610, *The Practice of Piety* appeared in nearly sixty editions by the end of the seventeenth century and had been translated for use in proselytizing among Native American Indian tribes in the Northeast. Bayly's work also greatly influenced John Bunyan, whose *Pilgrim's Progress* was another best-seller during the seventeenth century. Bayly's book was not the only popular guide for holy living, but its consistent appeal means that it sent powerful signals to scores of individuals as they went about the business of constructing a religious worldview. *The Practice of Piety*, well over six hundred pages in length in some editions, aimed to assist individuals in self-examination to determine whether they were among God's elect, whether they had been converted. In addition, it sought to nurture devout living among those who recognized the signs of God's election in their lives. To this end, it contains numerous devotional aids such as meditations and prayers to be used by the faithful and urges such pious practices as fasting. Yet its content and style both reinforce a sense that the world was an arena where great supernatural powers were at work. *The Practice of Piety*, a melodramatic work, paints vivid, detailed word pictures of dangers that confront the unconverted not only in this life, but in the life to come. Especially potent are Bayly's descriptions of the torments of hell. Always there looms the threat of impending divine judgment. Bayly, for example, makes the traditional connection between sickness and sin, regarding physical illness as a form of divinely inflicted judgment to punish human wickedness.

Nowhere does the double-edged focus of *The Practice of Piety*, its simultaneously offering assurance to the elect and terrifying presumed sinners with the horrors of divine wrath, become more obvious than in Bayly's discussion of the Lord's Supper. On the one hand, Bayly claims that the Lord's Supper provides the elect with the "greatest assurance . . . of their salvation."[54] On the other hand, he warns of dire eternal consequences that will ensue should the unworthy, the unconverted, so much as even touch the elements used in the sacrament. It is as if there were a supernatural power, almost a magical force, attached to the sacrament itself. For those unsure of their election, to handle the elements was to risk God's wrath; they, Bayly counseled, should refrain from participating in the Eucharist. Bayly's perspective dovetailed with a popular religiosity based on a profound sensitivity to the presence of supernatural power in every aspect of life. Historians have long called attention to an apparent decline in church membership in New England in the later seventeenth century and the controversies over whether to admit to the sacraments those who had not entered into full membership. One can only speculate about the extent to which Bayly's admonitions scared those who harbored doubts as to their salvation and led them to refrain from owning the church covenant.

Other dimensions of Puritan devotional life were also reflective of popular religiosity. Charles Hambrick-Stowe, whose study of such remains standard, claimed that Puritanism could be construed as a "popular devotional movement."[55] He called attention to popular practices that are often overlooked because they were part of private life and hence largely beyond the control of the formal religious institutions of the day.[56] There were, for example, private meetings held in neighborhood homes, some on a weekly basis, some biweekly, some monthly. Here ordinary folk had an opportunity to share their personal hopes and fears, their convictions and their doubts, and seek mutual support. In a study of Charlestown, Massachusetts, in the seventeenth century, Mary Macmanus Ramsbottom emphasized the importance to religious nurture of these lay devotional societies, almost entirely composed of men and some but not all directed by the clergy.[57] Hambrick-Stowe also reminds us of the extent to which individuals sought out personal spiritual counselors to whom they could bare their souls. While some went to religious professionals, the clergy, for such counsel, many did not. Rather, lay persons who were noted for their piety, their spirituality, and perhaps their ability to tap into the reservoir of supernatural powers so frequently filled the role of spiritual adviser that clergy often saw them as a threat.

Then, too, there were family devotions, prayers before and after meals, and discussions of sermons carried out in homes after Sabbath worship in the meeting house. One wonders how much ordinary people comprehended the fine points of doctrine propounded in sermons, even if they used the same religious vocabulary as the clergy. Traditional interpretation has assumed a high degree of understanding, but Kenneth Lockridge has argued the contrary.[58] Along with these devotional practices were private, "secret exercises" carried out by individuals on their own.[59] These included reading and study of the scriptures, personal meditation and prayer, perhaps poring over the pages of works like Bayly's *Practice of Piety*, and even engaging in devotional acts such as secret fasting. On the one hand, clergy extolled the virtues of family and private devotion. Such were means to discern the signs of God's providential presence and election. On the other hand, the clergy could not control what transpired in family activities or in individual minds in such secret exercises. Perhaps no other activities so fostered popular religiosity, with its blend of formal Puritan doctrine and an affirmation of supernatural power that pervaded the universe. That power was part of personal devotion cannot be denied. Hambrick-Stowe again is helpful in highlighting the near magical understanding of prayer that permeated popular Puritan devotion.[60] By bringing the individual directly into the presence of God, one had access to divine power, the same power that could be so threatening if turned against the unworthy. But sincere prayer could in effect channel that sacred power to the benefit of the devout.

The place of secret exercises and private devotional practices, the thrust of devotional works like Bayly's *Practice of Piety*, and the fascination with the occult are all of a piece. They point to popular belief in a supernatural realm of great power that could work to the advantage of those who had access to it or that could bring dire, even evil, consequences to those who misused it. They push the locus of religiosity away from the public sector and into a private, personal, and hence individual realm. In a word, they all promote popular religiosity. They also reinforce each other. And, the concern of those identified with "official religion," like Increase and Cotton

Mather, for such popular belief and practice not only testifies to its prevalence, but also suggests that there was not a tremendous gap between clergy and laity when it came to making sense out of the world.

From this vantage point, we can also shed light on two seventeenth-century movements that Peter Williams saw as illustrative of his understanding of popular religion: the Antinomian Controversy associated with Anne Hutchinson and the concern of the religious establishment for keeping Quakers out of New England.[61] Anne Hutchinson had followed her pastor Increase Mather from England to Boston. Ostensibly devout, she organized a female devotional society where women could discuss their own religious experience. But Hutchinson was also a lay spiritual counselor, and by all accounts those who came to her home regarded her as a spiritual authority. Yet as a woman, she was excluded from the ranks of official religious leadership; moreover, her group was not guided by Increase Mather or any other member of the clergy. The character of the group itself was enough to make it suspect, for it was hard to know what "heresy," or from our perspective what forms of popular religiosity, might be fostered by Hutchinson and her followers.

What brought Hutchinson into public view and ultimately led to her banishment from the Bay Colony was her claim to receive direct revelation from God, guidance from God that was not mediated through scripture nor the ministrations of the clergy. In a word, Anne Hutchinson claimed direct access to supernatural power. The biggest danger, though not expressed in so many words, was that Anne Hutchinson dared to make private religiosity public. She symbolized the sort of popular religiosity that official religion could not control.[62] When Anne Hutchinson gave birth to a deformed child, those who prosecuted her felt vindicated, for surely this event signaled God's displeasure. That view received confirmation when Mary Dyer, one of Hutchinson's followers, also gave birth to a malformed child. This misfortune was noted in a 1648 almanac's chronological table that included reference to Dyer's "horned-foure-talented monster" along with a "great and general Earth-quake."[63] Both reinforced the popular perception that beneficent and maleficent supernatural forces exerted tremendous power over human life.

So, too, with the Quakers.[64] Followers of George Fox were perceived as such a threat to political and religious order that some were hanged on Boston Common and others banished from Massachusetts Bay before legislation prohibited them from settling there. Other colonies in New England followed suit. Why were Quakers so dangerous? Their awaiting guidance from the "light within" or direct apprehension of God so interiorized religious experience, so made it a part of the private sphere, that official religion could not control it. The "inner light" was an authority superior to any other, even to scripture. Hence in a different way from Hutchinson,

Quakers symbolized the essence of popular religiosity, for they determined for themselves as individuals those beliefs, values, and practices by which they would endow their experience with meaning. To outsiders, emphasis on direct apprehension of the Divine, the "inner light," betokened potentially dangerous association with powerful supernatural forces.

Our attention has concentrated on Puritan New England for several reasons. Patterns of settlement there clustered people in cities and towns in a way that facilitated early development of a printing, publishing, and book distribution industry. The Puritan leadership encouraged literacy (and hence the purchase and reading of books) so the faithful could study the scriptures for their own edification. An unintended result was leaving behind a large body of written materials that later scholars have zealously scrutinized. The religious life of no other region of colonial America has received the same attention as New England. But many of the assumptions that undergirded popular religiosity there in the seventeenth century prevailed elsewhere in those colonies that became the United States.

Some surviving materials from colonial Virginia, for example, are similar to those from New England. Both offer diaries and estate inventory lists.[65] But there is an important difference. Colonial southern life had a more clearly defined social class structure than New England. As a result, the bulk of surviving materials come from those identified among the upper classes.[66] But we should not conclude that there was a wide gap between the worldviews of an aristocratic elite and those of the lower classes of white colonists or even of African-American slaves. As Richard Davis has pointed out, in the colonial South literacy among the lower classes of white colonists was higher than we long assumed.[67] There is no reason either to think that they did not own some books, including religious ones, even if we lack the same evidence for them that exists for the emerging aristocratic elite.

Jon Butler has identified numerous titles treating occult belief and practice that are found in surviving southern book lists.[68] Again caution is in order, for we have no way of discerning what persons did with these books, but as with New England, we can assume that people purchased works on the occult because they had interest in the subject. Butler has documented ownership of books dealing with astrology and astronomy, with alchemy and magic, with the healing arts, and even with Rosicrucian belief and practice. In some cases, he found persons who owned works describing occult practice in detail and books that attacked it. Obviously many Virginians, like their New England counterparts, shared a lively interest in the occult. Why? The reality of a supernatural realm of power was also part of the worldview these colonists fashioned, one that had plausibility in part because it was rooted in the cultural heritage they brought with them from Europe.

The practice of magic was fairly commonplace among Virginia colonists. Historian Darrett Rutman, in a provocative essay on the development of religious life in the early years of Virginia colonial life, found that:

In sound mind and with clear conscience a Virginian could ascribe his poor hunting to the spell of another (1626), hold that only the horseshoe over his door protected his sick wife from the evil intentions of a neighbor woman who perforce passed under it on her way to saying black prayers at his wife's bedside (1671), could attribute to a witch the death of his pigs and withering of his cotton (1698), and, in court, faced with a suit for slander, insist that "to his thoughts, apprehension or best knowledge" two witches "had rid him along the Seaside & home to his own house" (again 1698).[69]

In Virginia, then, as in New England, some persons were thought to possess extraordinary power that could be used in a variety of ways, from curing illness to bringing misfortune to farmers. Here, too, ordinary folk found it prudent to take steps to thwart malevolent use of supernatural power. It was, as Rutman noted, all part of a "generalized thirst for an ordering of the unknown."[70]

While the documentation is not as extensive as for New England, cases reported in court records offer additional evidence that belief in the power of witchcraft formed part of popular religiosity in seventeenth–century Virginia.[71] A 1626 case in which Goodwife Wright was accused of possessing the powers of a witch is the earliest known legal episode of witchcraft in the English North American colonies.[72] In Virginia, as elsewhere, it was difficult to prosecute persons accused of witchcraft because of a lack of firm evidence. Important for understanding popular religiosity is the belief that there were persons who had access to a realm of supernatural power, that such power pervaded the world and could be used for the benefit or detriment of ordinary folk. As well, many among the first Europeans to settle in Virginia believed that their Native American Indian neighbors routinely practiced black magic, engaged in witchcraft, and allied themselves with the Devil.[73] Samuel Clarke, describing life in the Virginia colony to an English audience, claimed that for the Native American Indians: "their chief God is the Devil whom they call *Oke*, and [they] serve him more for fear than love. In their Temples they have his image in ilfavoured [sic] shape, and adorned with chains, copper, Beads, and covered with a skin."[74] Colonists' failure to appreciate the dynamic of tribal rituals and ceremonies led some to conclude that ritual dances clearly demonstrated satanic influence. Alexander Whitaker, a clergyman of Puritan sympathies, ended a description of Indian rituals with the observation, "All which things make me think that there be great witches amongst them and they very familiar with the divill [sic]."[75] Such perceptions reinforced popular belief in the reality and power of the supernatural, especially in demonic form.

Institutional religious life in seventeenth-century Virginia differed considerably from that in New England. The Church of England, legally established in Virginia in 1624, never exerted the same influence as the Puritan churches in New England. Plagued by a shortage of clergy, challenged by the difficulties of ministering to a population that was widely dispersed rather than concentrated in towns and cities, and organized into parishes that were quite vast in the land area included in them, the Church of England as a religious institution in Virginia remained weak throughout the seventeenth century. Institutional weakness did not mean that individuals failed to develop a religious consciousness or that popular religiosity was absent. To the contrary, many of those even nominally associated with the Church of England were influenced by the contours of Puritan thought. Intricacies of theological debate and fine points of formal doctrine did not captivate Virginians, regardless of rank in society, any more than they did New Englanders. As in New England, so in Virginia—persons were interested in a practical religiosity, one that enabled them to make sense out of life and have some framework of meaning through which to interpret their experience. Consequently we find many similarities in terms of devotional materials, works of practical piety, and the like between the libraries of Virginia planters and those of New England Puritans.

Louis B. Wright, who made exhaustive studies of the reading habits of colonial Virginians, noted: "The amount of interest in controversial theology, even in Puritan New England, has been greatly overestimated, and Virginia planters were not likely to be much concerned over the hairsplitting of argumentative preachers. They were interested, however, in treatises that prescribed a way of attaining the good life and perhaps an eternal reward. That explains why nearly everybody who owned any books at all had Lewis Bayly's *Practice of Piety*."[76] Interest in a practical religion meant that Virginians, like New Englanders, frequently drew on Bayly and other Puritan writers for clues in constructing a workable religion. Wright further suggests that this practical interest, not congruence of formal Puritan and Anglican doctrine, accounts for the high proportion of Puritan authors other than Bayly found in southern libraries. Yet as in New England, signals sent by this practical literature to individuals who were formulating ways of understanding and interpreting their experience are important. Bayly's keen sense of the supernatural and the almost magical character he attached to the celebration of the Lord's Supper also informed the worldview of southern planters, even those nominally associated with the Church of England. A similar perspective undergirded another very popular religious classic of the age, Richard Allestree's *The Whole Duty of Man*.[77]

Given the general shortage of clergy in the southern colonies and the geographically diffuse nature of most parishes, the home and the sanctuary it offered from external authority figured prominently in southern religiosity, although evidence is more fragmentary for the seventeenth than the eighteenth century. Fairly early on the planter class that exercised control over the institutional structures of the Church of England apparently promoted some home-based religious activity, most frequently daily prayers for the household.[78] Informal discussions of matters of religious belief and practice, generally without the benefit of clerical influence, also were part of household life in developing plantation society. The home also became the site for celebrating religious ceremonies such as baptism, marriage, and funerals that a later age would associate with religious institutions. In the southern colonies, as in New England, women had a significant role in religious nurture, for to them fell the role of instructing children and sometimes slaves in the rudiments of acceptable belief.[79]

The traditional understanding sees southern religious life centered on the legal establishment of the Church of England, with its struggles to create a viable institution, and on the tacit genteel allegiance to Anglican tenets. That view misses much of the dynamic of what nurtured the religiosity of ordinary people in the seventeenth century. For in the South, especially in Virginia as we have seen, widespread popular acceptance of a supernatural realm and of persons possessed of extraordinary powers that could be used for the benefit of humanity or the reverse prevailed. Here, too, apart from the formal doctrines of the established church, evidence suggests that people read devotional literature, particularly Bayly's *Practice of Piety* that reinforced a sense of the supernatural. The same combination of official doctrine and informal belief, of practical piety grounded in formal theology and protocols associated with the occult, formed the cultural reservoir from which individuals drew to fashion a personal religiosity that made sense out of their experience.

In the southern case this popular religiosity was congruent with dimensions of the worldviews generally associated with African-American slaves. After 1619, when the first slave ship bearing Africans arrived in Virginia, popular religiosity cannot be sharply distinguished along racial lines. While scholars are steadily adding to our understanding of the religious perspectives of African tribal cultures that shaped the religious consciousness of black slaves, the experience of forced migration and the system of chattel slavery meant that transformation of worldviews occurred—as it had for the white Anglo colonists who came to New England. Two dimensions of the popular religiosity that sustained African-American slaves, the phenomenon of conjure and the idea of the slave as trickster, must concern us.[80]

Until well into the eighteenth century, efforts to Christianize slaves were minimal. Slaveholders balked at the idea of providing Christian nurture for slaves. To do so would have meant tacit acknowledgment of the humanity of those whose personhood the slave system categorically denied. Then, too, there was the fear that conversion on the part of slaves, signaled by baptism, might bring equality with slaveholders. Slaveholders understood the radical equality affirmed by St. Paul in Galatians 3: "There is neither

Jew nor Greek, there is neither slave nor free, there is neither male nor female; for you are all one in Christ Jesus." Although colonial assemblies enacted laws declaring that Christian baptism did not alter one's status as a slave, there was no upsurge in efforts to encourage African Americans to become Christians. The result was that especially in the seventeenth century, slave religiosity developed under those conditions that advance popular religiosity, especially the syncretism that often characterizes it.

Conjure offers a prime example. Drawing on the myriad African religious worldviews that saw empirical reality intertwined with a spiritual realm, conjure has as its base the affirmation of supernatural power and its presence in daily life. Simply put, spirits fill the world, and those possessed of spiritual power could tap into that realm of power through ritual, trance, and vision. Here, too, the spiritual had dangerous potential since its force could be detrimental or beneficial to human welfare. One could consult a conjurer for advice, for healing, for gaining revenge, or for any number of other situations where ordinary power was unavailable or ineffectual. Conjurers readily earned the respect of fellow slaves because of their ability to enter the supernatural arena and direct if not control its power. From an analytic perspective, conjure is part of the occult that so fascinated white colonists and sustained many cognate popular beliefs and practices. Like the occult, conjure was a way to give meaning to experience for it assumed that there was a cause for all that happened. There was no randomness. As with the occult, the ability to manipulate or control this power granted a semblance of control over one's life and thus endowed it with meaning.[81] This element of control figured prominently in notions of sickness and healing. Here, too, we find magical phenomena as part of the worldview associated with conjure—reliance on good luck charms and other amulets, the conviction that some persons had second sight, the acceptance of witchcraft. In the context of slavery, conjure represented a power that was superior to the power of the slaveholder, although it operated on an entirely different level. We cannot know how contact with African-American slaves reinforced or even enhanced white colonists' own belief in the supernatural. But it would be foolhardy to deny such interaction. In time, conjure was easily amalgamated with aspects of formal Christianity and the prevailing spirits readily identified with the spirit of Christ and the Holy Spirit. In time, too, slave preachers frequently absorbed the role of the conjurer since they were the ones possessed of extraordinary spiritual gifts. While some Christian slaves eventually rejected conjure, they did not have to abandon conjure's affirmation of a realm of superior spiritual power. For African-American slaves, as for many if not most of the white colonists, there was no disjunction between formal religion and the popular religiosity based on conjure or the occult. They were complementary for they both affirmed that power other than the merely human lay behind all that happened.

A similar understanding undergirds the notion of the slave as trickster.

While most of the known stories where slaves appear as trickster figures come from a later period, they have earlier roots for they reflect the age-old process of oral transmission and embellishment even when a particular incident lies behind them. Tales about animal trickster figures abound. They have a base in the African heritage and serve as a prototype for the slave as human trickster. Traditionally, the popularity of the trickster has been traced to its serving as a mechanism by which African Americans adapted to their slave status even if the trickster also represents a primal vehicle for cosmic justice or even cosmic revenge. There is more. Critical for understanding the place of the trickster in popular religiosity within slave culture is the power of deception that the trickster has and the source of that power. The trickster, powerless in empirical terms, outwits someone perceived as much stronger or in a position of greater power. Many of the later tales concern food. They share a common structure in that slaves outwit slaveholders by tricking them into thinking that, for example, a chicken they have stolen is really a possum or that an animal intentionally slaughtered for surreptitious slave consumption died of some sickness. In the empirical realm, the slaveholder is the one with power and intelligence; in the story, there is reversal, and the powerless, uneducated slave manifests superior power and a greater, albeit different kind of intelligence.

Where does the trickster's power originate? The trickster and the conjurer both represent figures who have access to a realm of superior power. Both assume that supernatural forces are prevalent in the world and that humans with proper knowledge can draw on that spiritual might to effect specific ends. While there is a greater playfulness to the trickster and what the trickster accomplishes than with the conjurer, both represent ways supernatural power intrudes into the empirical realm. This appreciation of the supernatural and the ways a supernatural presence enlivens daily life provide a point of congruence between the reservoir of beliefs, values, and practices that shaped popular religiosity among African Americans and that which sustained popular religiosity among Euro-Americans.

Jon Butler argues that the intrigue with magic, astrology, and other occult phenomena declined in the colonial period, particularly in the eighteenth century when Enlightenment currents began to influence formal education and the intellectual interests of the upper classes. But he reminds us that this interest remained strong among the common people.[82] As we have seen, there was less of a gap between the elite and the common people in the seventeenth century than has usually been assumed and institutional religion provided unwitting support for a popular religiosity based on a keen sense of the supernatural. If we look more closely at the eighteenth century, we shall find less of a gap there as well. Behind the presumed decline of elite interest in the occult there remained a substratum affirming the power of the supernatural. Such continuing affirmation of the reality of the supernatural was common to Euro-Americans, regardless of their formal identification with a particular religious institution, and to African Americans. And preachers and writers representing official religion continued to support a popular religiosity grounded in the power of a spiritual realm, often unintentionally.

NOTES

1. Some scholars suggest that Puritanism itself was a manifestation of popular religion in England that emerged as an alternative to the established Church of England. See Stephen Foster, "The Godly in Transit: English Popular Protestantism and the Creation of a Puritan Establishment in America," in *Seventeenth-Century New England*, edited by David D. Hall and David Grayson Allen, *Publications of the Colonial Society of Massachusetts* 63 (Boston: Colonial Society of Massachusetts, 1984), pp. 185–238.

2. Jon Butler, "Magic, Astrology, and the Early American Religious Heritage," *American Historical Review* 84 (1979): 317–46. This essay forms the nucleus of chap. 3 of his *Awash in a Sea of Faith: Christianizing the American People* (Cambridge, Mass.: Harvard University Press, 1990). Butler's subtitle reveals his hypothesis, namely that the low incidence of formal Christian affiliation among Americans until well into the nineteenth century meant that they were a people to be "Christianized."

3. See Ephesians 3:10, 1 Corinthians 2:8, and Colossians 2:8.

4. Such condemnation is found, for example, in 1 Timothy 1:4, where the author exhorts readers not "to occupy themselves with myths and endless genealogies which promote speculations rather than the divine training that is in faith" and in 1 Timothy 6:20, where the devout are told to "avoid the godless chatter and contradictions of what is falsely called knowledge, for by professing it some have missed the mark as regards the faith."

5. The standard work for understanding the English background for colonial interest in astrology, magic, and related phenomena is Keith Thomas, *Religion and the Decline of Magic* (New York: Scribners, 1971). Such interest was not restricted to England and also formed part of the cultural baggage of colonists who came from other parts of Europe. While this aspect of popular religiosity in Europe deserves fuller study, an important beginning is Robert Muchembled, *Popular Culture and Elite Culture in France, 1400–1750*, translated by Lydia Cochrane (Baton Rouge: Louisiana State University Press, 1985).

6. Butler's work has been noted above in note 2. For Hall's views, see especially *Worlds of Wonder, Days of Judgment: Popular Religious Belief in Early New England* (New York: Knopf, 1989). Sections of that work appeared earlier in his "A World of Wonders: The Mentality of the Supernatural in Seventeenth-Century New England," pp. 239–74. My own thinking grows out of an appreciation for the work of both Butler and Hall, although I am less concerned than Butler with the non-Christian aspects of colonial popular religiosity. Hall devotes more attention than I to how this amalgamation of beliefs and values was transmitted in both oral and print forms. On that process, see also Hall, "Toward a History of Popular Religion in Early New England," *William and Mary Quarterly*, 3d ser. 41 (1984): 49–55.

7. Butler, *Awash*, chap. 3.

8. See Ronald Sterne Wilkinson, "The Alchemical Library of John Winthrop, Jr. (1606–1676) and His Descendants in Colonial America," *Ambix* 11 (February 1963): 33–51, 13 (October 1966): 139–86; idem, "New England's Last Alchemists," *Ambix* 10 (October 1962): 128–38.

9. See Charles L. Nichols, "Notes on the Almanacs of Massachusetts," *Proceedings of the American Antiquarian Society*, n.s. 22 (1912): 15–134; and Marion Barber Stowell, *Early American Almanacs: The Colonial Weekday Bible* (New York: Burt Franklin, 1977). Also see Milton Drake, comp., *Almanacs of the United States* (New York: Scarecrow, 1962), 1:v–xviii; N. W. Lovely, "Notes on the New England Almanacs," *New England Quarterly* 8 (1935): 264–77.

10. Michael G. Hall, *The Last American Puritan: The Life of Increase Mather, 1639–1723* (Middletown, Conn.: Wesleyan University Press, 1988), p. 161.

11. Nichols, p. 16; Stowell, p. x.

12. See William D. Stahlman, "Astrology in Colonial America: An Extended Inquiry," *William and Mary Quarterly*, 3d ser. 13 (1956): 551–63.

13. M. Hall, p. 160. See also Robert K. Merton, "Puritanism, Pietism and Science," in his *Social Theory and Social Structure* (New York: Free Press, 1968), pp. 628–60.

14. Stowell, p. 61.

15. Butler also makes this point in "Magic, Astrology, and the Early American Religious Heritage."

16. Stowell, p. xii.

17. Some of these issues became more prevalent in eighteenth-century almanacs. Among the more successful almanac-makers of the eighteenth century were Nathaniel Ames and the Christopher Sauers (Sr., Jr., and III). The Sauers were of a Dunker background and produced almanacs initially targeted for a German immigrant audience. Almanacs published by Ames treated such topics as links between planetary movement and personality type as well as the influence of the stars and planets on the human body.

18. I do not wish to imply that almanacs were valued only for such information. Many of the colonial almanacs contain fairly weighty essays on points of doctrine and moral behavior, along with much practical material.

19. John Sherman, *An Almanack of Coelestial Motions of the Sun and Planets with Some of Their Principal Aspects* (Cambridge, Mass.: J. Sherman, 1677).

20. Stowell, p. 42.

21. Nichols, in his extended essay on Massachusetts almanacs, argued that astrology maintained a hold over ordinary people precisely because they saw the movement of stars and planets as direct messages from God.

22. Peter W. Williams, *Popular Religion in America: Symbolic Change and the Modernization Process in Historical Perspective* (Englewood Cliffs, N.J.: Prentice-Hall, 1980), pp. 151–55, sees the Salem episode as a popular movement reflecting response to manifold social, religious, political, and economic tensions in Salem Village and hence a manifestation of popular religion as he understands it.

23. See, for example, Wallace Notestein, *A History of Witchcraft in England from 1558 to 1718* (1911; reprinted, New York: Russell and Russell, 1965, and New York: Thomas Y. Crowell, 1968); and Alan D. J. MacFarlane, *Witchcraft in Tudor and Stuart England* (New York: Harper and Row, 1970).

24. For the Plymouth statute, see Samuel G. Drake, *Annals of Witchcraft in New*

England and Elsewhere in the United States (1869; reprinted, New York: B. Blom, 1967), p. 56.

25. For Massachusetts Bay, see William H. Whitmore, ed., *The Colonial Laws of Massachusetts* (Boston: City Council, 1889), p. 55; for Connecticut, see J. Hammond Trumbull, ed., *Public Records of the Colony of Connecticut, 1636–1776* (Hartford, Conn.: Case, Lockwood and Brainard, 1850), 1:77. The Massachusetts ordinance was part of the well-known 1641 "Body of Liberties."

26. See also Richard Weisman, *Witchcraft, Magic, and Religion in Seventeenth Century Massachusetts* (Amherst: University of Massachusetts Press, 1984), pp. 12–13.

27. This point is highlighted by David D. Hall in the introduction to *Witch-Hunting in Seventeenth-Century New England: A Documentary History, 1638–1692* (Boston: Northeastern University Press, 1991), p. 9.

28. For a provocative treatment of the larger story of colonial witchcraft, see John Putnam Demos, *Entertaining Satan: Witchcraft and the Culture of Early New England* (New York: Oxford University Press, 1982). See also Richard Gildrie, "Visions of Evil: Popular Culture, Puritanism, and the Massachusetts Witchcraft Crisis of 1692," *Journal of American Culture* 8 (Winter 1985): 17–33; and Frederick C. Drake, "Witchcraft in the American Colonies, 1647–62," *American Quarterly* 20 (1968): 694–725.

29. Hall, *Worlds of Wonder*, pp. 98–100.

30. On the prevalence of such popular belief in England, see Butler, *Awash*, pp. 21–23.

31. "Wonder books" were also popular in seventeenth-century England. See Hall, *Worlds of Wonder*, p. 81.

32. Hall, *Worlds of Wonder*, p. 100.

33. See, for example, David D. Hall, *The Faithful Shepherd: A History of the New England Ministry in the Seventeenth Century* (Chapel Hill: University of North Carolina Press, 1972).

34. Increase Mather, *An Essay for the Recording of Illustrious Providences* (Boston: Samuel Green, 1684).

35. Increase Mather, *Cases of Conscience Concerning Evil Spirits Personating Men, Witchcrafts, Infallible Proofs of Guilt . . .* (Boston: B. Harris, 1693), pp. 12–16.

36. Robert Middlekauff, *The Mathers: Three Generations of Puritan Intellectuals, 1596–1728* (New York: Oxford University Press, 1971), pp. 146–47.

37. *Illustrious Providences*, pp. 99–100.

38. On the fondness of Mather and other clergy for seeing natural disasters as indications of divine presence, see Weisman, p. 34.

39. Increase Mather, *Kometographia, Or a Discourse Concerning Comets* (Boston: Samuel Green, 1683). See also his *Heavens Alarm to the World* (Boston: John Foster, 1681), *The Latter Sign Discoursed of* (Boston: For Samuel Sewall, 1682), and *Doctrine of Divine Providence Opened and Applyed* (Boston: Richard Pierce, 1684).

40. *Heavens Alarm*, pp. 1–16; *Kometographia*, pp. 129–33.

41. *Kometographia*, p. 136.

42. M. Hall, p. 170.

43. Cotton Mather, *Memorable Providences, Relating to Witchcrafts and Possessions* (Boston: [R.P.], 1689).

44. Cotton Mather, *The Wonders of the Invisible World* (Boston: Benjamin Harris, 1693). This work appears also as the first volume of Samuel Drake, ed., *The Witchcraft Delusion in New England* (reprinted, New York: Burt Franklin, 1970).

45. Cotton Mather, *Magnalia Christi Americana* (London: T. Parkhurst, 1702). The first American edition appeared in 1820, and the first two books were issued in a scholarly edition by the Belknap Press of Harvard University in 1977, ably edited by historian Kenneth B. Murdock.

46. Quoted in Michael G. Hall, *The Last American Puritan: The Life of Increase Mather, 1639–1723* (Middletown, Conn.: Wesleyan University Press, 1988), p. 161.

47. Cotton Mather, *MDCLXXXIII. The Boston Ephemeris. An Almanac for the (Dionysian) Year of the Christian AEra M.DC.LXXX.III* (Boston: S. Green for S. Sewall, 1683).

48. Cotton Mather, *A Midnight Cry* (Boston: John Allen for Samuel Phillips, 1692), p. 60.

49. See Michael P. Winshop, "Cotton Mather, Astrologer," *New England Quarterly* 63 (June 1990): 308–14.

50. The manuscript is in the library of the American Antiquarian Society. The work published under this title in 1722 consists only of the fifth chapter of the manuscript.

51. Weismann, pp. 53–60.

52. Charles E. Hambrick-Stowe, *The Practice of Piety: Puritan Devotional Disciplines in Seventeenth-Century New England* (Chapel Hill: University of North Carolina Press, 1982), p. vii.

53. On colonial best-sellers, see Frank Luther Mott, *Golden Multitudes: The Story of Best Sellers in the United States* (New York: R. R. Bowker, 1947), pp. 12ff.; and James D. Hart, *The Popular Book: A History of America's Literary Taste* (New York: Oxford University Press, 1950), chap. 1. Both list Bayly's work as a best-seller. Mott uses as a standard for identifying a best-seller as a work with sales equaling one percent of the population. For the colonial period, of course, precise records do not exist.

54. Lewis Bayly, *The Practice of Piety*, 27th ed. (London: [J. Legat for] R. Allot, 1631), p. 521.

55. Hambrick-Stowe, p. 113.

56. Hambrick-Stowe, pp. 136–55.

57. Mary Macmanus Ramsbottom, "Religious Society and the Family in Charlestown, Massachusetts, 1630 to 1740" (Ph.D. diss., Yale University, 1987).

58. Kenneth Lockridge, *Literacy in Colonial New England: An Inquiry into the Social Context of Literacy in the Early Modern West* (New York: Norton, 1974).

59. Hambrick-Stowe, chap. 6.

60. Hambrick-Stowe, pp. 176–77.

61. Williams, pp. 104–8.

62. For a more complete view of Hutchinson, see David D. Hall, ed., *The Antinomian Controversy, 1636–1638: A Documentary History* (Middletown, Conn.: Wesleyan University Press, 1968); and William K. B. Stoever, *"A Faire and Easie*

Way to Heaven": *Covenant Theology and Antinomianism in Early Massachusetts* (Middletown, Conn.: Wesleyan University Press, 1978).

63. [Samuel Danforth], *An Almanacke for the Year of Our Lord 1648* (Cambridge, Mass.: [Matthew Daye], 1648).

64. For a brief account of the early Quaker experience in New England, see Charles H. Lippy et al., *Christianity Comes to the Americas, 1492–1776* (New York: Paragon House, 1992), pp. 280–81.

65. An important source for book lists from estate inventories as well as advertisements from book sellers is Marvin Yeoman Whiting, "Religious Literature in Virginia, 1685–1786: A Preface to a Study in the History of Ideas" (M.A. thesis, Emory University, 1975).

66. Louis B. Wright, "Pious Reading in Colonial Virginia," *Journal of Southern History* 6 (1940): 383–92; Richard B. Davis, *A Colonial Southern Bookshelf: Reading in the Eighteenth Century* (Athens: University of George Press, 1979), pp. 3–6.

67. Davis, p. 3.

68. Butler, *Awash*, pp. 77–80.

69. Darrett Rutman, "The Evolution of Religious Life in Early Virginia," *Lex et Scientia: The Journal of the American Academy of Law and Science* 14 (1978): 194–95.

70. Rutman, p. 197.

71. See E. D. Neill, ed., "Witchcraft in Virginia," *William and Mary Quarterly*, 1st ser. 2 (July 1893): 58–60.

72. See H. R. McIlwaine, ed., *Minutes of the Council and General Court of Colonial Virginia, 1622–1632, 1670–1676* (Richmond: The Colonial Press, Everett Waddley Co., 1924), pp. 111–14, 125–29. Also see Richard B. Davis, "The Devil in Virginia in the Seventeenth Century," in his *Literature and Society in Early Virginia, 1608–1840* (Baton Rouge: Louisiana State University Press, 1973), pp. 25–30.

73. Davis, "Devil," pp. 15–18.

74. Samuel Clarke, *A True, and Faithful Account of the Four Chiefest Plantations of the English in America* (London: For R. Clavel et al., 1670), p. 10.

75. Alexander Whitaker to William Crashaw, 9 August 1611, in Alexander Brown, *Genesis of the United States* (Boston and New York: Houghton, Mifflin, 1877), 1:499.

76. Louis B. Wright, *First Gentlemen of Virginia: Intellectual Qualities of the Early Colonial Ruling Class* (San Marino, Calif.: Huntington Library, 1940; reprinted, Stanford, Calif.: Stanford University Press, 1949), p. 240.

77. [Richard Allestree], *The Whole Duty of Man, Laid Down in a Plain and Familiar Way for the Use of All, but Especially the Meanest Reader* (London: For T. Garthwait, 1659); first published in 1658 as *The Practice of Christian Graces*.

78. Wright, *First Gentlemen*, pp. 66–69.

79. Joan R. Gunderson has examined the role of women in day-to-day religious activity in Virginia in the eighteenth century, but what she discusses began to emerge in the seventeenth century as the plantation model began to shape the structure of society. See her "The Non-Institutional Church: The Role of Women in Eighteenth-Century Virginia," *Historical Magazine of the Protestant Episcopal Church* 51 (1982): 347–57.

80. My thinking here has been influenced by Lawrence Levine, *Black Culture*

and Black Consciousness: Afro-American Folk Thought from Slavery to Freedom (New York: Oxford University Press, 1977), especially chap. 1 ("The Sacred World of Black Slaves") and pp. 121–33 on the slave as trickster.

81. See Bruce Jackson, "The Other Kind of Doctor: Conjure and Magic in Black American Folk Medicine," in *American Folk Medicine: A Symposium*, edited by Wayland D. Hand (Berkeley: University of California Press, 1976), pp. 259–72.

82. "Magic, Astrology, and the Early American Religious Heritage," pp. 345–46.

Chapter 3

Popular Religiosity in the Age of Awakening and Revolution

American culture of the eighteenth century offered much to sustain the inchoate, but lively sense of the supernatural that fuels popular religiosity. In many ways religious currents of that century especially augmented the ongoing emphasis on private experience as the locus of vital religiosity. Rarely, however, have those currents that buttressed popular religiosity received careful scrutiny in studies of American religion. Rather, four themes dominate the usual analysis of religious life in eighteenth-century colonial America.[1] One is the evangelical surge known to later generations as the Great Awakening. With roots in the ministry of Jonathan Edwards in Northampton, Massachusetts, in the 1730s, the Awakening became a more general movement through British colonial America through the preaching tours of George Whitefield in the 1740s and continued to support scattered religious revivals into the 1750s.[2] Because of its calls for an inner experience of conversion, initially couched in the Calvinist language of election and predestination, the Awakening receives much credit for stamping on American religious life its emphasis on personal religiosity and for creating the environment that nurtured the growth of the Baptists and Methodists, both of whom stressed the importance of a distinct experience of conversion.

Historians entranced by the Awakening have gone to local church records to see if formal membership actually increased as a result of the evangelical preaching of Edwards, Whitefield, Gilbert Tennant, and others associated with the revivals. In some cases, the results have been fruitful; in other cases, they have been meager. As with the seventeenth century, the most diligent work has centered on New England, with secondary consideration given to the middle colonies. For the southern colonies the record is much more spotty, largely because the nominal Anglican establishments there were generally less disposed to the evangelical style and population dispersion and parish size made it difficult to bring people together for preaching services outside the fledgling urban centers. Even the "grand itin-erant" George Whitefield reportedly commented that there was "no stirring among the dry bones" in the South when it came to enthusiasm for the evangelical message.[3]

The lack of a uniformly consistent record to document the results of the evangelical revivals has led some historians to question whether the Great Awakening actually existed as a discrete religious movement among those who lived in the eighteenth century. As well, the designation of the revivals as the "Great Awakening" did not become commonplace until nearly a century later when Joseph Tracy published a study of early New England evangelicalism.[4] Hence Jon Butler has claimed that the Awakening is an "interpretive fiction," a label manufactured by later analysts to categorize what in reality was a spate of local phenomena that had mixed results.[5] Others, however, continue to regard the revivalism of the mid-eighteenth century as a signal episode, albeit a multifaceted one, that etched the evan-gelical style deeply into the American religious consciousness.[6] Peter Wil-liams has highlighted the way the emphasis on direct, personal religious experience associated with the revivals demolished the boundaries between what official religion saw as acceptable and unacceptable practice and thus challenged traditional religious authority. Consequently he sees the Awak-ening revivals as a popular religious movement.[7]

For our purposes, it makes little difference whether the Great Awakening was a distinct movement or not. What does matter is the way evangelically inclined preachers like Edwards and Whitefield made inner, personal ex-perience the sine qua non of being religious, for that has enormous con-sequences for understanding the dynamics of popular religiosity in American life. By encouraging persons to look inward for the heart of authentic spiritual experience, revivalist advocates were wittingly or un-wittingly encouraging the privatization or interiorization of religiosity. If conversion—the quintessential religious experience—is a matter of individual encounter with the Holy, then authentic religion becomes a mat-ter that ordinary people themselves determine, regardless of external au-thority or official religion. Who can deny the authenticity of that which an individual claims to have experienced within the inner recesses of the self? In essence, the evangelical style creates an ideal ethos for popular religiosity to come to the fore since it makes the individual rather than the religious group the locus of genuine religion.

As well, accounts from revival proponents and opponents alike abound with cases of persons who found themselves in a spiritual frenzy because of the process of scrutinizing their inner lives to discern the gracious work of God. In the extreme, the dramatic intensity of such introspection had unfortunate results. Jonathan Edwards' uncle, Joseph Hawley, was driven to suicide. Others, sometimes while under the spell of the oratorical majesty of evangelical preaching and sometimes while engaged in personal meditation, were possessed by powers beyond their control. In a well-known discussion of the religious experience of his wife written after the evangelical fever had subsided, Edwards described her situation:

The soul in the meantime has been as it were perfectly overwhelmed, and swallowed up with light and love and a sweet solace, rest and joy of soul, that was altogether unspeakable; and more than once continuing for five or six hours together, without any interruption. . . . The soul dwelt on high, and was lost in God, and seemed almost to leave the body . . . the strength of the body taken away, so as to deprive of all the ability to stand or speak; sometimes the hands clinched, and the flesh cold, but senses still remaining; animal nature often in a great emotion and agitation . . . as to cause the person (wholly unavoidably) to leap with all the might, with joy and mighty exultation of soul.[8]

The mood evoked by Sarah Pierpont Edwards' experience will be familiar to persons of the twentieth century captivated by charismatic phenomena. Jonathan Edwards saw her experience and others like it as evidence of the mighty work of God, of supernatural forces beyond human control that stirred the sense of the heart to new heights. Detractors, of course, regarded such an unbridled emotionalism, as much deception wrought by demonic power as reception of divine power. Yet here we see the second consequence of the evangelical style for nurturing popular religiosity, for the dramatic, intense religious experience reinforced popular belief in the supernatural, in a realm of spiritual power that had direct influence on the course of human life. It matters not whether one attributes the source of that supernatural power to God or to the Devil. What matters is that many who were identified with official religion, as Edwards was, buttressed popular belief in the reality of the supernatural.

A second theme that has received considerable attention among interpreters of eighteenth-century American religious life is the rise of rationalism, one consequence of the impact of the Enlightenment on American culture.[9] Generally two strands of Enlightenment influence receive emphasis: the emergence of a presumed liberal strain in New England Puritan thought that eventuated in the birth of Unitarianism in the nineteenth century and the mild Deism regarded as characteristic of the thinking of such "founding fathers" of the United States as Thomas Jefferson and Benjamin Franklin. Both represent vital currents that left their imprint on official or institutional religion. As was the case with the evangelical style issuing from the revivals of the mid-eighteenth century, here, too, what is important is the way these various Enlightenment currents sent signals to ordinary people that nurtured popular religiosity.

The liberal strand within New England Puritan thinking owes its genesis in large part to those who were leery of the kind of intensive, personal religious experience promoted by revival advocates. Charles Chauncy, pastor of Boston's prestigious First Church where Whitefield had preached on one of his tours of New England, regarded this dramatic personal experience of conversion as nothing more than emotional excess. For Chauncy, the search for inner signs or assurance of God's work in the soul that preceded conversion resulted from emotional coercion that made individuals "subjects of terror" if they had not evidenced "bodily effects" as part of their experience.[10] Strongly influenced by the English "supernatural rationalism" advocated by Samuel Clarke and others, Chauncy believed that human reason was more important than human emotion in responding to the Divine. Chauncy never doubted the existence of supernatural power at work in the world and in human life. Indeed, in some instances he sounded remarkably like his forebears, particularly in seeing extraordinary natural occurrences as signs of supernatural intervention. For example, when an earthquake struck Massachusetts in 1755, Chauncy claimed that it was a direct sign of divine displeasure with human shortcomings.[11] But by and large, Chauncy's supernaturalism concerned how God worked on the minds of people in different ways. Chauncy's mild rationalism led him to assert that God might use as many different methods to prompt conversion as there were people since God tailored divine activity to the individual personality.[12] In other words, Chauncy's rationalist tendencies promoted the privatization of religiosity as much as did the evangelical emphasis on dramatic conversion.

Jonathan Mayhew, Chauncy's younger colleague who served as pastor of Boston's West Church from 1747 until his death in 1766, was more explicit in delineating the kind of individualism at the heart of this rationalistic approach to religious experience. In 1749 he published a collection simply titled *Seven Sermons*.[13] In one of those sermons, "The Difference Betwixt Truth and Falsehood," he argued that because all people possessed a rational faculty, they must evaluate all religious truth claims for themselves—regardless of formal doctrine or the teachings of preachers and churches—and decide what was the truth for them to believe. Another of the sermons, "The Right and Duty of Private Judgment," went further in dismissing as irrational any attempt to gain uniformity of belief or adherence to formal doctrine. Only individual use of reason, what Mayhew called "private judgment," could bring spiritual happiness. Like Chauncy, Mayhew was essentially consigning authentic religiosity to the private sphere, making belief a matter of individual appropriation of those doctrines or interpretations of doctrines that made sense on a case-by-case basis. In doing so as a preacher, a voice of official, institutional religion, Mayhew, too, was bolstering what we have called popular religiosity.

So also with the more Deistic rationalism associated with figures like

Thomas Jefferson and Benjamin Franklin.[14] Jefferson is perhaps the best example, since he left behind more extensive writings that allow us to grasp his understanding of religion and personal religiosity. While Jefferson had little truck with much of what made up the religious worldviews of ordinary people—their fascination with occult phenomena in particular—he retained a belief in a supernatural providence expressed in the natural order of things and in the grand design of human history. More an aloof architect of the universe than a personal power intervening in the daily lives of people, Jefferson's deity was a distant supernatural entity that, having endowed humankind with the powers of reason, was content to let individuals use that reason to ferret out truth for themselves. That Jefferson assumed the right of the individual to tamper personally with the received doctrines of religion and the authoritative documents on which those doctrines are based is evidenced in his publishing a highly edited version of the Christian New Testament.[15] In that personal abridgment of sacred writ, Jefferson deleted all that he found repugnant and retained only what he felt deserved belief or promoted common morality.

Jefferson represents but a single example of the way a moderate Deism infiltrated southern religiosity. Richard B. Davis, in his study of book lists of personal libraries owned primarily by persons we would classify as an unofficial southern aristocracy, noted the popularity of "rational theologians" in numerous private collections. He found numerous copies of William Whiston's *A New Theory of the Earth* (1696), Samuel Clarke's *Demonstration of the Being and Attributes of God* (1705–6), William Wollaston's *Religion of Nature Delineated* (1722), Matthew Tindal's *Christianity as Old as Creation* (1720), and Joseph Butler's *Analogy of Religion* (1736), which represented a curious blend of moderate Deism and mild Calvinism.[16]

Precisely what Jefferson and his fellow Deists classified as rational and therefore worthy of appropriation for themselves is less important than the sanction given to the privatization of religion, the basis for popular religiosity. Simply put, individuals did not all have to believe the same things; they did not all have to accept the same religious truths; they did not even have to identify with formal religious institutions. They were free to construct for themselves private worlds of religious meaning by which they could make sense out of their personal experience. Granted, Jefferson, Mayhew, Chauncy, and others swayed by Enlightenment currents no doubt assumed that proper use of reason would yield a broad consensus of what was rational and therefore worthy of personal belief. But such does not necessarily follow once one grants to the people the right to determine for themselves what they will believe. What remains crucial is the imprimatur emerging from American Enlightenment rationalism for the private, individual pursuit of truth that forms the core of popular religiosity.

A third theme marking traditional interpretation of eighteenth-century

American religious life is growing religious pluralism, the flourishing of a variety of forms of institutional religion competing in an open marketplace for adherents. The pluralism of the eighteenth century is intertwined with patterns of immigration to the American colonies that began in the seventeenth century. This immigration brings to the fore another set of signals that influence much popular religiosity, those related to ethnicity. We shall note two examples. In 1681 William Penn received a land grant in the New World from Britain's King Charles II. At once he laid plans for what was dubbed a "holy experiment," a proprietary colony intended not only as a refuge for Quakers, but as a place where Christians of a variety of persuasions might settle. Penn advertised his venture widely, and, as a result, in 1683 he attracted a small group of German immigrants to his colony. Providing a safe place for Quakers alone would have been significant, for the Quaker conviction of the "inner light," of the "truth within," offers fertile ground for the cultivation of a highly personalized popular religiosity. But Penn's opening the doors to persons from a variety of ethnic backgrounds is also significant.

Numerous clusters of German immigrants were to come to Pennsylvania in the ensuing decades after Germantown was organized in 1683, many of them followers of particular religious leaders who had their own idiosyncratic versions of Christian truth. Mennonites and Moravians, the Ephrata communitarians, Dunkers and Schwenkfelders, German (and Swedish) Lutherans—all made their way to Pennsylvania. What is important about Penn's welcoming German immigrants (and those from other areas of northwestern Europe) is the matrix of popular beliefs and practices many brought with them. Some of the German communities had a mystical flavor, promoting a sense of direct apprehension of the Divine that is another expression of the sense of the supernatural basic to popular religiosity. Others were of a pietist persuasion, emphasizing that private, personal devotion that also feeds popular religiosity. As well, the German ethos had its own reservoir of beliefs regarding persons possessed of extraordinary powers, even of witches, and of the need for ordinary people to be able to have access to the supernatural realm in order to harness its power for the welfare of individuals and the community. Such popular belief dovetailed nicely with the keen appreciation of the supernatural in seventeenth-century settlements elsewhere in British North America and helped give it a wider base and sustain its plausibility in the eighteenth century.

Penn's welcoming all who believed in God meant that the colony quickly became home to a wide range of institutional forms of Christianity. Although Maryland had earlier been established ostensibly as a colony where Roman Catholics would be free to live and worship without governmental interference, Pennsylvania became the center of colonial Roman Catholic life by the second quarter of the eighteenth century. The formal beliefs of institutional Catholicism in time were to mix with beliefs, practices, and values that pervaded American culture and with those grounded in various European ethnic cultures to breed a popular Catholic religiosity in the United States. Scotch-Irish immigrants began coming to the New World in the later seventeenth century (and were to constitute the largest single non-African ethnic group coming to American shores in the eighteenth century). Their presence meant that when Presbyterian Protestants organized their first synod, they made Philadelphia its headquarters. Early in the eighteenth century (1707), Philadelphia also became home to the first organized association of North American Baptists. A decade earlier, the flourishing Anglican community in Philadelphia had welcomed its first permanent rector.

This pluralism is of tremendous significance in the story of popular religion. With a variety of forms of official, institutional Christianity all promoting their own brands of Christian teaching and in varying degrees claiming their own version to be the sole legitimate one, the result was that none carried absolute status. None was able to force conformity to its own formal doctrines and practices. Rather, individuals were able to determine for themselves which, if any, of the manifestations of institutional Christianity they wished to accept. Or they could create their own private cluster of beliefs, drawing from many of the versions of official belief available in the religious marketplace. Simply put, pluralism set the ideal stage for the syncretism that characterizes popular religiosity. Immigration patterns, along with changes in British policy that ultimately required colonies to extend a modicum of religious toleration to all Protestant forms of institutional Christianity, meant that pluralism prevailed throughout the colonies that became the United States, not just in Pennsylvania. The extent of pluralism, the sheer variety of public forms of religious expression, figured prominently when political leaders of the new republic offered for adoption what became the First Amendment to the Constitution with its provision that "Congress shall pass no law respecting an establishment of religion, or prohibiting the free exercise thereof." The so-called separation of church and state that is based on this clause would have critical consequences for sustaining a cultural environment in which popular religiosity could flourish.

The fourth theme that marks much analysis of eighteenth-century American religious life concerns the interaction of religious and political forces in the movement resulting in American independence. The issue is much broader than "religion and politics" or "religion and the Revolution." In its larger framework, it has to do with a religious understanding of the meaning of the American nation, of the presumed uniqueness of the United States in the history of nations. As well, this interplay of religious and political factors draws on the theological vocabulary of institutional Christianity, for it helped imprint a millennialist strain on popular religiosity.[17] As with so much else, the roots of this theme lie in the seventeenth century. New England Puritans, for example, were fond of seeing their colonial enterprise as an ideal model for both church and state, a model that when duplicated universally would help usher in the millennial age.[18] A more grim picture of the millennial age came with the publication in the 1660s of Michael Wigglesworth's *The Day of Doom*, an extended poem that dramatically portrayed Christ's return to earth for the judgment day that would inaugurate the millennial reign of Christ.[19] By most accounts, Wigglesworth's poem was printed in an edition of 1,800 copies that sold within a year of publication, with subsequent reprintings also selling well. If so, *The Day of Doom* stands as the first "best-seller" in British North America.[20]

For our purposes, the particular millennialist theology of Wigglesworth's work is less significant than its role in sending signals to readers and others familiar with the poem about the nature of reality present and future. There is a heightened supernaturalism in *The Day of Doom* that extends well beyond its vision of Christ's sensational return to earth to judge humanity. Wigglesworth portrays humanity as involved in an ongoing, often violent struggle against the evil supernatural forces of the Devil; temptation lurks on every front. Only the faithful few will be able to resist and therefore be judged worthy of eternity in the heavenly realm. The import of the poem, then, rests in the way it reinforced the supernaturalism basic to popular religiosity. Life was precarious, and supernatural forces did make a difference.

In the eighteenth century, millennialist thinking received a boost from the evangelical revivals. The presumed increase of interest in religion, as evidenced by dramatic personal conversions, was given a millennial cast, interpreted by some as a clear indication that the end of all things was near. One example of this line of thinking is found in the writings of Jonathan Edwards. In *Some Thoughts on the Revival of Religion in New England*, Edwards claimed that the evangelical revivals portended the nearness of Christ's return and set the locus of Christ's millennial rule in America.[21] Millennialist notions gained greater currency in the mid-eighteenth century with the popular attention given to works like Richard Clarke's *The Prophetic Numbers of Daniel and John Calculated*, Christopher Love's *The Strange and Wonderful Predictions of Mr. Christopher Love*, and Joseph Bellamy's published sermon, "The Millennium," though none would be classified as a best-seller.[22] Love had been beheaded in 1651, and his unusual death may well have lent an added aura of mystique to his apocalypic projections.

Some looked to events in nature and others to the political sector for clues that the end was near. One should recall Charles Chauncy's sermon regarding the earthquake of 1755; the quake was not only a sign of God's supernatural involvement in the natural order, but also an omen of impending millennial judgment. Even the more rationalistically oriented Jonathan Mayhew described the French and Indian wars in millennialist terms. Mayhew rekindled a popular anti-Catholic sentiment that was never far beneath the surface when he argued that the struggle with the French and their Native American allies was symbolic of the struggle between authentic Christianity (Protestantism) and the Antichrist (Roman Catholicism). A British-American victory would mean the triumph of good over evil and hence serve as a prelude to the millennial age.[23]

After armed conflict between Britain and those colonies that became the United States issued in American independence, some explained the movement in millennialist terms. Perhaps the most well-known is Ezra Stiles, whose 1783 sermon "The United States Elevated to Glory and Honor" saw the independence effort as a religious purification of the American people and their government to ready them for the millennium. Revolution and millennium together gave the United States a unique status among nations as one especially favored by God. Popular millennialism was surely not a causative factor in revolutionary politics, but part of a larger complex of ideas and beliefs that enabled persons of the revolutionary generation to make sense out of their common experience. Historian Clarke Garrett has suggested that the peculiar fusion of religious and political millennialism in the new United States had a dual role in giving a sense of purpose to the cultural upheaval of the day and thus allowing many unresolved issues to fester beneath the surface. "Religion, revolution, democracy, and millennialism," he wrote, "were conflated in popular culture into a sense of shared national purpose and common destiny that obscured, for a very long time, the tension and incongruities that had in fact accompanied the revolution that created the United States."[24]

For a time, too, millennialist ideas were attached to the revolutionary movement that rocked France beginning in 1789. Here as well the anti-Catholic dimension came into play, for what drew Protestant writers to see the French Revolution as a precursor of the millennium was its assault on the established Roman Catholic Church. Many treatises published in England and elsewhere in Europe that gave the French Revolution a millennialist meaning were reprinted in the United States. Englishman Richard Brothers' *Revealed Knowledge of the Prophecies and Times*, a classic example of this genre, went through seven American editions in 1795 alone, despite Brothers' being generally regarded as somewhat deranged.[25] We have no way of knowing the extent to which this brand of millennialism penetrated the thinking, the worldviews, of ordinary people. The point is simply that voices coming from the arena of institutional religion, voices of pastors and would-be theologians, helped give currency to the sensational supernaturalism that marked the millennialist dimension of popular religiosity. To people trying to make sense out of their own experience, to those who already regarded the stage on which life was played out as one where supernatural forces were constantly at work for weal or for woe, the religious-political millennialism that came from the circles of official religion could not but have reinforced popular belief.

This review of the traditional themes students of American religion have identified as characterizing eighteenth-century life reveals the ways in which currents associated with official religion perpetuated the keen supernaturalism that is a hallmark of popular religiosity. But there are other strands of that supernaturalism that flourished in the eighteenth century, many representing ongoing development of the supernatural sense central to seventeenth-century popular religiosity. We should note, for example, the continuing and expanding popularity of almanacs. If New England had produced most of the American-published almanacs in the seventeenth century, in the eighteenth, almanacs were produced throughout those colonies that became the United States.[26] In Pennsylvania, for example, Christopher Sauer, of German Dunker background, was printing almanacs for a German-language population by the 1740s. His enterprise was continued in turn by his son and grandson, both also named Christopher. Evidence suggests as well that almanacs, perhaps in part because they were relatively inexpensive, were also the most widely purchased domestic publication in Virginia by midcentury, counting sales from four thousand to six thousand copies per year in the 1750s and 1760s.[27] In New England, the press most noted for almanac production in the eighteenth century was that of Nathaniel Ames in Cambridge.[28]

As earlier, some of the popularity of almanacs stemmed from the astrological charts and other occult-related data that they contained. As Marion Stowell has noted, "The eighteenth century almanac-makers were particularly competitive. Astrology intrigued the common man. The almanac-maker, to survive in the new world of free competition, could not ignore it: he could (1) embrace astrology wholeheartedly, (2) reject it, (3) reconcile it with astronomical science and religion, (4) ridicule it, or (5) double-talk so that the reader could believe whatever he wanted."[29] The first choice would bring the wrath of the religious establishment, the second and fourth would anger ordinary folk and therefore endanger sales, and the third involved too high a level of sophisticated argument. Most followed the example of Nathaniel Ames in opting for the fifth choice, providing material that customers wanted in such a fashion as to avoid criticism from the religious establishment. After all, what readers made of astrological phenomena was their own business.

The reasons for the ongoing fascination with astrology are complex and go well beyond a simple intrigue with the occult and the supernatural world.[30] There was, for example, an interest in some forms of astrology in academic circles. Here we need to note a distinction that was commonplace in the eighteenth century, a distinction between natural astrology and judicial astrology. Natural astrology was perceived to be closer to a science, if not a science itself, for it concerned such matters as how planetary movement might affect weather conditions and climatic changes. Judicial astrology, however, focused on the influence of the planets and stars on human life, human personality, and human events. Natural astrology was discussed in textbooks used in the science curriculum at both Harvard and Yale in the early eighteenth century. Most students of natural astrology rejected judicial astrology as unscientific and without any verifiable basis.

Both natural and judicial astrology had an appeal for ordinary folk. The weather calculations based on natural astrology, for example, were helpful to those engaged in agricultural pursuits, the bulk of the colonial population of the day. As well, some who were taken with natural astrology sought to make connections between planetary phenomena and disease and hence drew on astrological understanding in suggesting medical treatments for particular ailments. The link between natural astrology and medicine represents a forerunner of what in the later twentieth century would be described as holistic medicine and the use of natural, herbal-based concoctions for the treatment of certain types of disease and physical conditions. Almanacs helped popularize astrological medicine.[31] But there remained an abiding fascination with judicial astrology. A perusal of almanacs produced by Nathaniel Ames is instructive since Ames was one who provided material demanded by the market while attempting to fit it into a framework acceptable to official religion. Numerous editions of Ames' almanacs contain material relating to the possible influence of the planets and stars on the human body, particularly in determining personality type. Here we are dealing with the form of astrology still familiar in the twentieth century through horoscopes. Yet Ames made an important contribution, perhaps unwittingly, to the fusion of astrology and formal theology in popular religiosity by insisting that even if the stars and planets exerted some form of control over human life, they were nevertheless means used by God to impress the divine will on humanity. After all, traditional doctrine affirmed that God had fashioned planets and stars in the act of creation. Few colonial almanacs, however, ever got into the risky business of making specific predictions based on astrology; that was left to the reader.

On a popular level, then, interest in judicial astrology remained strong, and those individuals who were regarded as skilled in understanding the workings of the planets and stars, the fortune tellers of the day, were both revered and feared. How widely consulted such colonial fortune tellers were we do not know, but they did exist in the eighteenth century and in some areas enjoyed considerable plausibility. Rhode Island's Ezra Stiles, a voice of official religion as Congregational pastor and Yale president, rehearsed in his diary the standard biblical injunctions used to attack all sorts of occult phenomena, but went on to note in his entry for 13 June 1773: "Something of it subsists among Almanack Makers and Fortune Tellers, as Mr. Stafford of Tiverton lately dead who was wont to tell where lost things might be found and what day, hour and minute was fortunate for vessels to sail &c."[32] Herbert Leventhal has found evidence that the reliance of shippers on astrologers to determine propitious times for dispatching merchant vessels continued well into the nineteenth century, at least in Rhode Island.[33]

What is important about both judicial and natural astrology for understanding the dynamic of popular religiosity in the eighteenth century is very much what it was in the seventeenth. Astrology reinforced a sense of the supernatural, an understanding that the world inhabited by human beings was a world controlled by forces that were indeed more than human. As with all popular religiosity, there is a pragmatic element here. To make sense out of life and to achieve happiness entailed being in harmony with these supernatural forces. In practical terms, it was useless to plant crops when poor weather conditions prevailed. But if one understood and heeded the proper astrological signs, one might be reasonably assured of an abundant yield. With adequate food, a degree of happiness would follow, and life would have meaning. A similar way of thinking no doubt undergirded the practical use of judicial astrology in dealing with people and creating an environment conducive to human happiness. To live in harmony with the supernatural forces that governed the world simply made sense, all the more so if one could fuse notions drawn from popular astrology with aspects of formal religious belief into a personal worldview that worked.

The popularity of almanacs extended well beyond their inclusion of astrological material. In the eighteenth century, it became commonplace for almanacs to include several formal essays, excerpts from serious theological treatises, and pieces treating health, medicine, manners, morality, current events, and items of general interest. Stowell dubbed Christopher Sauer the "greatest exponent of almanac religion" in the eighteenth century because he included the largest proportion of theological and doctrinal material.[34] The more theologically oriented essays buttressed a syncretistic popular religiosity. Many of them, for example, played on the popular interest in millennialism, and some gave aspects of natural astrology an eschatological cast. Rhode Island almanac-maker Joseph Stafford in 1738, for example, suggested that two forthcoming eclipses might well foreshadow political disorder and other disruptions similar to those associated with the eschaton in those areas most directly affected by the eclipses.[35] Of course, earthquakes, the appearance of comets, and other such natural phenomena were also open to an eschatological interpretation.

Herbert Leventhal has suggested that astrology was on the decline in the eighteenth century largely because "its primary vehicle was the lowly almanac, the literature of the semiliterate" and "no learned tracts were written about it."[36] Leventhal's conclusion, however, reflects an elitist perspective since it assumes that what is important cannot be what has appeal to the "semiliterate" but what requires "learned tracts" for its analysis. Since those Leventhal classes as the "semiliterate" constituted the bulk of the colonial population, it would seem rather that what had appeal there is of immense import in understanding the popular mind and the pulse of popular religiosity. If published discussions of astrology and presentation of astrological data declined, what lay behind popular interest in astrology both natural and judicial—an intense sense of the supernatural and its power in human life—surely did not disappear or decline, but simply manifested itself in new and different ways. There has also prevailed the assumption that belief in witchcraft and other occult phenomena declined as Enlightenment rationalism gained ground in intellectual circles because of a sharp drop in legal accusations of witchcraft in surviving court records after the Salem hysteria. This assumption, too, is open to challenge. Legal proceedings may not accurately reflect popular belief, but, as in the seventeenth century, more the difficulty in producing sufficient evidence to sustain an accusation of witchcraft. Persons may have been reluctant to press charges of witchcraft in the courts because it was virtually impossible to prove them. Statutes dealing with witchcraft, however, remained on the books in several colonies. In some, the English common law tradition, where precedent decreed that witches should be burned, remained in effect. As well, surviving book lists indicate wide use in the colonies of one English handbook for justices of the peace first published in the seventeenth century and reissued several times in the eighteenth, *The Country Justice* by William Dalton. This work offered clues not only on how to identify genuine witches through body markings, behavioral patterns, or ownership of certain paraphernalia, but also on how to identify conjurers, sorcerers, and other practitioners of the magical and occult.[37] American printers produced similar handbooks, though none had the extent of use as did Dalton's.

Other evidence supports the contention that belief in the reality of witchcraft remained strong. There are occasional references to suspected witches in some surviving colonial diaries, letters, newspapers, and manuscripts.[38] Francis LeJau, while serving in South Carolina as an agent for the Anglican Society for the Propagation of the Gospel early in the eighteenth century, commented negatively on the failure of authorities to pursue suspected cases of witchcraft.[39] Benjamin Franklin's *Pennsylvania Gazette* in 1730 reported that a crowd of three hundred persons had witnessed a purported testing of two suspected witches in New Jersey, though there is no other evidence to suggest that this episode actually occurred and most think the account a satire on popular belief in witchcraft written by Franklin himself.[40] Several newspapers and magazines, however, recorded an incident in New York in 1787 in which a mob attacked and killed a woman suspected of witchcraft.[41] One study of southern newspapers noted the frequency with which reports of witchcraft episodes in England appeared throughout the eighteenth century.[42] Another indication of ongoing belief in witchcraft is the continuing popularity of John Hale's *A Modest Enquiry into the Nature of Witchcraft.* First published in 1702, about a decade after the Salem witch trials, Hale's work was reprinted in 1771. The need for reprinting seven decades after initial publication is one indicator of the continuing interest in witchcraft and suggests that two generations later Hale's arguments resonated in the lived experience of readers. Hale did not simply rehash the Salem episode, but built a case for the plausibility and reality of witchcraft, discussed techniques used by witches, and offered specific methods to counter its deleterious effects.[43]

The point, of course, is not whether these accounts—especially Franklin's—were accurate reports of real incidents. What matters is that they were reported at all. Newspapers then as now carried material of interest to readers, whether fact or fiction, that reflected an understanding of the world through which readers could organize and interpret their experience. Comments on witchcraft in diaries and letters and the continuing demand for treatises like Hale's analysis of the nature of witchcraft cannot be understood unless we recognize that they portrayed the lived reality of the people of the eighteenth century. That reality included acceptance of witchcraft as one expression of a cosmos inhabited by humans and spiritual powers alike.

Much of the surviving literature on popular belief in witchcraft in the eighteenth century comes in the genre of local legends. The lore of countless small communities includes tales of individuals, usually elderly women, who were reputed to have supernatural powers, thus incurring the fear of other folk lest they use that power to ill effect. As with accounts in newspapers and diaries, it does not matter whether such legends have a firm basis in historical fact. Herbert Leventhal, who mined old local histories to find such legends, was on target when he insisted: "Although these local legends present quaint and picturesque details of bygone days, they are important for far more than that. They illustrate the widespread extent of witchcraft belief and provide valuable information as to the types of damage witches were believed to do and the folk countermeasures that were taken against them."[44]

Simply put, ordinary people continued to blend popular assumptions of the reality of witchcraft with beliefs and practices associated with formal religious traditions. Even the more intellectually inclined, who may well have been dubious about specific claims of witchcraft, were hard put to deny its reality. After all, the Bible, the sacred text of the Christian tradition, talked about witches and affirmed the power of supernatural forces that could work against the best interests of individuals.[45] The popular religiosity that included affirmation of the supernatural, both good and evil, was at least consonant with scriptural precedent. To deny the reality and thus the power of the occult might well have seemed a denial of the authority of scripture itself.

Witchcraft and astrology were not the only forms through which magical and occult phenomena found expression in eighteenth-century popular religiosity. Among the German communities established in Pennsylvania, numerous occult practices remained current and apparently gained credence among their Quaker neighbors. Especially well-known is Christopher Witt, an English convert to the community headed by Johannes Kelpius who remained in Germantown after Kelpius's followers had abandoned their communal endeavors. Witt purportedly offered training to others eager to develop their magical powers, including some who remained convinced of the supernatural cause of disease.[46] Amelia Mott Gummere, in her now-dated study of *Quakerism and Witchcraft*, noted cases in which Quaker meetings had to discipline members who had picked up a range of occult skills from their German immigrant neighbors.[47]

Among Pennsylvania German colonists and New England Puritans in the eighteenth century we find evidence of intrigue with forms of divination, especially the use of the dowsing rod.[48] While common knowledge associates such with the search for water, in the eighteenth century dowsing rods were thought to be able to locate buried treasure or lodes of precious metals. How to use such rods properly was knowledge reserved for the few, and scattered references to procedures for employing divining rods included ritual incantations to be repeated, some of which (such as the Lord's Prayer) came from the realm of formal religious traditions. As with so much else, the roots of these practices, most noticeable perhaps among Pennsylvania Germans but widespread throughout the colonies, are found in popular belief in Europe.

Lest we dismiss such practices as having plausibility only among those of lower socioeconomic standing, we should recall that divining, conjuring, and other magical practices were the subject of a popular satirical comic-opera published in 1766 for the Philadelphia stage, *The Disappointment; or, the Force of Credulity*.[49] Even in dismissing the validity of magic and ridiculing its efficacy, by taking occult phenomena as its subject, the play reveals the extent of popular belief in divination and related practices and describes in some detail ritual procedures to be used, for example, when engaged in a treasure hunt. Apparently the play hit home, for Leventhal has found evidence that those most thoroughly satirized, those who were adept at occult practice, apparently managed to halt production of the play. After all, occult knowledge available to the multitudes loses its power.

As was the case with presumed instances of witchcraft in the eighteenth century, it makes little difference whether anyone ever actually found a buried treasure or uncovered veins of gold or silver by using a magical rod. What does matter is the kind of worldview that makes such plausible and possible. And that worldview is precisely one in which there is a keen sense of the reality of supernatural power and its availability to those who are willing to learn how to muster it. As well, the suggestions that rituals for performing certain occult acts drew on prayers and other devotional acts associated with Christianity points once again to the syncretism at the heart of constructing and maintaining a religiosity born in the experience of ordinary people.

More difficult to document is probably what was the most common manifestation of the occult: popular assumption that some men and women were what a later age would label "white witches." Such persons were thought to have extraordinary powers to effect cures of various ailments or to bring either good fortune or misfortune to those to whom they directed their energies. According to Herbert Leventhal, there is evidence, albeit very scant, that some of these persons worked as professionals.[50] Most, however, were likely individuals who led very ordinary lives and who drew on their presumed knowledge and skills to assist friends or perhaps to wreak havoc in the lives of foes. Rarely, however, was such practice identified with satanic influence, though preachers from the seventeenth century on repeatedly linked witchcraft with the Devil. Missing as well is any evidence that ordinary people found these beliefs and practices incompatible with the teachings of a formal religious institution like Christianity, though the Christian establishment did not encourage them but frowned on them. Instead, we have simply a popular religiosity that sustained a multifaceted appreciation of the supernatural and both respect for and fear of persons who were able to draw directly on that supernatural power. The world of popular religiosity is always a world of wondrous power.

Mention of intrigue with conjuration especially among German settlers in Pennsylvania recalls the role of conjure in the religiosity of African Americans. What happened there in the eighteenth century? As in the seventeenth century, white slaveholders generally showed little interest in carrying the Christian gospel to their African-American slaves in the eighteenth century until the time of the evangelical revivals of the Great Awakening. Even with increased efforts then to Christianize the slaves, by "the close of the colonial period in North America, only a handful of slaves had been introduced to Christianity."[51] But as was also the case earlier, the lack of overt white interest in their spiritual lives did not mean a lack of religiosity among slaves. Rather, practices adapted from the African heritage continued to inform the worldview of African Americans, including magic, conjure, and attributing extraordinary powers to individuals such as tricksters.[52] Those slaves whose journey to the North American mainland took them first to islands in the Caribbean may have augmented popular African-American religiosity greatly, for the Catholic culture in much of the Caribbean fostered a profound syncretism. The Catholic religious world, with its array of saints and sacramentals, blended well with the strains of African religiosity brought across the Atlantic, fashioning a popular worldview rooted in a vital sense of the supernatural. A venerated saint and one possessed of power to heal or curse were functionally equivalent.

Evangelical revivalists from the 1740s on who were among the first actively to seek converts among the African-American slave population found that just as emphasis on an affective experience of conversion resonated with the conviction that supernatural power could invade human life basic to white popular religiosity, the conversion experience itself drew African Americans into the evangelical orbit.[53] One did not have to be literate and read scripture, nor did one have to understand the intricacies of doctrine. All one had to do was experience the power of God within. Albert Raboteau ably summarized the compatibility of the evangelical style with the popular religiosity grounded in the African experience of supernatural forces: "The religious ecstasy of the revivals was not unlike the behavior characteristic of spirit possession in the festivals honoring the gods of Africa. In both cases, participants manifested bodily the presence and power of the divine. Moved to ecstatic trance by drumming, singing, and dancing, African mediums spoke and acted in the person of one of their gods. Similarly, Afro-American evangelicals were seized by the Spirit and driven to act, speak, and move under its power."[54] It matters not that in the one case the source of supernatural power is regarded as the God of Christianity and in the other, a god of African tribal origin. What is significant is that in both instances the reality of supernatural power comes to individuals in visible and mighty ways, reinforcing the perception that spiritual forces, not humans, are the center of the universe.

In effect, the process of "Christianizing" African-American slaves was a process that promoted the syncretism fundamental to popular religiosity. On the one hand, it is a commonplace that white preachers were quick to satisfy slaveholders, skeptical about the benefits of slave conversions, by stressing a postconversion life oriented to submission to authority (whether divine or human) while awaiting rewards in heaven. Simply put, a Christian slave would be a more obedient slave. On the other hand, and much more significant for understanding the dynamics of popular religiosity, slaves "Africanized" the Christianity they received and fitted it into their own worldviews. Raboteau emphasizes this process in describing the worship patterns that developed among "Christian" slaves in the wake of the evangelical revivals:

The rhythmic drumming, repetitive singing, and continuous dancing, characteristic of possession ceremonies in Africa, were replicated in the American South. Slaves used hands and feet to approximate the rhythms of the drum, substituted spirituals for hymns to the gods, and danced in a counterclockwise, circular ring called the shout, the steps of which bore a striking resemblance to those of possession dances in Africa and the Caribbean. The analogy between African styles of worship and the evangelical revivals enabled the slaves to reinterpret the new religion by reference to the old, thus making Christianity seem more familiar.[55]

Prayer was central to religious expression in both the African and evangelical settings. But here, too, we see the process of creating a popular religiosity at work, for the style of prayer that came to mark Africanized evangelical Christianity at least in some areas followed a familiar "call/response" format found frequently in West African tribal religions.[56] This rhythmic pattern became a means to invoke the presence of the Christian God, just as it was a way of summoning the spirits and making them part of present reality.

Some doctrines that were part of the evangelical message received reinterpretation in popular slave religiosity because they echoed beliefs that were part of African tribal worldviews. One example concerns the basic evangelical Christian conviction of the divinity of Christ and the relationship between Christ and the Creator God. From the African perspective, the issue never focused on the metaphysical dilemma that has plagued much formal Christian theologizing. How Jesus Christ could be both human and divine, how Christ could be a vehicle through whom the supernatural power of God could find expression, did not raise the same intellectual problems for African-American slaves as it did for many Euro-Americans over the centuries. Among West African tribal cultures there recurs a conviction that the high god, the manifestation of supernatural power in the fullest, was linked to creation. Even more, it was not uncommon for this high god to act through lesser gods, to take on a multiplicity of spiritual forms whose presence was more directly part of ordinary human experience.[57] It was logical for African-American slaves converted by evangelical preachers to recognize in Christ another manifestation of divine power, to filter that belief through the lenses of African religiosity, and even to replace African spiritual forces with Christ as the most effective means for gaining access to supernatural power and therefore for having a sense of control over one's destiny.

Another example is found in the notion of afterlife. Basic to much African religiosity was the conviction that at death one left behind existence in a physical body and entered the realm of the spirits. Spirits of the ancestors, like other spiritual forces, continued to influence what happened in the empirical world and were thus integral to the supernatural sensibilities.[58] Syncretism with a Christian idea of afterlife was natural and easy and may have even spurred some interest in Christianity on the part of African-American slaves.[59] In the African context, life in a spiritual realm after physical death was a real survival, just as in evangelical belief. As well, popular African belief excluded the grossly immoral from the benefits of such spiritual existence even as evangelical preachers consigned the unconverted—and disobedient, unsubmissive slaves—to hell.[60] One way to marshal the power of the spirits of the ancestors for the benefit of the living was through magic and occult ritual. What Charles Joyner noted about slave life in antebellum South Carolina applies as well to the eighteenth century: "If Africans brought with them . . . beliefs that the spirits of the ancestors regulated life in this world, Europeans brought with them beliefs in omens and witchcraft; both learned and common folk attempted to regulate their lives with signs, charms, and exorcisms."[61] The force exerted by the spirits of the ancestors and the concomitant need to control that force for the well-being of the living helps explain why in time funerals became major ritual celebrations among African-American slaves.

The evangelical surge also spawned the first African-American preachers, some of whom would in time help form independent African-American congregations and denominations. Such preachers were part of what is known as the "invisible institution."[62] Slave preachers might exhort while working in the fields or lead secret praise meetings when the work day was done. Slave preachers also frequently took on the role of conjurer and thus represented the syncretism of the African and the Christian in a vital way. If the conjurer was one adept at seeing the signs of the supernatural that filled the world, the preacher added to that role the ability to implore the God of Christianity to make the supernatural power of Jesus Christ and the Holy Spirit visible in human experience now.[63] This fusion of belief, this amalgamation of the African and the Christian, in the person of the African-American slave preacher points precisely to the presence of popular religiosity. In practice, it is unlikely that the Christian preacher who was also conjurer would see the two identities, the two roles, as incompatible. Far more likely the identities and roles were mutually compatible, for both preacher and conjurer bridged the empirical world and the supernatural world of God and the spirits. In doing so, they acquired great prestige and respect and not a little fear, for they symbolized the potential to unleash sacred power to the advantage or detriment of ordinary folk. Accepting the extraordinary abilities of the preacher/conjurer was another way to give sense to the world of everyday reality.

Before the eighteenth century closed, other sources that would later help disseminate the core values, beliefs, and practices of popular religiosity were making their appearance in American culture. The eighteenth century, for example, saw the birth of the first American religious periodicals. *Christian History*, although published only very briefly in Boston beginning in 1743, is among the earliest American periodicals of any sort. Philadelphia in 1789–90 was home to the short-lived *Arminian Magazine* that was devoted to theological discourse on the doctrine of the freedom of the will. Both these publications, while never reaching a large audience, were targeted for a fairly sophisticated readership. But they set the stage for using the medium of the magazine as a way to reach ordinary people, to send signals to them about what they should think and believe. In the nineteenth century, religious periodicals became a major conduit feeding popular religiosity. The eighteenth century also saw the novel make inroads into American culture. At first scorned by the religious establishment because it represented a form of amusement that detracted from the pursuit of holiness, the novel in the early nineteenth century would assume greater importance as a source on which ordinary people could draw to formulate a religious worldview that enabled them to make sense out of their own experience.

Then, too, before the eighteenth century closed another strand of official Christianity, the Roman Catholic tradition, began to generate written materials for the private use of Catholics who faced not only the difficulties confronting all immigrant peoples, but the added one of often overt hostility from official Protestantism. While the ostensible aim of these Catholic devotional materials may have been to bring the belief, behavior, and practice of Catholics in line with the formal teaching of the religious institution, they became tools used by Catholics to forge their own popular religiosity.[64] Among the first was one that would be quite influential in the nineteenth century, the *Pious Guide to Prayer and Devotion, Containing Various Practices of Piety Calculated to Answer the Various Demands of the Different Devout Members of the Roman Catholic Church*.[65] Even the reference in the extended title to "various demands" and "different devout members" points to the development of popular religiosity emerging from a Catholic base.

What all of these confirm is the growth and increasing complexity of American cultural and religious life. From the Awakening to the Revolution, from evangelicalism's turning religious experience inward to rationalism's stress on private judgment, conditions in the eighteenth century continued to nurture popular religiosity in America. The continuing acceptance of witchcraft, astrology, and other occult phenomena among numerous ethnic communities and in virtually every region of the country also indicates that popular religiosity remained a viable supplement to the official religion advanced by preachers and churches. Especially among African Americans, the eighteenth century provided fertile ground for the syncretism that lies at the heart of popular religiosity. The eighteenth century may have witnessed the end of the colonial period in the history of the United States, but it also was an age when popular religiosity flourished.

NOTES

1. An overview of Christian developments in British colonial America during the eighteenth century is found in Charles H. Lippy, Robert Choquette, and Stafford Poole, *Christianity Comes to the Americas, 1492–1776* (New York: Paragon House, 1992), pp. 317–65.

2. The best single-volume study, albeit geographically restricted, remains Edwin S. Gaustad, *The Great Awakening in New England* (New York: Harper and Row, 1957).

3. Quoted in Sydney E. Ahlstrom, *A Religious History of the American People* (New Haven, Conn.: Yale University Press, 1972), p. 315.

4. Joseph Tracy, *The Great Awakening: A History of the Revival of Religion in the Time of Edwards and Whitefield* (Boston: Tappan and Sennet, 1842).

5. Butler's most cogent statement of his position is his "Enthusiasm Described and Decried: The Great Awakening as Interpretive Fiction," *Journal of American History* 69 (1982–83): 305–25. This article also includes a valuable survey of secondary literature on the Awakening published prior to 1982. Another helpful overview of material on the Awakening is Allan C. Guelzo, "God's Designs: The Literature of the Great Awakening," *Evangelical Studies Bulletin* 9 (Spring 1992): 7–10.

6. See Stephen A. Marini, "The Great Awakening," in *Encyclopedia of the American Religious Experience*, edited by Charles H. Lippy and Peter W. Williams (New York: Scribners, 1988), 2:775–98.

7. Peter W. Williams, *Popular Religion in America: Symbolic Change and the Modernization Process in Historical Perspective* (Englewood Cliffs, N.J.: Prentice-Hall, 1980), pp. 110–13.

8. Jonathan Edwards, *Some Thoughts Concerning the Present Revival of Religion in New England*, in *The Great Awakening*, edited by C. C. Goen, *The Works of Jonathan Edwards* 4 (New Haven, Conn.: Yale University Press, 1972), p. 332.

9. Among the standard studies are Henry F. May, *The Enlightenment in America* (New York: Oxford University Press, 1976); and Gustav Adolf Koch, *Republican Religion: The American Revolution and the Cult of Reason* (New York: Henry Holt and Co., 1933).

10. See Charles Chauncy, *Seasonable Thoughts on the State of Religion in New England* (Boston: Rogers and Fowle, 1743), pp. 97–99.

11. Charles Chauncy, *Earthquakes a Token of the Righteous Anger of God* (Boston: Edes and Gill, 1755).

12. Charles Chauncy, *The New Creature Describ'd and Consider'd as the Sure Characteristick of a Man's Being in Christ* (Boston: G. Rogers, 1741), pp. 23–25.

13. Jonathan Mayhew, *Seven Sermons* (Boston: Rogers and Fowle, 1749).

14. The best study of the religion and religiosity of the "founding fathers" is Edwin S. Gaustad, *Faith of Our Fathers: Religion and the New Nation* (San Francisco: Harper and Row, 1987). Gaustad discusses Franklin on pp. 59–71 and Jefferson on pp. 97–107.

15. See Dickinson W. Adams, ed., *Jefferson's Extracts from the Gospels* (Princeton, N.J.: Princeton University Press, 1983).

16. Richard B. Davis, *A Colonial Southern Bookshelf: Reading in the Eighteenth Century* (Athens: University of Georgia Press, 1979), pp. 78–81.

17. The most sustained treatment of the interaction of millennial ideas and revolutionary politics is Ruth H. Block, *Visionary Republic: Millennial Themes in American Thought, 1756–1800* (Cambridge, Eng.: Cambridge University Press, 1985). Larry Murphy, "Apocalypse and Millennium in America," *Explor* 4 (Spring 1978): 58–65, argues, however, that millennialism was not a vital theme in American life until the twentieth century.

18. On American Puritan apocalyptic thinking, see Charles H. Lippy, "Waiting for the End: The Social Context of American Apocalyptic Religion," in *The Apocalyptic Vision in America: Interdisciplinary Essays on Myth and Culture*, edited by

Lois Parkinson Zamora (Bowling Green, Ohio: Bowling Green University Popular Press, 1982), pp. 40–43.

19. Michael Wigglesworth, *The Day of Doom; or, a Poetical Description of the Great and Last Judgment* (Cambridge, Mass.: S. Green, 1666).

20. Frank Luther Mott, *Golden Multitudes: The Story of Best Sellers in the United States* (New York: R. R. Bowker, 1947), p. 12. Stephen Foster, however, has suggested that sales estimates and the popular influence of Wigglesworth's epic have been overestimated. See his "The Godly in Transit: English Popular Protestantism and the Creation of a Puritan Establishment in America," in *Seventeenth-Century New England*, edited by David D. Hall and David Grayson Allen, *Publications of the Colonial Society of Massachusetts* 63 (Boston: Colonial Society of Massachusetts, 1984), pp. 185–238.

21. In Jonathan Edwards, *The Great Awakening*, *The Works of Jonathan Edwards*, 4:353.

22. Richard Clarke, *The Prophetic Numbers of Daniel and John Calculated*, 2d ed. (Charleston, S.C.: Peter Timothy, 1759); Christopher Love, *The Strange and Wonderful Predictions of Mr. Christopher Love* (Edinburgh: A. Robertson, 1785); Joseph Bellamy, "The Millennium," in *Sermons Upon the Following Subjects, viz. The Divinity of Jesus Christ. The Millenium [sic]. The Wisdom of God, in the Permission of Sin* (Boston: S. Kneeland, 1758).

23. Jonathan Mayhew, *Two Discourses Delivered November 23d 1758* (Boston: R. Draper, [1758]). A millennialist understanding is found even earlier in the introduction to Mayhew's *A Discourse Concerning Unlimited Submission to the Higher Powers* (Boston: D. Fowle and D. Gookin, 1750).

24. Clarke Garrett, "Popular Religion in the American and French Revolutions," in *Religion, Rebellion, and Revolution*, edited by Bruce Lincoln (New York: St. Martin's, 1985), p. 77. See also Nathan O. Hatch, "Millennialism and Popular Religion in the Early Republic," in *The Evangelical Tradition in America*, edited by Leonard I. Sweet (Macon, Ga.: Mercer University Press, 1984), pp. 113–47.

25. Richard Brothers, *Revealed Knowledge of the Prophecies and Times* (Philadelphia: Francis and Robert Bailey, 1795). There were at least three more American editions, including one German translation, published by 1797, along with those published in England and Ireland.

26. See Chester Noyes Greenough, "New England Almanacs, 1766–1775, and the American Revolution," *Proceedings of the American Antiquarian Society* 45 (October 1935): 288–316.

27. See Gregory A. Stiverson, "Books Both Useful and Entertaining: Reading Habits in Mid-Eighteenth Century Virginia," *Southeastern Librarian* 24:4 (Winter 1975): 52–58.

28. See, for example, Nathaniel Ames, *An Astronomical Diary; or Almanacke for the Year of Our Lord 1736* (Boston: J. Draper, 1736).

29. Marion Barber Stowell, *Early American Almanacs: The Colonial Weekday Bible* (New York: Burt Franklin, 1977), pp. 162–63.

30. The best sustained treatment of astrology, witchcraft, and other occult phenomena in the eighteenth century remains Herbert Leventhal, *In the Shadow of the Enlightenment: Occultism and Renaissance Science in Eighteenth Century America* (New York: New York University Press, 1976).

31. See Leventhal, pp. 27–30.

32. Ezra Stiles, *The Literary Diary of Ezra Stiles*, edited by Franklin Bowditch Dexter (New York: Charles Scribner's Sons, 1901), 1:385–86. Joseph Stafford published almanacs for many years in Newport, R.I. See *The Rhode-Island Almanack for the Year* . . . (Newport: Joseph Stafford).

33. Leventhal, p. 58.

34. Stowell, p. 171. See any of the almanacs published by the Sauer family: *Die Hoch-Deutsch Americanische Calendar auf das Jahr* . . . (Germantown, Pa.: C. Sauer). The Sauers began producing almanacs in English in 1755 under the title *Pennsylvania Town and Countrymen's Almanack*. Also see Clair Gordon Frantz, "The Religious Teachings of the German Almanacs Published by the Sauers in Colonial Pennsylvania" (Ph.D. diss., Temple University, 1955).

35. Joseph Stafford, *The Rhode-Island Almanack* . . . *for 1738* (Newport: Joseph Stafford, 1738).

36. Leventhal, p. 64.

37. See, for example, Michael Dalton, *The Country Justice* (In the Savoy: E. & R. Nutt, and R. Gosling, 1727), pp. 513–16. The 1731 edition eliminated the section on witchcraft since English statute law had halted prosecution of witches in 1736, yet it did note new legislation on "pretenders" not only to witchcraft but other occult practices. See Michael Dalton, *The Country Justice* (London: H. Lintot, 1742), p. 360.

38. The most thorough compilation of this evidence is rehearsed in Leventhal, pp. 84–101.

39. Francis LeJau, *The Carolina Chronicle of Dr. Francis LeJau, 1706–1717*, edited by Frank J. Klingberg (Berkeley and Los Angeles: University of California Press, 1956), pp. 25, 30.

40. See the account in Benjamin Franklin, *The Papers of Benjamin Franklin*, edited by Leonard W. Labaree et al., 1 (New Haven, Conn.: Yale University Press, 1960), pp. 182–83.

41. Several of the papers and magazines reporting this incident are noted in George Lincoln Burr, ed., *Narratives of the Witchcraft Cases, 1648–1706* (New York: Barnes and Noble, 1968), p. 88; and Brooke Hindle, *The Pursuit of Science in Revolutionary America, 1735–1789* (Chapel Hill: University of North Carolina Press, 1956), p. 253.

42. Judith Ward-Steinman Karst, "Newspaper Medicine: A Cultural Study of the Colonial South, 1730–1770" (Ph.D. diss., Tulane University, 1971), pp. 62–63.

43. John Hale, *A Modest Enquiry into the Nature of Witchcraft* (Boston: Kneeland and Adams, 1771; first published, Boston: B. Green and J. Allen for B. Eliot, 1702).

44. Leventhal, p. 101. See also Betty Oliver, "Grace Sherwood of Princess Anne: She Was a Witch, They Said," *North Carolina Folklore* 10 (July 1962): 36–39.

45. Probably the most well-known reference to a witch in the Bible is the story of "witch" of Endor recorded in 1 Samuel 28, although the biblical text does not here use the word "witch." There are numerous other references in both the Old and New Testaments to divination, sorcery, necromancy, witchcraft, magicians, and soothsayers.

46. See Leventhal, pp. 107–9.

47. Amelia Mott Gummere, *Witchcraft and Quakerism* (Philadelphia: Biddle Press, 1908), pp. 50–53.

48. Again Leventhal, pp. 107–18, has uncovered the relevant evidence for such practices.

49. The published play gives the author as Andrew Barton; Leventhal, however, attributes it to Thomas Forrest, who himself had a reputation for purporting to be a conjurer. Andrew Barton, *The Disappointment; or the Force of Credulity* (Philadelphia: Francis Shallus, 1766).

50. Leventhal, p. 120.

51. Leonard E. Barrett, "The African Heritage in Caribbean and North American Religions," in *Encyclopedia of the American Religious Experience*, 1:184.

52. See Hans Baer, "Toward a Systematic Theology of Black Folk Healers," *Phylon* 43 (Winter 1982): 327–43.

53. A good review essay that emphasizes the compatibility of African religiosity with the evangelical style and similarities between the African and evangelical Christian worldviews is Robert M. Calhoon, "The African Heritage, Slavery, and Evangelical Christianity among American Blacks, 1700–1870," *Fides et Historia* 21 (June 1989): 61–66.

54. Albert J. Raboteau, "Black Christianity in North America," in *Encyclopedia of the American Religious Experience*, 1:636.

55. Raboteau, p. 636.

56. This pattern has long endured and has continued in some areas well into the twentieth century. See Patricia Jones-Jackson, "Oral Tradition of Prayer in Gullah," *Journal of Religious Thought* 39 (1982): 21–33.

57. Lewis V. Baldwin ably argues this point in " 'Deliverance to the Captives': Images of Jesus Christ in the Minds of Afro-American Slaves," *Journal of Religious Studies* 12 (1986): 27–45. See also Barrett, p. 185.

58. On the influence of spirits on human affairs in African tribal religiosity, see John Mbiti, *African Religion and Philosophy* (Garden City, N.Y.: Doubleday, 1969), p. 83.

59. Preston L. [McKever-]Floyd, "The Negro Spiritual: Examination of Theological Concepts," *Duke Divinity School Review* 43 (1978): 102–11, shows how African ideas of afterlife found their way into religious song in the American context.

60. This point is carefully articulated by Lewis V. Baldwin, " 'A Home in Dat Rock': Afro-American Folk Sources and Slave Visions of Heaven and Hell," *Journal of Religious Thought* 41 (1984): 38–57.

61. Charles Joyner, *Down by the Riverside: A South Carolina Slave Community* (Urbana: University of Illinois Press, 1984), pp. 142–43.

62. The best overall study of this phenomenon remains Albert J. Raboteau, *Slave Religion: The "Invisible Institution" in the Antebellum South* (New York: Oxford University Press, 1978).

63. See Lawrence Levine, *Black Culture and Black Consciousness: Afro-American Folk Thought from Slavery to Freedom* (New York: Oxford University Press, 1977), p. 58.

64. The emergence of materials geared specifically toward American Catholics is the focus of Joseph P. Chinnici, "Organization of the Spiritual Life: American Catholic Devotional Works, 1791–1866," *Theological Studies* 40 (1979): 229–55.

65. *Pious Guide to Prayer and Devotion, Containing Various Practices of Piety Calculated to Answer the Various Demands of the Different Devout Members of the Roman Catholic Church* (Georgetown: James Doyle, 1792).

Chapter 4

The Flourishing of Popular Religiosity in Antebellum America

The prominence of evangelical Protestantism dominates the usual story of American religious life in antebellum America. It is a tale of Methodists and Baptists, of camp meetings and revivals, of voluntary societies geared toward social reform whose membership crossed over denominational boundaries. Historians call attention to shifts in the theological underpinnings of American Protestantism, especially the movement away from a Calvinist base, inroads made by romanticism, and the fascination with Transcendentalism that directly affected only a few but had significant literary influence. Increased Catholic and Jewish immigration receives consideration, as does the reaction to that influx in nativism, anti-Catholicism, and anti-Semitism. A nod goes to the more sustained efforts to evangelize African-American slaves and to the emergence of indigenous African-American denominations. Standard histories also concern themselves with a number of new religious movements in the form of communitarian experiments (for example, the Shakers and the Oneida Perfectionists), the intrigue with spiritualism, and the birth of the Latter-day Saints or Mormons. Few, however, explore how these currents relate to popular religiosity, yet all gave plausibility to that constellation of symbols, beliefs, and values grounded in a lively, but inchoate sense of the supernatural.

Nor do most analyses look beyond formal religious institutions and groups, writings of the theologians and preachers, and pronouncements of religious judicatories and agencies. Virtually ignored are religious periodicals that had increasing prominence and the spate of religious literature geared to the antebellum mass market. So, too, the rise of popular novels usually escapes notice, yet many had religious themes. Students of popular culture have explored the multifaceted ways such literature both shapes and reflects the beliefs and values of ordinary people, even more than literature exalted as "great." More important, many popular novels in the antebellum period were written by, about, and largely for an audience of women. Hence they offer considerable insight into the cultural signals that informed women's understanding of what it meant to be religious. A few have also looked at the drive toward public education, acknowledging that the common schools became vital conduits of popular values. All these phenomena merit scrutiny if we hope to understand the richness of popular religiosity in antebellum America, just as we need to look at the themes and motifs that dominate the standard recounting of American religion to see how they sustained the vitality of popular religion.

The camp meetings and the urban revivals that brought Methodists and Baptists to the fore among American denominations have significance well beyond their impact on institutional religious life and as a form of popular entertainment. Most important is the way the evangelical style they promoted buttressed the emphasis on intensive, personal religious experience. From the camp meetings that erupted on the Kentucky frontier in the opening years of the nineteenth century to the urban revivals of Presbyterian evangelist Charles G. Finney beginning in the 1830s, individual experience of conversion was paramount. Peter Cartwright, Methodist itinerant on the frontier, recorded his impressions in his autobiography, now a classical source for understanding the dynamics of the early camp meetings:

Just in the midst of our controversies on the subject of the powerful exercises among the people under preaching, a new exercise broke out among us, called the *jerks*, which was overwhelming in its effects on the bodies and minds of the people. No matter whether they were saints or sinners, they would be taken under a warm song or sermon, and seized with a convulsive jerking all over, which they could not by any possibility avoid, and the more they resisted the more they jerked. If they would not strive against it and pray in good earnest, the jerking would usually abate. I have seen more than five hundred persons jerking at one time in my large congregations. Most usually persons taken with the jerks, to obtain relief, as they said, would rise up and dance. Some would run, but could not get away. Some would resist; on such the jerks were generally very severe.[1]

Cartwright was far from alone in documenting such dramatic occurrences, and the western frontier was not the only place where they transpired. George Peck, another itinerant, helped plant Methodism in Pennsylvania's Wyoming Valley before becoming a prominent editor and publisher for his denomination. He sketched this account of a camp meeting held near Forty Fort, Pennsylvania, in 1817:

A company of young people from Forty Fort had a tent on the ground, and, for persons who made no pretensions to religion, were unusually interested in the exercises. At the close of the meeting it was evident that the Spirit of God was at work in their hearts. Not being sufficiently humbled to come out and seek religion openly, and yet feeling so deeply awakened as to resolve upon a change of life in some form, the leading spirit in the group [Betsey Myers] fixed her plan to escape from the camp-ground early on the morning of the close without exposing herself to the multitude, and to seek religion at home. The Myers tent was early taken down, and everything was in readinesss to lead the procession of wagons and carriages down the mountain into the settlement. Betsey was so deeply wounded that she lost her power of self-control and wept bitterly. In passing through the deep ravine called Carpenter's Notch she sobbed and cried aloud. As the carriage moved out of the dense shade and entered the outskirts of the valley settlement, her cries became so loud that they were heard by those who were next in the train. The carriage paused, and on the invitation of a female friend, a daughter of Colonel Denison, Betsey Myers alighted from the wagon and fell upon her knees in the shade of a clump of oak and pine shrubs by the side of the road, crying "God have mercy upon me a poor wicked sinner!" The way was soon blocked up. The whole train was arrested and the attention of all was attracted to a little group of young ladies by the wayside weeping and praying. The preachers came along and they found agreeable work upon their hands there on their way from the encampment. Other penitents joined the group, and there the voice of prayer, earnest prayer, ascended to heaven. It was not long before shouts of victory and songs of praise varied the exercises, and now here was the rare scene of a miniature camp-meeting by the wayside.

The attention of the neighborhood was attracted, and people came to the spot to see what was the matter who there sought and found salvation. For several hours the scene of the camp-meeting altar was witnessed in that apparently changed collection of people on the highway. Cries of penitents were succeeded by shouts of deliverance until some ten or a dozen were happily converted to God.[2]

Witness as well Charles G. Finney's account of his own conversion experience, which took place in the confines of a law office where he was then working as a clerk:

I went to my dinner, and found that I had no appetite to eat. I then went to the office, and found that Squire W—— had gone to dinner. I took down my bass-viol, and, as I was accustomed to do, began to play and sing some pieces of sacred music.

But as soon as I began to sing those sacred words, I began to weep. It seemed as if my heart were all liquid; and my feelings were in such a state that I could not hear my own voice in singing without causing my sensibility to overflow. I wondered at this, and tried to suppress my tears, but could not. . . .

Just at dark Squire W——, seeing that everything was adjusted, bade me good-night and went to his home. I had accompanied him to the door; and as I closed the door and turned around, my heart seemed to be liquid within me. All my feelings seemed to rise and flow out. . . .

There was no fire, and no light, in the room; nevertheless it appeared to me as if it were perfectly light. As I went in and shut the door after me, it seemed as if I met the Lord Jesus Christ face to face. It did not occur to me then, nor did it for some time afterward, that it was wholly a mental state. . . .

I returned to the front office, and found that the fire that I had made of large wood was nearly burned out. But as I turned and was about to take a seat by the fire, I received a mighty baptism of the Holy Ghost. . . . I could feel the impression, like a wave of electricity, going through and through me. Indeed it seemed to come in waves and waves of liquid love; for I could not express it any other way. It seemed like the very breath of God. I can recollect distinctly that it seemed to fan me, like immense wings.[3]

Little wonder that as an evangelist Finney would adapt the techniques of the frontier camp meeting for his urban revivals. Finney's "anxious bench," where those who felt the stirring of the Spirit could gather, replaced the "pen" that set apart those under conviction at a camp meeting. Thus the ecstatic fervor of the camp meeting experience came to mark Finney's urban revivals.[4]

Physical manifestations of profound religious experience were not an innovation of the camp meeting or urban revivals; they had roots in the evangelical revivals of the eighteenth century. But they did underscore popular acceptance of the reality of the supernatural. It was not just the preaching of itinerant evangelists that effected religious experience, but the way the divine moved the senses so powerfully that one might lose control over one's body. We have recurring examples of what we earlier identified as ecstatic experience, of possession by supernatural forces. Yet because these times of ecstasy came in a religious context, Cartwright, Peck, Finney, and others readily attributed them to the work of God and saw revivals as battlegrounds between the supernatural forces of Satan and those of God. Finney would later argue that revivals themselves were not supernatural in origin, but could be orchestrated by humans through the proper use of means such as powerful preaching.[5] But such does not undercut the popular belief that those who experienced a dramatic conversion had directly encountered supernatural power. As with the evangelical revivals of the eighteenth century, critics were skeptical, recognizing that any supernatural power beyond human control could have consequences other than those that were spiritual. Leonard I. Sweet reminds us, for example, that nineteenth-century commentators noted how in the camp meetings the sway of ecstasy "led to more souls being made than saved."[6] Mark Twain, in *The Adventures of Huckleberry Finn*, satirically dismissed the frontier camp meetings for pandering to the ignorant and gullible.[7] Yet even their dismissal suggests something of the force the camp meetings and their urban counterparts had in sustaining the belief of ordinary folk in the reality and power of the supernatural.

Traditional treatments of this evangelical surge in antebellum America stress that the camp meetings and revivals stamped a particular style on denominations that most vigorously promoted them and led to their numerical dominance for decades to come. But the institutionalization of revivalism, especially among Methodists and Baptists and, to a lesser extent, Presbyterians, represented a way to control the power it unleashed, and looking at the story primarily from the perspective of organized religious bodies obscures understanding the extraordinary impact of the evangelical ethos in nurturing a popular religiosity centered on the awesome reality of the supernatural that came directly to the believer through the intense, personal experience of conversion.

In evangelical circles in the nineteenth century, the popular religiosity propelled by camp meetings and the urban revivals of Charles G. Finney and others found additional expression in the Holiness movement that swept much of the nation just before the outbreak of the Civil War.[8] What makes the Holiness movement so central to popular religiosity is its looking to intense, personal, and often dramatic experience as integral to the religious life even after conversion. As well, it was a movement that initially began outside the formal structures of the institutional church and looked to laity, especially women, rather than clergy or other religious professionals for its leadership. The quest for holiness began to emerge in the 1830s in the Tuesday Meeting for the Promotion of Holiness, started by two Methodist sisters, Sarah Lankford and Phoebe Palmer.[9] Palmer quickly became a major voice for the movement, publishing several influential works geared to a lay audience. Her *The Way of Holiness*, first published in 1835, was so popular that it went through some fifty editions within twenty-five years.[10] Theologically the Holiness movement hearkened back to the early Methodist emphasis on sanctification, an experience of the constant presence of God that followed on conversion or justification. Although Phoebe Palmer insisted that sanctification need not be an emotional experience, for many it became almost a second conversion or at least an experience as profound and intensely personal as conversion. Sanctification, grounded in biblical promises that the Holy Spirit was perpetually present to those who had faith, came when one already converted surrendered the whole self to possession by Christ. In short, sanctification was another expression of religious ecstasy, of the keenly felt power of the supernatural invading and controlling human life.

That the elusive power of the supernatural was the controlling influence in the Holiness movement finds testimony in the issues it raised, issues debated more among theologians than ordinary folk. If entire sanctification, as Palmer frequently spoke of the matter, meant that one's life perfectly conformed to the divine will, had one attained a state of perfection? Did perfection in turn mean a life free of sin? In theological circles, Christian perfection became a major subject of discussion, much of it centering around Charles Finney and his colleague, Asa Mahan, who were now working from Oberlin College in Ohio. In time, some captivated by the possibility of perfection fused an understanding of sinlessness with one strain of popular millennialism in the communitarian enterprise spearheaded by John Humphrey Noyes at Oneida, New York. For thousands of men and women, what nurtured the pursuit of holiness with its sense of the abiding presence of the supernatural were religious periodicals. Especially significant in this regard was the *Guide to Christian Perfection*, first published in Boston in 1839. Moving its publication offices to New York in the 1840s, the periodical changed its name to *Guide to Holiness* and remained a powerful voice for the movement until the opening of the twentieth century.[11] The *Guide to Holiness* was also a vehicle for Phoebe Palmer to promote her views after her husband, Dr. Walter C. Palmer, purchased it in 1858. The *Guide to Holiness* attained a peak circulation of around thirty thousand, making it one of the most widely read popular religious journals of the day. As Jean Miller Schmidt has pointed out, popular periodicals with wide circulations, like the *Guide to Holiness*, numerous popular biographies that were testimonies to the power of the Divine in the lives of those who had attained holiness, and the writings of Phoebe Palmer and others helped "create a supportive network and a spirit of contagious enthusiasm" for the movement.[12]

While Holiness found its most receptive denominational home within Methodism, this network made it something of a grass-roots movement that tapped into religious sensibilities across denominational lines. It gained additional appeal in the so-called Holiness revivals of 1857–58 that swept across urban areas from coast to coast, especially in the northern half of the nation. Many of these revivals catered to businessmen who gathered for noontime prayer meetings and other religious activities and thus paved the way for the later development of male-oriented, nondenominational groups such as the Full Gospel Business Men's Association. As well, by the 1850s many camp meetings were focused on the quest for holiness, and in 1867 Methodists would take the lead in organizing the National Camp Meeting Association for the Promotion of Holiness. Although this institutionalization of Holiness in time enabled clergy and key lay persons to exert some control over the way in which the pursuit of sanctification was presented and channeled, the use of a structure like the camp meeting that was so geared to popular religiosity assured that Holiness would have an enduring influence in evangelical circles.

The Holiness movement not only reinforced the penchant toward intensive, personal experience at the heart of popular religiosity. Drawing its strength from lay leadership, not religious professionals, it spoke to ordinary men and women. Holiness was a powerful means of sustaining belief in the imminent power of the supernatural, particularly at a time when immigration was swelling the ranks of American Catholics, who entertained their own, very different sense of the supernatural and whose presence challenged the institutional dominance of Protestant denominations. It also bonded the sanctified together spiritually as slavery and abolition divided the nation. By stressing the individual experience of holiness, the movement gave additional momentum to the American propensity to relegate authentic religiosity to the private sphere.

Holiness was primarily an urban phenomenon at first, but even in frontier areas, camp meetings and revivals were not the only venue for sustaining the supernatural sense basic to popular religiosity. In much of rural America there remained a fascination with the enchanting, perhaps demonic power of the rattlesnake. Like the evangelical revivals, this fascination had roots in an earlier period, and Jon Butler argues that rattlesnake "gazing" was a manifestation of occult belief that originated in America.[13] One early commentator, John Lederer, who in the late seventeenth century explored areas of western Virginia unsettled by Europeans, claimed that attributing a charm to the rattlesnake akin to the "evil eye" of popular European belief was prevalent among some of the Native American peoples he encountered.[14] In the eighteenth century, some who wrote about attributing supernatural power to the rattlesnake fused scientific and religious perspectives. On the one hand, they sought to discern a rational basis for the popular belief; on the other hand, they were inclined to consign any power the rattlesnake did possess to its being an agent of Satan, a view that no doubt unwittingly perpetuated assignment of extraordinary power to the serpent.[15] Harvard professor Samuel Williams, in the initial 1794 edition of his *The Natural and Civil History of Vermont*, merely noted the existence of belief in the supernatural powers of the rattlesnake and indicated that there was little evidence to support it.[16] But according to Herbert Leventhal, Williams received so many letters from individuals testifying to the powers of the rattlesnake that when he published the second edition of the book in 1809, he added a ten-page appendix summarizing the evidence.[17]

In the nineteenth century, attribution of occult power to the rattlesnake shifted to the frontier and followed the movement of Euro-Americans westward.[18] Indeed, the few studies that have examined this phenomenon in the nineteenth and into the twentieth centuries have concentrated on areas farther to the west even than the Kentucky frontier.[19] The important point, however, is not where such popular belief prevailed or amazement at its endurance, but the simple fact of its existence.[20] While some might offer a psychological interpretation that links the intrigue with rattlesnake gazing to expression of repressed sexuality, a people familiar with the biblical story of the serpent's tempting Eve might well be predisposed to assume that the rattlesnake and other serpentine creatures did indeed possess supernatural power. Their experience in watching the rattlesnake at work, seeming to enchant its prey before striking, confirmed that perception. It also makes little difference whether one consigns this supernatural power to satanic forces; what matters is how this popular fascination reinforces the underlying conviction that the natural world is a realm of power where the supernatural invades everyday life.

The popular, though unsystematic, belief that supernatural power was real and ever-present also buttressed some features of new religious movements that emerged in antebellum America. Numerous scholars, for example, have called attention to the sense of the supernatural that pervaded the early experience of Joseph Smith and his followers in the Church of Jesus Christ of Latter-day Saints, better known as the Mormons. Smith, a religious seeker, found a ready audience for his proclamation that God had granted him special, direct revelation. Smith's basic claim was that in 1827 the angel Moroni led him to the golden plates containing the untranslated text of the *Book of Mormon*. Mormon tradition has it that Smith used a seer stone, called by the biblical terms "Urim" and "Thummin," to assist in the mysterious process by which he rendered the text of the plates into English. Smith was also widely known to have dabbled in magical practices, particularly treasure-seeking or using occult devices to discern the location of treasures that escaped detection by ordinary means.[21]

Smith's reputation as one who had access to supernatural power and could use that power for the welfare of others helps account for the appeal of the early Mormon movement. Accounts of his extraordinary power, evidenced in purported miracles such as faith healing and the ability to exorcise demons, abound. Combined with Smith's genius in transforming American space into the sacred space of God's primal revelation in the *Book of Mormon*, such supernatural phenomena propelled interest in the Mormon enterprise and drew hundreds into its orbit.[22] During the great migration to the Utah desert after Smith was lynched, miraculous events sustained the Mormon pilgrims, further convincing them that they had tapped a reservoir of supernatural power. The crowning evidence was the sudden descent of sea gulls that destroyed crickets threatening to ravage the first crop planted by the faithful after arriving in Utah. Detractors ever since have challenged the empirical reality of these extraordinary phenomena. But, as with any form of the occult, empirical reality counts for less than perceived reality. What remains significant is how Smith and his adherents were able to draw on popular belief in the presence and power of the supernatural to fashion a worldview that today, in its institutional form, ranks among the larger American religious denominations. People believed Smith because they believed in the supernatural and its pervasive presence in human life. People accepted Smith's claim to leadership based on special revelation because they inhabited a world in which it was a matter of course for some individuals to have unusual gifts in calling on supernatural forces and manipulating their power.

Joseph Smith was far from alone in his insistence that he enjoyed direct communication with supernatural powers. The vitality of popular belief in the possibility of the supernatural's immediate presence received additional support from the upsurge of interest in spiritualism that came first to western New York in 1848 when two young sisters, Catherine and Margaretta

Fox, claimed abilities to communicate with the dead in their "spirit rappings."[23] Their extraordinary powers received much publicity in newspapers of the day. Even those who had no direct encounter with spiritualism knew about it and no doubt found their own belief in the supernatural buttressed by such activity. Later historians have mustered considerable evidence suggesting that fraud and deception were part of this enterprise from the start. Yet that dismissal ignores the real point, for the widespread public intrigue with seances and spiritualist programs did not depend on empirical verification for its plausibility, but on popular religiosity's sense of the supernatural.

Part of the background for the interest in spiritualism lay in the teaching of Emmanuel Swedenborg, whose Church of the New Jerusalem had attracted a small number of American followers since its first group formed in Baltimore in 1792, and in the fascination with Mesmerism. Swedenborg argued that everything in the material world had a counterpart in the spiritual realm, an idea with roots in ancient philosophy. Consequently, material effects could have spiritual causes, and spiritual forces (especially those of the deceased) could communicate with the living. American intrigue with Swedenborg's theories reached its zenith in the 1840s and was especially strong in the Midwest. But the notion that there was a correspondence between everyday reality and a realm of spiritual power fed the inchoate popular belief in the supernatural, and Swedenborg's conviction that humans could actively communicate with the spiritual realm supported the claims of the Fox sisters to do precisely that. As an organized religion, Swedenborgianism has remained numerically small, but its core ideas have resurfaced many times since in such phenomena as Theosophy, New Thought, the New Age movement and intellectual concern with the "perennial philosophy" of the later twentieth century, and wherever else there are assertions of direct links between the empirical and spiritual orders.[24]

Mesmerism's contributions are even more wide-ranging.[25] Franz Mesmer's fascination with hypnotic states, for example, contributed to the development of scientific theories of hypnosis that in turn had an impact on the psychological sciences. For our purposes, what is important is Mesmer's belief that a spiritual force directly gave humans both life and health. While Mesmer did not speak in today's vocabulary about psychosomatic illness, he insisted that sickness resulted from a deficiency of this spiritual force and offered a means of access to its power through the phenomenon of "animal magnetism," usually manifested in a hypnotic-like condition, which revived this spiritual energy. With such power at its fullest, humans would not only experience physical health, but also have supernatural abilities of perception and understanding. Mesmer's stress on hypnotic states and Swedenborg's insistence on the possibility of communication between the corresponding empirical and spiritual spheres undergirded the plausibility of the trances that spiritualist mediums entered to communicate with the spirits of the dead. Although critics frequently panned such episodes as fraud, and no doubt some of them were, as Robert Ellwood has noted, we should also link spiritualist trances to the phenomenon of possession or ecstatic religious experience, which depends on a fundamental belief in the reality of the supernatural and in the power of supernatural forces to seize control of human life. By the 1840s, when Mesmerism, Swedenborgianism, and spiritualism were all at their antebellum height, possession already had a long history as an expression of American popular religiosity. Ellwood also reminds us that we should link continuing popular acceptance of the possibility of possession to contact with Native American peoples where possession in the form of shamanism had long been accepted. Since Swedenborgianism took hold especially in areas where westward migration was strongest and contact with surviving tribal cultures more likely, his analysis is right on target.[26] Then, too, witchcraft and other occult phenomena also drew on belief in spiritual possession.

That strain of popular religiosity oriented toward millennialism likewise found vital expression in antebellum America. Perhaps the most well-known example is that of William Miller, the evangelical preacher and popular lecturer who scrutinized biblical prophecy to determine the exact date Christ would return to earth to launch the millennial age.[27] In the 1830s and early 1840s Miller worked the revival, camp meeting, and popular lecture circuit, fascinating thousands with his predictions of the Lord's return in March 1843. When that date passed without the dawn of the millennium, Miller changed his prediction first to March 1844 and then to October 1844. When these expectations did not come to fruition, many of Miller's devotees abandoned the movement in the wake of this "great disappointment." Most historical accounts treat Miller as an eccentric whose obsession with the second advent of Christ represents an example of the distortion of formal Christian doctrine. Although that may be the case, we must also understand what drew ordinary people to pay attention to Miller in the first place. While a range of sociological and psychological reasons such as a yearning for community and a need for identity may help account for the attraction to popular millennialism, we should not underestimate its grounding in popular belief in the supernatural, in the conviction that supernatural forces could and would indeed intervene in human history at some point.

That understanding also pervaded the thinking of those of Miller's adherents who did not abandon strident millennialism following the "great disappointment," particularly Ellen G. (Harmon) White and her devotees who coalesced into the Seventh-Day Adventists.[28] White herself was not only a convinced millennialist, but one who was subject to states of trance or possession in which she received direct revelation. In such a trance state, for example, she learned that health and diet reform, in addition to keeping the Sabbath on the seventh day, were preconditions for Christ's return.

Essentially White endowed such seemingly ordinary phenomena as diet and hygiene with a supernatural aura. The most ordinary matters could be vehicles that led to the inbreaking of supernatural power in human life, a notion basic to popular religiosity. That the Seventh-Day Adventists as an organized body have grown at a rate far faster than the general population for decades testifies to the enduring strength of this style of popular belief.[29]

Another variant of millennialism and, at times, of spirit possession found expression in one of the better known communitarian experiments of the nineteenth century, the United Society of Believers in Christ's Second Appearing or the Shakers.[30] Their founder, Ann Lee, received the basic teaching that would guide the Shakers, the insistence on celibacy and separation of the sexes, in a vision she had while in prison in England before coming to North America. Her ecstatic experience also included the revelation that she was Christ returned to earth in female form as Holy Mother Wisdom, destined to launch the millennial reign on earth in which women and men would share full equality. In the 1830s and 1840s the disciplined order of the Shaker communities was disrupted when a large number of the brothers and sisters were seized by the supernatural and fell into frenzies of religious ecstasy. Many claimed that Mother Ann had spoken to them. Several produced spirit drawings now regarded as prime examples of American folk art. Others received gifts of song and dance, for which the Shakers are also renowned. Many of the communities began to celebrate a ritual of the heavenly banquet believed to accompany the millennial reign of Christ, sharing an imaginary meal to mark their participation in the rule of God in human affairs. At their numerical peak as this time of "Mother Ann's Work" drew to a close, the Shakers counted only some six thousand members. Hence in a narrow sense they hardly rate as a popular movement of the masses. Yet they received considerable public attention from their inception to the present. Their importance in the story of American religion exceeds their numbers, for what we see in the Shakers is an example of the syncretism common to popular religiosity in their fusion of millennial expectation and ecstatic experience, both signs of presence of the supernatural.

The Oneida Perfectionists also demonstrate the millennialist strain in popular religiosity, albeit in a rather different way than the Shakers.[31] Led by John Humphrey Noyes, who believed that Christ's second coming had occurred in A.D. 70, the men and women who settled at Oneida, New York, in the 1840s insisted that they had only restored New Testament Christian practice by holding all things in common. Further, they believed that they had established the living patterns that marked heavenly life by jettisoning traditional marriage. Since those who had mysteriously experienced perfect love were already living the celestial life, no one could be the exclusive partner of another. Rather, each male must regard each female as his wife, and every female see every male in the community as her husband. Contemporary critics who condemned Oneidans for this practice of "free love" missed the point entirely. From the perspective of the women and men who had been made perfect, what Oneida was all about was transforming empirical reality into a supernatural realm. Those who had truly experienced salvation from sin were no longer bound by the conventions of earthly society, but obligated to live in the present the life that would be normative under Christ's supernatural millennial reign.

A very different venue supporting features of popular religiosity emerged in the movement for common or public schools. By the 1830s many urban areas of the nation were embarking on programs to provide basic education for children. The greater population density in the North and the Northeast made public education more viable there than in the South, where the diffusion of the population and the aversion of slaveholders to instruction of African Americans impeded the development of common schools. Schools required curriculum materials, and among those that first appeared in the middle third of the nineteenth century, none had a more enduring impact than the well-known McGuffey *Readers* that ranked next to the Bible as the most widely read literature of the century. Indeed, estimates are that the various *Readers* sold some 120 million copies through 1920 and in reprint editions have been selling some 30,000 copies per year since 1961.[32] William Holmes McGuffey, who published his first reading textbook in 1836, was a devout Presbyterian as committed to inculcating a broadly evangelical moral stance as providing materials to teach children how to read. As Peter W. Williams has argued, because the *Readers* were designed for use in common schools theoretically open to children from families of all religious persuasions, they could not espouse an explicit doctrinal position, but they could present models of appropriate behavior derived from an evangelical Protestant worldview.[33] In other words, they could offer instruction in those values basic to the "central zone" of symbols and beliefs of American culture.[34] Most of the values presented in the *Readers* dealt with personal behavior, indirectly buttressing the dimension of popular thought that regards religion as a private, personal matter. McGuffey's texts stressed self-discipline, personal honesty, individual kindness, hard work, patriotism, and obedience to authority. The *Readers* had some explicit religious content, pointing to a generalized belief in God who was creator, preserver, and governor of the universe and who, in keeping with postulates of the formal Christian theological tradition, was omnipotent, omnipresent, and omniscient.[35]

Historians have long argued that the common or public schools of the nineteenth century—indeed perhaps until well into the twentieth century— were incubators of beliefs and values broadly associated with both evangelical Protestantism and an emerging middle-class sensibility. The McGuffey *Readers* were primary agents nurturing those values. But we need to look more closely at the worldview implicit in the *Readers*. On closer examination it is evident that, besides extolling specific moral virtues, the *Readers* were a powerful means of perpetuating the inchoate sense of the supernatural basic to popular religiosity. Although devoid of specific denominational content, the *Readers* portray a world where powerful forces of good and evil are constantly at work. The forces of good are associated with the moral values and fairly nebulous religious beliefs the *Readers* extolled, as well as with the American system of government and capitalist economics. Even the natural world is an arena of supernatural power, identified by the *Readers* with a providential God. Adhering to the virtues promoted by the *Readers* is a means of securing both happiness and success, but also a way to assure that the prevailing powers treat one with beneficence. Equality as real, however, is the temptation to abandon moral virtue; the danger of succumbing to evil powers is always present, though with the message that evil never pays. Simply put, the *Readers* etched into the minds of generations of American school children an understanding of the world as a place of power and offered a set of general values that would allow one to live in harmony with that power. Even in the nineteenth century, American Roman Catholic leaders recognized how the *Readers* fostered a popular worldview, one broadly linked to evangelical Protestantism that was not denomination-specific; the widespread use of the *Readers* may have been one factor prompting American Catholics to develop an alternative system of education. Catholic parish schools would foster a sensibility to an even more expansive realm of supernatural power, but one in keeping with the official worldview advanced by Catholic theology.[36]

Issues of Catholic education gained greater importance because from the 1830s to the outbreak of the First World War, immigration patterns brought increasing numbers of Roman Catholics to the United States. Consistently they encountered a religious ethos that was suspicious of, if not outright hostile to, Catholic belief and practice. This anti-Catholic sentiment was fueled by a spate of popular works attempting to expose official Catholic doctrine as dangerous superstition, Catholics (particularly priests and nuns) as crassly immoral, and both individual Catholics and their church as enemies of democracy. The most well-known of these spurious assaults was Maria Monk's *Awful Disclosures of the Hotel Dieu Nunnery of Montreal* that Frank Luther Mott lists as a "best-seller" for 1836.[37] A host of factors spurred this paranoia, ranging from gross misunderstanding of the nature of Catholic belief (and the power of the Catholic hierarchy to control adherents) to generalized xenophobia to fears that newer immigrants would destroy chances for economic success for those born in the United States by usurping job opportunities.[38] There is yet another plausible explanation, namely that the Catholic ethos supported a popular religiosity different from that nurtured by evangelical Protestantism, that it offered a different and perhaps even richer understanding of the supernatural, and that it provided different means to harness supernatural power on behalf of those who entered its realm.

It is important to understand something of how the worldview of official Catholicism stood apart from that of the predominant evangelical Protestantism in order to see how Protestant sensibilities came to regard a popular religiosity springing from a Catholic perspective as a threat. At the same time, however, Catholic popular religiosity strengthened the kind of belief in the supernatural that is basic to all forms of popular religiosity in American culture. At least from the medieval period on, Catholic spirituality was oriented to a supernatural realm. At its heart was an understanding that ordinary folk could have access to a limitless repository of supernatural, divine grace. The church itself was a supernatural institution, the agency through which an all-powerful God offered to mortals a glimpse of the divine dominion and the hope of immortality. Saints and sacraments, priests and pilgrimages, even language itself all provoked a profound sense that within the church and its offices lay the possibility of invoking supernatural strength and power to aid ordinary men and women in their struggle to combat the forces of evil that penetrated to the core of life in a human nature corrupt since the Fall.

The sacraments, especially the Mass where ordinary bread and wine became transformed into the supernatural body and blood of Christ, grafted supernatural power onto the souls of the faithful. The priests who presided over the sacraments were not mere men but symbols of the Divine who could bestow power on the devout or withhold it from the unworthy. Intoning the sacred words of the Mass in Latin, a language endowed with mystery and power since no one used it in ordinary life and few understood it even within the sacred space of the church, the priest represented the aura of divine terror that strikes those who stand in the presence of the Holy. Dwarfed by the majesty of the supernatural, ordinary folk through prayer and devotional acts could call on the saints, whose own inscrutable power could aid in the struggle against the forces of sin and evil that otherwise would surely prevail. Pilgrimages to shrines where such power had manifested itself in a particular place at a particular time helped make visible this invisible realm of power. Relics and rosaries were also concrete means through which the intangible, but real world of the supernatural became part of ordinary life. The Catholic world was one filled with mystery, magic, and miracle, its power released through this host of mediatorial agencies. But this power remained essential, indeed necessary, to combat the equivalent demonic power that could easily keep the unvigilant under its sway.

The formal traditions of Protestantism, particularly in the stark Puritan form that undergirded the Puritanism of much official American Christianity, had stripped away much of the mystique surrounding the Catholic world. In so doing, however, it had demolished the buffer between ordinary people and not only the divine, but also the demonic. Whereas Catholics could summon the saints to stand with them in their struggles of life, Protestants stood alone, confronting directly the majesty of the Almighty and the equally frightening might of the Devil. An unsystematic sense of the supernatural was real to both, basic to popular Catholic and Protestant sensibilities. But Protestants saw the rich Catholic realm of power as one fraught with a demonic superstition precisely because it was mediated to people in so many concrete ways. Thus it became a threat to the more austere power that nurtured Protestant popular religiosity. This difference combined with the xenophobia that penetrated American culture and misunderstanding of formal Catholic doctrine to create an environment that encouraged Catholics to retreat into the security of their own religious world, there to foster another strand of popular spirituality. Aiding the process was the increasingly diverse ethnic composition of the American Catholic community as the nineteenth century progressed, although in the first half of the century, adherents of English, Irish, and German backgrounds predominated. In part the ethnic dimension added a variety of popular understandings of the supernatural that flourished in the European cultures from which the immigrants came, giving rich nuance to strains of Catholic popular religiosity.

Print materials that were made available for personal use of Catholics provide one entree into Catholic popular religiosity. Another comes from the range of devotional practices that gained currency among rank and file Catholic Americans in the first half of the nineteenth century. For the first, the familiar caveats hold true. We cannot with any certainty know precisely how those who purchased and read such materials actually used them. As Ann Taves reminds us, this array of devotional books may reveal more about what the Catholic hierarchy wanted to teach their faithful than what ordinary Catholic Americans actually thought and did. But there would have been no market for them if there had not also been a demand. Further, even if all these works appeared with the endorsement of church authorities, individuals used them selectively, finding in them reinforcement of the worldviews that they had already personally constructed. Hence Taves rightly argues that these works helped create a separate subculture in which Catholic popular religiosity could prosper.[39] Although many of the Catholic devotional manuals published in the United States in the first half of the nineteenth century were translations of materials first appearing in Europe, there were some designed specifically for an American audience.

Among the earliest was the *Roman Catholic Manual, or Collection of Prayers, Anthems, Hymns, etc.*, first published in 1803.[40] While this work apparently had limited appeal, it went through three editions by 1837, suggesting that it filled a need. One matter of great importance about this manual—indeed about the earlier *Pious Guide to Prayer and Devotion*

(1792) and others that followed—is the use of the vernacular rather than Latin. Abandoning the mystique of Latin reduced dependence on priests for access to the supernatural realm and placed in the hands of ordinary people one means through which to approach the saints, indeed even the Almighty. Nonetheless the *Manual* was insistent on the need to look to the church and its sacraments (particularly penance and the Eucharist) for strength. The constant presence of powers that would prey on fallen human nature (and hence the need for strength) is a major focus of *True Piety or, The Day Well Spent, Being a Catholic Manual of Chosen Prayers, Devout Practices, and Solid Instructions*, prepared for publication in 1809 by one identified only as a "Catholic clergyman of Baltimore."[41] Joseph Chinnici has pointed out that all these early American devotional manuals shared a "bleak apocalypticism" in their view of the world, not only because of the prevalence of Protestant "error" in the American context, but also because of the precarious political situation in Europe resulting from the advance of Napoleon and his assault on the Roman Catholic Church.[42] How could one gain order and control over life amid this demonic chaos? The answer provided by the devotional manuals was to seek refuge in the supernatural realm of the church, made visible and concrete in reciting litanies of the saints, novenas, use of medals, seeing the Blessed Sacrament, and the like.

By midcentury the supernatural aura surrounding Catholic spirituality reflected the romanticism that influenced much of official Christianity, Protestant and Catholic, and directly fed into increased emphasis on devotion to the Sacred Heart as well as Marian devotion.[43] Availability and promotion of devotional materials also gained ground as a result of the parish mission movement, in some ways a Catholic counterpart to the revivalism promoted by Protestant evangelists in urban areas and camp meetings. Priests conducting parish missions would frequently bring devotional materials for sale, with some of the proceeds remaining with the local parish. The parish missions fostered organization of parish devotional societies (confraternities and sodalities) that in turn nurtured the private devotional life of adherents. Such societies proved particularly attractive to Catholic women and were most common among German parishes.[44]

Marian devotion received a significant boost in the United States when in 1846 the feast honoring the Virgin gained patronal status and throughout Catholic Christianity after 1854 with the promulgation of the doctrine of the Immaculate Conception. Increased interest in Marian devotion in the United States ultimately led to the founding of *Ave Maria*, a periodical started in 1865 that was, as its name implies, devoted to the Blessed Virgin and designed for family use in the home. Much Marian devotion was centered on the rosary. But it also promoted novenas and meditation on the Sacred Heart of Mary. Although some might classify Marian devotion as a manifestation of the ongoing fantasy of returning to the security of the womb, we should also note that Mary, the divine Mother, became a symbol of escape from the empirical realm into a supernatural one that offered transcendent security amid the warfare against evil that prevailed in life. Such, for example, is the recurring motif in *The Golden Book of the Confraternities* that appeared in 1854.[45] As Ann Taves has written, a "resurgence of affective spirituality underlay the popularization of such a devotional cosmos."[46]

Coupled with Marian devotion came the idealization of the family in which husband and father paralleled God the Father, wife and mother found a counterpart in Mary, and Jesus became an elder brother to all the faithful, past and present. Such mutuality, which transforms mundane reality into the supernatural, was a major theme in the extraordinarily popular devotional writings of Frederick William Faber. A missionary preacher among the Irish community in London and a convert who was contemporary with John Henry Cardinal Newman, Faber had an extensive American audience for his works. His *All for Jesus*, for example, which extols the virtues of popular devotions for ordinary people and makes much of the mutuality between Catholic families and the divine household, was in its twenty-third American edition in 1854.[47] Again, while we do not know precisely how many copies made their ways into the hands of Catholic folk or how individuals actually used Faber's work, the demand alone suggests that ordinary Catholic men and women were finding their religiosity sustained by such devotional writing.

Some materials portrayed the power of the supernatural realm in such a way that it took on a magical aura, one that Protestant critics who failed to recognize the prevalence of similar phenomena among themselves would label as superstition. In *The Sacramentals of the Holy Catholic Church* by Cincinnati priest William Barry, candles, relics, holy water, blessed palms, and the like took on a magical power that can be mustered on behalf of the faithful.[48] Devotional articles themselves became means of access to the supernatural. Simply put, they allowed users to draw on supernatural strength for their own well-being. Yet so much of this popular devotion stemmed from individual practice that Taves has described it as highly individualized lay worship.[49] Ordinary folk could use prayer books and devotional guides during the Mass. Since few understood Latin, the books provided an alternative to worship led by priests that the people could understand. Precisely how individual Catholics combined the world of the liturgy executed by priests with their personal world of devotion we cannot know. But the practice spurred a disjunction between official religion and the religion of the people, between the formal Catholic tradition and the popular religiosity that, one Catholic writer claims, has continued to play "a disproportionate part in the lives of many."[50] Taves reminds us that Roman Catholic convert Isaac Hecker, a tireless writer promoting Catholic belief and practice, believed that popular devotions made the spiritual world, the supernatural arena, present to Catholics in a much more vivid way than Protestant worship allowed.[51]

An equally vivid striking of the supernatural sustained the popular religiosity of African-American slaves in antebellum America. Although the antebellum period witnessed the first sustained efforts among some Protestant leaders to evangelize among the slaves, African Americans continued to appropriate those features of official Christianity that meshed with the religious worldviews that echoed the African heritage and resonated with the realities of slavery. Charles Joyner's careful study of the antebellum slave community in South Carolina demonstrates how this syncretism cultivated a popular religiosity that retained a vivid sense of the supernatural.[52] For example, as more Africans came to the United States by way of Caribbean communities, voodoo made deep inroads into slave spirituality. Most analysts see the practice of voodoo as confined primarily to Louisiana, where there was in the antebellum period greater contact with the Haitian culture in which voodoo took shape, to the Sea Islands off the coasts of South Carolina and Georgia, where relative isolation created circumstances that allowed this syncretistic fusion of African and Christian elements to flourish. They also claim that more widespread fascination with voodoo awaited a resurgence of interest that came in the later twentieth century. But more recent evidence suggests that some features of voodoo were also part of African-American spirituality much earlier and on a more widespread basis than once believed.[53]

At the heart of voodoo is an understanding of the world as pervaded by what in Haiti are called *loa*, supernatural powers or manifestations of supreme divinity that control not only such processes as fertility, sickness, and death, but also natural phenomena such as weather and agriculture.[54] One enters this realm of power through liturgical dance in which supernatural forces seize control of the physical bodies of dancers, thrusting them into ecstatic trance. Those thus possessed became conduits for the gods to speak to others; they also while under possession can demonstrate supernatural power. Detractors have tended to highlight the role of animal sacrifice in the practice of voodoo; such is a part of voodoo as it is part of much traditional African religion. But to single out sacrifice is to miss its role in linking the empirical realm to the supernatural just as the trance induced by frenzied dance opens access to the supernatural. Some voodoo included belief in the supernatural powers attributed to snakes, akin to the fascination with rattlesnake gazing that formed one substratum of popular religiosity in many frontier areas. Joyner notes, for example, that snake imagery pervades much voodoo ritual and argues that the attribution of supernatural power to snakes has deep African roots.

For our purposes, what is important about voodoo is the visionary experience that is akin to the ecstatic possession that comes with the shout in Christian worship, often generated by powerful preaching, and the supernatural knowledge attributed to herb doctors and those endowed with the ability to conjure. All depend on popular religiosity's affirmation of the reality of supernatural spiritual beings who dominate every aspect of life. What is also important is that for those who find access to supernatural power through these means there is no discontinuity with Christian identification, for central even to the belief systems of organized Christianity is the reality of the supernatural. All are manifestations of a world of power superior to any force in the mundane world of empirical reality.

Joyner has also called attention to the continuing belief that illness had supernatural origins and could therefore be countered only by a stronger supernatural power. Popular practices extending well beyond voodoo gave credence to this claim. Conjure doctors, for example, remained important for they brought the world of the spirits into the empirical world through potions and cures that were more powerful than the malevolent supernatural forces responsible for illness.[55] So, too, with any misfortune. Stronger magic, stronger supernatural intervention could overcome any evil power that brought misfortune. Joyner rightly notes that these popular beliefs and practices remained vital, even though some conjure doctors and others who exercised extraordinary power were "acknowledged to have been frauds and extortionists."[56] Whether they in fact had unusual power was beside the point; that African Americans ordered their lives based on the conviction that some could possess such power endowed conjure with enduring plausibility.

Also significant is the way much of this popular religiosity endured, albeit in modified form, as Christian preachers stepped up their efforts to seek slave conversions despite efforts of many slaveholders to keep slaves from involvement in institutional Christianity. Some came to see voodoo and conjure as inimical to Christian affirmation; they regarded conjure doctors and others believed to have unusual powers as having entered into compacts with the Devil. Some substituted reliance on the power of God for reliance on magical powers to counteract evil influence. In keeping with the syncretism basic to popular religiosity, many selectively combined this rich heritage of belief in the supernatural with basic Christian belief. Often the African-American preacher who exhorted slaves as they labored in the fields or as they gathered clandestinely at night for praise meetings was also the one who could tap into the realm of the supernatural power to effect cures and bring relief in times of distress. In other words, preacher and conjurer often fused into one.

As well, the evangelical orientation of much of the Christianity that was brought to African Americans bolstered a popular religiosity with roots in Africa and in the slave experience in America. The emphasis on an intense, personal experience of conversion, often expressed in dramatic ways, drew on popular belief in spirit possession. For slaves, the reality of spirit possession had deep antecedents in the Yoruba, Bantu, and Ashanti-Fanti cultures of Africa and gave credence not only to the powers of conjure doctors and others, but also to the dynamism of the Christian conversion experience. With African Americans, as with others drawn into the evangelical orbit, possession was a manifestation of broader ecstatic experience in which supernatural powers seized control temporarily over human life so that those possessed became vehicles through whom these powers communicated.

Historians have long demonstrated that the Christianity presented to slaves was skewed in its heavy emphasis on submission to both earthly and divine power and in its grandiose promises of heavenly rewards in return for faithful obedience even to oppressive force in this life. But other features of evangelical Christianity resonated with the religiosity nurtured by the slave experience. Belief in angels, those supernatural intermediaries between the human and divine, not only echoed the African openness to polytheism, but also gave fresh support to the continuing acceptance of conjure doctors who seemed to have the same power. Christian attribution of evil to Satan and kindred demonic spirits readily fused with belief in the power of hags, haunts, and plat-eyes. Hags, the disembodied spirits of witches, could work great destruction, as could haunts or the spirits of the dead. If the biblical account told of the Devil's tempting Eve in the form of a serpent, could not plat-eyes, malevolent spirits that could change shape at will, likewise endanger human life? There was no need here to leap from one worldview to another or to abandon one in order to espouse the other. Rather, individuals simply appropriated ideas, beliefs, and practices from both to form what Joyner called a "unique and creative synthesis."[57] Among African Americans, then, popular religiosity with its abiding sense of the supernatural remained vital to antebellum slave life. African Americans readily drew on beliefs and practices forged long before in African tribal cultures and adapted them to the environment of oppression to create a worldview that allowed them to make sense of their own experience. Even when Christians launched efforts to convert slaves, African Americans appropriated those beliefs that reinforced an understanding of the world as an arena of supernatural power, power that those possessed of extraordinary ability and experience could harness for the well-being of themselves and others, but power that could also have malevolent results.

Other peoples who endured oppression as Euro-Americans extended their control over North America also manifested the ability to fuse elements of Christianity with those grounded in tribal cultures in creating other strains of popular religiosity. One example from among the Native American Indian peoples who found tribal life increasingly shaken by the presence of Euro-Americans centers around the figure of Handsome Lake in the opening decades of the nineteenth century.[58] Handsome Lake was a Seneca, one of the tribes forming the Six Nation Iroquois Confederacy.

Located primarily in what is now New York state and the Canadian province of Ontario, the tribes comprising the Iroquois confederacy had long been at the center of much political conflict among European powers occupying North America. In the eighteenth century, when the contest between the French and the British for control of Eastern North America came to a climax, the various Iroquois tribes had been caught in the middle. Both the French and the British sought alliances, exploited the tribes economically, and attempted to subdue them by providing alcohol and other "gifts" to ameliorate the tribal peoples as their cultures were being destroyed. Protestant and Roman Catholic missionaries had, with varying degrees of success, brought the Christian message to the Native American Indians, who were always seen as more likely converts than African-American slaves because of the less obvious difference in skin color.[59] But there was a price to pay. Tribal worldviews began to erode as tribal cultures disintegrated.

Handsome Lake's life illustrates this disintegration. Once a respected leader among the Seneca, Handsome Lake had become an alcoholic. But in 1799, while near death, he experienced the first of a series of ecstatic visions that would transform his own life and enrich the popular religiosity of his people. As anthropologist Anthony F. C. Wallace has demonstrated, visions were central to much tribal religiosity, often experienced by shamans who communicated to their people the truths received while in a state of visionary possession or who became endowed with healing powers while in a trance.[60] Handsome Lake's visions were precisely of this sort, but reveal a syncretism with aspects of Christian teaching. In his visions, Handsome Lake encountered supernatural beings who urged the people to return to many traditional tribal ways and abandon cultural patterns (including abuse of alcohol) taken over from encroaching whites. Other visions, in one of which Handsome Lake conversed with Jesus, brought exposure to the afterlife. Those who remained faithful to tribal values and ethical standards imparted in the visions (called the *gaiwiio*) would enter a heavenly paradise after death. For those who did not, there awaited an eternity in a hell more frightening than any described by a camp meeting revivalist. Handsome Lake became a zealous preacher for the way of life that would issue in eternal bliss until his own death in 1815, pleading especially for adoption of ethical values that would allow the Seneca to retain their tribal ways while living in harmony with those who occupied the lands around them. His worldview caught on among his people and, although it lost some of its potency after Handsome Lake died, remains part of Seneca spirituality to the present.

What stands out is the way Handsome Lake fused tribal and Christian notions to fashion a popular religiosity that gave meaning to his own experience and that of the Senecas. His visions of a heavenly paradise and a hell of torment derive from Christian notions, albeit cast in a way consistent with the tribal heritage. Handsome Lake's message also gave followers a sense of having control over their lives. The political situation and relative military weakness of the Seneca and other Iroquois tribes meant that there was no hope of defeating the whites who had disrupted tribal life. In one sense, the British in Canada and the Americans exercised effective power. But there was a sense in which the Senecas could exercise a superior power, one with supernatural rather than mundane consequences. That came through following the *gaiwiio*, those ethical values given to Handsome Lake by supernatural beings encountered in ecstatic visions. The religion of Handsome Lake reveals not only the syncretism fundamental to popular religiosity, but also the primary function of popular religiosity in providing individuals with a sense of control over their ultimate destiny, even if they may lack power to control their empirical situation.

Another sign of the ferment of the first half of the nineteenth century with enormous consequences for popular religiosity is the proliferation of the publishing industry. We have already noted ways in which publishing had an impact on popular religiosity through the McGuffey *Readers*, journals like *Ave Maria* that were geared to a Catholic immigrant audience, the dissemination of devotional materials, and the appearance of periodicals such as the *Guide to Holiness* that promoted a particular religious perspective. Such tell only a fraction of the whole story. The growth of the nation and the increase in literacy rates created an expanding market not only for periodicals and newspapers, but also for popular novels and other print materials that could be purchased relatively inexpensively. The number of religious periodicals published in the United States, for example, mushroomed from approximately ten in 1800 to 850 in 1840. Here, too, we need to keep familiar cautions in mind. We can with some accuracy assemble lists of journals and newspapers that first appeared in the antebellum period and also of titles produced by book publishers (along with some inventory records of book sellers). Yet in precious few cases we do have any accurate records of circulation, sales, or readership. Given the rate at which periodicals and religious newspapers were founded and folded, securing a circulation base sufficient to meet publication and distribution costs was a recurring problem. In many cases those with lengthier publication runs were subsidized by denominations. Even figures for book sales are rough estimates, though repeated printings and multiple editions presumably signal an ongoing demand. But even if accurate sales and circulation statistics were available, we could only guess at total readership and speculate as to what readers actually made of these materials and how they used them. Nevertheless the proliferation of all sorts of print materials in the first half of the nineteenth century suggests both increasing demand and use, and, as in every age, one may rightly conclude that persons did not spend money on items that they thought had no value. Examination of representative popular religious periodicals will yield fruitful clues for discerning how they helped sustain popular religiosity.

Among the earliest nineteenth-century religious periodicals was the *Massachusetts Missionary Magazine*, published from 1803 until June 1808 when it merged with the *Panoplist*. Ostensibly designed to secure support for Congregationalist missions among Native American Indians and religious work in newly settled areas, the *Massachusetts Missionary Magazine* sought "compositions addressed to the conscience and heart" that were "calculated for the level of children and persons of but common information."[61] In other words, articles were intended for the edification of a popular rather than an elite audience. Along with news of mission activities and revivals, prominent in every issue were biographies of persons whose lives exemplified genuine religiosity and accounts of conversions (not by any means limited to the objects of missionary activity). Many of the pieces were reprinted from other religious newspapers and periodicals; indeed most such journals drew on each other for a good bit of their material.

The *Virginia Evangelical and Literary Magazine* (later the *Literary and Evangelical Magazine*), although intended by editor John Holt Rice to promote Calvinist tenets when he published the first issue in 1818, focused on efforts of numerous "voluntary societies" to effect social reform in the United States that would transform society into a distinctively evangelical, Christian culture. Consequently, its pages devoted considerable attention to delineating ways in which God was at work in American common life, ways in which one could see supernatural power creating a Christian society. In its eleven-year history, Rice's magazine enthusiastically reported on revivals, for it viewed the conversion of individuals as an important means of Christianizing culture. As well, other signs of supernatural providence came in reports of mission work among southern Native American tribal groups such as the Choctaws and Cherokees. Only in the theologically oriented articles could one discern any real traces of a Presbyterian, Calvinist focus. Like the *Massachusetts Missionary Magazine*, the *Virginia Evangelical and Literary Magazine* was really concerned with providing those who believed in a pervasive supernatural presence with evidence of where that power was actually at work.

Among the more long-lived periodicals was one that began self-consciously as a religious newspaper designed to compete with the secular press, the *Boston Recorder*. Founded in 1816, the *Recorder* underwent many mergers with other newspapers and periodicals over the years, ultimately taking the name *Congregationalist and Herald of Gospel Liberty*, its title when the final issue appeared in 1934. Like the *Virginia Evangelical and Literary Magazine*, this New England publication had an ostensible theological commitment, but to Congregationalist orthodoxy rather than Presbyterian Calvinism. Yet for much of its publication life, this link to official religion operated more as a subtle means to give coherence to content rather than as an obvious thematic focus. For more than a decade, the weekly looked much like any other newspaper, combining national and local news briefs, except for offering coverage of religious events and activities. In that arena, the same concerns that dominated cognate publications loomed large: reports of missionary achievements, news of revivals, and discussion of the work of numerous voluntary societies. And the same theme comes through: these are concrete ways in which one can discern the power of the supernatural actively effecting transformation of human life.

Although men controlled the voluntary societies that produced many of these popular periodicals, women constituted a majority of the active membership. Women also no doubt comprised the bulk of the readership of popular religious periodicals even if their content was not directed specifically to a female audience. At the same time, however, there was a burgeoning popular literature that was intentionally oriented to women. Among such periodicals founded in the antebellum period, the most prominent is that generally known as *Godey's Lady's Book*.[62] Sarah Josepha Hale, previously associated with the *American Ladies' Magazine*, began a forty-year tenure as its editor when the magazine first appeared in 1837. By midcentury, the magazine boasted a circulation of seventy thousand; that figure more than doubled by the time the Civil War began. These numbers alone indicate its influence. *Godey's Lady's Book* does not appear at first glance to be an explicitly religious magazine, for short stories, articles on fashion, pieces on household management and decoration, and the like fill its pages. Yet religious values underlie its contents and are readily apparent in editor Hale's column at the back of each monthly issue. Repeatedly Hale argued that authentic religion was a matter of the private sphere. That sphere was identified with the home where, for Hale, the innate religious sensibility of women could mold the character of the entire family. If for Phoebe Palmer the "beauty of holiness" was an intense personal experience of sanctification, for Hale and her readers it was the genteel refinement that came through the love and good taste nurtured by wives and mothers.[63]

An obvious Victorian middle-class base lies behind the values Hale espoused. Equally important, though, are the implications for popular religiosity. By identifying pure piety with domesticity, Hale and her magazine furthered that privatization of religion. As well, the association of spirituality with emerging stereotypes of women bolstered the sense that religiosity was primarily a matter of inner feeling, not of intellectual assent to formal doctrine. Most important, however, is the way the domestication of religion indirectly challenged the role of male-dominated clergy and official religious institutions. Hale did not overtly attack the churches or the clergy; indeed she endorsed and/or was personally actively involved in many religious causes such as missionary societies. But shifting the locus of religiosity away from formal religious institutions reoriented the central zone of beliefs, values, and practices away from organized religion and promoted a religiosity based in the private experience of ordinary people. Barbara Welter's study of antebellum women's magazines and of novels written by women, while not specifically focusing on popular religiosity, came to a parallel conclusion, namely that a piety based on feeling and nurtured in a domestic context became the model for all authentic religiosity.[64]

Many of the popular novels from the 1840s on promoted a similar notion of religion as essentially a matter of the private sphere. The dominant religious institutions had long criticized the novel and other genres of fiction, ostensibly because their diversionary and seemingly frivolous character could detract one from the pursuit of true spirituality. Yet such critiques may have masked the real reason for suspicion, namely the inability of official religious leaders to control what readers made of the ideas they received from novels and the like since they were read in the privacy of the home. Then, too, it is clear that women constituted the bulk of the readership of novels. Hence they also represented ways in which women could create a personal identity and nurture beliefs and values without direct interference from males.[65] Although the focus of popular novels reveals some shifts in the nineteenth century, those appearing before the Civil War supported much the same kind of popular religiosity as did popular magazines. Susan Warner's *The Wide, Wide World*, labeled a "best-seller" for 1850,[66] centered around a heroine, Ellen Montgomery, whose intense personal piety not only elevates private feeling as the primary source of genuine spirituality, but also allows her to triumph over an extraordinarily unpleasant domestic situation.[67] Demand for *The Wide, Wide World* was so high that it underwent thirteen editions in two years. Later critics panned Warner for promoting a mawkish sentimentality, but contemporary reviews claimed that she had made inner feeling seem both the natural and appropriate locus of religiosity.[68] A similar understanding undergirded Mary Jane Holmes' 1854 best-seller, *Tempest and Sunshine*, and *Lena Rivers*, her best-seller of 1856.[69] Confronted with crises and stock villains, Holmes' female characters exemplified a religiosity rooted in private feeling that fosters a morality that ultimately provides the strength to triumph over adversity.

Not all popular novels advanced heroines who were meekly submissive to domestic roles. Even when they did not, they tended to represent a personal religiosity based in private feeling. An example is found in southern novelist Augusta J. Evans' (Wilson) *Beulah*, published in 1859 and selling more than five hundred thousand copies.[70] Here the lead character married and therefore took on a culturally defined role only after establishing herself as a teacher and writer. She also provided a model for personal religiosity. Following a quest to find rational grounds for the style of faith perpetuated by formal religious institutions, Beulah finally concluded that her search was fruitless, for religiosity is primarily a matter of sensibility, not the intellect. Evans' later novels, especially *St. Elmo* that chalked up sales in excess of one million copies,[71] advanced female characters who even more aggressively confronted the frustration wrought by cultural stereotypes of women. But Evans' women consistently derived inner strength from a religiosity grounded in private feeling. Even Harriet Beecher Stowe, whose *Uncle Tom's Cabin* was among the best-sellers of 1852, articulated a vision in which the private home replaced the church as the symbol of morality and religiosity.[72]

In all of these examples, religiosity rooted in private, personal feeling reveals its strength in confronting crises and decisions that require self-sacrifice by providing the inner energy that allows sacrifice to be a positive rather than negative expression of spirituality.[73] Both Barbara Welter and Ann Douglas have argued that this privatization of religiosity reflects the feminization of American religion and culture in the nineteenth century.[74] Welter, for example, claims that the emphasis on a religiosity grounded in inner feeling that provides the strength to endure self-sacrifice transforms the popular vision of Christ into the sacrificial victim who is the paragon of meekness and humility. As well, she finds popular hymns with lyrics by women, such as "Nearer, My God, to Thee" written by Sarah F. Adams in 1841, extolling that feeling of dependence on God that had its cognate in women's empirical experience. Popular Catholic piety of the period fostered similar values. Both may represent ways in which romantic currents penetrated popular consciousness by legitimating sensibility as the most vital expression of authentic religiosity. But sensibility is first and foremost a matter of the private sphere, and the presumed feminization of American religion reinforced the privatization of spiritual experience fundamental to popular religiosity.

Douglas highlights another shift, though her focus falls more on the period from the mid-nineteenth century on. She argues that this domestication of religiosity undercut the role of the male clergy by transforming the popular image of the ideal clergy from one who was a virile and tough voice for God to one who manifested the love and nurture identified with women. Douglas claims that this change represented a symbolic emasculation of the clergy. In the Northeast, the gradual end of state support for religious institutions in the first three decades of the nineteenth century also helped alter the status of the clergy, removing them from the public sector into an ecclesiastical sphere where, as in women's sphere, the ability to influence replaced empirical power. Douglas's thesis helps illuminate many subtleties of nineteenth-century cultural change that most traditional scholarship has ignored, but there is another possible interpretation. As suggested earlier, the evangelical style, predicated on an individual experience of conversion, fed a popular religiosity that flourished alongside the religion advanced by religious institutions. The values that permeated many of the popular magazines and novels buttressed that same privatization of religiosity. Whatever bolsters popular religiosity always challenges the hegemony of official religion over defining what constitutes authentic spirituality. The domestication of religion, whether or not also labeled the feminization of religion, is another way of making private experience the arena where contact with the supernatural most likely occurs. Even in the South, where general cultural patterns were somewhat different, the evangelical ethos perpetuated the domestication of religion, encouraging not only a sense of community among women (both white and black, though the specifics varied greatly), but also the privatization of religiosity.[75]

Along with magazines and novels, the religious newspaper geared toward a mass audience blossomed in the first half of the nineteenth century.[76] Religious papers existed in the major cities of the Northeast relatively early in the century, but many could not compete with the secular press as newspapers and gradually evolved into periodicals oriented to a denominational audience or targeted toward clergy and educated laity. But in areas like the Old Northwest, religious newspapers in the antebellum period often preceded the establishment of a secular press and served a dual function of reporting news of general interest and promoting a religious worldview. Many had denominational ties, some rather loose and often dependent on the personal affiliation of editors who frequently were their proprietors and publishers as well. Most were Protestant, but a handful represented Roman Catholic and Jewish perspectives.[77] Wesley Norton's study of religious newspapers published in the Old Northwest is instructive for understanding the entire genre.[78] He found that virtually all the papers eschewed essays that were heavily theological or doctrinal. Even those with formal connections to religious institutions tended to avoid a narrowly sectarian focus. The religiously pluralistic ethos of the region meant that papers whose denominational bias was too obvious restricted their appeal and ultimately their financial success. The papers implicitly promoted an understanding of religiosity. Norton demonstrated, for example, that most of the papers with a Protestant background shared a commitment to an evangelical piety broadly based in revivalism. They therefore tended to promote a religiosity that saw religious experience as a highly individual and personal matter and advanced a piety that was likewise private and individualistic. Personal religiosity had public ramifications, and the papers routinely stressed an individualistic morality that eschewed vices such as dancing, attending the theater, reading popular literature, participating in violent activities like prize fighting and dueling, and use of tobacco.[79] On the moral issue that ultimately divided the nation, the matter of slavery, the papers generally opted for a moderate position that reflected a pragmatism on the part of owners and editors who wished to refrain from alienating potential customers.[80]

The approach of the newspapers promoted the development of a popular religiosity. By focusing on the individual, whether in terms of religious experience or moral behavior, the papers tacitly endorsed the privatization of religious expression. At the same time, by emphasizing the social ramifications of individual moral behavior, the papers could identify signs of supernatural involvement in the everyday world; when public morals improved because of individual piety, God was clearly at work. The converse was more implicit than explicit: supernatural forces of evil represented constant temptation and propelled immoral behavior. In other words, the public arena reflected the ways supernatural forces both good and evil influenced the lives of private individuals. Hence the papers in essence helped strengthen the notion that private, individual experience was the primary locus of supernatural activity.

Thus far we have made no mention of popular religiosity among American Jews in the antebellum period. The reason is not that persons identified with the formal traditions of Judaism lacked a sense of personal religious expression. Rather, the number of American Jews, while increasing in the antebellum United States, remained so small proportionately that it is difficult, though not impossible, to identify trends. Estimates indicate that in 1830, for example, there were only 6,000 Jews residing in the United States, approximately .05 percent of the total population. By 1860 the figure had risen to just 150,000, or .47 percent of the population,[81] though already there was a popular Jewish press as the newspaper the *Israelite* had begun publication in Cincinnati in 1854. Yet given the relatively small number of Jews in the United States prior to the Civil War, we shall defer the story of how Judaism also fostered a popular religiosity until we look at the closing decades of the nineteenth century when a massive Jewish immigration from Central and Eastern Europe swelled the ranks of American Judaism and brought a diversity to the various Jewish communities that enabled a popular religiosity to flourish.

In the first half of the nineteenth century, American popular religiosity found increasing avenues of expression. From camp meetings and evangelical revivals to the piety nurtured by Catholic devotional materials and popular novels attractive especially to a female readership, forces strengthened the privatization of authentic spirituality. Print materials as diverse as the McGuffey *Readers* and the religious newspapers of the Old Northwest bolstered the personal morality and emphasis on individual behavior as the locus of supernatural activity central to much popular religiosity. The occult dimension found expression in varied forms as Mormonism, spiritualism, and Mesmerism, while the supernaturalism at the heart of millennial expectation fed a strand of popular religiosity that took concrete shape in the experience of men and women who identified with the Shakers and the Oneida Perfectionists. Syncretism found powerful manifestation in the religious experience of many African Americans who combined conjure and voodoo with aspects of Christianity to forge another enduring strand of popular religiosity. The increasing emphasis on the home rather than religious institutions as the forum for vital religiosity also strengthened the private and individual character of popular piety. In antebellum America, formal religious institutions may have grown rapidly, but the pulse of American religion remained centered on the manifold ways ordinary women and men experienced the power and presence of the supernatural in daily life.

NOTES

1. From Peter Cartwright, *Autobiography of Peter Cartwright* (1856), excerpted in *The America Evangelicals, 1800–1900,* edited by William G. McLoughlin (New York: Harper and Row, 1968), p. 49.
2. George Peck, *Early Methodism within the Bounds of the Old Genesee Conference from 1788 to 1838* (New York: Carlton and Porter, 1860), pp. 312–13.
3. Charles G. Finney, *Memoirs* (New York: Fleming H. Revell, 1876), pp. 18–21.
4. On the importance of Finney to American evangelicalism and on the issues regarding the role of women in the revivals, see Garth M. Russell, "Charles G. Finney: His Place in the Stream," in *The Evangelical Tradition in America,* edited by Leonard I. Sweet (Macon, Ga.: Mercer University Press, 1984), pp. 131–47; Carroll Smith-Rosenberg, "Women and Religious Revivals: Anti-Ritualism, Liminality, and the Emergence of an American Bourgeoisie," in ibid., pp. 199–231; and Nancy A. Hewitt, "The Perimeters of Women's Power in American Religion," in ibid., pp. 233–56.
5. Charles Grandison Finney, *Lectures on Revivals of Religion,* edited by William G. McLoughlin (Cambridge, Mass.: Belknap Press of Harvard University Press, 1960), especially "What a Revival of Religion Is," pp. 9–23.
6. Leonard I. Sweet, "Nineteenth-Century Evangelicalism," in *Encyclopedia of the American Religious Experience,* edited by Charles H. Lippy and Peter W. Williams (New York: Scribners, 1988), 2:889.
7. Samuel Langhorne Clemens, *Adventures of Huckleberry Finn,* edited by Sculley Bradley, Richmond Groom Beatty, and E. Hudson Long (New York: W. W. Norton, 1961), pp. 105–7. *Huckleberry Finn* was first published in England in 1884 and in the United States in 1885.
8. On the Holiness movement in general, see Melvin E. Dieter, *The Holiness Revival of the Nineteenth Century* (Metuchen, N.J.: Scarecrow, 1980).
9. On Palmer, see Charles E. White, *The Beauty of Holiness: Phoebe Palmer as Theologian, Revivalist, Feminist, and Humanitarian* (Grand Rapids, Mich.: Zondervan [Francis Asbury Press], 1986); and Harold E. Raser, *Phoebe Palmer: Her Life and Thought* (Lewiston, N.Y.: Mellen, 1987). Margaret McFadden, "The Ironies of Pentecost: Phoebe Palmer, World Evangelism, and Female Networks," *Methodist History* 31 (January 1993): 63–75, places Palmer's work in a larger context.
10. Phoebe Palmer, *The Way of Holiness* (New York: Foster and Palmer, [1835]).
11. See Stephen D. Cooley, "*Guide to Holiness,*" in *Popular Religious Periodi-*

cals of the United States, edited by Mark Fackler and Charles H. Lippy (Westport, Conn.: Greenwood, forthcoming).

12. Jean Miller Schmidt, "Holiness and Perfection," in *Encyclopedia of the American Religious Experience*, 2:816.

13. Jon Butler, *Awash in a Sea of Faith: Christianizing the American People* (Cambridge, Mass.: Harvard University Press, 1990), p. 86. See also George C. S. Adams, "Rattlesnake Eye," *Southern Folklore Quarterly* 2 (March 1938): 37–38; H. P. Beck, "Herpetological Lore from the Black Ridge," *Midwest Folklore* 2 (1952): 141–50; James R. Masterson, "Colonial Rattlesnake Lore, 1714," *Zoologica* 23 (July 1938): 213–16; Frank G. Speck, "Reptile Lore of the Northern Indians," *Journal of American Folklore* 36 (1923): 273–80.

14. John Lederer, *The Discoveries of John Lederer*, edited by William P. Cumming (Charlottesville: University of Virginia Press, 1958), pp. 15–16.

15. See, for example, Paul Dudley, "An Account of the Rattlesnake," *Philosophical Transactions* 32 (March–April 1723): 292–95. Dudley, a Massachusetts lawyer and then superior court justice, was an avid naturalist and also a fellow of the Royal Society.

16. Samuel Williams, *The Natural and Civil History of Vermont* (Walpole, N.H.: Isaiah Thomas and David Carlisle, 1794).

17. Herbert Leventhal, *In the Shadow of the Enlightenment: Occultism and Renaissance Science in Eighteenth-Century America* (New York: New York University Press, 1976), p. 143. See Samuel Williams, *The Natural and Civil History of Vermont*, 2d ed. (Burlington, Vt.: Samuel Mills, 1809), pp. 483–93.

18. See "The Rattlesnake & Its Congeners," *Harper's New Monthly Magazine* 10 (March 1855): 470–87.

19. See, for example, Calvin Claudel, "Tales from San Francisco," *California Folklore Quarterly* 2 (April 1943): 117–18.

20. Much of the popular belief is summarized in Laurence M. Klauber, *Rattlesnakes: Their Habits, Life Histories, and Influence on Mankind* (Berkeley and Los Angeles: University of California Press for the Zoological Society of San Diego, 1956), 2:1220–25.

21. The best general study is Jan Shipps, *Mormonism: The Story of a New Religion* (Urbana: University of Illinois Press, 1985), but also valuable for the present discussion is Richard L. Bushman, *Joseph Smith and the Beginnings of Mormonism* (Urbana: University of Illinois Press, 1984).

22. See D. Michael Quinn, *Early Mormonism and the Magic World View* (Salt Lake City, Utah: Signature Books, 1987).

23. See Slater Brown, *The Heyday of Spiritualism* (New York: Hawthorne Books, 1970); Earl W. Fornell, *Unhappy Medium: Spiritualism and the Life of Margaret Fox* (Austin: University of Texas Press, 1964); Howard Kerr, *Mediums, and Spirit-Rappers, and Rearing Radicals: Spiritualism in American Literature, 1850–1900* (Urbana: University of Illinois Press, 1972); Geoffrey K. Nelson, *Spiritualism and Society* (New York: Schocken Books, 1969).

24. Swedenborg's teaching lacks a sustained contemporary analysis. Still worth examining is George Trobridge, *Swedenborg: Life and Teaching* (1907; 4th rev. ed., New York: Swedenborg Foundation, 1935).

25. The best full-length study of Mesmerism remains Robert C. Fuller, *Mesmerism and the American Cure of Souls* (Philadelphia: University of Pennsylvania Press,

1982). More generally see Robert C. Fuller, *Alternative Medicine and American Religious Life* (New York: Oxford University Press, 1989).

26. Robert S. Ellwood, "Occult Movements in America," in *Encyclopedia of the American Religious Experience*, 2:716.

27. Helpful guides to millennialism in general and its manifestation in American popular religion are Hillel Schwartz, "The End of the Beginning: Millenarian Studies, 1961–1975," *Religious Studies Review* 2 (July 1976): 1–15; David E. Smith, "Millenarian Scholarship in America," *American Quarterly* 17 (1965): 535–49; and Leonard I. Sweet, "Millennialism in America: Recent Studies," *Theological Studies* 40 (1979): 510–31. On Miller, see the sympathetic if not hagiographic study by Francis D. Nichol, *The Midnight Cry: A Defense of the Character and Conduct of William Miller and the Millerites* (Washington, D.C.: Review and Herald Publishing Association, 1944).

28. Several valuable essays are found in Edwin S. Gaustad, ed., *The Rise of Adventism: Religion and Society in Mid-Nineteenth Century America* (New York: Harper and Row, 1974).

29. In 1981, for example, the Seventh-Day Adventists reported a membership of approximately 553,000; ten years later, the denomination reported just over 701,000 members, representing a growth rate of 26.8 percent.

30. A recent, provocative study is Stephen J. Stein, *The Shaker Experience in America: A History of the United Society of Believers* (New Haven, Conn.: Yale University Press, 1992).

31. On Oneida, see Maren Lockwood Carden, *Oneida: Utopian Community to Modern Corporation* (Baltimore: Johns Hopkins University Press, 1969).

32. John H. Westerhoff, *McGuffey and His Readers: Piety, Morality, and Education in Nineteenth Century America* (Nashville: Abingdon Press, 1978), p. 18.

33. Peter W. Williams, *Popular Religion in America: Symbolic Change and the Modernization Process in Historical Perspective* (Englewood Cliffs, N.J.: Prentice-Hall, 1980), p. 170.

34. Westerhoff noted that until the various *Readers* underwent extensive revision in 1879, values were the theme for over half the lessons offered.

35. Other studies, some of them uncritical, of McGuffey and the impact of the *Readers* on American culture include Harvey C. Minnick, *William Holmes McGuffey and His Readers* (Cincinnati: American Book Co., 1936); Alice McGuffey Ruggles, *The Story of the McGuffeys* (New York: American Book Co., 1950); Richard D. Mosier, *Making the American Mind: Social and Moral Issues in the McGuffey Readers* (New York: King's Crown Press, 1947); and Carol Billman, "McGuffey's Readers and Alger's Fiction: The Gospel of Virtue According to Popular Children's Literature," *Journal of Popular Culture* 11 (1971): 614–19. Also valuable is the introduction by historian Henry Steele Commager to the *Fifth Eclectic Reader* (New York: Signet Classics, 1962).

36. This point is made by Robert D. Cross, "Origins of the Catholic Parochial Schools in America," *American Benedictine Review* 16 (1965): 195.

37. Maria Monk, *Awful Disclosures of the Hotel Dieu Nunnery of Montreal* (New York: Howe and Bates, 1836). See Frank Luther Mott, *Golden Multitudes: The Story of Best Sellers in the United States* (New York: R. R. Bowker, 1947), p. 306.

38. Among the more compelling studies of this hate literature and one that places

it in a larger historical context is David Brion Davis, "Some Themes of Counter-subversion: An Analysis of Anti-Masonic, Anti-Catholic, and Anti-Mormon Literature," *Mississippi Valley Historical Review* 47 (1960): 205–24.

39. See Ann Taves, *The Household of Faith: Roman Catholic Devotions in Mid-Nineteenth Century America* (Notre Dame, Ind.: University of Notre Dame Press, 1988).

40. *Roman Catholic Manual, or Collection of Prayers, Anthems, Hymns, etc.* (Baltimore: Fielding Lucas, Jr., [1803]).

41. A Catholic Clergyman of Baltimore, *True Piety or, The Day Well Spent, Being a Catholic Manual of Chosen Prayers, Devout Practices, and Solid Instructions, Adapted to Every State of Life. Taken Partly from the French* (Baltimore: Warner and Hanna, 1809).

42. Joseph P. Chinnici, "Organization of the Spiritual Life: American Catholic Devotional Works, 1791–1866," *Theological Studies* 40 (1979): 229–55.

43. One can readily detect the significant increase of devotional material oriented to the Sacred Heart in those editions of the *Pious Guide to Prayer and Devotion* (first published, Georgetown [Washington, D.C.]: James Doyle, 1792) that appeared after 1815. Seven editions appeared between 1815 and 1875, compared with two prior to 1815.

44. Taves, pp. 17–18.

45. *The Golden Book of the Confraternities* (New York: Dunigan, 1854).

46. Taves, p. 71.

47. Frederick William Faber, *All for Jesus: or, The Easy Ways of Divine Love*, 23d ed. (Boston: John Murphy, 1854).

48. William J. Barry, *The Sacramentals of the Holy Catholic Church, or Flowers for the Garden of the Liturgy* (Cincinnati: John P. Walsh, 1858). The subtitle alone reflects the heightened romantic sentiment that flows through the work.

49. Taves, pp. 42–45.

50. Donald Attwater, ed., *A Catholic Dictionary* (New York: Macmillan, 1942), p. 154.

51. Taves, p. 47.

52. The following discussion relies heavily on Charles Joyner, *Down by the Riverside: A South Carolina Slave Community* (Urbana: University of Illinois Press, 1984), pp. 144–50.

53. For example, the reminiscences in Zora Neale Hurston, *The Sanctified Church* (Berkeley, Calif.: Turtle Island, 1981), give evidence of some voodoo practices in parts of rural mainland South Carolina and Florida after the Civil War.

54. A valuable exposition of Haitian voodoo is Jean Price-Mars, *So Spoke the Uncle*, translated by Magdalino W. Shannon (Washington, D.C.: Three Continents Press, 1983; first published, 1928).

55. Also see Leonora Herron and Alice M. Bacon, "Conjuring and Conjure Doctors," *Southern Workman* 24 (1895), beginning in the November issue and ending in the December issue.

56. Joyner, p. 148.

57. Joyner, p. 154. See also pp. 150–55, 161–66.

58. On Handsome Lake, see Anthony F. C. Wallace, *The Death and Rebirth of the Seneca* (New York: Knopf, 1970). For a cognate understanding of how Handsome Lake represented a strain of popular religion, see Williams, pp. 27–32.

59. Winthrop D. Jordan, *White over Black: American Attitudes toward the Negro, 1550–1812* (Chapel Hill: University of North Carolina Press, 1968), definitively demonstrated that skin color was the decisive factor in determining the difference in attitudes toward Africans and Native Americans.

60. See John R. Swanton, "Religious Beliefs and Medical Practices of the Creek Indians," *U.S. Bureau of Ethnology Annual Report* 42 (1924–25): 473–672.

61. *Massachusetts Missionary Magazine* 1 (May 1803): 159.

62. During its publication history, the magazine had several name changes. The most familiar titles are *Godey's Lady's Book*, *Lady's Book*, and *Godey's Magazine*. There are two secondary studies of the impact of *Godey's Lady's Book*: Ruth E. Finley, *The Lady of Godey's* (Philadelphia: Lippincott, 1931); and Angela Marie Howard Zophy, "For the Improvement of My Sex: Sarah Josepha Hale's Editorship of Godey's Lady's Book, 1837–1877" (Ph.D. diss., Ohio State University, 1978). See also Kathryn Long, "*Godey's Lady's Book*," forthcoming in *Popular Religious Periodicals of the United States*.

63. See, for example, *Godey's Lady's Book* 23 (November 1841): 236; 33 (November 1846): 235; and 34 (March 1847): 173.

64. Barbara Welter, "The Cult of True Womanhood, 1820–1860," *American Quarterly* 18 (Summer 1966): 151–74.

65. A thoughtful study with import beyond that suggested by its title is Nina Baym, *Woman's Fiction: A Guide to Novels by and about Women in America, 1820–1879* (Ithaca, N.Y.: Cornell University Press, 1978).

66. Mott, p. 307.

67. Susan Warner, *The Wide, Wide World* (New York: G. P. Putnam, 1850). See also Beatrice K. Hofstadter, "Popular Culture and the Romantic Heroine," *American Scholar* 30 (Winter 1960–61): 100–102.

68. Mott, pp. 122ff.

69. Mary Jane Holmes, *Tempest and Sunshine* (New York: D. Appleton, 1854); *Lena Rivers* (New York: Miller, Orton and Co., 1856).

70. Augusta J. Evans, *Beulah* (New York: Derby and Jackson, 1859).

71. Augusta J. Evans, *St. Elmo* (New York: George W. Carleton, 1867).

72. Gayle Kimball, *The Religious Ideas of Harriet Beecher Stowe* (Lewiston, N.Y.: Mellen, 1974), p. 84.

73. A similar emphasis on seeing religion as a private matter and looking to the domestic sphere of the home as the place where authentic religiosity was nurtured but tested through suffering prevailed in popular novels published in England in the 1840s, according to Kathleen Tillotson, *Novels of the Eighteen-Forties* (Oxford: Clarendon Press, 1954).

74. Barbara Welter, "The Feminization of American Religion, 1800–1860," in *Clio's Consciousness Raised: New Perspectives on the History of Women*, edited by Mary S. Hartman and Lois Banner (New York: Harper and Row, 1974), pp. 137–57; Ann Douglas, *The Feminization of American Culture* (New York: Knopf, 1978).

75. See Jean E. Friedman, *The Enclosed Garden: Women and Community in the Evangelical South, 1830–1900* (Chapel Hill: University of North Carolina Press, 1985). In a broader context, Friedman argues that in the South the "evangelical community survived because [white] women adopted traditional roles that oriented them toward family concerns" (p. 37). In other words, parallel forces that linked

domesticity with women's roles and thus with personal spirituality and popular religiosity prevailed in both North and South.

76. Several such newspapers are profiled in the forthcoming *Popular Religious Periodicals of the United States.*

77. The well-known Catholic and Jewish papers, the *Catholic Telegraph* and the *Israelite*, were both published in Cincinnati.

78. Wesley Norton, *Religious Newspapers in the Old Northwest to 1861: A History, Bibliography, and Record of Opinion* (Athens, Ohio: Ohio University Press, 1977).

79. See Norton, pp. 67–89, 134–37.

80. See Norton, pp. 111–33.

81. Deborah Dash Moore, "The Social History of American Judaism," in *Encyclopedia of the American Religious Experience*, 1:294.

Chapter 5

Challenge and Change in Traditional Religion: Nurturing Popular Religiosity in the Later Nineteenth Century

As the United States became more urban and industrialized in the decades after the Civil War, forces both related to and distinguished from institutional religion continued to nurture the unsystematic, but lively sense of the supernatural at the heart of popular religiosity. Even the cultural currents that had great influence on the formal religious traditions in their own way fostered popular religiosity, though that dimension has rarely received scrutiny. Usually immigration, urbanization, industrialization, and the challenges to the intellectual foundations of religious faith wrought by Darwinism, the emerging study of comparative religion, and higher criticism are the themes that loom large in traditional interpretations of American religion in the last half of the nineteenth century. Most often emphasis falls on how the heavy immigration from Central, Southern, and Eastern Europe challenged the Protestant hegemony in American religious life, since those who came to American shores from 1880 until the outbreak of the First World War were by and large identified with the Roman Catholic, Eastern Orthodox, and Jewish traditions. How these traditions coped with the influx of immigrants and how in turn the gradual process of Americanization affected both the immigrant and the religious group informs most treatments of American religious history. Because immigrants flocked to the cities where burgeoning factories and business enterprises associated with industrialization offered jobs, often at low pay and under hazardous working conditions, the standard accounts also dwell on the impact of urbanization and industrialization on the various denominations. Generally some attention falls as well on movements, such as the social gospel or the work of the Evangelical Alliance, that crossed denominational lines. Usually, too, note is taken of the emergence of some new religious movements, such as Christian Science and Theosophy, that were born in the cultural and intellectual tumult of the later nineteenth century.

Those who focus on the history of religious thought fix on showing how American theological thinkers responded to the perceived threats to Christian belief posed by new intellectual currents. Darwinian theory, for example, reared its challenge to the orthodox understanding not only of divine creation, but also of the Fall of humanity into sin. Yet the theory of evolution resonated strongly with the sense of progress prevalent in the larger culture. The danger of comparative religion, which received a boost in the 1893 Chicago World's Parliament of Religions, came in its emphasis on the underlying unity among religions. If all religions shared a common base, then claims for the superiority of Christianity, especially in its Protestant forms, lost ground. Application of higher criticism to biblical texts, so the traditional story goes, provoked fears that the authority of scripture itself was being undermined. All of these movements, however, provoked greater fear among the religious professionals, the clergy and the theologians, than among the people themselves.[1]

As usual, the story of how ordinary men and women went about the business of developing and sustaining worldviews that allowed them to make sense out of their experience receives short shrift in standard analysis. Immigration, urbanization, industrialization, and the new intellectual currents did have an impact on the popular level, albeit different from that felt by the official religious institutions and their professional leaders. To understand the dynamics of popular religiosity in this era, we need to look beyond immigration and industrialization, urbanization and new intellectual currents. We must also look at how people maintained a sense of being religious in the midst of movement westward to the Pacific coast, how African Americans forged ways of being religious appropriate to the African heritage and the cultural context of freedom from slavery, how immigrants fused dimensions of their ethnic backgrounds with traditional belief in a new setting. We also have to be sensitive to the complex ways men and women appropriated religious ideas in popular novels, popular periodicals, tracts, Sunday school literature, and devotional materials to create their own religious worldviews. And we must examine such diverse phenomena as home life—private life—and the interest in fraternal organizations if we hope to gain an understanding of the religious pulse that coursed through American life on a popular level.

To respond to the urbanization of the later nineteenth century many Protestant leaders rekindled the fires of revivalism. The premier evangelist of the age, Dwight L. Moody, had been a shoe salesman in Chicago before embarking on his religious career.[2] A product of the new urban environment of the age, Moody did not simply draw on the techniques advocated by Charles G. Finney in urban revivals earlier in the century. Finney had always been concerned with reaching those who were in positions of power and influence in the communities where he preached; Moody, while by no means eschewing the emerging urban middle class, extended his message to include those on the fringes of urban culture who found the city threatening to established ways of viewing the world. For those accustomed to the kinship and familial relational patterns of the village and small town, where a certain predictability to life brought a sense that one did control one's destiny, the city because of its sheer size and the factory with its lack of personality left many convinced that they lived in a world over which they had little control. External forces determined the course of life; individuals had little say in charting their own destinies. But aligning with the supernatural power of God, becoming identified with God through conversion, placed a superior power at the disposal of the believer. The call for conversion, the gospel of individual salvation, was as central to Moody's preaching as it had been to Finney's. Hence Moody's style, like Finney's, promoted the privatization of religiosity basic to Protestant evangelicalism in the United States by giving individuals access to a realm of sacred power that offered if not control over empirical reality at least a means of dealing with it.

Integral to Moody's brand of evangelical revivalism was music, and he was among the first to employ a professional musician to assist in leading revivals. In retrospect, Ira D. Sankey, Moody's musical associate, was every bit as vital to the revivals as Moody himself. Song leader, composer, and hymnal compiler, Sankey helped etch the gospel hymn into the popular religious consciousness.[3] Examining some of the hymns that emerged from the Moody-Sankey era, now regarded by many as "old favorites," is instructive in understanding how they reinforced both the sense of the supernatural basic to popular religiosity and the primacy of individual experience as the locus of authentic religion. Two well-known hymns with words written by Fanny J. Crosby are illustrative.[4] In the still-popular "Blessed Assurance," penned in 1873, Crosby proclaimed:

> Blessed assurance, Jesus is mine!
> O what a foretaste of glory divine! . . .
>
> Perfect submission, all is at rest;
> I in my Savior am happy and blest,
> watching and waiting, looking above,
> filled with his goodness, lost in his love.
>
> This is my story, This is my song,
> Praising my Savior all the day long.

The following year, Crosby wrote "Close to Thee," the second and third stanzas of which read:

Not for ease or worldly pleasure, nor for fame my prayer shall be;
gladly will I toil and suffer, only let me walk with thee.

Lead me through the vale of shadows, bear me o'er life's fitful sea;
then the gate of life eternal may I enter, Lord, with thee.

The sense of personal possession of Jesus in these hymns brings the supernatural presence into everyday life and endows the heavenly sphere with greater meaning and power than empirical reality. For the urban laborer, perhaps somewhat adrift because of the anomie attendant on city life, these gospel hymns offer a transcendent security that results from "praising my Savior all the day long." One might feel lost amid the seeming chaos of factory and city, but those who tapped into the reservoir of supernatural power knew that they were in actuality "lost in his love" and hence not lost at all in an ultimate sense but, rather, at "the gate of life eternal." Persons who knew firsthand what it was like to feel powerless because of the necessity of submitting to the seemingly arbitrary control of the factory boss could regain power and indeed possess greater power in "perfect submission" to the supernatural Savior. If many left behind the familiar for the promised ease and greater prosperity of life in the industrializing city, they found that the long hours of labor were demanding and brought their own kind of suffering. But that sort of ease, that "worldly pleasure," paled in comparison with the bliss of having access to supernatural power for which one would "gladly . . . toil and suffer." Total trust in the reality of the supernatural realm brought, as Crosby put it in another hymn, "a sweet relief" from the vagaries of ordinary life and hence a sense of control over them.

Such hymns did not necessarily reflect the formal theology of institutional revivalism. Easily remembered by the masses, they did become vehicles for developing not only a common vocabulary for much popular Protestant religiosity, but also powerful cohesive bonds among those for whom they captured a way of viewing reality that gave personal experience rich meaning. Sandra Sizer has argued convincingly that the hymnody of the later nineteenth century nurtured a "community of feeling" that extended well beyond the boundaries of organized religion.[5] By speaking to the heart, gospel hymns buttressed an inner purity among those for whom the experience of individual salvation brought a sense of ultimate control over personal destiny. The easily remembered phrases of the hymns, often dismissed by scholars as cliches, were, as Richard Rabinowitz noted in a different context, "far more important than theological or ecclesiastical concepts in organizing the daily lives of Christians—how they felt and expressed themselves, how they acted and interacted with others."[6] They were a way of maintaining the pure life through intense awareness of the perpetual power of the supernatural to protect and sustain the human enterprise.

That personal purity had social ramifications. Sizer emphasizes a point already made, namely that this privatization of religiosity reinforces the social bonds of home and family, the base of the private sphere in urban culture. Beyond that, however, the emphasis on private religious experience also made evangelical social ethics primarily personal ethics. The larger culture remained alien space, but individuals, supported by the supernatural power of the Divine, could remain pure and make their way through the morass of a corrupt society by avoiding, for example, the use of tobacco or alcohol or attending worldly amusements such as the theater or dances.[7] The threat of temptation always loomed large, however, and one had constantly to be on guard lest the supernatural forces of evil overpower one intent on a personally pure life.

Another of Fanny Crosby's hymns is relevant. "Rescue the perishing," she wrote in 1869, "care for the dying, snatch them in pity from sin and the grave." It was not physical death that concerned Crosby nor an earthen grave, but the presumed spiritual death and grave that came from yielding to temptation. One by one individuals could be rescued by those who knew that "Jesus is merciful," and one by one those who were patient could bring the erring ones "back to the narrow way" of personal (not societal) morality. When evangelicals inspired by the urban revivalism of Moody sought to develop institutional forms to advance the conviction that inculcation of private, personal morality preceded any societal change, it is little wonder then that they organized city "rescue missions" or settlement houses to serve those in slum areas or worked, as had Moody, through already existing institutions like the YMCA. Indeed, part of the rationale for establishing the Moody Bible Institute was to train "city evangelists" or "city missionaries" who would "rescue the perishing" of urban America and bring them individually under the sway of popular supernaturalism. As well, the popularity across religious lines in the later nineteenth century of the temperance movement reflects this passion for individualized, personal morality.

The major thrust within American religion that did look to social transformation, not just the conversion of individual souls, bears the label of the "social gospel."[8] Most standard analyses give considerable attention to the social gospel as a major strand of American religious life in the late nineteenth and early twentieth centuries. While its influence stretched into Roman Catholic and Jewish circles, the social gospel was largely a movement guided by prominent clergy (such as Washington Gladden), professors (such as Walter Rauschenbusch), and officials of denominational or interdenominational agencies (like Josiah Strong). Largely a response to the same effects of urbanization and industrialization that spurred the revivalism of Moody and others, the social gospel called for changes in the very structures of business and society in order to create a cultural order in which minimal justice and equality would prevail. With the proper environment in place, individuals would be more open to the message of the Christian gospel for individual transformation. One could argue, however, that the social gospel's major impact was precisely among the circle of those who provided its leadership rather than among the rank and file of ordinary Americans. As denominational leaders became more sensitive to the plight of folk in urban, industrial America, they urged adoption of social creeds and the like that addressed especially labor issues. Part of the impetus for the formation of the Federal Council of Churches in 1908 was the widespread belief among theologians and religious professionals that denominations needed to work together to effect social change. In other words, the primary inroads that the social gospel made in American religion came within the formal structures of religion. Hence as significant as the social gospel is to institutional religious life in the United States, it is imperative to ask whether it had an impact on popular religiosity and, if so, how that impact was manifested. Did the social gospel filter down from bureaucratic levels to ordinary folk?

As is so often the case, there is no precise way to measure the way the social gospel nurtured popular religiosity. There are some clues, ones similar to those that reveal the way evangelical revivalism penetrated popular consciousness. As had evangelicalism, the social gospel spawned its own hymnody, and some of the hymns that emerged from the movement remain in use today. In 1879 Washington Gladden wrote:

O Master, let me walk with thee in lowly paths of service free;
tell me thy secret; help me bear the strain of toil, the fret of care.

Help me the slow of heart to move by some clear, winning word of love;
teach me the wayward feet to stay, and guide them in the homeward way.

Methodist Frank Mason North, a prime mover behind the effort to have both the Federal Council of Churches and the various denominations adopt formal social creeds, early in the twentieth century (1903), penned these words:

Where cross the crowded ways of life, where sound the cries of race and
    clan,
above the noise of selfish strife, we hear your voice, O Son of man.

From tender childhood's helplessness, from woman's grief, man's burdened
    toil,
from famished souls, from sorrow's stress, your heart has never known
    recoil.

Till all the world shall learn your love and follow where your feet have
    trod,
till, glorious from your heaven above, shall come the city of our God!

What leaps out from Gladden's text is the way in which he has individualized what was essentially the corporate message of the social gospel and thereby rendered it accessible to those for whom religiosity remained a private, personal matter. It is the individual who seeks paths of service, who experiences the toil of labor, and who in turn brings other individuals into the secure realm of supernatural power. North's text at first glance seems to maintain the more corporate focus of the social gospel, especially in its obvious urban and industrial orientation. But North introduces one element that recurs in popular religiosity, namely the millennialist impulse that awaits direct divine intervention to transform the social order. Even Walter Rauschenbusch, whose writings in the opening decades of the twentieth century gave the social gospel its more formal theological base, drew on the millennialist impulse. He closed his *Christianity and the Social Crisis* (1907) with an apocalyptic vision:

Last May a miracle happened. At the beginning of the week the fruit trees bore brown and greenish buds. At the end of the week they were robed in bridal garments of blossom. But for weeks and months the sap had been rising and distending the cells and maturing the tissues which were half ready in the fall before. The swift unfolding was the culmination of a long process. Perhaps these nineteen centuries of Christian influence have been a long preliminary stage of growth, and now the flower and fruit are almost here. If at this juncture we can rally sufficient religious faith and moral strength to snap the bonds of evil and turn the present unparalleled economic and intellectual resources of humanity to the harmonious development of a true social life, the generations yet unborn will mark this as the great day of the Lord for which the ages waited, and count us blessed for sharing in the apostolate that proclaimed it.[9]

Rauschenbusch also produced what was arguably the most popular single piece of social gospel writing, his *For God and the People: Prayers for the Social Awakening*.[10] Appearing in 1910, this slender volume quickly became a devotional classic. While the corporate dimensions of the social gospel figure prominently in the subtitle, one must recall that a book intended for devotional purposes readily nurtures popular religiosity, for its primary use comes in the privacy of the home at the hands of individuals seeking to enrich their personal religious worldviews. Even if the ostensible content of Rauschenbusch's prayers pointed to widespread social transformation, it was a transformation inwardly appropriated in a variety of ways by individuals who used the prayers to strengthen their own understanding of the supernatural presence in everyday life.

Persons whose religiosity was shaped by Protestant currents were not the only ones to respond to the challenges of urbanization, industrialization, and immigration. The bulk of immigrants who came to American shores in the later nineteenth and early twentieth centuries brought with them worldviews and a corresponding popular religiosity molded by various strains of European Catholicism, Eastern Orthodox Christianity, and Judaism. How these various clusters of immigrants fused dimensions of formal religious traditions, popular modes of belief and practice originating in their cultures of origin, and ways of thinking and acting drawn from their perceptions of the alien American culture around them forms a vital part of the story of popular religiosity in American culture. In many cases, efforts of religious professionals to sustain a particular faith tradition unwittingly helped feed that sense of the supernatural basic to popular religiosity. The sheer number of Roman Catholic immigrants and the diversity of ethnic backgrounds from which they came provide ready illustrations.

Among American Catholics, an analogue to Protestant evangelical revivalism was the parish mission movement.[11] The aims of Catholic revivalism differed from those of Protestant evangelicals, for the primary goal was not to seek conversions.[12] Rather Catholic parish missions sought in the midst of a hostile religious environment to strengthen commitment to Catholic ways of those who were already numbered among the faithful and in more subtle ways to enable Catholics to adjust to the American religious context. Yet much Catholic revivalism promoted that private, individually oriented religiosity, even as it encouraged Catholics to remain identified with the church as an institution. Historian Jay Dolan points out, for example, that those who preached the missions stressed attendance on the sacrament of penance.[13] Penance, of course, is inextricably linked to the practice of confession. Done in the confines of the confessional booth with a screen separating the penitent from the confessor, confession is among the most private of the sacraments in its very structure. It is private also in the sense that individuals scrutinize their personal lives to identify shortcomings and sins. Hence confession and penance promote that introspection fundamental to popular religiosity and provide a vital awareness of supernatural power, both in the fear of the wrath of God that awaits the unrepentant and the awareness of evil powers that continually thwart the spiritual pursuits of the faithful. There follows as well a conviction that with divine assistance, one may triumph over these evil forces.

Emphasis on the Eucharist promoted its own form of devotionalism, one that on the surface represented an attempt both to maintain a distinctive Catholic identity in a hostile Protestant environment and to enhance priestly power, since priests, visible symbols of the authority of the institutional church, officiated at the sacrament.[14] Many commentators on American Catholic life have noted the efforts of the church leadership in the mid- and later nineteenth century to shift popular devotion away from the Marian fascination that followed promulgation of the doctrine of the Immaculate Conception in 1854 and toward the Blessed Sacrament and exercises centered on Jesus. Part of the rationale for that change of emphasis was to standardize devotional practice in the midst of the tremendous ethnic diversity the American church confronted. Standardization in turn would enhance the control of the hierarchy over popular practice, though Ann Taves reminds us that some Catholic leaders were content to promote uniformity in doctrinal affirmation and pluralism in devotional practice to accommodate ethnic differences.[15] Yet stressing devotion to the Blessed Sacrament could not fail to promote that sense of supernaturalism basic to popular religiosity. At the heart of Catholic belief lay the conviction that at the moment of consecration, the bread and wine of the Eucharist miraculously became the body and blood of Christ. The bread and wine ceased to be symbols of sacred power; they became concrete, visible manifestations of the reality of the supernatural here and now. Devotion to the Blessed Sacrament became a constant reminder of the perpetual invasion of ordinary reality by divine power, and attendance on the sacrament itself became a means through which ordinary men and women could align themselves with the power of the supernatural and draw on its strength to survive in an outer world fraught with danger.

Another feature of Catholic institutional life that enhanced devotional practice was the formation of numerous societies for lay persons whose primary purpose was to promote personal devotion. These confraternities (male) and sodalities (female), according to Taves, accounted for approximately 60 percent of all organizations formed within American Catholic parishes in the nineteenth century.[16] Although more women than men were drawn to these devotional societies, they have signal importance as vehicles for sustaining popular religiosity framed by Catholic ways. In many ways the parish missions and these auxiliary parish organizations functioned for ordinary Catholics the way revivals and gospel hymns worked for Protestants in sustaining a sense of the sacred. Ann Taves adroitly captured the parallelism: "Where Catholics held parish missions, promoted popular devotions, established confraternities and sodalities, and emphasized the infallibility of the pope, mid-nineteenth-century evangelical Protestants held revivals, sang gospel hymns, established prayer groups and mission societies, and emphasized the authority and infallibility of the Bible."[17] Popular periodicals geared to a Catholic audience, such as *Ave Maria* and the *Messenger of the Sacred Heart*, enthusiastically supported the formation of devotional societies in local parishes especially in the decades after the Civil War. Stories and columns in both routinely reported dramatic, indeed supernatural, results that came from the active practice of devotion ranging from direct answers to prayer to miraculous cures. Simply put, devotional societies became mechanisms that routinized access to the supernatural realm for the faithful, and if the hierarchy thought that they could exert greater control over devotion through such organizations, they could not control what people actually thought and what they appropriated while engaged in devotional exercises. For many immigrants, the life of devotion promoted by confraternities and sodalities filled a gap that was not there in many of their cultures of origin. Popular practice in much of European Catholicism looked to pilgrimages to shrines of the saints or to such sources of sacred power as the water of Lourdes as ways to maintain regular contact with the supernatural. In the American setting, shrines were few and pilgrimages rare. In their place, the practices promoted by devotional societies became concrete ways to tap into supernatural power on a regular basis. Like the pilgrimage in Europe, devotional practice reinforced the nearness and accessibility of the benevolent spiritual world.

Opportunities for pilgrimage in the American context were not entirely absent, however, for there were eleven shrines established prior to 1880, most of them associated with parish churches.[18] One that became a center of controversy within institutional Catholicism, however, reveals something of the power of the pilgrimage within popular religiosity and the ways in which popular religiosity endures despite a lack of sanction from formal traditions. Adele Brice, a devout Catholic lay woman from Robinsville, Wisconsin, claimed to have had a visionary experience of the Blessed Virgin and sparked much popular interest when she began to travel about speaking of her encounter with the sacred. After her father built a chapel on the spot where she reportedly had received her vision, pilgrims—mostly women—began to visit the shrine, much to the consternation of church authorities who dismissed Brice's reports as figments of the imagination and hoped to discourage women from making pilgrimages to Robinsville. Perhaps to gain validity for her ecstatic experience and the religiosity of the women drawn to her, Brice eventually joined the Third Order of St. Francis, along with several of her female supporters. On the one hand, Brice's shrine was the only one established by a lay person; hence her role could be construed as a challenge to the authority of the institutional clergy. And since Brice was female, her brief prominence clearly threatened the male priesthood. But the institution in the end was unable to thwart her, a strong indication that ordinary people remained unaffected by the pronouncements of the institutional church and would continue to seek access to the sacred realm on their own terms.

Catholic parochial schools also had a prominent role in nurturing a distinctive popular religiosity that drew on Roman, American, and ethnic components, for the last half of the nineteenth century witnessed a concerted effort among American Catholics to develop a parish school system.[19] Providing educational institutions of any sort was not a high priority in American culture until the 1830s when impetus to organize public or common schools swelled, particularly in the cities of the Northeast. After the Civil War, the public school movement expanded considerably. Most schools had a distinctly Protestant cast in part because of the dominance of Protestants in the population (and hence in the teaching staffs), but also because of the religious overtones in curricular materials such as the widely used McGuffey *Readers*. Irish Americans, who remained the primary ethnic cluster within the Catholic ranks, were less suspicious of public education than many of the newer immigrants. Although the Irish had experienced sometimes violent anti-Catholicism during the heavy waves of immigration from Ireland in the 1830s and 1840s, in the years after the Civil War they were well on their way to assimilating into the larger culture and tended to regard public schools as appropriate vehicles to prepare immigrant children (now mostly from other ethnic groups) for the realities of American life.[20] For newer immigrants, however, parish schools offered distinct advantages. Since immigrants tended to cluster in ethnic parishes, provoking a crisis in parish organization and control that usually dominates the telling of the story, parishes often became cultural as well as religious centers, places where one not only entered sacred space to connect with supernatural reality, but where one could nurture and sustain customs and traditions brought from the home country.[21] Hence parish schools became a vehicle to preserve and protect a cultural heritage as much as a way to provide basic education. With the increase in non-English-speaking immigrants, some parish schools offered instruction in languages of origin, while also teaching English, and thus aided the transition from one culture to another. Given the Protestant ethos of public schools, they also served as agencies to promote commitment to a Catholic worldview and maintain a Catholic identity. Despite their hesitation over the wisdom of parochial education, Irish-American Catholics provided much of the financial backing necessary to developing a parish school system. In many cases the schools and the devotional societies together helped perpetuate a popular religiosity that blended ethnic, Catholic, and American ways, for festivals and other special activities often associated with patron saints or popular practices brought to the United States from Europe often depended on parish school involvement and the organizational leadership of devotional societies.

The *contadini*, the peasant folk of Southern Italy who flocked to places like Italian Harlem in the closing decades of the nineteenth century, provide a good example. Scholars have long noted that Italian immigrants brought with them a strident anticlericalism that went well beyond mere suspicion and questioning of priestly authority. It spilled over into a seeming disregard for traditional doctrine and sometimes even open hostility to the church as an institution because of the association of formal belief and institutional practice with a system of oppression that marked peasant life in Italy. This ambivalent relation to Catholicism as a formal religious tradition did not mean an absence of vibrant religiosity, one that the people themselves might have defined as Christian even if church professionals saw it as pagan.[22] It was, as Robert Anthony Orsi put it, a popular religiosity shaped by Catholic sensibility, not by the Roman Catholic Church.[23] Rudolph Vecoli has pointed out that within the "sacred cosmos" of the *contadini*, "every moment and every event was infused with religious and magical significance."[24] In the homeland, remnants of ancient fertility cults, local deities, and demonic forces such as were manifested in the *malocchio*

or evil eye provided the foundation on which a Roman Catholic Christian
tradition had been erected. That substratum never vanished. *Santa Maria*,
the blessed Madonna, replaced the goddess of the old fertility cults and
saints took the roles of one-time village gods, but the primal supernatural
power they all represented remained constant. The prominence of Mary in
Italian immigrant religiosity emerged in part from seeing her as the personal
mother who knew firsthand the depths of suffering because of the brutal
crucifixion of her child. Mary thus became a supernatural force with whom
the people could identify because of their own life situation. Like the gods
of centuries past, the saints were real personalities who possessed extraordinary supernatural power that provided hope and assistance for those for
whom daily life was a routine of suffering.

In Italy, much of this popular religiosity found expression in devotions
and pilgrimages, in erecting shrines and placing holy pictures and other
sacred objects in one's home. In the American city, it found expression in
the *festa*, the great street festival, such as that dedicated to the Madonna
of Mount Carmel on East 115th Street in New York City that lasted for
several days, though the primary procession was held each 16 July. The
sacred theater of the *festa* operated on many levels. On the one hand, it
maintained a sense of connection to the Italian cultural heritage in the midst
of an alien environment. That, long after "Americanization" occurred and
Italian Americans had left Harlem for the suburbs, later generations would
return for the *festa* bears witness to the power of this connectedness.[25]
Then, too, the *festa* socialized children into the community, yet not just
into an ethnic community but into a sacred community where the supernatural was real and its power pervasive. The *festa* and the sacred power
it unleashed signaled stability and the possibility of control over one's destiny in a world where instability held sway and control seemed too often
in the hands of oppressors. Festival and procession kept alive a popular
religiosity grounded in a persistent belief in the supernatural and the power
of the supernatural to influence ordinary life.

Popular devotion took cognate forms among Polish Catholic immigrants.[26] Working-class Polish Americans brought with them their own
brand of anticlericalism that in the American context manifested itself most
prominently in resistance to the control of Irish Americans over much of
the institutional apparatus of American Catholicism, including parish
schools. Polish immigrants were particularly adept at organizing national
parishes, often to the consternation of church authorities who repudiated
such lay initiative in parish life.[27] For many Polish Americans, religious
identity and Polish patriotism were inseparable; the connection is especially
obvious, for example, in the title given to the newspaper targeted to a Polish
audience that began publication in Chicago in 1887: *Faith and Fatherland*.
In some areas, such as Scranton, Pennsylvania, the nationalist element became so strident that the result was schism.[28] But for Polish immigrants,

ethnic parishes also served to perpetuate a popular religiosity centered on feasts and festivals. Such celebrations were integral to life in the land of origins where parish and village were often contiguous. In the American urban context, that tight relationship vanished. Hence festival occasions assumed even greater import. At the center of much Polish-American popular religiosity, as with that of Italian Americans, stood the Blessed Virgin Mary. John Bukowczyk has suggested that Mary figures so prominently in part because she and the doctrines surrounding her were "malleable." On the one hand, as the idealized maternal symbol, Mary was nurturing and protective. Her supernatural power would see the immigrant through the travails of adjusting to a strange environment and offer assistance to the faithful in coping with the vagaries of daily life, perhaps even with an Irish religious hierarchy. On the other hand, Mary also had a redemptive dimension. In much popular piety, Mary assumed a role that made her virtually a co-redemptor with Jesus Christ. In other words, Mary signaled not only the possibility of survival but also ultimate triumph over all the forces that impeded control over one's destiny and, for many, the destiny of the fatherland. Ultimately some strains of Polish-American popular religiosity centering on Mary were brought in tandem with other forms of Marian devotion through the efforts of the Polish Resurrectionist Fathers, who emerged in Chicago and fused this popular religiosity with the "cult of sorrows" that was basic to much Marian piety. Indeed part of what sustained popular religiosity focused on Mary among all immigrant groups was the Marian devotion that was part of a larger Catholic sensibility in American culture.

In Czech immigrant communities, similar patterns recur. As in Polish culture, so in Czech culture: the congruence of village and parish often meant that feast days and a panoply of patron saints supported not only religion as an institution or tradition but a popular set of values predicated on supernatural power. In turn these values supported a network of relationships connecting families and villages together and also linking them to the realm of sacred power. In the American setting, the parish church and parochial school again became vehicles to support these connections. Josef L. Barton has called attention especially to the role of the child's first communion and other family-oriented ritual occasions in maintaining these networks of vertical and horizontal relationships.[29] I would suggest that the first communion is important for another reason, one directly related to the dynamics of popular religiosity. What is important to recall in this context is the mystical, if not near-magical understanding of the Eucharist that prevailed in much popular religiosity. To ingest the body and blood of Christ was the most concrete means of accessing the power of the supernatural realm and appropriating it for human benefit. In the miracle of the Mass, the supernatural quite literally became part of the stuff of ordinary life. Hence the significance attached to first communion stems in part from its signaling that one could now draw on the reservoir of divine power to give order and significance to life and to have a modicum of control over what transpires from day to day.

The ethnic overlays that immigration brought to popular religiosity shaped by Catholic sensibilities have parallels and differences in the American Jewish experience. The large-scale immigration of the later nineteenth and early twentieth centuries also swelled the Jewish population of the United States, pushing it from an estimated 250,000 in 1880 to 1,058,000 in 1900 and to 3,390,000 by 1920.[30] As was the case with Catholic immigrants from Southern, Central, and Eastern Europe, the American environment proved a catalyst for the development of several strands of a Jewish popular religiosity. To understand the distinctive character of Jewish popular religiosity, we must first be aware of some of the forces that had molded Jewish religiosity and Jewish identity over the course of many centuries. Central to the story is a dual conviction that finds powerful biblical expression in the accounts telling of Moses' leading the ancestors of the Jews out of bondage in Egypt, the covenant between God (Yahweh) and the children of Israel made at Sinai, symbolized in Torah, and the awkward and often difficult interaction the Hebrew people had with other cultures in and around the promised land. That dual conviction insists first that Yahweh and the Hebrew people had a special relationship with each other that was different from the way God related to other peoples and the way other peoples related to their gods. As God's chosen people, the Hebrews were set apart from others and were to remain so. The second affirmation concerns the importance of history. Just as Yahweh had acted in history to bring the Hebrew people from Egypt to the promised land, so God would continue to act in history. Concomitantly, as God's special people, the Hebrews must live out in history their commitment to God's way, to Torah. Even the most mundane and routine affairs of daily life, such as the food one ate and how one prepared it, became vehicles for manifesting the holiness that God required. As in tribal cultures the world over, there was no sense that religion was a discrete component of individual and social life. All of life had a supernatural base in the God who called Israel into being.

From the start, there were challenges in maintaining this sense of separation and holiness. As interaction brought exposure to other cultures, it was difficult to avoid adopting or adapting other ways, even if such endangered the sense of separation and holiness basic to God's way. Political conflict with neighboring peoples and empires brought dangers of another sort, for conquerors often scattered those whose lands they took over. At least from the time of the Babylonian conquest in the sixth century B.C.E., one speaks of the diaspora or the scattering of the Jewish people outside the promised land, making them aliens in often hostile cultures and hindering the ability of even the most committed to follow Torah. Always, though, there loomed a hope that God would act in history to restore the promised land to the chosen people and gather those dispersed on holy ground. Further complications arose when Judaism gave birth to Christianity, for quickly early Christians laid claim to being the heirs to God's promises to Israel and saw themselves as superseding Israel as the special people of God. When Christianity established itself as the dominant formal religion in the Roman Empire and maintained that status even after the empire's political demise, Jews again saw themselves pushed to the periphery of social structures as heinous anti-Semitism came to mark Christendom in Europe. By the Middle Ages that anti-Semitism led increasingly to the confinement of Jews to ghettos, areas of cities often enclosed by walls where laws required Jews to live, the exclusion of Jews from certain occupations and participation in much public life, and other restrictions. Too frequently, in many places there occurred violent efforts to eradicate the Jewish population or to demand conversion to Christianity on penalty of death or expulsion, often forcing Jews to migrate to other areas. In Eastern Europe such hostility and forced migration gave birth to the *shtetl*, the peasant agrarian community of Jews. The obverse of anti-Semitism and societal exclusion in many cases was the deepening of internal bonds and a fierce sense of Jewish identity, but an identity that knew well the reality and prevalence of evil forces in the world. In Western Europe at least, the Enlightenment's emphasis on reason highlighted the irrationality of this anti-Semitism and exclusion. Gradually opportunities for fuller participation in society opened to Jews, bringing anew the challenges faced by the Hebrew people centuries earlier when interaction with other cultures threatened to undermine the sense of holiness and separateness basic to Israel's covenant with Yahweh.

Germany was among the first areas where an easing of restrictions offered the possibility of greater participation in the larger culture, and from German lands came the bulk of Jewish immigrants arriving in the United States prior to the last third of the nineteenth century. German Jewish immigrants tended to form congregations separate from the synagogues of the small number of English-speaking Jews who had planted Jewish life in those colonies that became the United States. They thus set the stage for what became a recurring pattern later: the formation of congregations based on place of origin. Because there was no central authority akin to pope and bishops that sought to control the public aspects of Jewish life, the autonomy of local congregations made organizing synagogues and auxiliary agencies along ethnic lines easier than was the case with Catholic immigrants. But like the Catholic parishes that catered to the needs of a specific ethnic clientele, the synagogues became not only religious institutions but agencies to sustain some association with traditions and customs of the lands of origin.

Other factors at work in the American Jewish experience propelled the privatization of religiosity basic to popular religion, albeit in a way so elusive as to frustrate those who would try to analyze it. Perhaps the most significant was the theoretical equality of Jewish citizens before the law, a result of the "separation of church and state" grounded in the First Amendment to the federal Constitution. In principle, Jewish citizens confronted no legal disabilities to full participation in American public life, though all too frequently anti-Semitism, both overt and covert, worked to narrow opportunities, especially in private education and employment. Jewish immigrants readily recognized that the separateness that lay at the heart of being God's holy people, reinforced by centuries of exclusion in the European context, could foster a different kind of separation from the social order in the American context, almost a sense of aloofness and superiority. All too aware from history that surface acceptance could quickly evaporate, some American Jews began to question whether all the trappings associated with Jewish life were essential to Jewish identity and religiosity. In many instances, circumstances forced the issue. Dietary practices, or the observance of *kashruth* (Jewish dietary laws), are a good case in point. As Jewish immigrants became dispersed throughout the population, they frequently found themselves in communities where it was difficult to procure kosher foods. Itinerant peddlers especially found it next to impossible to adhere to a kosher diet. As well, avoidance of certain foods set Jews apart from other folks; simply put, they stood out and called attention to themselves because of their diet. Would that kind of separateness trigger discrimination? Was it not easier to abandon kosher ways in order to fit into the larger society? On an intellectual level, questions emerged about whether the dietary regimen of the Jewish tradition was essential to Jewishness. The dietary codes that were part of Torah may have played a vital role in the ancient world in giving a disparate tribal culture a sense of cohesion (as well as holiness). But that function had long since disappeared. With the rationale for *kashruth* no longer operative, had the practices associated with it lost their meaning?

These concerns were among many that spurred the development of what has become known as Reform Judaism.[31] We cannot here sketch the full story of the emergence of Reform, which is part of the history of Judaism as a formal religious tradition. But the impulse to Reform is emblematic of the tensions that smoldered for more than a generation within the German-American Jewish community, where many eager to assimilate fully into the culture around them were willing to rethink, if not abandon some of the formal religious tradition. What brought those tensions into sharpest relief was the rapid expansion of the Jewish population with the immigration of the later nineteenth century that brought millions whose homeland experience was very different from that of even the poorer, less well-educated German Jewish immigrants of even a generation earlier, millions for whom Reform appeared as alien as the new American culture around them. But we risk losing sight of the larger point. As institutional Judaism took on more and more the character of the other religious institutions of the nation, as ancillary benevolent and fraternal agencies organized along lines parallel to their Protestant and Catholic counterparts, and as many jettisoned practices such as *kashruth* that set Jews apart from other people, religiosity was essentially becoming a matter of the private sphere. Religious experience was more and more what men and women did in the confines of their homes, more and more how individuals chose to relate to the supernatural realm apart from the structures of organized Judaism. And such, of course, is central to popular religiosity wherever it appears.

We do not have the wealth of clues about the contours of this popular religiosity that we have, for example, about popular religiosity shaped by Catholic sensibilities. While we gain valuable information about the thrust of Catholic popular religiosity from the spate of devotional materials and the like that nurtured personal piety, the host of prayer books that emerged from within the Jewish immigrant community were intended more for use in Sabbath services and other communal activities. Just as there was a Catholic immigrant press, so from 1843 when the *Occident* first appeared, there was a Jewish immigrant press, but the early papers especially were clearly more intent on reporting events, both domestic and foreign, of interest to an immigrant constituency than on perpetuating religious devotion. But the religiosity of the people was influenced by the same forces that stirred the institutions of American Judaism, namely wrestling with what it meant to identify with the people of the covenant in an American context. In this vein, it is important to note that even the major festivals of the formal Jewish tradition, unlike the *festa* of Italian-American Catholics, for example, are home-based and therefore prone to adaptation within the orbit of popular religiosity. A prime example is the observance of the Passover seder, by tradition a family celebration, which vividly links contemporary Jews with those whom Yahweh led from bondage in Egypt to the freedom of being God's holy people.[32] But marking Passover reminds even the most secularized Jew of claims regarding supernatural intervention in history.

The immigration of the later nineteenth and early twentieth centuries made the picture much more variegated. On the one hand, because this wave of immigrants brought with them the trappings of various *shtetl* cultures much different from that of the earlier German immigrants, they could not help but stand out in American life, at least initially. If earlier immigrants had been willing to modify traditional practice in order not to seem so visibly separate, there was no way that could be avoided now. As well, these immigrants poured into a few urban areas, like New York City, rather than quickly diffusing themselves throughout the population. The concentration of Jews in New York alone meant that burgeoning industries there counted a large percentage of Jewish immigrant workers in their labor force. A Yiddish subculture rapidly developed that gave birth not only to a Yiddish press, but to Yiddish theater (and in turn to vaudeville), and a host of other expressions of popular culture. For many years it was fashionable to argue that this later wave of immigrants brought with them either a fierce commitment to orthodoxy as far as formal religious observance was concerned or an extraordinary willingness to abandon all obvious religious identity, clinging to Jewishness more as a cultural or ethnic identity. The former receives some confirmation in the division of institutional Judaism into its familiar tripartite configuration of Orthodox, Conservative, and Reform during this period. The latter gains plausibility because of the heavy involvement of Jewish immigrants in the labor movement and radical politics, prompting the conclusion that these more secular arenas replaced the ostensibly religious realm as the focal points of Jewish life. While there is some value in both observations, they also oversimplify the richness of Jewish immigrant life.

Peter Williams, for example, has noted that popular religiosity among European Jews had for centuries contained a substratum of "magical lore, based on the manipulation of the names of God and on the harnessing of the angelic inhabitants of the spirit world to human ends," although he also rightly reminds us that there had long been an "attitude of caution" toward such practices to avoid charges of sorcery at the hands of anti-Semitic Christians.[33] A dimension of that magical heritage survived in the popular religiosity of Jewish immigrants from Eastern Europe, as did the heritage of Jewish mysticism (to which it is related), with its sense of awe in the presence of the Almighty. Even the now widely practiced custom of saying "Gesundheit" when another person sneezes owes part of its transmission into American life from the Yiddish culture of Jewish immigrants and reflects an appreciation of the reality of the supernatural. While the word itself (as much Yiddish) has roots in the German language and technically offers wishes of good health, its appropriateness as an acknowledgment of a sneeze stems from the popular belief that the act of sneezing involved the expulsion of evil spirits from the body. Hence a wish of good health was in order.

More complicated is the way Zionism relates to popular religiosity once the call for the establishment of an independent Jewish nation gained ground near the close of the nineteenth century. On the one hand, Zionism had a distinct political focus. On the other hand, it raised anew the messianic strain within Judaism that has direct bearing on popular religiosity. Debates within the Jewish community centered around whether the reestablishment of a Jewish nation should come from human activity in the political sector or await divine intervention, God's sending the messiah to restore Israel just as supernatural action in history had initially brought the Hebrew people to the promised land. At the risk of oversimplification, those who held more strictly to Orthodoxy, particularly the Hasidim, were more skeptical about political Zionism and more insistent on awaiting direct supernatural intervention, while those who had become more secularized saw Zionism as a political rather than a religious endeavor, if they supported its premises at all. A messianic element has buttressed much of the millennialist impulse in other forms of popular religiosity. When it found expression in Jewish popular religiosity, with Zionism serving as a catalyst to bring it to the fore, messianism was a vital reminder of the reality of the supernatural and of the power that supernatural forces could release in human history. It thus served to reinforce that lively sense of the supernatural that quickens much popular religious sensibility. Messianic expectation clearly did not enliven all Jewish religious consciousness any more than millennialism has been at the center of all expressions of popular religiosity shaped by a Christian orientation. But its intrusion into the debates over Zionism signals both its continuing presence in Jewish life and its role in the way some American Jews went about the business of creating a world of meaning through which they interpreted the events of daily life.

Alternative forms of messianism and millennialism also nudged popular religiosity among some Native American tribal peoples in the later nineteenth century. Fused with ideas drawn from traditional forms of tribal religious expression and from the Christianity of the Euro-American invaders who encroached on tribal lands, a sense of the supernatural imbued with millennialist tones came to the surface among tribes in the Northwestern United States in the 1870s, in the first manifestation of the Ghost Dance in Nevada and California around 1870, and in the more familiar expression of the Ghost Dance that began in 1889–90, also in Nevada. Among the Wanapum in Washington, a popular millennialism coalesced around the figure of Smohalla (b. circa 1815–20) whose personal experiences reveal the syncretism of tribal and Christian sensibilities.[34] As a youth, Smohalla attended Catholic mission schools where he was introduced to some of the core ideas of Christianity. In true shamanistic tradition, he experienced numerous ecstatic visions that emboldened his commitment to tribal ways. At one point, while in the Southwest, he had a powerful vision that confirmed his prophetic call. In this dramatic encounter with the supernatural, Smohalla claimed to have visited the spiritual realm and directly encountered the Divine, the Great Chief. He returned to his people and in the 1850s proclaimed a message calling for recommitment to tribal traditions, an abandonment of Euro-American agricultural techniques, and the practice of some new ritual forms. The payoff would come in the future when divine intervention would destroy the Euro-American invaders and their civilization and then restore tribal life to a pure form. In practical terms, Smohalla's millennialist religiosity was essentially a mechanism that would promote accommodation with the encroaching white culture, for the destruction of the alien peoples was cast in an unspecified, but distant future. But harnessing supernatural power for the benefit of some and the destruction of others is inherently dangerous. Others saw in this claim to ultimate supernatural intervention a call to active resistance against further white intrusion; governmental authorities sensed the potential danger for revolt and took steps to quash the movement.

It is not clear the extent to which the ideas of Smohalla influenced the first known outbreak of the Ghost Dance among the Paviotso of western Nevada, though the parallels in some instances are striking. Again there is a central figure, Wodziwob, who developed the ritual form of the Ghost Dance that was, in a sense, an attempt at inducing tribal ecstasy or possession.[35] In the frenzy generated by the ritual dance, participants gained access to supernatural power. The more they danced, the more they could call upon the supernatural forces unleashed to intervene in history by destroying the culture of the demonic white oppressors, bringing the tribal dead back to life, and restoring tribal life to its pristine form in a terrestrial paradise. While this manifestation of the Ghost Dance generated much excitement, that enthusiasm was short-lived. When divine action to suppress the oppressor was not immediately forthcoming, tribal interest in the Ghost Dance waned. But the millennialist impulse at its base in popular religiosity did not die out.

Nearly twenty years later a much more widespread fascination with Ghost Dance millennialism spread among numerous tribal groups. It took hold especially among many tribes of Plains Indians and ultimately became part of tribal life in cultures stretching from Nevada to the Dakotas where the government had recently forced the Sioux onto reservations.[36] At the center of this revitalization of the Ghost Dance was another charismatic shaman, a Paiute named Wovoka (Jack Wilson). Wovoka, the son of one of Wodziwob's disciples, described his own encounter with the supernatural, which occurred in the winter of 1888–89: "When the sun died, I went up to heaven and saw God and all the people who had died a long time ago. God told me to come back and tell my people they must be good and love one another, and not fight, or steal, or lie. He gave me this dance to give my people."[37] Like the message of the earlier Ghost Dance, that of Wovoka was essentially pacifistic, offering endless life in a paradise devoid of Euro-Americans to those who practiced the simple virtues of getting along with each other and fervently participated in the Ghost Dance ritual. But once the Ghost Dance spread, the ecstatic power it generated turned the dance into a call to militant resistance to American Indian policy and the usurpation of ancient tribal lands by the government and Euro-American settlers.

Precisely what prompted the transformation of Wovoka's message into one of militant resistance is difficult to assess. Part of the shift stemmed from increasingly restrictive Indian policy on the part of the government as settlers moving westward demanded access to more land. As well, the Ghost Dance rekindled a sense of tribal pride and a desire to restore the integrity of tribal cultures. The dance took many forms as it spread among numerous tribes, and in some cases, it revived belief in impending divine intervention to thwart further white oppression. As was the case with earlier millennialist currents in Native American popular religiosity, the danger inherent in the release of supernatural power became all too clear to U.S. officials who feared massive rebellion. As is well known, the Ghost Dance among the Sioux was brutally suppressed in the massacre of Wounded Knee in December 1890. The violent response of the American military, along with the failure of the dance to usher in a paradisiacal age, subdued public participation in the ritual not only among the remaining Sioux, but among most of the other tribes where it had captured popular imagination. In muted form, it continues among a few western and Plains tribes.

What made these forms of millennialism and expectation of supernatural action in history plausible? We need simply to recall the abiding sense of the reality of the supernatural realm fundamental to tribal religiosity and the belief that some persons (shamans) were endowed with extraordinary powers to access supernatural forces and muster them to work for the benefit of all. The long tradition of the acceptance of charismatic shamans helps us understand why individuals such as Smohalla, Tavibo, and Wovoka were able to garner popular belief in their millennialist message. As well, longstanding popular belief in a spiritual realm, inhabited not only by supernatural powers but also by the tribal dead, buttressed popular acceptance of the claim that the dead would return at a time when supernatural invasion of empirical reality would destroy oppressors and restore tribal life to its pure form. The Indian policies of the U.S. government and the attitudes of Euro-Americans might have undermined the integrity of tribal culture, but they could not annihilate the pulse of popular religiosity that always beat beneath the surface. Indeed contact with the Christianity of the oppressors provided the syncretistic base that may well have augmented the plausibility of the Ghost Dance and its kindred expressions of popular religiosity.

Another form of ecstatic religiosity that reflects a blending of traditional tribal religiosity with dimensions of Christian belief and practice came with the growth of peyote religion among numerous tribal groups near the end of the nineteenth century.[38] Ingestion of peyote buttons in a religious context had a long history among some Mexican tribal societies, where it was used in healing rituals and as a catalyst for shamanistic prophecy, and some Apache groups had incorporated its use in tribal ceremonies as early as 1870. But in the 1880s and especially after the collapse of the Ghost Dance movement, peyote religion in a form that fused aspects of indigenous tribal worldviews with some Christian beliefs and practices made significant inroads among Native American cultures in the United States and Canada, prompting many analysts to regard it as an important instance of a nearly pan-Indian popular religiosity.

A cactus found primarily in northern Mexico and parts of the Rio Grande valley, peyote is also a hallucinogen, now classified by the U.S. government as a controlled substance. Under its influence, as Peter Williams has noted, "Those aspects of the external world which users perceive . . . seem to contain a personal meaning, giving them a feeling that they are communicating with a universe that has something important to reveal to them about themselves."[39] In other words, peyote is a catalyst to bring users into direct contact with the realm of supernatural forces and power. Because peyote religion spread from Southwestern tribes such as the Comanche and Kiowa to tribes to the north in Wisconsin and on into Canada, it remained one of the most prevalent expressions of Native American popular religiosity and took on many different ritual forms and the like, depending on the particular tribal context. In 1918 one expression of peyote religion became institutionalized when the Native American Church received a charter in Oklahoma. Chartering granted legal standing to adherents and allowed them use of the controlled substance in ritual contexts until there were court challenges in the late 1980s that culminated in the U.S. Supreme Court decision (*Oregon v. Smith*) in 1990 that granted individual states the right to restrict use of peyote in religious rituals. In 1993, however, new federal legislation restored to Native Americans the right to ritual use of peyote. All manifestations of peyote religion share some fundamental assumptions about the nature of reality and the power of the supernatural realm as well as some recurring ritual patterns. Male tribal members gather on a specified Saturday evening in a tepee arranged with symbols and other materials drawn from both native and Christian traditions (e.g., fire, mounds of earth, and sometimes Christian trinitarian symbols such as a cross). Peyote may be placed on an altar-like arrangement, reverenced in part for the supernatural power it can unleash. The most significant part of the ceremony is the distribution and ingestion of the peyote buttons in a fashion reminiscent of the distribution of the bread and wine of the Christian Eucharist. Through the night, those participating alternate between active involvement in corporate ritual activity and private meditation spurred by the visions and hallucinatory experiences generated by the mescaline alkaloid in the peyote. Practitioners, though, see the common bonds created through shared experience and the presumed healing power of peyote as more important than the private visions. Some rituals identify the source of visions with the Christian God or with Jesus Christ, a sign of the syncretism inherent in peyote-based religiosity. Prayers may be offered to the spirit present in the peyote, beseeching it to endow those ingesting the buttons with wisdom and power; prayers to Jesus are also common.[40] Then sometime the following morning the men will join others of the tribe for a time of eating and socializing, bringing the encounter with the supernatural to a formal close.

While some have constructed formal belief systems based on peyote religion, such are tangential to understanding how all this manifests recurring elements of popular religiosity. Peyote religion, like all popular religiosity, is about power, a transcendent power that is superior to and not contingent upon the power manifested in empirical reality. In this case, the peyote spirit represented a power superior to that of the white oppressor, no matter how much that power seemed to hold sway in daily life. Peyote religiosity works no differently than forms of Christian popular religiosity that regard the world as a place where satanic forces are constantly at work thwarting and oppressing those who believe in a superior power. In both instances those who tap into the realm of supernatural power have access to a greater power, even if that is not readily acknowledged by outsiders. Through vision and hallucination, one enters that superior world and gains a practical power that allows the individual to cope with the vicissitudes of ordinary life, including a sense of empirical powerlessness. What grants peyote religiosity plausibility is the worldview of tribal cultures that affirms the presence and reality of spiritual forces in all dimensions of existence. In a sense, then, the peyote is only a catalyst akin to the devotional exercises in popular religiosity shaped by Catholic sensibilities that transports one into an alternative space where divine power reigns supreme. The fact that individual experiences under the influence of peyote differ also brings its use into the arena of popular religiosity where private, personal experience is paramount. Tribal members may participate in a corporate ritual of ingestion, but no two persons will have precisely identical encounters with the supernatural spirit believed accessible through the visions induced by peyote.

The same vibrant sense of a spirit-filled world was, as we have seen earlier, also part of the African-American religious consciousness, and a popular religiosity grounded in African-American culture found continued expression in the later nineteenth century. Here again traditional interpretation tends to focus on institutional developments, especially on the emergence of independent black denominations and the growth of those founded before the Civil War, the establishment of numerous church-related educational institutions and other auxiliary agencies, and the centrality of the church and the preacher to black community life. All that is important, to be sure, but overemphasis on formal religious institutions in the African-American experience can easily cause us to lose sight of the vital popular religiosity that prevailed among ordinary people. Still central was that constellation of values, beliefs, and practices that assumed the reality and power of the supernatural realm. When northern black preachers embarked on missions among the former slaves, frequently they were taken aback by what seemed an excessive emotionalism in worship. Daniel

Alexander Payne, a bishop of the African Methodist Episcopal Church who returned to his native South Carolina after the Civil War, was critical of the "heathenish" shouting that marked much public worship.[41] But the shout reflected the continuity of that ecstatic experience that had its roots in African religiosity and had long been blended with Christianity as a means of directly accessing the supernatural power of God. If ecstatic worship became more a hallmark of independent African-American denominations, the reason is simply that the context of legal freedom and the absence of white attempts to control black religiosity allowed ecstatic experience fuller expression.

Much else from the syncretistic popular religiosity of the antebellum period also remained. Indigenous black preachers were often respected not only for their power to preach the gospel, but also for their ability to mediate between the realm of the supernatural and that of ordinary human beings. It is the old popular tradition of conjure melding with Christian regard for the pastoral role that endowed black preachers with this added aura of sacred power. Documents dating from the 1930s and 1940s but reflecting back on the religious style of postbellum America suggest as well that, especially in the rural South, reliance on herbs and herb doctors for their healing powers continued to shape a popular religious worldview in which supernatural power pervaded all there is.[42] In many communities, men and women with the special knowledge that went with conjure and healing might be consulted in particular circumstances, along with preachers who could call on the power of prayer to effect healing or other forms of transformation. The vital role of song in black worship, often the spontaneous expression of the inner experience of the presence of divine power, likewise nurtured a lively sense of the supernatural. Words and music alike were often "given" to the singer in another manifestation of spirit possession. As is well known, the musical expression of African-American popular religiosity gradually gave birth to what we now call "black gospel" music as well as the blues.[43] Although the casual listener may find the plaintive character of the blues haunting, one must remember that it is really suggesting that there is another world, a spiritual and supernatural one, where the frustrations and pain of this life vanish. While drawing on similar themes, many popular gospel hymns emerging from the African-American context emphasize the immanence of supernatural power, usually through a Jesus who is always ready to aid those who call for assistance, and the way such forces enable believers to make sense out of and cope with everyday experience.

Two examples will suffice. Charles Albert Tindley (1856–1933), a prominent African-American Methodist pastor in Philadelphia, wrote many gospel hymns that address these concerns in the context of black popular religiosity. Among them is the well-known "Stand by Me," which has a blues variant melody:

When the storms of life are raging, stand by me,
When the storms of life are raging, stand by me,
When the world is tossing me,
Like a ship upon the sea,
Thou who rulest wind and water, stand by me.

Tindley in turn was a major influence on Thomas A. Dorsey (1899–1993), one of the foremost composers of early blues and black gospel.[44] Dorsey echoes African-American popular religiosity and Tindley's work in his widely known "Precious Lord, Take My Hand," composed in 1932, which portrays God as a force gently guiding the weary believer through the storms and vicissitudes of life to a final heavenly abode.[45]

The possibility of the immediate presence of the Divine took a different shape in African-American popular religiosity and influenced popular religiosity more generally when Pentecostalism became fashionable.[46] Pentecostalism broadly speaking had some of its roots in the earlier Holiness movement, with its quest for a discrete experience of sanctification of holiness akin to the initial experience of personal conversion, but one that transported the believer to a higher spiritual plane. Many of the early leaders of the modern Pentecostal movement, both African-American and Euro-American, were first drawn to Holiness teaching before moving in a Pentecostal direction. Hence casual observers have often mistakenly viewed the two movements as synonymous. There are distinctive features to Pentecostalism that moved its emphases away from those of Holiness, though in time adherents of both organized new denominational structures to promote their perspectives. The most important of these is the reception of the gifts of the Spirit discussed in the New Testament, especially the gift of speaking in tongues or glossolalia.[47] The movement derives its name from the story in the New Testament book of Acts that records the first reported account of glossolalia in the Christian tradition as occurring during the Jewish festival of Pentecost.

While there is evidence of Pentecostal expression among African-American churches around Durham, North Carolina, as early as the mid-1880s, more directly at the center of the origins of the modern Pentecostal movement nationally is an African-American Holiness preacher named William J. Seymour (1870–1922).[48] Among Seymour's ministerial mentors was Charles Fox Parham, who was thoroughly committed to Holiness of a Methodist stripe in his ministry in Topeka, Kansas, and Houston, Texas. Parham had become convinced that those who attained perfect sanctification, the goal of Holiness experience, could expect a direct sign of the baptism of the Holy Ghost, usually the ability to speak in tongues, although Parham also believed in the gift of healing. Seymour brought similar expectations with him when he founded the Apostolic Faith Gospel Mission in an abandoned Methodist chapel on Los Angeles's Azusa Street in 1906.

Nightly meetings at Seymour's mission emphasized the reality of spiritual power, the giving of spiritual gifts to those who earnestly sought them. When experiences of glossolalia became common at the mission's revivals, hundreds of persons came to Los Angeles to see firsthand this miraculous invasion of supernatural power in human life. Awareness of this outburst of Pentecostal fervor became common, thanks to the media attention it generated. Within a decade Pentecostalism had spawned a host of popular periodicals, its own hymnody, a network of itinerant preachers who traveled throughout the country, and several associations of Pentecostal churches that ultimately coalesced into denominations.

Several features of this early Pentecostalism merit comment. The revivals at Azusa Street and many of those that followed in their wake broke both the racial and gender barriers of the day. Women and men, blacks and whites came together and experienced the gift of tongues, though as denominational groups formed out of the movement, the persistent racism in American culture meant that they tended to organize along racial lines. More important for understanding how this movement nurtured strains of popular religiosity is the nature of the experience of speaking in tongues. Here is archetypal ecstatic experience. No one consciously orchestrates the experience; those who speak in tongues claim they do not do so under their own power. Rather, the supernatural takes control, and while under the sway of that power, individuals are not conscious of the sounds they are uttering. Peter Williams captured the way this experience is set apart from ordinary reality: "In the repudiation of rational discourse for the ecstatic utterance of a rapid flow of syllables with no discursive content, the forms of structured, everyday modes of communication are left behind in favor of pure, unmediated flow. Whatever communication thus achieved is at the prerational level; what is valued above all is a 'pure experience,' uncontaminated by any attempt at interpretation or structuring."[49] Essentially glossolalia is direct, unmediated apprehension of supernatural power, one that endows the recipient not with an empirical superiority to others, but with access to a realm that is more potent than anything empirical. At the same time, even if glossolalia occurs in the context of group worship, it is an individual and hence private experience. That is, not everyone who attends a Pentecostal gathering automatically will speak in tongues; the experience comes only to individuals one at a time, though many speak simultaneously. Nor does the experience always occur in such a public context. As well, no two experiences are exact duplicates. This unmediated, individual character of glossolalia, like the dramatic experience of conversion promoted by much popular evangelicalism, makes Pentecostal experience a phenomenon of popular religiosity.

Not all popular interest in the power of the Holy Spirit found expression in religiosity associated with Pentecostalism. Two other manifestations merit brief mention: "higher life" thinking and the calls for "victorious life" in some evangelical Protestant circles, and the fascination with dispensationalist premillennialism. The "higher life" theology attracted many prominent clergy of the day, including Reuben Torrey, a Minneapolis Congregationalist, and J. Wilbur Chapman, a Presbyterian pastor in Philadelphia, both of whom were well-known speakers at a number of "higher life" conferences and published sermons and tracts outlining their thought.[50] Proponents, rooted more in Reformed traditions than in Wesleyan Holiness thought, insisted that following the experience of personal conversion there came a number of subsequent individual experiences that drew one into the "higher life," into the presence of the Holy Spirit. Part of the excitement that surrounded "higher life" thinking was its eschatological bent; the increasing power of the Spirit in ordinary life was a sign of the nearness of the end. Hence "higher life" religiosity also drew on the millennialist fervor that long weaved into popular religiosity, even as it emphasized the centrality of inner, personal experience of supernatural power. But it also gave those who incorporated it into their personal religiosity a sense of aloofness from the turmoil of empirical reality.

By the 1870s some "higher life" conferences also began to tap the earlier evangelical quest for perfection that had more obvious connections to Holiness teaching and, following Charles G. Trumbull, spoke of the possibility of the "victorious life," a life in which individuals would triumph here and now over the stresses, anxieties, and insecurities accompanying life in urbanized, industrialized America.[51] As Douglas Frank has argued, "victorious life" religiosity emphasized a "privatized and spiritualized means of dealing with a wicked world."[52] Left to their own devices, individuals would be unable to measure up to divine standards of living in the midst of an evil culture. But through absolute surrender to the power of the Holy Spirit, by giving the self over to possession by the supernatural, one could triumph and thus attain power and control over the course of one's life. A "victorious life" hymnody helped carry the message to ordinary folk. Witness this text, written by J. M. Van Deventer in 1896, still found in many Protestant hymnals:

> All to Jesus I surrender; all to him I freely give;
> I will ever love and trust him, in his presence daily live.
>
> All to Jesus I surrender; make me, Savior, wholly thine;
> let me feel the Holy Spirit, truly know that thou art mine.
>
> All to Jesus I surrender; Lord, I give myself to thee;
> Fill me with thy love and power; let thy blessing fall on me.

In speaking of possession by the Spirit through surrender to Jesus and explicitly claiming that one received power in return, "victorious life" thinking was buttressing elements that had long nurtured popular religiosity.

The widespread use of "victorious life" language among evangelicals a century later testifies to the imprint this understanding of religiosity made on popular consciousness.

Premillennial dispensationalism was also to a large degree about spiritual power, but perhaps on a larger scale.[53] With a background in the teaching of John Nelson Darby and his British followers known as the Plymouth Brethren, premillennial dispensationalists looked at the total scheme of world history from the perspective of their interpretation of biblical prophecy. They divided all human history into dispensations, or large epochs detailing different ways God dealt with humanity. By transposing their interpretation of prophecy onto specific events of world history, they concluded that they were living in the final dispensation that would precede Christ's return to earth in total victory. Theologians have long debated whether dispensationalists, with their emphasis on the imminent rapture of the church and believers, distort the meaning of the biblical texts. That concern, however, does not detract from the impact of a broad dispensationalist understanding on many rank and file Protestants in forging their own worldview. In essence, what this line of thinking does is to allow believers to recapture control of history itself.[54] Human destiny is not in the hands of governments or those who control the economy, but under the control of the supernatural power of God. Those who believe will ultimately achieve victory over not just an evil social order, but over history itself.

What made premillennial dispensationalism an enduring presence within American religion was the publication in 1909 of the *Scofield Reference Bible*, called by Ernest R. Sandeen "the most influential single publication in millenarian and Fundamentalist historiography."[55] Cyrus I. Scofield, a mainstay of the Bible Conference movement, prepared an edition of the King James Version of the Bible with introductory materials, notes, annotations, and other apparatus based on the schemes developed in premillennial dispensationalism.[56]

With an updated edition published in 1967 following the revision of the King James translation, total sales by all reasonable estimates are around eleven million copies. One did not need to be a convinced premillennial dispensationalist to be influenced by the *Scofield Reference Bible* since for generations of American Protestants it was the only edition of scripture to use for reading and study of the sacred text of Christianity, etching deeply into the popular religious consciousness an understanding of the reality of supernatural power and its ultimate control over history.

Intellectual and social issues confronting the organized religious traditions in the later nineteenth century may well have offered challenges to religious professionals and leaders of the day. But they also nourished many currents of popular religiosity among ordinary women and men. So, too, did the changes that redirected African-American life in the United

States once slavery had been eliminated. As well, the continued interaction between Native American and Euro-American cultures had an enduring impact on the religiosity of indigenous peoples. In every case that unsystematic but abiding sense of the supernatural that underlies popular religiosity in American life, that constellation of values, beliefs, and practices by which ordinary folk give meaning to their world and their experience, received sustenance. But other dimensions of American life in the later nineteenth century that cultivated various strains of popular religiosity also merit attention.

NOTES

1. Ferenc Morton Szasz, in *The Divided Mind of Protestant America, 1880–1930* (University: University of Alabama Press, 1982), argues that the issues raised by evolutionary theory, comparative religion, and higher criticism did not have any significant impact on popular thought (and hence on the religiosity of ordinary folk) until after 1900, although they troubled theologians earlier.

2. See James F. Findlay, Jr., *Dwight L. Moody: American Evangelist, 1837–1899* (Chicago: University of Chicago Press, 1969).

3. On Sankey, see Rupert Murrell Stevenson, "Ira D. Sankey and 'Gospel Hymnody,' " *Religion in Life* 20 (1950–51): 81–88; and Mel R. Wilhoit, "Sing Me a Song: Ira D. Sankey and Congregational Singing," *The Hymn* 42 (January 1991): 13–19.

4. All hymns cited are found in *The United Methodist Hymnal* (Nashville: United Methodist Publishing House, 1989), and direct quotations are taken from the texts therein.

5. Sandra Sizer, *Gospel Hymns and Social Religion: The Rhetoric of Nineteenth-Century Revivalism* (Philadelphia: Temple University Press, 1978). Sizer provides a cogent summary of her argument in "Politics and Apolitical Religion: The Great Urban Revivals of the Late Nineteenth Century," *Church History* 48 (1979): 81–98.

6. Richard Rabinowitz, *The Spiritual Self in Everyday Life: The Transformation of Personal Religious Experience in Nineteenth-Century New England* (Boston: Northeastern University Press, 1989), p. 179.

7. A similar concern for personal morality also marked English evangelicalism. See Michael Hennell, "Evangelicalism and Worldliness, 1770–1870," in *Popular Belief and Practice*, edited by G. J. Cuming and Derek Baker, *Studies in Church History* 8 (Cambridge, England: Cambridge University Press, 1972), pp. 229–36.

8. An overview of the movement is found in Charles H. Lippy, "Social Christianity," in *Encyclopedia of the American Religious Experience*, edited by Charles H. Lippy and Peter W. Williams (New York: Charles Scribner's Sons, 1988), 2: 917–31.

9. Walter Rauschenbusch, *Christianity and the Social Crisis*, edited by Robert D. Cross (1907; New York: Harper and Row, 1964), p. 422.

10. Walter Rauschenbusch, *For God and the People: Prayers for the Social Awakening* (Boston: Pilgrim, 1910).

11. The basic study remains Jay P. Dolan, *Catholic Revivalism: The American Experience, 1830–1900* (Notre Dame, Ind.: University of Notre Dame Press, 1978).

12. A modest effort to gain Protestant converts to Catholicism in the closing years of the nineteenth century is appraised in Thomas J. Jonas, *The Divided Mind: American Catholic Evangelists in the 1890s* (New York and London: Garland, 1988).

13. Dolan, pp. 106–8.

14. See Ann Taves, *The Household of Faith: Roman Catholic Devotions in Mid-Nineteenth-Century America* (Notre Dame, Ind.: University of Notre Dame Press, 1986), especially pp. 113–20.

15. Taves, p. 116.

16. Taves, p. 17.

17. Taves, p. 126.

18. See Ralph L. Woods and Henry Woods, *Pilgrim Places in North America* (New York and Toronto: Longman, Green, 1939); and Taves, pp. 98–103.

19. A brief overview, albeit with a different focus, is Robert D. Cross, "Origins of the Catholic Parochial Schools in America," *American Benedictine Review* 16 (1965): 194–209.

20. Cross, pp. 201–3.

21. On the role of the parish in immigrant life more generally, see the essays collected in Brian Mitchell, ed., *Building the American Catholic City: Parishes and Institutions* (New York: Garland, 1988).

22. Rudolph J. Vecoli has wrestled with the nature of Italian immigrant religiosity, though he concludes that this religiosity reflects a "folk" religion rather than authentic Christianity. See Rudolph J. Vecoli, "Prelates and Peasants: Italian Immigrants and the Catholic Church," *Journal of Social History* 2 (Spring 1969): 217–68, and especially his "Cult and Occult in Italian-American Culture: The Persistence of a Religious Heritage," in *Immigrants and Religion in Urban Culture*, edited by Randall M. Miller and Thomas D. Marzik (Philadelphia: Temple University Press, 1977), pp. 25–47. My point, of course, is that such a distinction is artificial since it presumes that institutions, not the people themselves, provide the normative standards for authenticity.

23. Robert Anthony Orsi, *The Madonna of 115th Street: Faith and Community in Italian Harlem, 1880–1950* (New Haven, Conn.: Yale University Press, 1985), especially chap. 8 ("Theology of the Streets").

24. Vecoli, "Cult and Occult," p. 26.

25. On the gradual movement of Italian-American Catholics into so-called mainstream American Catholicism, see Silvano M. Tomasi, *Piety and Power: The Role of the Italian American Parishes in the New York Metropolitan Area, 1880–1930* (Staten Island, N.Y.: Center for Migration Studies, 1975).

26. Here I rely especially on John Bukowczyk, " 'Mary the Messiah': Polish Immigrants, Heresy and the Malleable Ideology of the Roman Catholic Church in America, 1860–1930," in *Disciplines of Faith: Studies in Religion, Politics, and Patriarchy*, edited by Jim Obelkevich, Lyndal Roper, and Raphael Samuel (New York: Routledge, 1987), pp. 371–89; and William H. Galush, "Faith and Fatherland: Dimensions of Polish-American Ethnoreligion, 1875–1975," in *Immigrants and Religion in Urban Culture*, pp. 84–102.

27. On the strong role played by laity in organizing ethnic churches that is not

limited to the Catholic experience, see Timothy L. Smith, "Lay Initiative in the Religious Life of American Immigrants, 1880–1950," in *Anonymous Americans: Explorations in Nineteenth-Century Social History*, edited by Tamara Hareven (Englewood Cliffs, N.J.: Prentice-Hall, 1971), pp. 214–49.

28. Other factors also contributed to schism, including some that from the perspective of the Catholic tradition would be regarded as promoting doctrinal heresy. See Bukowczyk, "Mary the Messiah."

29. Josef L. Barton, "Religion and Cultural Change in Czech Immigrant Communities, 1850–1920," in *Immigrants and Religion in Urban Culture*, pp. 3–24.

30. Figures are taken from Deborah Dash Moore, "The Social History of American Judaism," in *Encyclopedia of the American Religious Experience*, 1:294.

31. Traditional treatments of the emergence of Reform Judaism highlight changes associated with the more formal aspects of Judaism as a religious tradition, such as holding services on Sunday rather than on the Sabbath, use of instrumental music in services, the structure and format of such services, and the choice of prayer books for use in corporate worship. I single out dietary practice since it more directly involves what individuals themselves choose to do and hence is more specifically germane to a consideration of popular religiosity. A good overview is found in Abraham J. Karp, "The Emergence of an American Judaism," in *Encyclopedia of the American Religious Experience*, 1:273–90.

32. Scholars argue that the celebration of Passover has witnessed considerable transformation among American Jews. See Beatrice S. Weinreich, "The Americanization of Passover," in *Studies in Biblical and Jewish Folklore*, edited by Raphael Patai, Francis Lee Utley, and Dov Noy (Bloomington: Indiana University Press, 1960), pp. 329–66. Also see Wayland D. Hand, "Jewish Popular Beliefs and Customs in Los Angeles," in ibid., pp. 309–26.

33. Peter W. Williams, *Popular Religion in America: Symbolic Change and the Modernization Process in Historical Perspective* (Englewood Cliffs, N.J.: Prentice-Hall, 1980), p. 82. See also Joshua Trachtenberg, *Jewish Magic and Superstition: A Study in Folk Religion* (New York: Atheneum, 1974).

34. On Smohalla, see Vittorio Lanternari, *The Religions of the Oppressed* (New York: New American Library, 1963), pp. 110–13; Bryan R. Wilson, *Magic and the Millennium: A Sociological Study of Religious Movements of Protest among Tribal and Third-World Peoples* (London: Heinemann, 1973), pp. 278–83; and Williams, pp. 32–33.

35. On the Ghost Dance phenomenon, a helpful resource is Shelley Anne Osterreich, *The American Indian Ghost Dance, 1870 and 1890: An Annotated Bibliography* (Westport, Conn.: Greenwood, 1991). On the 1870 dance, see Cora DuBois, "The 1870 Ghost Dance," *Anthropological Records* 3:1 (Berkeley: University of California Press, 1939), pp. 1–131; Michael Hittman, "Ghost Dance, Disillusionment and Opiate Addiction: An Ethnohistory of Smith and Mason Valley" (Ph.D. diss., University of New Mexico, 1973), especially chap. 4; Lanternari, pp. 113–16; and Wilson, pp. 283–87.

36. See James Mooney, *The Ghost-Dance Religion and the Sioux Outbreak of 1890*, edited by Anthony F. C. Wallace (Chicago: University of Chicago Press, 1965); Paul Bailey, *Wovoka: The Indian Messiah* (Los Angeles: Westernlore Press, 1957); David H. Miller *Ghost Dance* (1959; reprint, Lincoln: University of Nebraska Press, 1985); Robert M. Utley, *The Last Days of the Sioux Nation* (New

Haven, Conn.: Yale University Press, 1963); Weston LaBarre, *The Ghost Dance* (New York: Dell, 1972); George A. Dorsey, *The Arapaho Sun Dance* (Chicago: Field Museum of Natural History, 1903); Joseph G. Jorgensen, *The Sun Dance Religion: Power for the Powerless* (Chicago: University of Chicago Press, 1972); Lanternari, pp. 128–32; and Wilson, pp. 292–306.

37. Quoted in Mooney, p. 2.

38. Among the standard analyses of tribal religiosity that incorporates use of peyote are David F. Aberle, *The Peyote Religion among the Navaho* (Chicago: Aldine, 1956); Weston LaBarre, *The Peyote Cult* (New York: Schocken, 1969); J. S. Slotkin, *The Peyote Religion: A Study in Indian-White Relations* (Glencoe, Ill.: Free Press, 1956); Omer C. Stewart, *Peyote Religion* (Norman: University of Oklahoma Press, 1987); idem, *Peyotism in the West: A Historical and Cultural Perspective* (Salt Lake City: University of Utah Press, 1984); Lanternari, chap. 2; and Wilson, chap. 13.

39. Williams, p. 35.

40. Sam D. Gill, "Native American Religions," in *Encyclopedia of the American Religious Experience*, 1:150.

41. Albert J. Raboteau, "Black Christianity in North America," in *Encyclopedia of the American Religious Experience*, 1:641.

42. See especially Zora Neale Hurston, *The Sanctified Church* (Berkeley, Calif.: Turtle Island, 1981).

43. See James H. Cone, *The Spirituals and the Blues* (New York: Seabury, 1972); and Tony Heilbut, *The Gospel Sound: Good News and Bad Times* (Garden City, N.Y.: Anchor Books, 1975).

44. See Michael W. Harris, *The Rise of Gospel Blues: The Music of Thomas Andrew Dorsey in the Urban Church* (New York: Oxford University Press, 1992).

45. Both hymns are found in a variety of hymnals serving both African-American and Euro-American churches. The text here is reprinted from *The United Methodist Hymnal* with permission.

46. The voluminous literature on modern Pentecostalism includes W. J. Hollenweger, *The Pentecostals: The Charismatic Movement in the Churches* (Minneapolis: Augsburg, 1969); Nils Bloch-Hoell, *The Pentecostal Movement* (London: Allen and Unwin, 1964); Robert Mapes Anderson, *Vision of the Disinherited: The Making of American Pentecostalism* (New York: Oxford University Press, 1979); Vinson Synan, *The Holiness-Pentecostal Movement in the United States* (Grand Rapids, Mich.: Eerdmans, 1971); Grant Wacker, "Pentecostalism," in *Encyclopedia of the American Religious Experience*, 2:933–45. On the larger impact of black Pentecostal expression, see Leonard Lovett, "The Spiritual Legacy and Role of Black Holiness-Pentecostalism in the Development of American Culture," *One in Christ: A Catholic Ecumenical Review* 23 (1987): 144–56. A helpful reference book is *Dictionary of Pentecostal and Charismatic Movements*, edited by Stanley M. Burgess and Gary B. McGee (Grand Rapids, Mich.: Zondervan, 1988).

47. On glossolalia as a manifestation of ecstatic experience, see especially John P. Kildahl, *The Psychology of Speaking in Tongues* (New York: Harper and Row, 1972); and Felicitas D. Goodman, *Speaking in Tongues: A Cross-Cultural Study of Glossolalia* (Chicago: University of Chicago Press, 1972).

48. See James T. Connelly, "William J. Seymour," in *Twentieth-Century Shapers*

of American Popular Religion, edited by Charles H. Lippy (Westport, Conn.: Greenwood, 1989), pp. 381–87.

49. Williams, p. 144.

50. A good introduction to "higher life" religiosity is Grant Wacker, "The Holy Spirit and the Spirit of the Age in American Protestantism, 1880–1920," *Journal of American History* 72 (1985): 45–62.

51. See Douglas W. Frank, *Less than Conquerors: How Evangelicals Entered the Twentieth Century* (Grand Rapids, Mich.: Eerdmans, 1986), chap. 4.

52. Ibid., p. 167.

53. See especially Timothy P. Weber, *Living in the Shadow of the Second Coming: American Premillennialism, 1875–1982,* enl. ed. (Grand Rapids, Mich.: Zondervan, 1983); and Frank, chap. 3.

54. Frank, p. 67.

55. Ernest R. Sandeen, *The Roots of Fundamentalism* (Grand Rapids, Mich.: Baker Book House, 1970), p. 222.

56. A brief sketch and appraisal of Scofield's work and larger influence is Larry V. Crutchfield, "C. I. Scofield," in *Twentieth-Century Shapers of American Popular Religion,* pp. 371–81.

Chapter 6

Popular Culture and Popular Movements: Advancing Popular Religiosity in the Later Nineteenth Century

American growth in the later nineteenth century expanded the ways various dimensions of popular culture found expression. On the one hand, there were a number of religious movements, often with a symbiotic relationship to organized religious institutions, which emerged to give voice to the experience of supernatural power that the traditional religions seemed to thwart. As well, population growth meant an increasing market for the materials of popular culture such as popular books and magazines. Then, too, the private and personal aspects of popular religiosity received fresh support as cultural images of gender roles and even the place of the home in American life shifted. While social historians in recent decades have expanded our awareness of how these forces shaped the overall culture, few have scrutinized their implications for understanding the religious pulse of the American peoples. Yet all these helped sustain vital strains of popular religiosity that allowed ordinary men and women to endow their lives and the world around them with meaning. We must look beyond traditional interpretation to examine how such forces have nurtured popular religiosity. Direct apprehension of sacred power pervaded manifestations of popular religiosity in the later nineteenth century in movements with a tangential relationship to the formal religious traditions. Rather than turning toward some physical expression of supernatural power as Pentecostals did with glossolalia, many turned inward to the mind or the inner self. Historians of American religion often cluster these expressions of popular religiosity together and speak of metaphysical movements or metaphysical religions because of their insistence on the spiritual nature of reality and the ability of the mind to tap into that reality. Catherine Albanese has suggested that the emphasis many of these movements placed on mental control of the body should lead us to think of them also as forms of a "physical religion."[1] Some, such as Christian Science and New Thought, represented new forms of that recurring phenomenon in popular religiosity that seeks harmony between the self and a realm of power, while others, such as Theosophy, represented a resurgence of the occult in popular religiosity.[2] We shall look briefly at just these three—Christian Science, New Thought, and Theosophy—though there are numerous other examples of similar styles of popular religiosity.

To a large extent, behind the emergence of both New Thought and Christian Science lie the popular teachings of two individuals, Warren Felt Evans and Phineas T. Quimby. Evans, a one-time Methodist who dabbled in Swedenborgianism, wrote several books of a popular nature on the idea of mental healing. While they would not be considered best-sellers, by all accounts they attracted a rather wide audience. Among them were *The Mental Cure, Mental Medicine,* and *The Divine Law of Cure,* all published between the close of the Civil War and 1881.[3] Combining elements of Mesmerism, hypnotism, and what that age called animal magnetism, Evans induced a hypnotic, trance-like state in clients who sought his assistance in healing. One needed simply to relax and surrender control to higher forces within. Then, using the power of suggestion, Evans sought to have clients exert that higher, mental power in order to cure their ailments. Hence in time, Evans' approach and those similar to it became known as mind-cure. *Mental Healing Monthly,* which began publication in August 1886, helped further popular fascination with mind-cure, even though its run ended in June 1888. While there is no solid evidence that Evans directly influenced Quimby or vice-versa, Quimby went further than Evans in drawing on Mesmerism to effect healing and in abandoning hypnotic trance for direct application of mental control over the body. Quimby also rejected much of traditional Christian teaching, convinced that its superstition and reliance on clergy prevented ordinary folk from recognizing the mental cause and cure of disease. He did, however, occasionally link his own thinking with that of Christ because of New Testament accounts of Christ's ability to heal. But as Stephen Gottschalk has pointed out, Quimby's primary interest was the particular therapeutic technique that he promoted, not the possible spiritual dimension in sickness and health.[4] Others would push links to an understanding of the pervasive presence of supernatural power more directly.

The spiritual aspects latent in Quimby's approach were developed more fully, for example, by Mary Baker Eddy and the early Christian Science movement. That Eddy chose to label her approach as "science" reflects the tenor of the age; science was perceived as offering explanations to human questions superior to those of traditional theology and formal religion. The details of Eddy's life, with its various personal ailments, dissatisfaction with the Calvinist religion of her upbringing, unfulfilling marriages, and occasional near poverty, need not concern us here. What is important, however, is how she fashioned ideas and approaches advocated by Evans and Quimby into a particular style of popular religiosity. In the early 1860s Eddy had direct contact with Quimby as she sought relief for her own health problems through his techniques, though evidence suggests that even earlier she had toyed with the idea that disease of all sorts had mental causes. Unlike Quimby, however, Eddy directly connected the mental power to effect healing with dimensions of formal Christian belief. Always an avid reader of the Bible, Eddy concluded that the numerous accounts in the New Testament of Jesus' effecting miraculous healing clearly revealed the power of the mind over disease. The mind housed a spiritual force that once unleashed would bring about health. For Eddy, the nature of authentic life was spiritual rather than physical or material. The common understanding that confined the spiritual to some heavenly realm and restricted empirical reality to the physical and material, a view Eddy found at the heart of both medicine and traditional religion, was the root cause not only of disease, but of human unhappiness. "Life in and of the Spirit," one of her favorite phrases to summarize her teaching, was the only authentic plane of existence.

By the mid-1870s Eddy began to reach a wider audience for her way of thinking. In 1875 she published the first edition of her *Science and Health with Key to the Scriptures*, a handbook of her teaching that tried to connect her thinking directly with the sacred text behind traditional Christian understanding.[5] Within four years, she organized what became the "mother church" of Christian Science in Boston, her headquarters of sorts since 1866. The desire to institutionalize the movement stemmed both from Eddy's conviction that she needed to distinguish her teaching from the presumably more secular mind-cure approach and her firm belief that she had recaptured the essence of authentic Christianity. To reach an even wider audience, in 1883 Eddy launched the *Journal of Christian Science*, later renamed the *Christian Science Journal* and the forerunner of today's *Christian Science Monitor* newspaper.[6] As with other periodicals intended for a mass audience, we have no way of knowing exactly how many people Eddy reached through her magazine. But it served as a potent mechanism to promote her notions of the spiritual nature of reality, and its influence extended well beyond the number of those who actively identified themselves as Christian Scientists.[7] Emma Hopkins, who edited the periodical briefly in the 1880s, went on to become a major advocate of New Thought. Hopkins in turn was a signal influence on such figures as Charles and Myrtle Fillmore, who founded the Unity School of Christianity, and Malinda Cramer, one of the primary movers behind Divine Science.

Eddy's decision to institutionalize her movement gives it a formal dimension that lies beyond our purview, but her recognition that in the 1880s and 1890s there was wide interest in a religiosity based on the power of the mind was on target, for as Christian Science expanded through organization, so, too, did other approaches to mind-cure and New Thought. In the 1880s mind-cure "institutes" were established in several cities from coast to coast, summer conferences like the Greenacre Conference in Maine in 1894 brought advocates together, and more informal clubs in numerous cities paved the way for the establishment of the National New Thought Alliance in 1908 (later the International New Thought Alliance). A better, though more elusive, indicator of the extent of interest is the spate of periodicals and popular books generated by mind-cure and New Thought. Although some were short-lived, periodicals such as *Practical Ideals*, *Eternal Progress*, and *New Man* (among others) brought this form of spirituality into countless American homes. Of the books spawned by the movement, none gained a wider readership than Ralph Waldo Trine's *In Tune with the Infinite*, which first appeared in 1897 and remained in print in the late twentieth century.[8] By the outbreak of the First World War, Trine's New Thought classic had already sold in excess of 135,000 copies.[9] By 1993 total sales were approaching the two million mark. Trine's work went beyond the assertion that mental power could cure disease to claim that mental suggestion could also produce material prosperity and all kinds of success. "Suggest prosperity to yourself," Trine wrote. "See yourself in a prosperous condition. Affirm that you will before long be in a prosperous condition. Affirm it calmly and quietly, but strongly and confidently."[10] The underlying conviction is that in time mental power will transform what one desires from mere suggestion into actual fact. As well, the focus on material success reflected the increasing hegemony of laissez-faire capitalism in American economic life.

Closer to the basic tenets of the formal Protestant tradition in the springboard for his thinking, but taking an approach close to Trine's is Russell H. Conwell (1843–1925).[11] Before entering the Baptist ministry, Conwell had been a lawyer in Massachusetts (where he numbered Mary Baker Eddy among his clients), a popular public lecturer, and author of several biographies of political leaders that were geared to a mass audience. Conwell's inordinate success as a pastor only enhanced his reputation as a lecturer and led to countless articles about him in newspapers and magazines and several hagiographic biographies even before his death in 1925.[12] He left an enduring mark on American popular religiosity through his lecture, *Acres of Diamonds*, that he reportedly delivered more than sixthousand times across the nation and that remains in print more than a century after its initial publication.[13] In a nutshell, Conwell's message was that anyone could achieve wealth through hard work and simple faith in the supernatural power of the Divine to assist those who believed. It was not only the few, such as the industrial barons of the day, who could reap great wealth, but ordinary men and women who, with God's help, could garner great economic gain. Such material success for Conwell was also a challenge, for

he believed that those who were rich had a responsibility to use their resources for the welfare of all. The underlying point remained that every
person who had a private, personal, inner faith in the Divine could reach
the heights of material prosperity, regardless of external circumstances. It
was a message for the individual par excellence.

What made mind-cure, Christian Science, the various forms of New
Thought, and the ideas found in *Acres of Diamonds* plausible? Why did
Mary Baker Eddy, Emma Hopkins, Ralph Waldo Trine, and Russell H.
Conwell gain such a widespread audience? From the perspective of popular
religiosity, the plausibility of all these approaches rests in their strident
affirmation of the power of the supernatural and their emphasis on the role
of the individual in tapping into that reservoir of power to effect results in
the empirical realm. For Eddy, it was the individual who had to realize
that all life was a spiritual force, that the physical with all its ailments was
ephemeral if not illusory. Even Trine's grandiose claims for the power of
suggestion elevate the individual, for it is the individual who, through calm
but strong suggestion, gains health and prosperity. That the supernatural
lay within the self and not necessarily in the doctrines or institutions of
formal religious traditions not only challenged the normative authority of
the churches and denominations, but also reinforced the primacy of private,
personal experience fundamental to popular religiosity. The notion underlying them all, that there is a correspondence between what we ordinarily
perceive as empirical reality and the spiritual realm, resonated with the idea
of the pervasive presence of a realm of power that underlies all popular
religiosity. As well, as Donald Meyer demonstrated, many of those who
were early "practitioners" of Christian Science or who were drawn to
mind-cure did not abandon other religious identification, but personally
blended ideas drawn from these alternative forms of religiosity with more
traditional religious teaching to create an idiosyncratic personal (and hence
popular) religious worldview.[14] After all, these metaphysical thinkers did
not require an individual to have membership in a group in order to appropriate their techniques. The vocabulary of New Thought and Christian
Science was also attractive to many who had been exposed to "higher life"
and "victorious life" teaching, for all spoke of surrender to a higher power
and the triumph that came from, in Eddy's words, "Life in and of the
Spirit."

What gave particular currency to these claims in the later nineteenth
century was the way they restored power and access to a superior realm
of power to ordinary men and women whose daily lives seemed devoid of
power as the impersonality of city and factory replaced the village and farm
as the locus of economic life. Conwell's *Acres of Diamonds* offered a powerful promise of success in an industrializing world where many found
themselves removed from the economic gains of the few. In this context, it
is important to note that by all accounts an inordinate proportion of those

drawn to mind-cure, New Thought, and Christian Science were women. As we shall see more fully later, urbanization and industrialization combined with other forces to alter the role of women in American life by undercutting the economic role coequal women played in an agrarian society and creating a sphere where women's social role was increasingly confined to domestic responsibilities. If society denied women access to some expressions of power, New Thought, mind-cure, and Christian Science provided entrees to a superior realm of power. This particular strain of popular religiosity is by no means limited to the later nineteenth century, though it then may have enjoyed greater currency than during other periods. The continuing interest in Trine's *In Tune with the Infinite* is one indicator of its ongoing presence. So, too, especially are the "positive thinking" of Norman Vincent Peale and the "possibility thinking" advocated by Robert Schuller in the mid- and later twentieth century. As well, some of the philosophy of the spate of "twelve-step" support groups and self-help, beginning with Alcoholics Anonymous and expanding to encompass a variety of real and perceived disorders, reflects the premise of mind-cure, New Thought, and Christian Science that there is a latent power within connected to a higher power that, when tapped, can grant the individual control over personal life and hence meaning and happiness.

In a different though related fashion, Theosophy and other expressions of religiosity that reached to Asian, expecially Indian, ways of thinking for part of their understanding of the world also buttressed the unsystematic, but lively sense of the supernatural at the heart of popular religiosity. Theosophy, institutionalized in the Theosophical Society established in 1875 in New York by Helena Petrovna Blavatsky and Henry Steel Olcott, also has links with spiritualism and other occult strands of popular religiosity discussed earlier.[15] Two works by Blavatsky, *Isis Unveiled* and *The Secret Doctrine*, sketch the worldview of Theosophy.[16] Here, too, mind is central, but in a more cosmic sense even than Mary Baker Eddy had envisioned. Generally called "Consciousness" by Blavatsky, this universal mind is the source of both matter and spirit. Indeed it is the single reality (reflecting the monism fundamental to much Hindu philosophy). One's present physical form expresses one's spiritual reality as it evolves toward ultimate union with Consciousness. Hence reincarnation becomes part of the worldview of Theosophy, for one's present state expresses how one has dealt with Consciousness in past lives as part of a continuing pilgrimage toward pure Consciousness. So, too, astrology is important, for it allows individuals to bring their lives into greater correspondence or harmony with cosmic Consciousness by ascertaining how spiritual powers are working at any given time. Especially through meditation, either alone or in groups, individuals can draw on spiritual energy that will move them in this life and lives to come toward ultimate Consciousness. Those whose evolutionary progress has advanced beyond that of most are acknowledged as masters whose wisdom can assist others in their own journeys. Theosophy's understanding of the self as constantly evolving, a notion in step with then current ideas of progress, endowed one with an ability to deal with the vicissitudes of one's present situation. Through study and meditation, one could increase one's spiritual dimension and hence gain power or control over the forces that on the surface seemed to control daily life. That knowledge of the true nature of reality was also secret, revealed only to the few through the great masters, also gave those drawn to this form of religiosity a certain superiority to others. That the secret was to be found within the self enhanced the importance of private, personal experience and thus elevated the individual of knowledge to a higher rank in the cosmic scheme than those who, although seemingly more powerful in an empirical sense, remained unaware of the truth. From an analytic perspective, the spiritual power enjoyed by the individual through Theosophy was no different than that special power enjoyed by evangelical Protestants of the time who found in Jesus a friend to guide them through the perils of daily life in a sinful world. Both buttressed popular religiosity.

While Theosophical centers were established in many cities in the final decades of the nineteenth century and opening decades of the twentieth, the movement represents just one of many expressions of an occult spirituality that resurfaced. Many alternative approaches came from the ranks of those who had been Theosophists, such as Jiddu Krishnamurti, Rudolf Steiner (founder of Anthroposophy), and Alice Bailey. In the later twentieth century this strain of popular religiosity would also feed into the fascination with New Age thought, another manifestation of the occult in American religious life. Outside the larger urban areas, Theosophy and its religious cousins, like New Thought and Christian Science, struck responsive chords in particular regions of the country. The form of New Thought known as Unity, for example, found the Midwest particularly receptive to its understanding of the world. All of these expressions of an alternative popular religiosity gained a hearing in the Far West, especially in California. Sandra Sizer Frankiel's *California's Spiritual Frontiers* calls attention to the inroads made especially by New Thought, Theosophy, Christian Science, and Unitarianism among Euro-American settlers coming to California between 1850 and 1910.[17]

Because they offered a greater personal sense of satisfaction, because the popular religiosity they inspired seemed to offer more viable access to the supernatural realm, these alternative ways of being religious not only challenged the efforts of churches aligned with formal religious traditions to establish their institutions in California, but they also frequently influenced so-called mainline churches to adapt their style to popular religiosity in order to garner a following. The California ethos in the later nineteenth century was complicated and enriched as well by the presence of Chinese immigrants intent on maintaining their own forms of religiosity and interacting with those around them. Other expressions of popular religiosity also flourished in California and the Southwest. Native Americans first introduced to Catholicism by Spanish missionaries during the age of colonialism had long fused their indigenous traditions with more formal Catholic belief and practice, adding yet another layer of ethnic diversity to the overall Catholic story.[18] One striking example is the *penitentes* of the Southwest who combined ancient initiation rites and blood rituals with Catholic devotion to the suffering of Jesus in a unique exercise of self-flagellation carried out in secret rituals in private structures apart from the organized church. What is important about this exercise for our purposes is the way in which inflicting pain on the body becomes a means of identifying with the supernatural, in this case with the Christ whose suffering brings redemption. While institutional Catholicism has long eschewed such expressions of religiosity, in some areas of New Mexico the secret brotherhood of *penitentes* still endures.[19] All of these dimensions of the religious landscape of California and the Southwest promoted the eclecticism and syncretism that shape popular religiosity.

Thus far we have looked at currents of popular religiosity in the later nineteenth and early twentieth centuries that had some direct or indirect relationship with formal religious traditions or recognizable movements. Other forces nurtured and sustained an abiding belief in the supernatural and a realm of power beyond the human. From the 1840s on, novels provide a vital source for discerning ideas and ways of thinking to which ordinary people had access.[20] Novels gained in popularity among American readers in the nineteenth century, despite both Protestant and Catholic religious leaders frowning on fiction of all sorts as frivolous and detrimental to genuine piety.[21] While it has long been assumed that women constituted the bulk of the readership of novels and other forms of fiction, women also wrote numerous novels with a religious focus that became best-sellers.[22] Hence the constellation of ideas found in popular novels of the later nineteenth century provides valuable clues not only about features of popular religiosity in general, but particularly about ways in which American women fashioned a religious world that brought meaning to their experience. Much traditional literary criticism has summarily dismissed a large body of this literature as sentimental and merely reflective of a Victorian cult of domesticity. On the contrary, although we cannot discern precisely how ordinary women—and men—appropriated the ideas in them, these novels represent an important entree into the religious consciousness of ordinary people. Indeed, even nineteenth-century critics recognized that novels often mirrored the "common" religious experience of the day.[23]

Augusta J. Evans (Wilson), a native of Mobile, Alabama, and an ardent supporter of the Confederate cause during the War between the States, penned several novels that gained a wide readership, beginning in 1859 with *Beulah*, which had sales in excess of one-half million copies.[24] *Beulah* is itself an intriguing journey into the realm of popular religiosity, for the title heroine on one level is seeking a rational, intellectual basis for her religious faith and concludes there is none. Rather, one must proceed through life without dependence on formal doctrine (or, in the novel, on other human beings), but rather on the inner strength an abiding, but nonrational sense of the supernatural and the self provides. Evans' most popular work, with sales of more than one million, was *St. Elmo*, published in 1867.[25] While the novel takes its name from the leading male figure, St. Elmo Murray, the story really centers on Edna Earl, an orphan taken in by the Murray family. At first glance, the novel appears to use Edna and St. Elmo as archetypes, she of piety and he of a nearly antireligious worldliness. Consequently Edna rejects St. Elmo's proposal of marriage and, in a challenge to the patriarchal assumptions of the larger culture, achieves considerable success and an identity in her own right as a governess in New York City and as a writer. Meanwhile, St. Elmo undergoes a religious conversion and, without Edna's knowledge, enters the ministry. Ultimately, now that their values appear in harmony, Edna and St. Elmo marry. To see Edna only as a paragon of traditional piety and St. Elmo as the rake who turned his life around obscures the real dynamic of the novel for underscoring popular religiosity. What makes Edna a genuine heroine is not her purity, but her ability to create a meaningful world for herself because her religiosity provides access to a realm of power superior to that which the early St. Elmo exemplifies. Meaning and success are not to be equated with wealth and social status. Rather, confidence in the assistance provided by the spiritual power that comes to the individual through faith and devotion yields the only authentic meaning and success. In emphasizing that the individual with a firm personal religious worldview can triumph without succumbing to fashionable currents, Evans buttresses the enduring belief in popular religiosity of the ultimate efficacy of the supernatural to bring genuine happiness to human life.

Less successful in terms of sales than *St. Elmo*, Elizabeth Stuart Phelps's *The Gates Ajar* nevertheless sold and estimated eightythousand copies in the United States and probably around one hundred thousand in Britain between its publication in 1868 and the end of the century.[26] Here heroine Mary Cabot, seeking to find meaning in the death of her brother in combat during the Civil War, rejects the understanding of both death and heaven offered by traditional Protestant theology for a highly personalized notion. Mary's heaven becomes an extension of earthly happiness, a place where one is surrounded by red balloons, pianos, and the enticing aroma of freshly baked ginger cookies. Because Phelps so thoroughly humanizes heaven, perhaps, as some critics have claimed, to avoid the brute reality of death, to demystify the unknown, or to preserve domestic, middle-class values through their correspondence with a heavenly realm, it is easy to dismiss her work as an expression of mere sentimentalism.[27] Such criticism

obscures the role of the novel in sustaining popular religiosity. It is important, for example, that Mary Cabot finds no meaning or satisfaction in the
formal teachings of institutional religion, represented in the novel by Dr.
Bland and Deacon Quirk, whose names are symbolic of the character of
traditional religion. Rather, she is forced to develop a highly individualized,
private understanding in order to make sense out of the death of her
brother. By transforming an unknown heaven into what is familiar, Phelps
created a bridge between empirical reality and the supernatural realm. The
supernatural is not distant and removed from ordinary life, but an extension of what brings inner contentment to personal life here and now. By
bringing the supernatural into ordinary life, Phelps reinforced the conviction fundamental to much popular religiosity that supernatural power is
available to women and men as they go about the business of creating a
world of meaning to make sense out of common experience, such as confronting death and grief.

In intellectual circles challenges to traditional doctrine stemmed largely
from the inroads made by various strands of scientific thought and the
application of critical methods of literary analysis to sacred texts. In a
rather different fashion than Augusta Evans' *Beulah*, the title figure of Mrs.
Humphrey Ward's *Robert Elsmere* also confronts such challenges. Although the author was British, the novel ranked among the most widely
read in the United States, selling more than a half million copies in 1888,
the year it appeared.[28] Elsmere, a priest in the Church of England, becomes
so distraught over what formal doctrine to accept, given the questions
raised by contemporary science, and what organized form of Christianity
is most legitimate that he finally rejects all official theology and all religious
institutions. His intellectual rejection of traditional expressions of Christianity does not render Elsmere devoid of religiosity, for he retains a commitment to the ethical teachings associated with Christianity. One may
discard formal religion, but not religiosity. There remains some way in
which individuals fashion a means of making sense out of their experience
as Robert Elsmere did through Christian ethics. In essence, Elsmere created
his own personal religion.

More practical challenges to being religious confront the larger cast of
characters in Charles M. Sheldon's *In His Steps*, often seen merely as a
"naive" *Robert Elsmere* or at best a "shoddy imitation" of it.[29] Originating
in a series of sermons Sheldon preached to his Topeka, Kansas, congregation on Sunday evenings, *In His Steps* details the trials that confront several
members of a Protestant church as they resolve to ask the question, "What
would Jesus do?" before making any decision, professional or personal.
Quickly they all realize that Jesus, in their understanding, would have little
to do with business as usual, but would abandon material security and
social position for ministry with the poor, whose apparent values also seem
at odds with traditional religious teaching. Although those who embark on

this experiment abandon their own positions of prestige and wealth, they are hardly successful in effecting radical social or personal change in those to whom they now minister. Yet they become personally transformed in the process, apart from the institutional expression of Christianity. By prevailing social standards, they exchanged power for impotence, but they found an inner satisfaction in giving themselves over to a supernatural Jesus and living as they thought Jesus would live. As Peter Williams has claimed, "At one level *In His Steps* can be read as a reaffirmation of the timeless Christian message of the Cross, the way of suffering which leads to earthly failure but ultimately to redemption in another realm. At another level, it can be seen as the attempt of a class of people which perceived itself as increasingly impotent—in this case, the middle-class Protestant clergy—to redefine success in terms that conform to its own perception of its situation in the world."[30] Wayne Elzey has cogently argued that the novel exalted the values of the emerging urban middle class by showing that these values represent a harmonization of the virtues and strengths of both the upper and lower classes, without the corresponding vices and weaknesses associated with those values.[31]

One can find a basis for all of these interpretations in Sheldon's novel, but none adequately accounts for its enduring success, as it not only remains in print, but was even published in comic book form in 1977, albeit with updated characters.[32] From the perspective of popular religiosity, what gives *In His Steps* its continuing plausibility is the way it makes the religious quest a purely private and personal one. It is up to individuals to ascertain what Jesus would do in their particular circumstances. Although such may have social consequences in terms of how one deals with other people and with the institutions of the larger society, part of the message Sheldon communicates is that authentic religiosity is not confined to creeds and churches. It finds its locus in how ordinary folk translate their beliefs and values into a way of life that enables them to endure whatever comes their way. Because the Jesus of institutional Christianity becomes a co-participant in the quest, the supernatural is again drawn into the ordinary, and the realm of power exemplified by Sheldon's Jesus becomes one that is ultimately superior to all other manifestations of power in the human realm, despite apparent failure and frustration. To follow "in His steps" is to live in that world of superior power basic to popular religiosity.

Before the end of the nineteenth century, historical fiction with a biblical base was gaining in favor among American readers and nourished popular religiosity in its own way. Like other forms of popular literature, historical fiction with a mass appeal has reaped considerable negative appraisal from both literary critics and representatives of formal religion. The former castigate the genre for a lack of literary quality; the latter for exaggeration and distortion of the biblical record. One prominent example is Lew Wallace's *Ben Hur*.[33] Wallace, a lawyer who eschewed formal affiliation with an organized religious group, never visited the Near East, where the novel was set, until after it was published. He began work on *Ben Hur* in 1878 after a conversation about the figure of Christ with Robert Ingersoll, the lawyer, orator, and sometime Republican politician noted for his virulent attacks on Christianity. Wallace completed the manuscript while serving as the appointed governor of the New Mexico territory. During its first year in print, *Ben Hur* sold in excess of a half million copies; within two decades it had been made into a play that both toured the country and was staged on Broadway. One estimate has it that more than twenty million persons saw the stage production.[34] In the twentieth century, two film versions were made, a silent one in 1926 and an extravagant color and sound remake in 1959. As historian Mark Noll has commented, *Ben Hur* represents the sort of religious book of which "the American people can never seem to get enough."[35] Why? Told from the perspective of the title figure, a contemporary of Jesus, *Ben Hur* on one level is a fictional biography of Jesus. As the lives of Ben Hur and Jesus intersect, Ben Hur (and the reader) gradually recognize that Jesus is no ordinary human being, but one endowed with tremendous courage, wisdom, and power—virtues that the culture of the day would have seen as desirable masculine characteristics. Although, thanks to the stage and film versions, the battles and especially the climactic chariot race produce greater excitement than the portrayal of Jesus, what is vital about *Ben Hur* and cognate works is the way they strip Jesus of the centuries of christological doctrine that mark formal Christianity and make Jesus accessible to ordinary men and women. It is easier to believe in the Jesus of historical fiction than in the Jesus of the New Testament. The Jesus of fiction cannot be identified as a Baptist or a Methodist or a Catholic; such labels are irrelevant. The Jesus of fiction, as in *Ben Hur*, is one whose power common folk can grasp, understand, and use. That is precisely the appeal of *Ben Hur* and the reason it promotes popular religiosity. *Ben Hur*'s Jesus is one who comes alive in the mind and imagination of the reader or viewer, one who can be fashioned into the kind of Christ that one wants or needs in the continuing pilgrimage to give meaning to life. Indeed one becomes so overwhelmed by the power of Lew Wallace's Christ that one scarcely notices that the novel perpetuates a mistaken stereotype of Judaism and Jews as a religion and people inferior to Christianity and Christians.[36]

Few novels written by Roman Catholics or treating religion from a Catholic viewpoint were best-sellers in the later nineteenth century, although several appeared that were targeted primarily to a Catholic readership and thus helped foster that strain of popular religiosity shaped by Catholic sensibilities. Much of it was, as Paul Messbarger put it in the title of his study, "fiction with a parochial purpose." Several forces helped generate this Catholic popular literature. Catholic leaders, aware of the growing body of popular materials coming from Protestant writers, were eager to offer something to counter both the explicit content of books with Protestant religious themes and also the frequent negative portrayal of Catholics and Catholicism even in works that were not religious in focus. Some assumed that any Catholic work by definition would be superior to that of a Protestant writer. The surge in immigration in the decades following the Civil War considerably increased the potential audience for Catholic writing, especially as parochial schools, Catholic reading unions, and other ancillary agencies labored to teach immigrants and their children the English language and help them adjust to the new society in which they lived. But there was always the fear that the Protestant tone of the larger culture would woo the once faithful away from their Catholic commitment; hence there was need for a literature that would assure in readers' minds the compatibility of a Catholic identity with an American identity.[37] Only a very few aimed to convert Protestants to Catholicism.[38]

Two novels by Mary Agnes Tincker, *House of Yorke* and *Grapes and Thorns*, both deal with Catholic fears of Protestant prejudice and the need for maintaining faith in Catholic ways to combat that prejudice, but the latter especially emphasizes the compatibility of a Catholic and an American identity.[39] Frances Tiernen's *Child of Mary*, the very title of which betrays its Catholic focus, demonstrates how simple devotion to Catholic supernaturalism ultimately brings personal triumph over adversity and despair even to those adjusting to life in the postbellum South where the Catholic population was small.[40] Perhaps because of the need to provide appropriate curriculum materials for children receiving instruction in parochial schools and to counter the Protestant tone of the popular McGuffey *Readers*, there were numerous works of fiction targeted for a young readership. The most widely known are those by the Jesuit writer Francis Finn, many of them set in Catholic boarding schools.[41] His *Tom Playfair*, with the name of the title character obviously suggesting the book's focus on moral behavior, deftly argues that Catholic belief provides the only sure foundation for the ethical life.[42] Finn also consistently created adolescent male characters who were active in devotional societies; his works especially promoted the devotion to the Blessed Virgin that marked much of the popular religiosity sustained by Catholicism.

Only one best-seller of the later nineteenth century treated explicitly Catholic concerns, *L'Abbé Constantin* by Ludovic Halévy, a French dramatist and novelist who also wrote the book for Bizet's *Carmen*. Although set in France, *L'Abbé Constantin* ranks as an American best-seller for 1882 and centers on two American characters.[43] The story line combines Catholic concerns with romantic interests. A French estate, the income from which supports a small church, passes into the hands of an American owner. The abbe presumes that the new owner is a Protestant, an assumption not without basis given the character of American society at the time. Accordingly, he fears that the financial base of the church will disappear. Much to his surprise and delight, the abbe learns that the new owner and his sister, once they take up residence, are devout Catholics. The romantic interest unfolds when the abbe's newphew falls in love with the sister. In one sense, then, the novel demonstrates that supernatural power protects and promotes Catholic interests.

All of these and the many other books that circulated in the closing decades of the nineteenth century reveal a good bit about the popular religiosity nurtured by Catholicism. While all ostensibly emphasize Catholic doctrine and the sacramental focus of the Catholic tradition, they suggest that for ordinary American Catholics, popular devotion and private faith were more important than the trappings of institutional Catholicism. Messbarger offers an explanation: the sense of dislocation that came to an immigrant minority prompted a need for sacred order that devotionalism, not doctrine, filled.[44] As we have seen earlier, the private and personal nature of Catholic devotionalism brought the faithful into the arena of supernatural power and gave a basis for gaining direct access to that power within a larger society where empirical power was in the hands of others. The moralism of the children's novels is to the point, for in devotional exercises even children can call upon sacred power to grant the strength needed to live a moral life in the midst of a hostile social order.

Since the Catholic and Jewish immigrant experience shared some common features, one might expect to find similarities in the ways a Jewish popular literature nurtured popular religiosity. The story is actually somewhat different. We have already noted the emergence of a Yiddish press and popular theater, where countless productions evoked memories of European Jewish culture and the religiosity that was intertwined with it. Although occasional Jewish characters figure into popular novels by non-Jewish writers of the later nineteenth century, most perpetuate negative stereotypes rather than offering insight into American Jewish religiosity. Among the first to explore the implications of the American experience for Jewish religious identity was *The Rise of David Levinsky* by Abraham Cahan.[45] Although not published until 1917, *The Rise of David Levinsky* offers a portrait of the Eastern European Jewish immigrant experience. It first lures readers into the religious and cultural life of the European ghetto and *shtetl* before exposing the challenge to traditional ways of being religious wrought by the American experience. The title character appears to abandon the formal trappings of religiosity for the pursuit of material gain, a secular pursuit easier in the New World than in the Old. Yet there remained elements of a distinctive Jewish identity, particularly an attachment to the religious festivals and holidays that marked the passage of the year. Peter Williams has suggested that this process of secularization signaled assignment of things religious to the realm of the sentimental and nostalgic.[46] It also signals the increasing privatization of religiosity. Since the core of Jewish religiosity has always been home and family based, the impetus to privatization that came from the immigrant experience was a natural development of an impulse basic to Jewish identity.[47]

Literature such as the novel and the magazine is a prime vehicle for nurturing popular religiosity since it is read primarily in the confines of the home, the epitome of the private sphere. Numerous analysts have examined how the home gradually became the locus of religious expression in later nineteenth-century American culture, especially as the larger society began to emphasize the role of women as wives and mothers who kept religiosity alive within the family circle.[48] Hence it is not surprising that the number of magazines targeting a female audience mushroomed in the later nineteenth century, that women constituted the majority readership of fiction, and that women writers wrote so many best-selling novels. Yet there was another realm of literature that addressed specifically female concerns, some of it focused on the wife and mother and some on the working woman, and it is important to see how that literature also helped promote dimensions of popular religiosity.

Colleen McDannell has scrutinized the home as the locus of religious expression in the Victorian era.[49] She notes, for example, that among evangelical Protestants, women were responsible for maintaining a family atmosphere conducive to personal piety, especially in encouraging the family to gather for daily Bible reading and prayer. Even if the husband and father presided at such devotions, the wife and mother was the primary motivating force. That such practice became more widespread receives some testimony when one looks at figures for the number of Bibles and New Testaments published and distributed by the American Bible Society during this period. In 1860, for example, the society produced some 700,000 Bibles and New Testaments; five years later, the total was 1,500,000.[50] Most presumably made their ways into Protestant homes. Mothers, of course, were thought also to bear primary responsibility for the religious nurture of children. One study of nineteenth-century Episcopal Sunday school literature, for example, reveals that a dominant theme is the inherent spirituality of women, a characteristic no doubt fostered by cultural expectations of women's role.[51] McDannell also shows that the Catholic wife and mother likewise had a religious responsibility within the home. If Catholic devotionalism was ostensibly more corporate because it centered on the sacramental life of the institutional church, devotional practices such as saying the rosary and the like were readily advanced through maternal influence. Mothers, Catholic and Protestant, usually determined what literature children would read. We have already seen how children's novels such as those of Francis Finn promoted personal devotion; an expanding array of other children's literature for Catholics reinforced this emphasis on personal devotion.[52] The Young Catholic, for example, was a Sunday school paper designed for Catholic children that began publication in 1870 and was edited by the sister-in-law of well-known convert to Catholicism

Isaac Hecker. Part of its purpose was to provide a basis for religious instruction conducted by mothers in the home.

Transforming the home into religious space signals that privatization of religious experience fundamental to popular religiosity. But there is more. Whatever transpires in the home is done without the direct control of religious institutions or authorities. Printed materials from denominational presses might advance the formal doctrines of a particular tradition, but how those doctrines were transmitted and interpreted became a private, personal, domestic matter. In actuality, elevating woman's role as the transmitter of religiosity and making the home sacred space undermined the necessity of religious institutions altogether. One could find sacred power in the confines of the most private space; one could think and believe however and whatever one chose. Protestants in Victorian America might read the Bible and pray just as Catholics might recite the rosary. But both engaged in essentially individualized acts of religiosity that allowed the individual direct encounter with divine power, however the individual understood that power.

A much larger body of literature promoted popular religiosity among women, some of it at odds with what formal religious institutions hoped to inculcate. Many Catholic women, particularly before marriage, found their way into the work force. Are there any clues about what might have shaped their personal religiosity? Paulist father George Deshon first published his *Guide for Catholic Young Women* in 1871; it saw more than thirty editions before the century's end.[53] While on the surface this handbook stressed submission to authority, whether that of church and priest or employer, and employed a highly moralistic tone, it also reinforced the idea basic to much popular religiosity that the world is a place of spiritual power. On the one hand, evil power is always waiting to tempt one, whether to be lax in one's employment or to neglect formal religious duties. But the individual working woman can tap a superior power through prayer, devotion, and discipline, for God is always present and available to assist the faithful. In other words, one can always call upon sacred power to assist in the business of daily life.

Somewhat different in tone is Elizabeth Wilson's *Fifty Years of Association Work among Young Women, 1866–1916*, written to celebrate the work of the Young Women's Christian Association (YWCA).[54] Founded in part to provide young, single Protestant women with socially acceptable places to live while they were employed in urban businesses and industries, the YWCA developed a host of programs, ranging from Bible study groups to classes in the "domestic arts," from English classes for immigrant women to prayer groups. Especially important is Wilson's focus on the ways the overall program allowed young women to develop an independent identity apart from male-dominated churches or other institutions. Women could develop their own spirituality, their own means of approaching the supernatural realm and drawing on its power to create a world of meaning for themselves. In a different vein, Annie Turner Wittenmeyer's *Women's Work for Jesus* (1873) makes the same point.[55] Wittenmeyer notes that while women accounted for two-thirds of the members of Protestant churches, their religiosity was denied expression in the public work of religious institutions, for precious few women were in positions of clerical or lay leadership. Echoing the then prevalent idea that a woman's first religious responsibility lay in the home, Wittenmeyer also claimed that womanhood was itself a divine calling and that women, because of their personal religiosity, were well equipped to battle the supernatural forces of evil that plagued the nation's cities. In brief, women had an access to the supernatural superior to that of men.

Perhaps no one recognized the ways in which the domestication and hence privatization of religiosity elevated the power of women than did Frances Willard, founder of the Women's Christian Temperance Union and later an advocate of woman's suffrage. Willard wrote several works that are illustrative of how personal, private religiosity was integral to authentic self-definition for women, how women—perhaps because of their domestic role—were less tainted by the forces of evil than men, and hence how the ability of women to maintain direct contact with the Divine gave them the power to be independent, even in a culture that stressed women's submission to men. Willard advanced her ideas in such works as *Home Protection Manual: Containing an Argument for the Temperance Ballot for Women and How to Obtain It as a Means of Home Protection* (1879), *Do Everything: A Handbook for the World's White Ribboners* (1885), and *How to Win: A Book for Girls* (1886).[56] Willard recognized that women's religiosity flourished apart from the formal institutions of religion, though in her case that led to a call for the ordination of women to the Protestant ministry.[57]

By relegating religiosity to the sacred space of the home, the Victorian culture of the later nineteenth century promoted the privatization of religious experience that feeds popular religiosity. It also, perhaps unwittingly, elevated women to a superior spiritual status, for removed from the turmoil of public life, women were able to develop a deeper spirituality based not only on a cultural sense of their innate piety, but also on the often unstated conviction that the personal religiosity nourished by women granted access to a divine realm more powerful than any force operating in the empirical world. To understand all the contours of popular religiosity in the later nineteenth century, one must appreciate the reinforcement given to private, personal religious expression by women's spirituality.

The Victorian home also brought new dimensions to the celebration of an explicitly Christian holiday, Christmas, and helped bring it into the orbit of popular religiosity even as it became more central to the organized Christian churches in the United States.[58] German immigrants, for example, brought the custom of the decorated Christmas tree to their Pennsylvania enclaves early in the nineteenth century, although the practice of decorating trees did not become widespread until midcentury. From Germany also came the popular "Silent Night," composed in 1818. Clement Moore penned the well-known "A Visit from St. Nicholas" in 1823, even though by then Santa Claus had already started to replace the Christian St. Nicholas as the symbol of gift-giving in popular children's lore. The personal and family dimensions of Christmas celebration gained much popular appeal when Charles Dickens published *A Christmas Carol* in 1843, and the story soon became a holiday favorite in both the United States and Britain. The Christmas card is also a Victorian phenomenon, with the first one produced by John Calcott Horsley in England in 1843. The manufacture of Christmas cards in the United States began in 1875, quickly making the exchange of such greetings as widespread in the United States as in Britain. Although it has become fashionable in the later twentieth century to bemoan the commercialization of the holiday and a concomitant loss of its pristine religious meaning, the home and family orientation of Christmas rooted in the Victorian age has made its celebration integral to much popular religiosity, for it reaffirms the role of personal relationships in shaping individual identity.

If the sacred space of the Victorian home was the domain of women, there were vehicles beyond home and family for nurturing adult male religiosity. Some evidence comes from the growth of fraternal orders open only to men in the last half of the nineteenth century. The roots of the fraternal movement stretch back in American life at least to the age of independence and its fascination with Freemasonry. Because of the secrecy that shrouded their gatherings, Freemasonry and similar societies had also long spurred suspicion if not outright condemnation by religious authorities. Purported links to nativism, the anti-Catholic, anti-immigrant movement that flourished briefly in the antebellum period, only exacerbated the problem. Indeed, so widespread was the hostility of organized religion to such secret societies that one periodical, *Christian Cynosure*, was founded in 1868 with an aim to combat their influence. Some of the popular apprehension abated when several formed cognate organizations, such as the Order of the Eastern Star (1869) for women.[59] Historians have recognized the religious dimension of such groups. "The rise of fraternal orders at mid-century," Mark Carnes has written, "provides evidence of the emergence of a middle-class institution parallel to evangelical Protestantism."[60] Carnes has noted that in the last third of the nineteenth century, somewhere between one-eighth and one-fifth of adult American men held membership in one or more of the seventythousand or so fraternal lodges that flourished in American culture. Another analyst, Fergus MacDonald, has claimed that by the early twentieth century, lodges outnumbered churches in all the major cities of the nation.[61] While many of these groups opened their membership only to Protestants, their popularity indicates that the values and understanding of the world that they promoted resonated with male experience, offering clues to another current of popular religiosity.

Carnes has suggested that much of the appeal of the fraternal movement rested in its providing rites of passage to male adulthood independent of, but not necessarily totally divorced from the religiosity of home and organized religion, both women's spheres. Fraternal rituals attracted men precisely because they offered "dramatic journeys in search of a distant god" that did not have the feminine orientation of the traditional church and home.[62] If Victorian women nurtured the religious and social identities of their male children through home and school, the lodges provided a means for men to sort out matters of their own identity in space that excluded women. They provided a mechanism for men to confront the realities and tensions of life.[63] They offered a place to develop values and fashion a way of constructing a meaningful world. The elaborate rituals, especially the initiation ceremonies, brought men into a realm of sacred power, usually one claimed to have ancient sources, which proponents believed complementary to that promulgated by the formal religious institutions and their doctrines. Filial duty, family responsibility, absolute loyalty, even an unconditional love for those who shared the bond of fraternal membership— all were popular values fostered by the societies. All could be realized in individual life and reinforced in practice through access to the supernatural realm found only within the confines of the fraternal hall. To be sure, among the practical consequences was the solidification of gender roles whose legitimacy a later age would question. Nevertheless, the lodges perpetuated an abiding sense of the supernatural for millions of American men for generations, for the rituals themselves and the role they played demonstrate many features of popular religiosity. Virtually all were syncretistic, blending language and symbols, usually drawn from Christianity, with presumed ancient myths and practices to fashion a particular understanding of sacred space and sacred power. All granted a sense of power to members. While most may have come from the ranks of the emerging urban middle class, members gained an identity independent of that conferred by family, occupation, or social standing within the society. Although men granted effective power to women in the home and were subject to the power of employers in the economic sector, in the fraternal bond, they had an entree to power that granted a way to see the world from a different perspective. If the formal religious institutions and even the home failed to provide men with a constellation of values and practices that gave coherence to their experiences, the lodges did so, at least until changing social conditions in the twentieth century weakened their plausibility.

Fraternal lodges flourished primarily in the cities and towns of the nation. But the later nineteenth and early twentieth centuries also witnessed a renewed, but idealized interest in things rural, especially awe at the presumed beauty of nature. This impulse, as so many others, had roots in an earlier period. The elite movement identified with the Transcendentalists of New England in the 1830s and 1840s provided one source in, for example, Ralph Waldo Emerson's provocative essay *Nature* that appeared in 1836 and Henry David Thoreau's sojourn at Walden and his treatise by the same name.[64] Also coming from New England was the rural cemetery movement of the same era, with its explicit connection between the repose of nature and the repose of the dead. In the wake of rapid urbanization in the closing decades of the nineteenth century, the realm of nature took on added dimensions. In the larger social context, the conservation/preservation movement, propelled by the likes of John Muir, elevated the world of nature in the public mind. There was also a new sensitivity to the natural realm in popular consciousness, and hence in popular religiosity, as the arena where one could experience sacred power directly.[65] Several works of popular fiction also extolled nature. In 1898 Canadian writer Ralph Connor, the pseudonym of the Rev. Charles W. Gordon, published *Black Rock*, which became a best-seller in the United States.[66] While the story line concerns the efforts of a crusading pastor to promote temperance among coal miners in the Canadian Northwest, the novel equates nature with purity and those who imbibe its power as the only "real" men (Connor's chief characters were male). He drew a similar literary sketch of the raw power of nature in *The Sky Pilot*, a popular though somewhat less successful novel that appeared the following year.[67] As well, images of nature contained in popular hymnody penetrated deeply into the religious consciousness of Americans. Witness these words penned by Maltbie D. Babcock in 1901:

> This is my Father's world, and to my listening ears
> All nature sings, and round me rings the music of the spheres.
> This is my Father's world: I rest me in the thought
> Of rocks and trees, or skies and seas; his hand the wonders wrought.

In a subsequent stanza Babcock proclaims that the Divine passes by "in the rustling grass" and "speaks to me everywhere" in nature. Three years later, following a visit to Pike's Peak, Katherine Lee Bates wrote the ever-popular patriotic hymn "America the Beautiful" with its paean to the glories of the natural world. In all these cases, nature is more than just a source of inspiration. Rather, nature is the location of sacred power. One can realize that power and be filled with its strength through contemplation of nature. One did not need formal religious institutions or the ministrations of its professionals; one did not need the privacy of the Victorian home or the secrecy of the fraternal lodge. One could experience and appropriate supernatural power on one's own, for nature offers directly to the individual that unmediated access to the supernatural that is at the core of popular religiosity. Giving nature a religious dimension in popular religiosity was hardly a new connection in Western culture, for identifying nature with the moral and spiritual stretches back to the pastoral tradition of Greek and Roman poetry and the literature of the Hebrew Bible. Seventeenth-century English humanists merged these two traditions in their own fascination with the pastoral mode. Later and rather different expressions of the purity and power of nature would come to the fore in the national parks movement, the explosion of suburbia in the mid-twentieth century, and even television programs like "Green Acres," "The Andy Griffith Show," and "Evening Shade."

The era between the close of the Civil War and the end of World War I also witnessed an enhanced regional consciousness, particularly in the part of the United States that had comprised the Confederacy. In the wake of military defeat in the Civil War and the consequent legal destruction of the system of slavery, white southeners especially engaged in a process of re-thinking their past and their values in order to reconstruct a world of mean-ing for their common experience. Charles Reagan Wilson has been the most insistent voice arguing that in the various ritual events celebrating the glo-ries of the defeated Confederacy there emerged a southern civil religion of the Lost Cause.[68] Scholars have long debated whether this or any version of so-called civil religion merits being called a religion in the same way formal traditions and institutions are so classified. Regardless, in the me-morial rites extolling the valor of the Confederate dead and the numerous other manifestations elevating the Lost Cause to the heights of the mythic, we have some of the ingredients of popular religiosity. Those who created an idealized vision of the antebellum "Old South" were attempting to im-pose on their world a coherence and meaning that empirical reality denied them. In bestowing popular sainthood on persons such as Robert E. Lee or "Stonewall" Jackson, white southerners were fashioning models of what human beings should be. The past became a prototype for a meaningful present, a means of reclaiming a sacred realm that seemed lost and non-existent to outsiders. One could cope with this life because one affirmed the values and mores of a past world that now seemed pure. Access to that realm of power was both inclusive and exclusive. Those not from Dixie could never appreciate its mystique and overarching strength; but to those who experienced within themselves the ways of the Old South, the array of rituals and events magnifying the Lost Cause became a means of entering the supernatural sphere.

Historical currents do not know the demarcation of time in years and centuries. The currents of popular religiosity nourished by new forms of expression in the later nineteenth century often cascaded across the century divide into the twentieth. In many ways, what marked the next transition point in the common life of Americans was World War I, the Great War to "make the world safe for democracy." Yet as was the case with other pivotal turning points in American history, this war and the transformed culture that followed in its wake had enormous impact on popular religious consciousness.

NOTES

1. Catherine L. Albanese, "Physical Religion: Natural Sin and Healing Grace in the Nineteenth Century," chap. 4 of her *Nature Religion in America: From the Algonkian Indians to the New Age* (Chicago: University of Chicago Press, 1990).

2. On New Thought and Christian Science, see Stephen Gottschalk, "Christian Science and Harmonialism," in *Encyclopedia of the American Religious Experience*, edited by Charles H. Lippy and Peter W. Williams (New York: Charles Scribner's Sons, 1988), 2:901–16; idem, *The Emergence of Christian Science in American Religious Life* (Berkeley and Los Angeles: University of California Press, 1973); Charles Braden, *Spirits in Rebellion: The Rise and Development of New Thought* (1963; reprint, Dallas, Tex.: Southern Methodist University Press, 1987); Gail Thain Parker, *Mind Cure in New England: From the Civil War to World War I* (Hanover, N.H.: University Press of New England, 1973); Horatio W. Dresser, *A History of the New Thought Movement* (New York: Thomas Y. Crowell, 1919); Donald Meyer, *The Positive Thinkers: Popular Religious Psychology from Mary Baker Eddy to Norman Vincent Peale and Ronald Reagan* (Middletown, Conn.: Wesleyan University Press, 1988); Raymond Cunningham, "From Holiness to Healing: The Faith Cure in America, 1872–1892," *Church History* 43 (1974): 499–513; Robert C. Fuller, *Mesmerism and the American Cure of Souls* (Philadelphia: University of Pennsylvania Press, 1982); John F. Teahan, "Warren Felt Evans and Mental Healing: Romantic Idealism and Practical Mysticism in Nineteenth-Century America," *Church History* 48 (March 1979): 63–80; and Williams, *Popular Religion in America: Symbolic Change and the Modernization Process in Historical Perspective* (Englewood Cliffs, N.J.: Prentice-Hall, 1980), pp. 130–33. On Theosophy, see Robert S. Ellwood, "Occult Movements in America," in *Encyclopedia of the American Religious Experience*, 2:717–18; idem, *Alternative Altars: Unconventional and Eastern Spirituality in the United States* (Chicago: University of Chicago Press, 1979); Robert S. Ellwood and Harry Partin, *Religious and Spiritual Groups in Modern America*, 2d ed. (Englewood Cliffs, N.J.: Prentice-Hall, 1988); and Bruce F. Campbell, *Ancient Wisdom Revealed: A History of the Theosophical Movement* (Berkeley: University of California Press, 1980). On the metaphysical movement in general, see J. Stillson Judah, *The History and Philosophy of the Metaphysical Movements in America* (Philadelphia: Westminster, 1967).

3. Warren Felt Evans, *The Mental Cure* (Boston: H. H. and T. W. Carter, 1869); *Mental Medicine* (Boston: W. White, 1872); and *The Divine Law of Cure* (Boston: H. H. Carter, 1881). *The Mental Cure* had nine editions in its first year of printing; *Mental Medicine* had four.

4. Gottschalk, "Christian Science and Harmonialism," p. 905.

5. Mary Baker Eddy, *Science and Health with Key to the Scriptures* (Boston: Christian Scientist Publishing Co., 1875).

6. See John Corrigan, "*The Christian Science Monitor*," in *Religious Periodicals of the United States: Academic and Scholarly*, edited by Charles H. Lippy (Westport, Conn.: Greenwood, 1986), pp. 124–28.

7. Also helpful in understanding the thought behind the early Christian Science movement are Mary Baker Eddy, *Retrospection and Introspection* (Boston: W. G. Nixon, 1891); and idem, *No and Yes* (Boston: J. Armstrong, 1891). The latter saw more than fifty editions printed in the first fifteen years after publication.

8. Ralph Waldo Trine, *In Tune with the Infinite* (New York: Thomas Y. Crowell, 1897). In 1985 Macmillan was still publishing *In Tune with the Infinite*.

9. James D. Hart, *The Popular Book: A History of America's Literary Taste* (New York: Oxford University Press, 1950), p. 168.

10. Quoted in ibid., p. 181.

11. See John R. Wimmer, "Russell H. Conwell," in *Twentieth-Century Shapers of American Popular Religion*, edited by Charles H. Lippy (Westport, Conn.: Greenwood, 1989), pp. 80–88; Clyde K. Nelson, "Russell H. Conwell and the 'Gospel of Wealth,' " *Foundations* 5 (1962): 39–51; Daniel W. Bjork, *The Victorian Flight: Russell H. Conwell and the Crisis of American Individualism* (Washington, D.C.: University Press of America, 1979); Mary Louise Gehring, "Russell H. Conwell: American Orator," *Southern Speech Journal* 20 (Winter 1954): 117–24; and Richard M. Huber, *The American Idea of Success* (New York: McGraw-Hill, 1971), pp. 55–61.

12. See, for example, Albert Hatcher Smith, *The Life of Russell H. Conwell* (Boston: Silver, Burdett, 1899); Thane Wilson, "Russell H. Conwell: Who Has Helped 3,000 Young Men to Succeed," *American Magazine* 81 (April 1916): 15.

13. Russell H. Conwell, *Acres of Diamonds* (New York: J. Y. Huber, 1890). In 1993 Tree of Life Press issued a new printing of *Acres of Diamonds*.

14. Meyer, pp. 39, 42–43.

15. The most recent appraisal of Blavatsky is Sylvia Cranston, *H.P.B.: The Extraordinary Life and Influence of Helena Blavatsky, Founder of the Modern Theosophical Movement* (New York: Jeremy P. Tarcher, 1993).

16. Helena P. Blavatsky, *Isis Unveiled* (New York: J. W. Boughton, 1877); *The Secret Doctrine* (New York: William Q. Judge, 1888). Both works were still in print in 1993, published by the Theosophical University Press.

17. Sandra Sizer Frankiel, *California's Spiritual Frontiers: Religious Alternatives in Anglo-Protestantism, 1850–1910* (Berkeley: University of California Press, 1988). More generally see her "California and the Southwest," in *Encyclopedia of the American Religious Experience*, 3:1509–23.

18. A model local religious history that examines the interplay between this form of Hispanic Catholicism with the more "Americanized" Catholicism of Euro-American settlers as well as a host of other issues is Michael E. Engh, *Frontier Faiths: Church, Temple, and Synagogue in Los Angeles, 1846–1888* (Albuquerque: University of New Mexico Press, 1992).

19. See Marta Weigle, *Brothers of Light, Brothers of Blood: The Penitentes of the Southwest* (Albuquerque: University of New Mexico Press, 1976).

20. On the problems and possibilities of discerning the popular religious mind through best-selling novels, see Ruth Miller Elson, *Myths and Mores in American Best Sellers, 1865–1965* (New York and London: Garland, 1985), pp. 1–2.

21. On Catholic antipathy to the novel, see Paul R. Messbarger, *Fiction with a Parochial Purpose: Social Uses of American Catholic Literature, 1884–1900* (Boston: Boston University Press, 1971).

22. Nina Baym, *Women's Fiction: A Guide to Novels by and about Women in*

America, 1820–1870 (Ithaca, N.Y.: Cornell University Press, 1978), notes that the novel replaced the poem and short story as the primary genre of American women's writing by the 1850s.

23. "The Influence of the Religious Novel," *The Nation* 47 (1888): 329–30.

24. Evans' first novel, *Inez, A Tale of the Alamo* (New York: Harper and Bros., 1855), repeated much of the popular Protestant antipathy toward and misunderstanding of Roman Catholicism; Augusta J. Evans, *Beulah* (New York: Derby and Jackson, 1859). See also William Perry Fidler, *Augusta Evans Wilson, 1833–1900: A Biography* (University: University of Alabama Press, 1951).

25. Augusta J. Evans, *St. Elmo* (New York: George W. Carleton, 1867). See also Beatrice K. Hofstadter, "Popular Culture and the Romantic Heroine," *American Scholar* 30:1 (Winter 1960–61): 98–116; Baym, pp. 276ff.; and Richard Weiss, *The American Myth of Success: From Horatio Alger to Norman Vincent Peale* (New York and London: Basic Books, 1969), pp. 65–67.

26. Elizabeth Stuart Phelps, *The Gates Ajar* (Boston: Fields, Osgood, and Co., 1868). A modern, critical edition is available, edited by Elizabeth Sootin Smith (Cambridge, Mass.: Harvard University Press, 1964).

27. Williams, p. 215; Baym, p. 297; Elmer F. Suderman, "Elizabeth Stuart Phelps and the Gates Ajar Novels," *Journal of Popular Culture* 3 (1969): 91–106; Wayne Elzey, "Popular Culture," in *Encyclopedia of the American Religious Experience,* 3:1737; Elson, pp. 179–80; Hart, p. 120.

28. Mrs. Humphrey Ward, *Robert Elsmere* (Chicago: J. S. Ogilvie, 1888). See also Hart, pp. 164–65; Elson, p. 181; Frank Luther Mott, *Golden Multitudes: The Story of the Best Sellers in the United States* (New York: R. R. Bowker, 1947), p. 311.

29. Charles M. Sheldon, *In His Steps: What Would Jesus Do?* (Chicago: Advance, 1897; published in serial form, 1896). See also Mott, pp. 193–97; Hart, pp. 165–66; Elzey, "Popular Culture," pp. 1737–38; Wayne Elzey, " 'What Would Jesus Do?' *In His Steps* and the Moral Codes of the Middle Class," *Soundings* 58 (1975): 463–89; Timothy Miller, *Following In His Steps: A Biography of Charles M. Sheldon* (Knoxville: University of Tennessee Press, 1987); Weiss, pp. 71–76; and Paul S. Boyer, "*In His Steps*: A Reappraisal," *American Quarterly* 13 (1971): 60–71.

30. Williams, p. 140.

31. See especially his " 'What Would Jesus Do?' "

32. The comic book version was published by Fleming H. Revell.

33. See Lee Scott Thiesen, " 'My God, Did I Set All of This in Motion?' General Lew Wallace and *Ben Hur*," *Journal of Popular Culture* 18:2 (1984): 33–41; Mott, pp. 172–74; Hart, p. 164; Henry Herx, "Religion and Film," in *Encyclopedia of the American Religious Experience,* 3:1345, 1349.

34. Hart, p. 164.

35. Mark A. Noll, *A History of Christianity in the United States and Canada* (Grand Rapids, Mich.: Eerdmans, 1992), p. 411.

36. Leo R. Ribuffo, "Religious Prejudice and Nativism," in *Encyclopedia of the American Religious Experience,* 3:1536.

37. All of these points are amplified in Messbarger, *Fiction with a Parochial Purpose.*

38. See Christina M. Bochen, *The Journey to Rome: Conversion Literature by*

Nineteenth-Century American Catholics (New York: Garland, 1988). Bochen notes that the bulk of this literature belongs in the genre of spiritual autobiography rather than fiction and that Protestant converts to Catholicism wrote much of it.

39. Mary Ann Tincker, *House of Yorke* (New York: Catholic Publication Society, 1872); and *Grapes and Thorns* (New York: Catholic Publication Society, 1874).

40. Christian Reid [Mrs. Frances Tiernen], *Child of Mary* (Notre Dame, Ind.: Ave Maria Office, 1885).

41. See Francis J. Molson, "Francis J. Finn, S.J.: Pioneering Author of Juveniles for Catholic Americans," *Journal of Popular Culture* 11 (1977): 28–41.

42. Fr. Francis Finn, *Tom Playfair; or Making a Start* (New York: Benziger Bros., 1892).

43. Two American editions appeared in 1882. J. W. Lovell in New York published a translation by Katherine Sullivan, and G. P. Putnam's Sons, also in New York, released a translation by Emily H. Hazen.

44. See Messbarger, p. 140.

45. Abraham Cahan, *The Rise of David Levinsky* (New York: Harper Colophon, 1960).

46. Williams, p. 83.

47. In a very different context, this point is also made by Naomi W. Cohen, *Jews in Christian America: The Pursuit of Religious Equality* (New York: Oxford University Press, 1992), p. 15.

48. In different ways, this point is made in Ann Douglas, *The Feminization of American Culture* (New York: Knopf, 1978); and Jean E. Friedman, *The Enclosed Garden: Women and Community in the Evangelical South, 1830–1900* (Chapel Hill: University of North Carolina Press, 1985).

49. Colleen McDannell, *The Christian Home in Victorian America, 1840–1900* (Bloomington: Indiana University Press, 1986).

50. Hart, p. 118.

51. Joanna B. Gillespie, "Carrie, or the Child in the Rectory: Nineteenth-Century Episcopal Sunday School Prototypes," *Historical Magazine of the Protestant Episcopal Church* 51 (1982): 359–70.

52. See Christa Ressmeyer Klein, "Literature for America's Roman Catholic Children (1865–1895): An Annotated Bibliography," *American Literary Realism, 1870–1910* 6 (1973): 137–52.

53. George Deshon, *Guide for Catholic Young Women* (reprinted, New York: Arno, 1978).

54. Elizabeth Wilson, *Fifty Years of Association Work among Young Women, 1866–1916* (New York: National Board of the Young Women's Christian Association of the United States of America, 1916; reprinted, New York and London: Garland, 1987).

55. Annie Turner Wittenmeyer, *Women's Work for Jesus* (New York: Nelson and Phillips, 1873; reprinted, New York: Garland, 1987).

56. These three are reprinted in Carolyn DeSwarte Gifford, ed., *The Ideal of "The New Woman" According to the Women's Christian Temperance Union* (New York and London: Garland, 1987).

57. See Frances Willard, *Women in the Pulpit* (Chicago: Women's Temperance Publishing Association, 1889), reprinted in *The Defense of Women's Rights to*

Ordination in the Methodist Episcopal Church, edited by Carolyn DeSwarte Gifford (New York and London: Garland, 1987).

58. See Patricia B. Stevens, *Merry Christmas: A History of the Holiday* (New York: Macmillan, 1979); James H. Barnett, *The American Christmas: A Study in National Culture* (New York: Macmillan, 1954); and Irene Chalmers et al., *The Great American Christmas Almanac* (Baltimore: Penguin, 1988).

59. The political dimension of the antifraternal movement is told in William Preston Vaughn, *The Antimasonic Party in the United States, 1826–1843* (Lexington: University Press of Kentucky, 1983). Representative of the many contemporary religious critiques is Rev. Joseph T. Cooper, *Odd-Fellowship Examined in the Light of Reason and Scripture* (Philadelphia: William S. Young, 1853).

60. Mark C. Carnes, *Secret Ritual and Manhood in Victorian America* (New Haven, Conn.: Yale University Press, 1989), p. 31.

61. Fergus MacDonald, *The Catholic Church and the Secret Societies in the United States*, edited by Thomas J. McMahon, United States Catholic Historical Society Monograph Series 22 (New York: United States Catholic Historical Society, 1946), p. 100.

62. Carnes, p. 79.

63. See Carnes, pp. 104–11.

64. See Albanese, *Nature Religion*, especially chap. 3, "Wilderness and the Passing Show: Transcendentalist Religion and Its Legacies."

65. See Peter Schmitt, "The Church in the Wildwood: The Nature Cult in Urban America, 1890–1930," *Journal of Popular Culture* 2 (1968): 113–18.

66. Charles W. Gordon [Ralph Connor], *Black Rock* (New York: Thomas Y. Crowell, 1898).

67. Charles W. Gordon [Ralph Connor], *The Sky Pilot* (New York: Fleming H. Revell, 1899).

68. Charles Reagan Wilson, *Baptized in Blood: The Civil Religion of the Lost Cause, 1865–1920* (Athens: University of Georgia Press, 1980).

Chapter 7

Into the Twentieth Century: Popular Religiosity in the Age of World Wars

War, retreat to isolationism, economic depression, and war again, both hot and cold—these broad themes suggest the larger social currents that nurtured popular religiosity in the first half of the twentieth century. From World War I to the Korean conflict and the Cold War, American culture was slowly coming to recognize the consequences of industrialization and urbanization that linked the destinies of various societies and nations. The same categories also are apt metaphors to describe the major movements and themes that analysts of American religion traditionally highlight. The raging battle between fundamentalists and modernists takes the place of World War I, while the moralism of Billy Sunday, the national experiment with Prohibition, and a surge of anti-Semitism and anti-Catholicism reflect the isolationist retreat of the 1920s. Historian of Christianity Robert T. Handy appropriated the metaphor of depression to discuss the presumed loss of influence and perhaps even decline in actual strength of the major denominations in the decades between the World Wars when economic depression gripped the nation.[1] If ultimately it was the second global conflict that brought the nation out of economic depression, so it was also the specter of "godless communism" that contributed to the widely touted religious revival of the 1950s, as Americans prepared to wage war against the forces of evil that threatened not only democracy but true religion as well.

These traditional emphases are all important in understanding the contours of American popular religiosity in the first several decades of the twentieth century. They are not, of course, the whole story. The advent of radio transformed the forces that shaped popular religiosity, the rapid expansion of the film industry brought new venues for influencing the popular imagination, while writers and journalists bombarded the American public with a dazzling array of novels and periodicals that also sustained a popular religiosity that existed alongside the struggles between fundamentalists and modernists that disrupted much of institutional Protestantism. To appreciate the abiding sense of the supernatural that has marked American popular religiosity, we must again give heed to the traditional interpretation to see how interwoven with the forces shaping the institutional life of the formal religious traditions were others that had a more immediate impact on ordinary people and how they went about the business of endowing their own experience with meaning. Then we must direct our attention to a variety of other cultural and religious currents that usually are pushed to the margins of any discussion of American religion, if they are discussed at all, to find other influences sustaining popular piety.

We have already noted some of the roots of fundamentalism. On the one hand, there was the negative reaction of theologians and many denominational leaders to the new intellectual currents of the later nineteenth century, especially the fascination with Darwin's theory of evolution in one form or another, the application of critical methods of analysis to biblical texts, and the more liberal theology issuing from German academic circles. On the other hand, there was the fascination with premillennial dispensationalism and its use in the *Scofield Reference Bible*, the series of pamphlets called *The Fundamentals* that appeared in the second decade of the twentieth century—with some two million copies distributed—defining the proper parameters of Christian belief, and a host of other currents primarily in intellectual circles. Not until the second and third decades of the twentieth century, however, did the controversy between fundamentalism and modernism filter down through the tomes of systematic theologians and through the denominational bureaucracies, where persons of a more liberal persuasion remained in control, to reach ordinary men and women.

At its base, fundamentalism was compatible with the religiosity of the people, for both assumed the reality of supernatural power and the prevalence of supernatural forces at work in the world. By stressing such theological notions as the virgin birth of Jesus, the bodily resurrection of Jesus, a literal and physical second coming of Christ, and miracles as proof of the divinity of Christ and the reality of sacred power, fundamentalism buttressed the supernaturalism that has long sustained popular religiosity. At the same time, that very sense of the supernatural prevalent in popular religiosity predisposed many, particularly those whose religious consciousness and experience were shaped by American Protestantism, to be drawn into the fundamentalist orbit. Seeing how the tenets of fundamentalism and its attendant social concerns were mediated to ordinary folk will enable us to see its impact on popular religiosity and the symbiotic relationship that has frequently prevailed between fundamentalism and popular religiosity. The devastation of World War I, for example, fueled an ongoing interest in biblical prophecy among many Protestants. To explore prophetic teaching, there continued to be an array of summer Bible conferences and the like that helped disseminate a premillennial worldview to ordinary believers eager to discern the meaning of the biblical text.[2] Many of these conferences drew on the network of summer Holiness camp meetings and the organizational structures that had developed to sustain them. The upshot was simply that the men and women who took their families to summer camp meetings, by then becoming the precursors of resorts of the later twentieth century, were absorbing a premillennialist perspective with its emphasis on the reality of the supernatural.

Then, too, a number of schools and other related educational institutions, some with roots in the nineteenth century, grew in influence among those drawn to premillennialism and its prophetic scheme that placed the present at a critical juncture leading to the final struggle between the forces of good and evil. The Moody Bible Institute in Chicago, founded in 1889, quietly trained hundreds of lay workers who took the premillennial understanding into countless local congregations and other forms of ministry. Of similar ilk were the Nyack Missionary College of the Christian and Missionary Alliance (now simply Nyack College) and especially the Bible Institute of Los Angeles (better known as BIOLA) whose board would ultimately be chaired by the popular fundamentalist radio evangelist Charles E. Fuller. Their role in perpetuating an abiding sense of the supernatural among the rank and file in the churches where their graduates worked should not be underestimated. Battles between fundamentalists and modernists over belief and control of denominational bureaucracies may have raged especially among northern Baptists and Presbyterians, but people in the pew were far more likely to imbibe a sense of the supernatural from a lay church worker trained at Moody Bible Institute, for example, than from a denominational executive or decree of some denominational general assembly.

Other forces also promoted a casual popular understanding of the reality of supernatural power. In the political and social sectors, the so-called Red Scare generated an irrational fear of Bolshevism and communism in the 1920s by identifying such forces with supernatural evil.[3] The concomitant was that men and women found reinforcement for the popular perception that the world was fraught with supernatural power, much of which was intent on undermining human well-being. By identifying Bolshevism and communism with the forces of evil, those who feared their deleterious political impact unwittingly bolstered the popular acceptance of the world as an arena for the cosmic conflict between good and evil. The popular perception that most Bolsheviks and Communists were persons involved in the labor movement or recent immigrants had far-reaching consequences. It contributed to calls to restrict civil liberties (in the hopes of containing the forces of evil), resulted in immigration quotas, and fueled xenophobia that took ugly shape in the Ku Klux Klan, anti-Semitism, and anti-Catholicism. While we shall examine several of those facets later, important here is the way the hysteria of the Red Scare and its attendant phobias kept alive a sense of the world as an arena where the powers of evil were always lurking and always threatening. Another social force that gave popular premillennialism a boost came in the 1930s when the economic crisis of the Great Depression convinced some that the eschaton was imminent. One need only scan the pages of *Our Hope*, a popular periodical that served as a vehicle for the fundamentalist voice of Arno C. Gaebelin, during the 1930s to see numerous accounts claiming that the economic turmoil of the Depression represented that dominance of evil believed to precede the return of Christ. Then, too, there was the array of publishing houses that produced literature for use in educational programs in Protestant churches as well as in homes that simply presumed a fundamentalist, if not always a premillennialist, perspective. Scripture Press (Wheaton, Ill.) and David C. Cook (Elgin, Ill.) became major producers of such materials, as did the press of the Moody Bible Institute.

Revivalism continued to fuel the religiosity of those drawn to evangelistic meetings. No evangelist of the early twentieth century better exemplifies the strident affirmation of the power of the supernatural found in popular religiosity than Billy Sunday (1862–1935).[4] Sunday, who spent a few years playing professional baseball, began his career in evangelism in the 1890s under the aegis of the YMCA. Although demand for Sunday's evangelistic services began to wane in the 1920s, he remained the most well-known revivalist of the first half of the twentieth century, bringing his message to more than one million Americans. Even in his own day, Sunday was noted for his flamboyant, almost theatrical style as he railed against the powers of evil that he found rampant in urban America. Sunday found them at work especially in efforts to thwart the rising passion for Prohibition, which became an American experiment in 1919,[5] and in any opposition to American support for the Allied cause in World War I. For Sunday, piety, patriotism, and Prohibition were mirrors of each other, vehicles through which a muscular Christianity could carry on the struggle against the powers of Satan and hell. Sunday looked at the changing world around him and shrank in horror at the inroads made by the forces of evil. Nothing less than a full-scale battle could save American urban culture from their ravages.

In retrospect, Sunday owed much of his popularity to adaptation of public relations and promotional methods drawn from the secular world he condemned.[6] But he also kept alive a powerful sense that American culture was caught in the grips of an ongoing struggle between the powers of good (the God of evangelical—if not fundamentalist—white Christianity) and those of evil (the Devil, Satan, and the like). One could, however, receive assurance of personal victory in that struggle by aligning with Sunday's

God through the simple experience of "hitting the sawdust trail." All one needed to do was come forward at the close of one of Sunday's evangelistic meetings and shake the revivalist's hand. Critics have long branded Sunday's approach as naive and simplistic. But that is precisely the point when it comes to popular religiosity. Using the slang of the people, Sunday painted verbal portraits of a world fraught with supernatural power. He was especially gifted at depicting the insidious ways forces of evil were always attacking individuals, particularly men who had abandoned public affirmation of religion as religiosity moved into the domestic sphere controlled by women in the Victorian era. Yet in insisting on the reality of the supernatural, Sunday provided additional support for the inchoate but lively sense of the supernatural at the heart of popular religiosity. Sunday's world, like that of ordinary men and women, was clear-cut in seeing the constant interplay between the powers of good and the powers of evil. Hence his message resonated with millions of Americans, regardless of denominational affiliation, who likewise inhabited a world where supernatural forces still reigned supreme.

Sunday designed his brand of fundamentalist Christianity in part to appeal to men who retreated from expressing their religiosity. But as Betty DeBerg has shown, there was another side to that masculine orientation.[7] Much of the social agenda of the early twentieth-century fundamentalism, according to DeBerg, was a thinly disguised effort to maintain the gender distinctions of the Victorian age and hence frequently portrayed women in negative terms. Fundamentalist attacks on theater and film (then a new entertainment medium) and on clothing fashions all cast women as particularly susceptible to the evil influences that sought to undermine traditional structures of belief and practice. The changing role and behavior of women, especially in the 1920s, became yet another sign of the moral collapse that signaled the nearness of the millennium. Such attacks reinforced the popular perception that supernatural forces were constantly at work in the larger society. One had always to be on guard against them. Through acceptance of the supernatural realities behind fundamentalism, however, one could tap into the forces of good that would preserve and protect the emerging urban middle class. As Douglas Frank argued, Billy Sunday interpreted the world his audience inhabited as a realm of supernatural power and gave them a simple formula to achieve control over that world for their own benefit.[8] Sunday's moralism focused on the individual and private, personal behavior that has always been central to popular religiosity.

One sign of the cultural change that so bothered some fundamentalists soon itself became a means of keeping before millions the supernaturalism basic to popular religiosity. When radio became part of American life, many condemned it as having the potential to spur idleness and leisure that would lead to the neglect of things religious. Some feared that religious broadcasting would erode commitment to local congregations, a concern that would resurface in the age of televangelism.[9] Others saw in the new medium a means of expanding the size of the audience reached with a particular message and the opportunity of bringing a religious service to those unable to attend public religious gatherings. By the era of World War II, manuals were available to guide those who wanted to make the most of radio for religious purposes.[10] It was not only fundamentalists who turned to radio. As early as 1922 Thomas F. Coakley urged American Catholics to consider the potential of radio in promulgating the Catholic message following a two-week series of sermons broadcast by Paulist Fathers in late 1921 on Pittsburgh's KDKA.[11] The first Catholic to gain fame through regular radio broadcasts, however, was Fr. Charles Coughlin, who used the airwaves for political as much as for religious purposes. Among Protestants, for many years Walter A. Maier was the regular voice of the "Lutheran Hour," while modernist Harry Emerson Fosdick and more moderate Ralph Waldo Sockman also reached millions with their own versions of the Christian gospel. Yet none equaled the appeal of fundamentalist Charles E. Fuller (1887–1968), who began broadcasting Sunday services from his independent Calvary Church in Long Beach, California, in 1930.[12] In time, the program became the "Old Fashioned Revival Hour" that at its peak in the 1940s was carried on nearly five hundred radio stations nationwide and that remained on the air until 1963. Radio made Fuller the most well-known evangelist in the United States between Billy Sunday and Billy Graham.

While Fuller's style was more polished than Billy Sunday's, his message was as simple and direct: the only way to survive in the modern world was to place one's full trust in the power of God who, through Christ, would meet all inner needs. Part of the appeal of Fuller's program, the model for later twentieth-century preacher Jerry Falwell's televised "Old Time Gospel Hour," came in the reading of letters sent in by listeners. Fuller's wife, Grace Payton Fuller, read excerpts from listeners' letters on each broadcast.[13] Without fail, every letter testified to the miraculous way God intervened for the good in the listener's life or in a situation involving the listener. The unstated message was obvious: without such supernatural intervention, forces of evil would dominate. By relying on God, however, listeners could gain control over the demonic elements of life and ensure that all would ultimately work for their benefit. In other words, the Christianity promulgated by Fuller on the airwaves was more pragmatic than dogmatic; it was practical, not a matter of debating fine points of theology. That very practicality brought Fuller and the "Old Fashioned Revival Hour" into the arena of popular religiosity.

Theologically, Harry Emerson Fosdick (1878–1969) was the antithesis of Charles E. Fuller.[14] Plunged into national prominence among the religious elite with his 1922 sermon, "Shall the Fundamentalists Win?" Fosdick represented all that fundamentalists dreaded about modernism for he refused to affirm publicly the five points of fundamentalism with their firm base in supernaturalism. Radio was also a ready forum for the evangelical liberalism of Fosdick, who headlined the "National Vespers Hour" from 1927 until his retirement in 1946, when estimates indicate that the program reached a weekly audience of up to three million listeners. A careful reading of Fosdick's published sermons suggests that, like Fuller, he aimed to present a practical religion, one that would give men and women a sense of direction and moral purpose and a conviction that they were in control of their lives.[15] But rather than emphasizing surrender to the supernatural power of God in Christ, Fosdick spoke of inner experience, of finding the power of God within the self. The theological constructs differed from those employed by Fuller, but the end result was remarkably similar: seeing a private, personal experience of sacred power as the basis for daily living. It was "a common-sense approach informed by gospel values."[16] By making private, personal experience the locus of faith and by seeing religion as something useful in dealing with everyday realities, Fosdick in his own way promoted the individualized piety and belief that mark popular religiosity.

The Roman Catholic Charles Coughlin, Canadian-born, established a base of operations near Detroit at the Shrine of the Little Flower in Royal Oak, Michigan, in the late 1920s and became "one of the master broadcasters of the period."[17] Coughlin's ostensible radio message, eventually carried on his own network, was political and economic, not religious. Shifting from ardent support of President Franklin Roosevelt to harsh criticism of the New Deal program and a strident anticommunism that came close to open endorsement of Nazi ideology, Coughlin built his appeal on hatred, though he always claimed simply to articulate the concerns and beliefs of the ordinary person.[18] His radio audience was vast; the largest estimates, undoubtedly exaggerated, put it in the range of thirty million. Especially prominent among Coughlin's targets were those identified with Judaism, the "synagogue of Satan."[19] Coughlin even saw to the republication of the highly anti-Semitic *Protocols of the Elders of Zion* that Henry Ford had previously issued and that had been demonstrated to be spurious even then.[20] In terms of popular religiosity, what is significant about Coughlin's xenophobia is his elevating the anxieties felt by millions during the Great Depression to the level of the cosmic conflict between the powers of good and evil. The devastation of the Depression meant that millions of Americans (indeed millions globally) felt they had lost all control over their personal destinies. Not only were great fortunes lost; millions of ordinary means also experienced an economic devastation that rendered them seemingly helpless amid the financial chaos of the day. Did it not make sense then not just to identify possible causes of that uncontrollable situation in order to have a scapegoat, but to give them cosmic significance? In other words, by linking his irrational xenophobia to the forces of Satan, Coughlin reinforced in the minds of his listeners and admirers a view of reality in which the world was under the domination of supernatural powers. At the moment, evil seemed ascendant; its defeat—for Coughlin, ultimately defeat of Franklin Roosevelt and the New Deal—would restore power to the powerless and again lift ordinary women and men to a higher plane where they could become partners with God in ordering the individual and corporate destiny of Americans.

The xenophobia Coughlin unleashed had a curious dimension, for while Coughlin's supporters had a range of religious affiliations, the bulk of them were Roman Catholics. The very hatred that Coughlin epitomized was of the same sort as the irrational hysteria of the Red Scare of 1919–20 that had readily included Catholic Americans in its net. Indeed the xenophobia of the 1920s and the 1930s, regardless of the form it took, had ramifications for much popular religiosity. For example, anti-Semitism, whether hawked by Father Coughlin and Henry Ford or creeping into public consciousness covertly through quotas on admissions to colleges and universities, housing covenants, and denial of membership in private clubs, made open affirmation of Jewish religiosity a liability. Those intent on seeking acceptance continued to minimize public demonstration of a Jewish religious identity that might bring attention to one's Jewishness and hence separate Jews from the larger culture. The net result was paradoxical. On the one hand, at precisely the time when children and grandchildren of the generation that came in that massive wave of immigration at the close of the nineteenth century were discovering something of their ethnic roots and in some cases seeking more traditional forms of religious expression, cultural signals nudged Jewish piety more and more into the private sphere. Even the longstanding sense of Jewish peoplehood could not stop a process in which Jews decided for themselves what it meant to be a Jew and whether being a Jew necessarily involved religiosity at all. Jewish leaders, in part to combat the incipient anti-Semitism of the age, sought interfaith conversations that continue to the present. For ordinary men and women with roots in the Jewish tradition, an ethos where anti-Semitism prevailed accelerated that privatization of religious experience basic to much popular religiosity and to a religion in which fundamental practice transpired in the confines of the home and family.

Three events of the 1920s provide a helpful frame for pondering not only the anti-Catholicism of the day but also the currents nurturing a popular religiosity grounded in Catholic sensibilities: the launching of a popular but intellectually inclined Catholic periodical, the *Commonweal*, in 1924; the Twenty-Eighth Eucharistic Congress that brought Catholic leaders from all over the world to Chicago in 1926; and the unsuccessful presidential candidacy of Catholic lay man Al Smith in 1928. The first two initially appear to mark the strength of Catholicism in American culture, while the latter seems to highlight a residual anti-Catholicism. The reality in all three cases is more complex.

Most analyses of the Catholic story suggest that the dawn of the twentieth century witnessed a gradual decline in the defensive attitude of official Catholicism, still caught up in melding an ethnically diverse constituency into a single religious institution. The emergence of numerous social welfare societies signaled Catholicism's acceptance of its responsibility for American common life in an age of progressive reform, while the cooperative endeavors that mobilized Catholic support for the Allied cause during World War I seemed to diffuse the most blatant Protestant suspicions of Catholicism. Indeed often the moral teaching of Catholicism as a formal religious institution dovetailed nicely with Protestant visions of a moral, if not Christian culture.[21] Even the expanding Catholic parochial school system, with a combined total of more than eight thousand elementary and secondary schools by the 1920s, seemed to bolster the conviction that Catholic moral teaching could create as solid a citizenry as anything advanced by evangelical Protestants, though the xenophobic Americanism of the 1920s did increase attacks on the parochial schools as subversive institutions.[22] There is an alternative reading of the evidence, however. The same years witnessed concerted efforts on the part of the Catholic hierarchy to bring the various lay societies under their own control, perhaps because the social reform that lay at their basis brought Catholic involvement in politics that official leaders feared would arouse dormant anti-Catholicism. Peter Williams has argued as well that the moral tone of parochial education exhibited a "preoccupation with virginity, which was carried to occasionally obsessive lengths by the celibate clergy and sisterhoods" and therefore "was another reflection of the generally defensive posture of the Church on an international scale."[23] The paradox was that the same forces that projected confidence to the larger culture internally supported what many have dubbed a "ghetto Catholicism."

What resulted for ordinary folk was the continuation of an understanding of Catholic identity that saw religiosity defined in terms of individual piety and devotionalism. We can see that individualistic element even in the thrust of a periodical that at first glance seems rather different. When the *Commonweal* began publication in 1924 as a lay-edited Catholic journal of opinion, its intent was simultaneously to apply formal Catholic principles to social issues and to trumpet what Catholicism could learn from the pluralistic ethos of American culture.[24] It aimed to present a Catholic perspective on issues of common interest to the American people, although its appeal (like that of cognate Protestant journals) was to an educated, if not elite readership. Within the pages of the *Commonweal*, though, one can discern a shift away from an ambivalence toward the larger culture because of an affirmation of a distinctive Catholic identity to an ambivalence toward a Catholic identity determined by the church as a formal institution because of an increasing affirmation of the right of individuals to determine for themselves what is an appropriate Catholic response to social issues. In other words, the *Commonweal* unwittingly elevated the individual as a religious authority. By asserting that the individual rather than the institutional church shapes Catholic identity, the *Commonweal* gave credence to the range of individual worldviews that persons construct to make sense out of their own experience.

That a vibrant sense of supernatural reality continued to be integral to Catholic identity is part of the import of the Twenty-Eighth Eucharistic Congress that drew in excess of a half-million people to Chicago in June 1926. In an editorial in the popular *Catholic World*, James Gillis proclaimed: "At Chicago we came, so to speak, out of our holes and corners, out of our catacombs into a blinding light."[25] While demonstrating the strength and confidence of the American Catholic Church as an institution was not its primary aim, the congress sent signals to Catholics and non-Catholics alike. Martin Marty has described an outdoor Mass that was part of the congress: "In a nation where the sight of a single Catholic cardinal could appear threatening to non-Catholics, the procession of forty-nine red-robed princes of the church on Michigan Avenue had to stun bystanders. At Soldier Field 150,000 faithful attended Mass. The magnificent pageantry of the church there unfolded before the faithful and the fearful alike."[26] All of this transpired in an era before popes routinely celebrated Mass in stadiums and other public arenas on their travels across the planet. The significance of the congress and the Mass at Soldier Field is paradoxical. On the one hand, the Mass is the central act in the worship life of Catholicism as a formal religious tradition. Hence the public nature of the event reinforced the perception that American Catholicism was no longer on the defensive. But when one recalls that the sacramentalism that undergirds the Mass was also central to popular Catholic devotionalism, it becomes clear that what came out of "holes and corners" was not just a formal religious institution. Rather, the congress became a potent public affirmation of the sense of the supernaturalism from which devotion and sacrament alike arise. The throngs who came to Chicago and the attendant publicity signaled to ordinary Catholic men and women, as the *Commonweal* gradually did to a more elite Catholic laity, that it was legitimate to construct a way of viewing the world through lenses crafted to the individual Catholic's understanding.

In most histories, the presidential candidacy of Al Smith represents one of the last hurrahs of anti-Catholic sentiment in American life, for Smith's detractors did not hesitate to dredge up old fears of Catholicism and Catholic power in their efforts to secure his defeat.[27] In addition to the long-standing anxiety that the pope would manipulate a Catholic president, Protestant concerns that Catholicism was by nature incompatible with American democracy resurfaced. Ironically, roughly half a century earlier that latter issue had troubled the highest level of Vatican leadership who saw democracy as inimical to Catholicism. But the 1928 presidential campaign contains clues about popular religiosity, both Protestant and Catholic. On the Protestant side, raising the specter of Catholicism as deleterious to authentic Christianity gave credence to popular religiosity's conviction that forces of evil were at work in the world and that one had to be on guard every moment lest they triumph, as they surely would were Smith elected. Having a concrete symbol of that evil in candidate Smith made such suspicions all the more real. Smith and his supporters generally refrained from adding to the hysteria through direct counterattacks. In one of the few published statements where Smith did reply to the anti-Catholic propaganda even before the formal campaign was underway, he called attention to his political record as four-term governor of New York, asking where there was evidence of church or papal interference and control.[28] More important is what is implicit in Smith's response, namely that religious belief and practice are in principle matters of the private sphere. While Protestants of an evangelical stripe had long claimed that the religious experience par excellence, conversion, was essentially a private matter and that the heart of genuine religiosity was individual and personal, now a prominent Catholic voice articulated a position based on the same assumptions.

The most potent symbol of the xenophobia, anti-Catholicism, anti-Semitism, and racial prejudice of the era following World War I remains the Ku Klux Klan, organized in 1915.[29] From public parades to purported involvement in lynchings, the Klan promoted itself as a white, Protestant body committed to biblical precepts that were reaffirmed in elaborately staged rituals. While the Klan drew on some of the fascination with secret societies that had mushroomed in Victorian America, it also had a distinct religious dimension. Commentators in the 1920s were well aware of the spiritual side of the Klan; among recent analysts, Martin Marty has called attention again to the religiosity or spirituality that accompanied the Klan.[30] In the 1920s those Klan adherents who promoted this religious aspect went well beyond noting that membership requirements restricted admission to white Protestant males (generally of a theologically and politically conservative bent). Some, for example, argued that the Klan was simply more aggressively pursuing the moral teaching inherent in all conservative Protestantism. In other words, the Klan for many was the logical extension of Protestantism as a religious institution. There were constant reminders of the connection between the Klan and Christianity in the style of Klan rituals, the use of the cross as a basic symbol, and even the language Klan leaders used to describe their mission. Another dimension of the Klan phenomenon brings us closer to popular religiosity, its powerful sense of the reality of evil, of supernatural forces that sought to thwart the well-being of ordinary men and women, of demonic threats that constantly lurked just beneath the surface of empirical reality. By blatantly identifying immigrants, African Americans, Catholics, and Jews with that arena of evil, the Klan helped sustain popular belief in an understanding of the world as a stage on which the forces of good and evil remain in constant contention. Historians have long pointed out that by the 1920s American society had become so religiously, ethnically, and racially pluralistic that it could not be accurately described as an Anglo-Saxon Christian (i.e., Protestant) culture. For those whose sense of identity, whose sense of place in the world, was most profoundly shaped by that misperception of the United States, it was not enough simply to label the enemy as such. It was necessary to take action on behalf of perceived forces of good. One had to join in the cosmic struggle against the powers of evil. It is easy, but simplistic, to dismiss the Klan as irrational hatred become fanaticism. The Klan in actuality represented the surfacing of those strong currents of popular religiosity that affirmed the reality and ever-present danger of the forces of evil, however they were named.

Not all popular religiosity was channeled into sustaining the style of supernaturalism touted by fundamentalists or the sense of evil so real to the Klan. From Pentecostals to popular writers, other expressions of an abiding, but inchoate sense of the supernatural came to the fore. Among those in the Pentecostal orbit who received much popular attention in the first half of the twentieth century were Aimee Semple McPherson (1890–1944) and Kathryn Kuhlman (1907–76), although Kuhlman may have had more enduring and wide-ranging influence.[31] In 1923 McPherson established her Angelus Temple in Los Angeles to serve as a base for her evangelistic work and the denomination she started, the Four Square Gospel Church International. That same year the younger Kuhlman held her first evangelistic revival under the auspices of her brother-in-law Everett B. Parrott and his traveling Parrott Tent Revival. But the two ultimately were rather different in style and impact.

Canadian-born McPherson was first married to Robert Semple, an evangelist from Ireland who included his wife as a partner in his revivals following their marriage in 1908. Early on Aimee demonstrated the power that would mark her later ministry. Before the Semples left for a missionary tour in China in 1910, she experienced the power of the Holy Spirit in healing her ankle and in granting her the gift of interpreting tongues. Robert Semple died after the couple had been in China less than a year, and his grieving widow returned to the United States with their newborn daughter. About a year after her return, Aimee married Harold McPherson in a union described as less than happy. When she again felt called by the Spirit to pursue an evangelistic ministry, Aimee left McPherson, from whom she was later divorced. In June 1917 she launched publication of the *Bridal Call*, a popular periodical that would carry her message into the nation's homes. As the major catalyst in giving her followers a sense of common identity, the *Bridal Call* helped transform her from an itinerant evangelist in the Holiness and Pentecostal traditions into the founder of a denomination. At the same time, when healings were reported at evangelistic services she conducted, both attendance and offerings increased. The latter allowed her to reap great advantage from one of the technological marvels of the day. She purchased a car that she dubbed the "Gospel Auto" and drove from town to town on her evangelistic rounds. Once she established her base in Los Angeles, a network of auxiliary agencies quickly emerged. Her own radio station, KFSG, ranks as the first radio station in the United States that was devoted exclusively to religious broadcasting. Although personal scandal and unhappiness plagued McPherson, she continued a steady schedule of services at the Angelus Temple, reserving one each week for healing.

Like McPherson, Kuhlman had no formal theological education and held ministerial credentials from a group independent of the more established Christian denominations. She began her evangelistic career as a teenager, but gained greater national recognition when, during the Great Depression, she settled in Denver, Colorado, where followers transformed a warehouse into the Kuhlman Revival Tabernacle that provided her with a home base. Kuhlman's optimistic message that the power of the Holy Spirit could effect miracles of all sorts in human lives resonated with a Depression audience whose seemingly hopeless lives needed miracles. However, in the late 1930s, Kuhlman watched her Denver ministry disintegrate as marital scandal undermined her credibility. Then in 1944 while in Los Angeles, Kuhlman had a dramatic experience of the presence of the Holy Spirit, more akin to the Holiness than the Pentecostal understanding of baptism of the Spirit. The experience revitalized her ministry even as it ended her marriage. Not until nearly two years later, however, in the Gospel Revival Tabernacle near Pittsburgh did success come, and Kuhlman determined to remain in the Pittsburgh area, embarking on intensive study of the phenomenon of divine healing. In April 1947 when Kuhlman preached a series of sermons on the power of the Holy Spirit, numerous individuals reported miraculous healings. Soon Kuhlman became a leading figure of the post–World War II healing and deliverance revivals, even launching a television series in 1967. Although the segment of Kuhlman's career that brought her the greatest fame lies in the post–World War II period, its roots lie earlier, and Kuhlman's understanding of the power of the Spirit to effect healing of all sorts stretches back to her Depression-era ministry in Denver.

Much of what McPherson and Kuhlman promoted is vital to understanding the continuing dynamics of popular religiosity in American culture. First, neither carried the imprimatur of a well-established formal religious denomination. Both gained a following because they felt they were individually empowered by the Spirit of God. This sense of access to supernatural power unmediated by formal institutions is basic to popular religiosity, as is the conviction of both McPherson and Kuhlman that the very same power could come to ordinary individuals. Indeed, Kuhlman's healing services became distinguished from those of other deliverance evangelists precisely because she eschewed rituals like laying on of hands or even offering individual prayers for those seeking healing. Supernatural power operated on its own terms. Those who sought miracles through the ministrations of McPherson and Kuhlman represented a cross-section of the American population, persons drawn from a wide range of formal religious affiliations, although some of McPherson's followers did make their way into the Foursquare Gospel denomination that she founded. Some estimates indicate that a majority of Kuhlman's audience in her later years came from the ranks of Roman Catholicism.[32] The point is simply that both reached ordinary people with a message of the reality and accessibility of supernatural power. It is also significant that both McPherson and Kuhlman were women. Given the gender roles that had become etched into American culture since the Victorian era and the efforts of early fundamentalists to regard such roles as divinely ordained, McPherson and Kuhlman's defiance of gender expectation under the claim of supernatural empowerment gave added credence to their respective, though different messages that anyone could not only hope for, but actually experience the reality of the transcendent. Such was not abstract, but pragmatic for it could effect change and transformation in ordinary human life.

A very different understanding of the supernatural, but one that also stressed the pragmatic element so important to popular religiosity, formed the ideological basis for the best-selling writings of Bruce Barton (1886–1967) and Lloyd C. Douglas (1877–1951). Barton remains known less for his distinguished career first in periodical editing and then in advertising and for his two terms in the U.S. House of Representatives than for his wildly popular *The Man Nobody Knows*. Likewise, the influence of Douglas on popular religiosity stems not from his highly successful career in the pastoral ministry, but for his many novels such as *Magnificent Obsession* and *The Robe*, both of which became successful Hollywood feature films. In the work of both, one clearly discerns a sense of how the power of the supernatural has practical consequences for everyday life. In other words, one sees again cultural supports for popular religiosity.

Barton's *The Man Nobody Knows* became a best-seller for two years after its publication in 1925, although for a time its publication in a format designed to reach a mass audience was in doubt.[33] Scribners rejected the original manuscript, and, prior to its publication in book form, it ran as a serial in a magazine targeted to a female audience, although analysts have emphasized how its portrayal of a masculine Jesus was intended to appeal primarily to men, especially businessmen.[34] Here was a Jesus, albeit fashioned from an Anglo-Saxon mold, who succeeded in attracting such a following that he was not only the most popular dinner guest in Jerusalem, but through unstinting service as well as shrewd strategy was able to create a demand for his product, a moral way of life. For decades students of

American religion and culture assumed that Barton, because of his own success in business, had created a Jesus who was the ideal businessperson of the 1920s when capitalism reigned supreme in the United States.[35] This interpretation, however, obscures the real reason why Barton's Jesus had such extraordinary popular appeal. Far from trying merely to endow the business world of the 1920s with religious sanction, Barton had created a very concrete Jesus. Here was no abstract ethereal divinity, but a Jesus who dealt with real-life situations and always triumphed, even when others saw defeat. Here was a Jesus always in control, confident, and possessed of a magnetic personality. To this extent, Barton's Jesus exemplified the practical supernaturalism characteristic of popular religiosity. Especially for the middle-class worker who was caught in the corporate morass and felt a loss of autonomy as big business took on a life of its own, the Jesus "nobody knows" was a concrete person who could enable persons struggling in business (and those whose lives were intertwined with them) to have a formula that would give them control over their lives. Feeling such control and order even in the face of contrary empirical reality is part of the practical dimension of popular religiosity. Gerald Sittser has argued that the optimism Barton's Jesus gave to ordinary folk resonated primarily with those who saw themselves in a position to rise in the business world, but had not yet done so. Barton's idealism had less appeal to those who were already at the pinnacles of business, since they already had one form of power, and to those, such as women and African Americans, for whom access to such power the culture of the day denied.[36] Nevertheless, for the millions who purchased *The Man Nobody Knows* and the millions more who have read it, Barton extended hope that a world seemingly out of control could be brought back under control.[37]

Although the Jesus who graces the pages of the many popular novels of Lloyd C. Douglas was not cut from the mold of the successful advertising executive as was Barton's, Douglas likewise "believed that the proof of Christianity lay in the practical value of Jesus' teachings as they affected individual lives . . . . If Jesus is to be the exemplar for humans, Douglas argued, then he has to live under human conditions . . . . In Douglas' view, the true importance of Jesus was that he was in touch with the divine spirit and that he showed that humans could be too."[38] Such becomes clear in both *Magnificent Obsession* and *The Robe*, arguably two of Douglas' most well-known works.[39] The story line of the first had its base in an episode reported in the popular press in which one individual died because the only available life-saving medical equipment was already being used for another patient. Douglas, always willing to fill in the blanks, took the incident and built a novel in which not only medical technology, but the power of Jesus could bring new life to individuals as well as to society. In a vital way, this practical power of Jesus superseded the results of medical science, for it was accessible to all. *The Robe* is also a story about power, but in a different vein. Its hero, Marcellus, is the Roman soldier overseeing the cru-cifixion of Jesus. After Jesus is declared dead, Marcellus receives the robe that Jesus had worn to the crucifixion. Although Marcellus attempts to return to business as usual and winds up far from Palestine in Rome, the image of the confident, courageous Jesus haunts him, and the robe becomes akin to a magical relic in its ability to keep such thoughts in Marcellus's thinking. Meeting the apostle Peter in Rome, Marcellus concludes that compared with Jesus, he himself is more cowardly, despite his being a sol-dier. Nudged by Peter, Marcellus becomes a Christian so that the same courage and control that Jesus exemplified will come to him. In an ironic twist, Marcellus has the opportunity to demonstrate that courage when he becomes a martyr for his new faith. Significant about both is the way they give a practical bent to belief in the supernatural. Some have noted, of course, that the Jesus of *The Robe* and of *The Big Fisherman*, which fol-lowed in 1948, was particularly apt for the era of World War II when extraordinary courage seemed in order. But the point to both *Magnificent Obsession* and *The Robe* is also that personal religiosity yields an inner peace, that the empirical forces that seem to control the world in which ordinary folk live can be conquered. The message of Douglas is essentially to reinforce the power that comes to the individual in popular religiosity.

We have repeatedly seen how the medium of print is particularly appro-priate for sustaining popular religiosity. The novels of Douglas and inter-pretive works, like those of Barton, are gleaned in private. They speak to the reader without the direct mediation of religious professionals or relig-ious groups. Hence they send signals at a very personal level, and readers are free to add whatever beliefs are communicated to their own personal views of the world. Literary critics have frequently panned the work of Douglas for its sentimentalism, and religious professionals have railed against the vapid theology and doctrinal distortion of both Barton and Douglas. But both reached a vast audience with their message. While one can never assess the extent to which the Jesus presented by Barton and Douglas replaced the Jesus of the New Testament and the churches in pop-ular consciousness, for millions the perspectives of Barton and Douglas influenced their own perceptions of Jesus and their sense of the power of the supernatural over the empirical.

The 1920s and 1930s were also the decades when the medium of film was gaining popularity. The first film version of *Magnificent Obsession* was released in 1935; a remake appeared in 1954. Independent producer Frank Ross purchased film rights to *The Robe* even before the book was pub-lished. They followed on Cecil B. DeMille's *King of Kings* of 1927, which went well beyond the fictional portrayals in its extravagant presentation of Jesus. Earlier best-sellers also provided subject matter for the developing film industry. Both *Ben Hur* and *Quo Vadis*, for example, were among the major films that helped launch a new entertainment industry. Like the medium of print, that of film is also especially appropriate for buttressing dimensions of popular religiosity. While prior to widespread use of the home videocassette recorder virtually all persons who viewed a film did so in a group context in a movie theater, the experience of watching a film is essentially a private, personal one. With lights dimmed so that what is projected on the screen may be viewed clearly and with conversation at a minimum (especially after films added sound), there is a mystique to the movie theater that gives it almost the same aura as a more traditional religious setting. The lack of communication with others—the primary communication is really between the film and the individual viewer—transforms the experience into a private one. Hence like the reader of a novel, the viewer of a film is able to absorb whatever is presented and accept, reject, or combine that with views and beliefs already held. Film becomes a way of seeing the subtle syncretism that weaves throughout popular religiosity.

That belief in the supernatural had practical ramifications for daily living is a recurring feature of popular religiosity. To some extent the continuing fascination with astrology and the occult also reflects that practical quality. Some have also argued, for example, that the optimistic message of Aimee Semple McPherson buttressed that same practical sense that would in the later twentieth century be labeled "self-help." It is there, too, in the confident Jesus of many of Douglas's novels and a central ingredient of Barton's successful Jesus. But another manifestation of that spirit came in a pungent book by Missouri native Dale Carnegie (1888–1955). *How to Win Friends and Influence People*, with aggregate sales now in excess of ten million, first appeared in 1936 in the midst of the Depression.[40] A virtual industry developed from this book in the form of courses and institutes where ordinary folk could learn the secrets of personal success. Carnegie's message had a different twist, however, but one that nevertheless blended well with many of the features of popular religiosity. Carnegie, like evangelists calling for personal conversion, emphasized the importance of the individual, for it was the individual alone who could develop techniques for dealing with other people that would bring success. More to the point is Carnegie's insistence that individuals can be in total control of their lives. What is vital is that they recognize that they already have such control. Then they can tap into it for their own benefit. But Carnegie gives a different twist to the notion of personal control. Like early Christian Science and the heady self-reliance of Russell Conwell, Carnegie essentially locates supernatural power within the self. It is a latent power that can be brought to life as one learns to believe in the self and in one's inner power. Carnegie's program for success also assumes that the majority of folk are unaware of this power within the self. Hence those who know this truth have an extraordinary ability to manipulate others. They actually extend the boundaries of the control they have over their own lives to attain control over others.

Carnegie's pitch, at least in the early editions of *How to Win Friends and Influence People*, was clearly directed at a male clientele. So, too, most of the key characters who draw us into the orbit of popular religiosity in the novels of Douglas were male. Barton drew his portrait of Jesus in such dominant masculine terms to some degree to demonstrate that the supernatural was not the exclusive domain of women. We have already seen how one undercurrent of the fundamentalism and conservative evangelical Protestantism of the first decades of the twentieth century had as an unstated goal the maintenance of gender roles carved out in the Victorian era. There were exceptions, of course, in such figures as Aimee Semple Mc-Pherson and Kathryn Kuhlman. But there was also another arena, especially for Protestant women, where the supernatural realm came alive in very practical terms, for the first half of the twentieth century witnessed a continuation in the production of a range of literature targeted primarily to a white Protestant female clientele. Popular periodicals, many with some loose denominational connection, continued to make their way into thousands of American homes. But there was also an entire genre of fiction that spoke to the ways in which simple trust supernatural power had beneficial practical results for women. A stunning example is the fiction of Grace Livingston Hill (1865–1947), who also wrote under the name of Marcia MacDonald (actually her mother's birth name).

None of Hill's works made the best-seller list, but she more than made up for that through the quantity of her publications. Hill published seventy-nine novels during her career, with total sales in excess of three million copies. At her most productive, she drafted three novels per year.[41] Some might argue, however, that in reality Hill wrote one novel and simply recast it with different settings and characters, for there is a recurring theme that runs through nearly all of her work. A later age would label her works as "Christian romance," and several have been reprinted by Christian publishing houses in the later twentieth century to compete with popular secular romance novels. For our purposes, however, what is central is that recurring theme. Most of Hill's novels center around a female figure who confronts some sort of adversity in life or high adventure (such as uncovering a plot to overthrow the U.S. government at the time of the Red Scare). Regardless of the tragedies that loom and the forces that would thwart any heroine's achieving happiness (albeit usually within the parameters of acceptable culturally defined gender roles), she always triumphs through her faith in the power of God. That power provides strength to confront and surmount any obstacle; in turn, strength becomes an inner control over the course of one's life, empirical evidence to the contrary. Usually by the conclusion of a Hill novel, the heroine has met and married or plans to marry a Christian (Protestant) husband who will provide her with a secure location in the social order. Hence the practical dimension of popular religiosity, the sense of control over one's life, is paramount. Important also is the lack of anything that is denominationally specific in the professed religiosity of Hill's characters. Their own religiosity, although often sustained through church involvement, could fit any denominational affiliation, though virtually all are Protestant. So, too, all women, regardless of formal religious identification, could through their personal religiosity experience power and control.

If women's sphere as traditionally defined in the first half of the twentieth century remained the home, there also developed another genre of popular literature aimed at personal devotional life centered in the home. In 1925, for example, Mrs. Charles E. Cowman published the first volume in a series called *Streams in the Desert*.[42] A series of daily readings for private devotion for a full calendar year, that initial volume attained sales of two million copies in 1931 alone.[43] Four years later came the first printing of what was destined to become the most popular magazine of daily devotional materials, the *Upper Room*.[44] Although begun under Methodist auspices, the *Upper Room* quickly adopted a nondenominational posture, printing daily devotional writings from more than three hundred individuals selected from among thousands received each year through an open solicitation process. The initial printing was onehundred thousand copies. With global distribution and editions published in languages other than English continuously since 1938, circulation exceeded three million within thirty years.[45] Like cognate periodicals such as *Our Daily Bread*, the *Upper Room* offers a suggested daily Bible reading, brief meditation, prayer, and "thought for the day." Four characteristics of materials in the *Upper Room* are significant for seeing how it nurtures popular religiosity. First, writers of the daily meditations are ordinary men and women, not theologians or professional writers. Hence they speak to the masses of the laity in language and terms they understand. Second, the broad guidelines for potential contributors encourage submissions based on personal experience. The meditations thus move into the private, personal realm where popular religiosity flourishes. Third, the experiences that writers discuss always demonstrate how their personal faith was directly related to dealing with a problem or gaining a sense of direction or control in a specific situation. In this way, the content of the *Upper Room* supports that aspect of popular religiosity that finds in simple reliance on supernatural power a sense of control over one's destiny. Fourth, the international character of the *Upper Room*, while ostensibly demonstrating that humans deal with similar problems in life the world over, also reminds us that the inchoate sense of the supernatural at the heart of popular religiosity is not uniquely American, though there may be expressions of popular religiosity that are. It is also worth noting that while daily devotions may be perceived as part of the domestic sphere of women, many of the contributors are male.

Increased efficiency in mass production brought not only a greater volume of printed material to ordinary women and men but also an array of art objects that could be used in home decoration as well as in more specifically religious contexts such as churches. Of these one stands out as having deeply impressed itself on the American religious consciousness: the "Head of Christ" by artist Warner Sallman (1892–1968). Originally sketched in charcoal as a cover illustration for the *Covenant Companion*, the magazine of the Swedish Evangelical Mission Covenant of America denomination, and based on an image of Jesus in a painting by the French artist Leon Augustin Lhermitte, Sallman's "Head of Christ" was painted in 1940.[46] In half a century, it had been reproduced more than five hundred million times in formats ranging from large-scale copies for use in churches to wallet-sized ones that individuals could carry with them at all times. The androgynous Jesus portrayed by Sallman bears little resemblance to a first-century Semite. But the image, with its near mystical illumination that David Morgan finds akin to that of a commercial studio photograph, has a haunting appearance. Jesus has eyes looking vaguely upward in what appears to be a combined gesture of awe of God and obedience to God. Although the facial expression communicates a feminine tenderness, the beard and flowing hair suggest a masculine dimension. Above all, the portrait is personal, and therein lies its potency as an expression of popular religiosity. For those whose religiosity is shaped by Protestant sensibilities, the majesty and power of God remain somewhat distant. But Sallman's thoroughly humanized Jesus has as well a mystical aura to betoken how Jesus partakes of the power of God. Whether in a religious setting or a home setting, in Sallman's "Head of Christ" the supernatural enters the realm of empirical reality in a way that suggests to the viewer that this same serene sense of power (and hence control) is available to all. There is, of course, no physical description of Jesus in the New Testament or in any other surviving early Christian literature. Yet for hundreds of millions, Sallman's depiction has become the basis for their visualization of Jesus, a Jesus who brings the sacred into the realm of the ordinary.

Additional insight into popular religiosity in the first half of the twentieth century comes from the classic studies of Muncie, Indiana, by Robert S. Lynd and Helen M. Lynd. The first of these, *Middletown: A Study in American Culture*, appeared in 1929 and was based on extensive sociological and anthropological work conducted in 1924–25. The Lynds offered a follow-up study, *Middletown in Transition: A Study in Cultural Conflicts*, published in 1937.[47] While the Lynds did not focus their analysis on religion, they were attentive to the role of formal religious institutions and to an understanding of religiosity that was measured mostly by participation

in religious institutions, although some came from interviews with informants. The Lynds' prognosis for religion in Middletown is well known
among students of American life. On the one hand, they recognized the
prominence of religious institutions within the local society, though they
concluded that they were declining in influence as other associations, such
as civic organizations, competed with them for the allegiance and loyalty
of the people. The Lynds also noted that many persons spoke nostalgically
of a past time when religion (again presumably in its institutional form)
seemed more vital and that many informants seemed increasingly less convinced of the ultimate truth of orthodox formulations of Christian doctrine.
Thus they concluded that religious belief was on the wane. In other words,
the Lynds saw a creeping secularism encroaching on their archetype of
American society.

If we look more deeply we will find, as did the team of researchers that
returned to Muncie (Middletown) in the 1970s, that looking at religious
institutions and formal doctrine obscures a vital religiosity that was not
only flourishing in the 1920s, but still thriving in the 1970s.[48] What was
clear in the 1970s was perhaps more nascent in the 1920s, namely that
behind the denominational apparatus that marked the public religious life
of Middletown, there was a popular religion predicated on an abiding sense
of the supernatural, on a conviction that God did provide all of life's meaning and that prayer and other practices that brought individuals into contact with divine power were efficacious in allowing individuals to gain a
sense of direction and purpose in life. More to the point, as Theodore
Caplow and the later researchers ascertained, there was no concern among
ordinary folk about whether this sense of meaning and the reality of the
supernatural could be proved in a logical or formal sense, nor about
whether their personal beliefs were related to the official theological positions of the denominations. What did matter was that people organized
and lived their lives on the assumption that the sacred power of God was
available to them and would work on behalf of those who believed. If all
of this went counter to what the Lynds had expected half a century earlier,
we should not be surprised, for what the Lynds did not see was the grounding of public religion in private religiosity and the staying power of that
popular, personal, private religiosity.

Thus far we have not looked closely at dimensions of popular religiosity
among African Americans in the first half of the twentieth century other
than to note that Pentecostal currents remained strong. In the rural South
especially, the sense of the supernatural continued to express itself in ways
we have already seen. Thousands continued to blend belief in conjure and
an almost tribal world of spirits and supernatural forces with their own
Christianity and its supernaturalism. In some areas, voodoo remained an
important part of the syncretistic blend of beliefs and practices that gave
meaning to life. But we must also note a phenomenon more obvious in

northern urban areas that witnessed a steady in-migration of African Americans in the first half of the century as employment opportunities in northern factories offered prospects for a more secure life than was to be found in the agrarian South. A classic study sketches the contours of the religious dynamics within the African-American community in one urban area, metropolitan Chicago, and serves as a prototype for other areas. *Black Metropolis*, by St. Clair Drake and Horace R. Cayton, resulted from extensive sociological research conducted in Chicago in the 1930s.[49] While by economic measurements there was evidence of a small, but not insignificant middle and upper class, nearly two-thirds of the African Americans living in Chicago in the 1930s fell into the lower class and by and large were concentrated in ghetto areas that the authors referred to as Bronzeville. This area grew significantly in terms of both the land area it encompassed and its total population because of the "great migration" of African Americans from the rural South to the urban North in the opening decades of the twentieth century. From their analytic perspective, Drake and Cayton emphasized the prevalence of Baptist and Holiness groups in Bronzeville, along with a large number of storefront churches and smaller sectarian bodies that usually had some tangential links to the Holiness/Pentecostal orbit, but often revolved around the ministry of a particularly charismatic male or female preacher. At the same time, they noted that many of their respondents revealed an ambivalent attitude toward organized or institutional religion. On the one hand, many were skeptical of the sincerity and intentions of religious professionals, as they were of any in positions of authority. Most were apt to claim that religious affiliation was not necessary to assure one's eternal destiny. At the same time, participation in formal religious activity had positive benefits in terms of identity, pride, and social acceptance.

What concerns us for exploring the continuing strength of a popular religiosity rooted in the African-American experience are the Holiness/Pentecostal ethos of much of the formal religion of Bronzeville and the claim that affiliation with a religious institution had no direct connection to one's eternal destiny. As we have already seen, the style of Holiness and Pentecostal expression that took root within African-American religious life accepted without question the possibility of a direct personal apprehension of God's Spirit, often in terms of some ecstatic experience, possession of presumed healing powers, and the like. For the thousands of African Americans who left the rural South for the alien culture of the urban North, the world of the city was one where there was a keen sense of power, but that power was often in the hands of an economic elite. Once again, popular religiosity opened avenues to a superior power for those who found new dimensions of life within their control. Especially important here are the number of Holiness healers and the countless storefront spiritualists. Those who had the power to heal or to manipulate people and external conditions for the benefit of clients in part represent a mutation of the longstanding belief in conjure with its mystical if not magical power to control external forces. Religiosity was not confined to formal institutions and for the majority of the African-American population of Chicago in the 1930s remained focused on the reality of supernatural power wherever and however it became manifest.

From the jazz clubs of the cities came the blues, a natural development musically from the spirituals of antebellum days and the gospel music of the late nineteenth and early twentieth centuries. While some have claimed that once blues musicians became perceived as artists they and their music stopped being religious, in reality the blues consistently evoke a realm of power.[50] If the lyrics of vocal blues music seem filled with tales of sex and lost love, they also are replete with hope for redirection, for bringing order to a world that seems out of control. So, too, with instrumental blues where haunting melodic lines draw listeners into an awareness of despair and near defeat, only to find triumph in a dramatic resolution of tremendous musical force. The blues mirror the experience of the African-American population of the northern cities, where conflict between the mores of a rural past and an urban present produced a world where effective control seemed wrested from the individual. Yet hope for resolution endured, just as popular religiosity, with its juxtaposition of good and evil supernatural forces, offered hope for tapping into a realm of power that would restore control to life.

Another movement that stood outside the formal religious institutions had a great impact on currents of African-American popular religiosity, but in a fashion very different from the blues. In 1916 Marcus Garvey came to the United States from Jamaica, with the goal of expanding his Universal Negro Improvement Agency (UNIA).[51] By the time he was deported just over a decade later, Garvey had built an organization existing alongside the churches with an estimated membership ranging anywhere from one hundredthousand to two million. He also founded a popular weekly, *Negro World*, to carry his message of pride in the African heritage and the effort to return African Americans to the continent of their origins. Garvey's movement had a distinctly religious dimension to it, one that reflects that constellation of beliefs and values associated with popular religiosity. While one specifically religious group, the African Orthodox Church, did spring from the work of the UNIA, it was not paramount, for Garvey recognized that many of those who would take an interest in the UNIA were already formal church members. Garvey and his associates spoke in highly personal and private terms when they talked about planting the Temple of God in the individual heart, with the result that inner peace and universal brotherhood would ensue. The important point is that persons of all formal religions or no formal religion could become Garveyites for where Garvey's program touched on religion, it resonated with that interior piety, that highly personal apprehension of the sacred, that is the core of popular religiosity. Although Garvey's immediate agenda was short-lived, he left an enduring heritage that decades later would feed into a renewed interest in things African, including African religions and spirituality, that in turn would enrich the syncretism that had long marked African-American popular religiosity.

Thus far we have also said little about strains of popular religiosity among Native American Indians in the first half of the twentieth century. Precious few commentators on American religious life offer any insight into the Native American experience during this period, largely because it was a time of basic neglect. Most Native Americans were consigned to reservations, and government policy was aimed more to make sure nothing rocked the boat than to enhance Native American life. Occasionally there were calls for renewed Christian missions among the Indians, again reflecting the larger cultural lack of sensitivity to the integrity of what remained of tribal life. Some insight into currents of popular religiosity, however, emerge from controversies that came to the fore. There was, for example, concern about the Native American Church and its ritual use of peyote, though as Martin Marty has noted, those who observed the rituals recognized that "worshipers in this sect gained from their rites what mainstream fellow Christians did from theirs: a sense of meaning and belonging along with heightened morale and incentive for moral action."[52] That, of course, is precisely what all popular religiosity provides in its keen sense of the supernatural and the involvement of the supernatural in ordinary affairs. Some Native American groups that were designed to promote Indian interests joined in the opposition to the Native American Church, in part because they feared broader regulation of internal Indian affairs would follow as government agents sought to suppress the use of an illegal substance.[53] The American Indian Defense Association, founded in 1923 by John Collier who later became the federal commissioner of Indian affairs, sought to combat attempts to restrict other traditional tribal rites, with their ceremony and dance.[54] The need for such a defense suggests that life on reservations had neither brought acculturation to Euro-American ways nor eradicated that indigenous sense of power woven throughout initiation rites, ceremonies, and tribal dances.

From fundamentalists who looked to miracle for proof of the supernatural to Native American Indians who struggled to maintain a sense of the sacred, the many streams of popular religiosity cascading through American culture continued in the first half of the twentieth century to provide ordinary men and women with a way to have some control over their daily lives and to endow their lives with meaning. The years between the two World Wars also provided glimmers of the forces that would help shape popular religiosity in numerous ways later. As religious leaders pondered the import of popular entertainment media such as radio and film, the means of sending signals to ordinary folk about what to think and what to believe, signals that would reinforce popular religiosity, expanded at an extraordinary rate. Even traditional religious institutions were aware of a new day, for analysts of American culture point to the apparent religious boom of the 1950s as an indicator of the renewed strength of religion in American life. If institutional religion prospered as the nation entered the second half of the twentieth century, the many currents of popular religiosity also experienced fresh vigor and strength.

NOTES

1. Robert T. Handy, "The American Religious Depression," *Church History* 29 (1960): 3–16. Handy's understanding receives expanded treatment in his *A Christian America: Protestant Hopes and Historical Realities*, 2d ed. (New York: Oxford University Press, 1984).

2. Three essays by Joel A. Carpenter survey the range of institutions that emerged to carry the fundamentalist message to the popular level: "Fundamentalist Institutions and the Growth of Evangelical Protestantism, 1929–1942," *Church History* 49 (1980): 62–75; "The Fundamentalist Leaven and the Rise of an Evangelical United Front," in *The Evangelical Tradition in America*, edited by Leonard I. Sweet (Macon, Ga.: Mercer University Press, 1984), pp. 257–88; and "Revive Us Again: Alienation, Hope, and the Resurgence of Fundamentalism, 1930–1950," in *Transforming Faith: The Sacred and Secular in Modern American History*, edited by M. L. Bradbury and James B. Gilbert (Westport, Conn.: Greenwood, 1989), pp. 105–25. Also see Ferenc Morton Szasz, *The Divided Mind of Protestant America, 1880–1930* (University: University of Alabama Press, 1982), pp. 84–91.

3. Robert K. Murray, *Red Scare: A Study in National Hysteria, 1919–1920* (Minneapolis: University of Minnesota Press, 1955), remains the standard analysis.

4. The most recent biography is Lyle W. Dorsett, *Billy Sunday and the Redemption of Urban America* (Grand Rapids, Mich.: Eerdmans, 1991), although it lacks the critical acumen of William G. McLoughlin, *Billy Sunday Was His Real Name* (Chicago: University of Chicago Press, 1955).

5. On the religious efforts to oppose repeal of Prohibition, see Martin E. Marty, *Modern American Religion 2: The Noise of Conflict, 1919–1941* (Chicago: University of Chicago Press, 1991), pp. 233–41.

6. Peter W. Williams, *Popular Religion in America: Symbolic Change and the Modernization Process in Historical Perspective* (Englewood Cliffs, N.J.: Prentice-Hall, 1980), p. 163, emphasizes this point.

7. Betty A. DeBerg, *Ungodly Women: Gender and the First Wave of American Fundamentalism* (Minneapolis: Fortress, 1990).

8. Douglas W. Frank, *Less than Conquerors: How Evangelicals Entered the Twentieth Century* (Grand Rapids, Mich.: Eerdmans, 1986), p. 183. On Sunday more generally, see pp. 169–224.

9. See, for example, Dave Berkman, "Long before Falwell: Early Radio and Religion—As Reported by the Nation's Periodical Press," *Journal of Popular Culture* 21:4 (1988): 1–11; Everett C. Parker, David W. Barry, and Dallas W. Smythe, *The Television-Radio Audience and Religion* (New York: Harper, 1955); George H. Hill, *Airwaves to the Soul: The Influence and Growth of Religious Broadcasting*

in America (Saratoga, Calif.: R & E Publishers, 1983); and William C. Martin, "The God-Hucksters of Radio," in *Side-Saddle on the Golden Calf: Social Structure and Popular Culture in America,* edited by George H. Lewis (Pacific Palisades, Calif.: Goodyear, 1972), pp. 49–55. A helpful reference tool is George H. Hill and Lenwood G. Davis, *Religious Broadcasting, 1920–1983: A Selectively Annotated Bibliography* (New York: Garland, 1984).

10. Representative is Wendell P. Loveless, *Manual of Gospel Broadcasting* (Chicago: Moody, 1946). This work reflects a fundamentalist orientation.

11. Thomas F. Coakley, "Preaching by Wireless," *Catholic World* 72:5 (January 1922): 516.

12. See L. David Lewis, "Charles E. Fuller," in *Twentieth-Century Shapers of American Popular Religion,* edited by Charles H. Lippy (Westport, Conn.: Greenwood, 1989), pp. 148–55. The only full biography is the mildly hagiographic one by Fuller's son: Daniel P. Fuller, *Give the Winds a Mighty Voice: The Story of Charles E. Fuller* (Waco, Tex.: Word, 1972).

13. A collection of these letters was published: Mrs. Charles E. Fuller, *Heavenly Sunshine: Letters to the "Old-Fashioned Revival Hour"* (Westwood, N.J.: Fleming H. Revell, 1956).

14. The standard study of Fosdick is Robert Moats Miller, *Harry Emerson Fosdick: Preacher, Pastor, Prophet* (New York: Oxford University Press, 1985). A brief analytical appraisal is found in R. Scott Appleby, "Harry Emerson Fosdick," in *Twentieth-Century Shapers of American Popular Religion,* pp. 141–48.

15. Of the several collections of sermons Harry Emerson Fosdick published, most of his representative themes are found in *The Hope of the World: Twenty-five Sermons on Christianity Today* (New York: Harper and Bros., 1933). Also see Richard H. Potter, "Popular Religion of the 1930s as Reflected in the Best Sellers of Harry Emerson Fosdick," *Journal of Popular Culture* 3 (1970): 712–28.

16. Appleby, p. 146.

17. Marty, p. 273. On Coughlin, see especially Charles J. Tull, *Father Coughlin and the New Deal* (Syracuse, N.Y.: Syracuse University Press, 1965); and Louis B. Ward, *Father Charles E. Coughlin: An Authorized Biography* (Detroit: Tower Publications, 1933). A fascinating contemporary account of Coughlin's popularity is "Father Coughlin (pronounced Kawglin)," *Fortune* 9:2 (February 1934): 34–39, 110, 112.

18. See Marshall W. Fishwick, "Father Coughlin Time: The Radio and Redemption," *Journal of Popular Culture* 22:2 (Fall 1988): 33–47; and Wilfred Parsons, "Father Coughlin and Social Justice," *America* 3:6 (18 May 1935): 129–31.

19. Quoted in Marty, p. 276.

20. The first U.S. edition appeared as *Praemonitus Praemunitus. The Protocols of the Wise Men of Zion* (New York: Beckwith, 1920).

21. See especially Alfred J. Ede, *The Lay Crusade for a Christian America: A Study of the American Federation of Catholic Societies, 1900–1919* (New York: Garland, 1988).

22. Fayette Breaux Veverka, *"For God and Country": Catholic Schooling in the 1920s* (New York: Garland, 1988), treats these issues in depth.

23. Williams, p. 76.

24. The most complete study, focusing on editorials that appeared in the periodical, is Martin J. Bredeck, S. J., *Imperfect Apostles: The Commonweal and the*

American Catholic Laity, 1924–1976 (New York: Garland, 1988). But also see Rodger Van Allen, *The Commonweal and American Catholicism: The Magazine, the Movement, the Meaning* (Philadelphia: Fortress, 1974). For a much briefer analysis, see Shelley Baranowski, "*The Commonweal,*" in *Religious Periodicals of the United States: Academic and Scholarly,* edited by Charles H. Lippy (Westport, Conn.: Greenwood, 1986), pp. 153–58.

25. James M. Gillis, "Out of the Shadows into the Light," *Catholic World* 123 (August 1926): 691, as quoted in Marty, p. 146.

26. Marty, p. 146.

27. Michael Williams, long-time editor of the *Commonweal,* collected statements representative of the range of Protestant attacks on Smith because of his Catholic affiliation in *The Shadow of the Pope* (New York: Whittlesey House, 1932).

28. Alfred E. Smith, "Catholic and Patriot: Governor Smith Replies," *Atlantic Monthly* 139 (May 1927): 721–28. The essay was a response to a hostile piece by Charles C. Marshall that had appeared in the previous issue: Charles C. Marshall, "An Open Letter to the Honorable Alfred E. Smith," *Atlantic Monthly* 39 (April 1927): 540–49.

29. An organization bearing the same name flourished briefly during Reconstruction, but the twentieth-century manifestation has no direct connection to that earlier incarnation.

30. Among earlier studies of the Klan that highlight the religious element are Stanley Frost, *The Challenge of the Klan* (Indianapolis: Bobbs-Merrill, 1923); and John Moffatt Mecklin, *The Ku Klux Klan: A Study of the American Mind* (New York: Harcourt and Brace, 1924). Marty, pp. 88–102, discusses the spirituality of the Klan.

31. The only comprehensive study of McPherson is Daniel M. Epstein, *Sister Aimee: The Life of Aimee Semple McPherson* (San Diego: Harcourt, Brace, 1993). Three short pieces offer a helpful overview of McPherson: William G. McLoughlin, "Aimee Semple McPherson: 'Your Sister in the King's Glad Service,' " *Journal of Popular Culture* 1 (Winter 1967): 193–217; the entry on McPherson also by McLoughlin in *Notable American Women: A Biographical Dictionary* (Cambridge, Mass.: Harvard University Press, 1971), 2:477–80; and L. DeAne Lagerquist, "Aimee Semple McPherson," in *Twentieth-Century Shapers of American Popular Religion,* pp. 263–70. Although Kuhlman was the subject of countless newspaper stories and articles in magazines including *MS, Coronet, People,* and *Redbook,* there is even less secondary scholarly literature about her than about McPherson. But see James Morris, *The Preachers* (New York: St. Martin's, 1973), pp. 235–52; and Deborah Vansau McCauley, "Kathryn Kuhlman," in *Twentieth-Century Shapers of American Popular Religion,* pp. 225–33. The several titles appearing under Kuhlman's name were all ghostwritten.

32. McCauley, p. 231.

33. Bruce Barton, *The Man Nobody Knows* (Indianapolis: Bobbs-Merrill, 1925).

34. Roger Burlingame, *Of Making Many Books: A Hundred Years of Reading, Writing, and Publishing* (New York: Charles Scribner's Sons, 1946), p. 141, notes that he was the editor at Scribners responsible for rejecting Barton's manuscript. For background, see especially Edrene S. Montgomery, "Bruce Barton's *The Man Nobody Knows*: A Popular Advertising Illusion," *Journal of Popular Culture* 19:3 (Winter 1985): 21–34, an article derived from her "Bruce Barton and

the Twentieth Century Menace of Unreality" (Ph.D. diss., University of Arkansas, 1984).

35. A classic example is Frederick Lewis Allen, *Only Yesterday* (New York: Blue Ribbon Books, 1931), pp. 180–81. For a cogent questioning of this interpretation, see James Ferreira, "Only Yesterday and the Two Christs of the Twenties," *South Atlantic Quarterly* 80 (1981): 77–83.

36. Gerald L. Sittser, "Bruce Barton," in *Twentieth-Century Shapers of American Popular Religion*, p. 27. See also James A. Neuchterlein, "Bruce Barton and the Business Ethos of the 1920's," *South Atlantic Quarterly* 76 (1977): 293–308; and especially Leo P. Ribuffo, "Jesus Christ as Business Statesman: Bruce Barton and the Selling of Corporate Capitalism," *American Quarterly* 33 (1981): 206–31.

37. My understanding of Barton has also benefited from Richard M. Huber, *The American Idea of Success* (New York: McGraw-Hill, 1971), pp. 196–209, and from conversations with my former colleague, Wayne Elzey.

38. D. G. Paz, "Lloyd Cassel Douglas," in *Twentieth-Century Shapers of American Popular Religion*, p. 121. There is a dearth of analytical material on Douglas. But see Carl Bode, "Lloyd Douglas: Lost Voice in the Wilderness," *American Quarterly* 2 (1950): 340–58, and four dissertations: Edward Richard Barkowsky, "The Popular Christian Novel in America, 1918–1953" (Ed.D. diss., Ball State University, 1975); Raymond Arthur Detter, "A Ministry to Millions: Lloyd C. Douglas, 1877–1951" (Ph.D. diss., University of Michigan, 1975); Mary Ann Underwood Russell, "Lloyd C. Douglas and His Larger Congregation: The Novels and a Reflection of Some Segments of the American Popular Mind of Two Decades" (Ph.D. diss., George Peabody College for Teachers, 1970); and Richard Leon Stoppe, "Lloyd C. Douglas" (Ph.D. diss., Wayne State University, 1966). There is also some perceptive discussion of Douglas, especially of *The Robe*, in Allene Phy, "Retelling the Greatest Story Ever Told: Jesus in Popular Fiction," in *The Bible and Popular Culture in America*, edited by Allene Phy, *The Bible in American Culture* 2 (Philadelphia: Fortress, 1985), pp. 42–83.

39. Lloyd C. Douglas, *Magnificent Obsession* (Chicago: Willett, Clark, and Colby, 1929); idem, *The Robe* (Boston: Houghton Mifflin, 1942).

40. Dale Carnegie, *How to Win Friends and Influence People* (New York: Simon and Schuster, 1936). On Carnegie, see Huber, pp. 226–50.

41. There is very little critical work on Hill. The only full-length study is hardly analytical, but does contain a complete bibliography of Hill's writings (pp. 119–34): Jean Karr, *Grace Livingston Hill, Her Story and Her Writings* (New York: Greenberg, 1948). There are biographical sketches in such standard reference works as *Notable American Women, 1607–1950*, vol. 2; *National Cyclopedia of American Biography*, vol. 40; *Who's Who in America, 1918–1919* (listed under Lutz, Hill's second husband's surname); and Durward Howes, ed., *American Women 1935–36* (Los Angeles: Richard Blank Pub. Co., 1935).

42. Mrs. Charles E. Cowman (Lettie Burd Cowman), *Streams in the Desert* (Los Angeles: Oriental Missionary Society, 1925). This book of devotions went through twenty editions by 1940, and in 1984 Zondervan (Grand Rapids, Mich.) published the most recent printing.

43. Alice Payne Hackett, *Seventy Years of Best Sellers, 1895–1965* (New York: R. R. Bowker, 1967), p. 18.

44. An uncritical brief history of this devotional pamphlet, containing both nar-

rative and heavy illustration, was prepared for its thirtieth anniversary: Leif Sevre, *The Story of the Upper Room* (Nashville, Tenn.: Parthenon Press, 1965). See also John Kloos, "*The Upper Room*," forthcoming in *Popular Religious Periodicals of the United States*, edited by Mark Fackler and Charles H. Lippy (Westport, Conn.: Greenwood).

45. In 1993 the *Upper Room* was still being published—in sixty-two editions in forty-one languages.

46. There are few secondary studies of Sallman's work. For its place in Christian popular devotion, see Cynthia Pearl Maus, *The Church and the Fine Arts* (New York: Harper and Bros., 1960). The most provocative analyses to date are by David Morgan: "Sallman's *Head of Christ*: The History of an Image," *Christian Century* 109 (7 October 1992): 868–70, and "Imaging Protestant Piety: The Icons of Warner Sallman," *Religion and American Culture* 3 (Winter 1993): 29–47. See also Williams, p. 142. In recognition of the tremendous influence of Sallman's work on the popular religious consciousness, Valparaiso University professor David Morgan in 1993 began a major study of the phenomenon, soliciting responses to Sallman's "Head of Christ" from ordinary Americans through advertisements placed in several religious publications.

47. Robert S. Lynd and Helen M. Lynd, *Middletown: A Study in American Culture* (New York: Harcourt and Brace, 1929); *Middletown in Transition: A Study in Cultural Conflicts* (New York: Harcourt and Brace, 1937). See also Marty, pp. 17–23.

48. Theodore Caplow et al., *All Faithful People: Change and Continuity in Middletown's Religion* (Minneapolis: University of Minnesota Press, 1983), especially pp. 91–93, 294–99.

49. St. Clair Drake and Horace R. Cayton, *Black Metropolis: A Study of Negro Life in a Northern City*, rev. ed., 2 vols. (New York: Harper and Row, 1962).

50. See James H. Cone, *The Spirituals and the Blues* (New York: Seabury, 1972); and especially Jon Michael Spencer, "A Theology for the Blues," *Journal of Black Sacred Music* 2 (Spring 1988): 1–20.

51. My understanding of Garvey has been aided by Judith Stein, *The World of Marcus Garvey: Race and Class in Modern Society* (Baton Rouge: Louisiana State University Press, 1986); and especially Randall K. Burkett, *Garveyism as a Religious Movement* (Metuchen, N.J.: Scarecrow, 1978). See also Amy Jacques-Garvey, ed., *The Philosophy and Opinions of Marcus Garvey*, 2 vols. (London: Frank Cass, 1967).

53. There is brief discussion of the controversy over peyote use in the Native American Church in Omer C. Stewart, *Peyote Religion* (Norman: University of Oklahoma Press, 1987).

54. Collier recounted his efforts in an autobiography, *From Every Zenith: A Memoir and Some Essays on Life and Thought* (Denver: Sage Books, 1963).

Chapter 8

After the War: Popular Religiosity and Cultural Currents in the Later Twentieth Century

While calls for a "return to normalcy" were popular following the close of World War I, most in the United States recognized that life after World War II could never be the same as it had been before the global conflict.[1] If 1945 brought an end to formal hostilities in Europe and the Pacific, it also ushered in what quickly became dubbed the Cold War. The specter of communism loomed everywhere, and religious folk were quick to pounce on its ideological rejection of religion and its public atheism to heighten the danger it posed. As Winston Churchill spoke of an Iron Curtain's being drawn over Eastern Europe and as American troops joined the United Nations forces to contain the spread of communism in Korea, it appeared that the mentality of war would continue to shape public consciousness and much public policy, even though peace formally prevailed. At the same time, commentators in the decade following the war spoke of a revival of religion.[2] The movement to the suburbs of a population eager to get on with life after Depression and war led to a boom in erecting religious structures, even as it left behind countless vacant buildings in the hearts of cities where a new urban poor quickly replaced those who sought happiness in suburbia. Those statistics that presumably measure religiosity—professed membership in a religious body, attendance at formal religious services, participation in personal acts of devotion, and the like—all pointed to an increased interest in religion that some hoped would match that intensified pursuit of things religious that historians attached to the Great Awakening of the 1740s. Mark Noll has captured well the spirit of excitement that prevailed among religious institutions and their leaders:

The vast surge in population—the postwar Baby Boom—created countless new families for whom attachment to church became as normal as increased personal prosperity and a move to the suburbs. Church membership and the building of new houses of worship both increased dramatically. From 1945 to 1949, Southern Baptists grew by nearly 300,000 members; Catholics baptized something on the order of 1,000,000 infants a year; and Methodists reported growing more rapidly in the four years after the war than in any period since the mid-1920s. By 1950 Protestant and Jewish seminaries were enrolling twice their prewar numbers, and Catholic institutions also experienced substantial increases.[3]

Even the religious divisions that had once separated Americans seemed muted; the formation in 1950 of that ecumenical Protestant body, the National Council of Churches, from the former Federal Council of Churches symbolized the diminished importance once attached to denominations and organized religious traditions. Among students of American culture, a popular representation of this postwar dimension of the nation's religious life is President Dwight D. Eisenhower, the first president to include a prayer, one of his own composition, at his inauguration in 1953. Eisenhower's remark that the U.S. "government makes no sense unless it is founded on deeply felt religious faith—and I don't care what it is," signified the general religiousness that seemed to sweep the nation.[4] Just a decade after the war ended, sociologist Will Herberg published what has since become an academic classic. Entitled *Protestant, Catholic, Jew*, Herberg's study forcefully argued that the three major faith families had for all practical purposes become functionally equivalent in American life.[5] What mattered in social terms was not with which of these three broad traditions one identified, but merely that one had a religious label. Herberg's point in part was that the sharp distinctions that had once prevailed had faded as Americans sought a common ground for a national identity. He went on to argue that this common identity fostered a deeper commitment to an American way of life predicated on materialism and consumerism than it did to a vital religiosity.

Herberg's hypothesis has had an enduring impact on the analysis of American religion. Numerous scholars have advanced the argument for a common religious base for American life, some in terms of a "civil religion" (Robert Bellah) and others in terms of a "religion of the Republic" (Sidney Mead).[6] Many have criticized Herberg for implicitly making the white middle class the norm for generalizations about what was even then a much more complex culture. Yet Herberg's appraisal is suggestive, for despite the seeming boom that religious institutions enjoyed in the first decade or so after World War II, formal traditions had deemphasized their distinctiveness in order to appeal to a broader spectrum of the population. In so doing, as Herberg claimed, groups identified with the longstanding major religious families had become functionally equivalent. But we do not have to conclude, as Herberg did, that an erosion of religiosity followed. Rather, religiosity simply became more firmly entrenched in the private sphere where unstructured, unorganized popular piety had long flourished.

One way to see this public-private division comes in what many have touted as a vibrant symbol of the postwar surge of piety, the evangelical revivalism associated with Billy Graham (b. 1918).[7] Graham emerged as a major player in evangelical circles following the publicity given to his revival crusade in Los Angeles in 1949 and the crowds that flocked to major crusades over the next decade, especially those in London (1954) and New York City (1957). In one sense, Graham's message over the years stands firmly within the evangelical heritage that stretches back in the American experience at least to Jonathan Edwards and the revivalists of the eighteenth century. From the start, Graham constructed a world in which evil is prominent and prevalent, lurking everywhere to tempt humanity. In the early years, Graham repeatedly pointed to such phenomena as communism and juvenile delinquency as evidence of the pervasiveness of the supernatural forces of evil in human life. At the same time, Graham offered a way out through what he called a "decision for Christ," a commitment to the Christian way advanced by evangelical Protestantism. Every preaching service closed with an invitation for those who wished to make such a commitment to come forward and then spend time in prayer and consultation with a personal counselor. As always in the evangelical style, the personal nature of such a commitment came to the fore; the decision was first and foremost an individual one.

Several other features of Graham's ministry merit attention. In order to avoid some of the popular criticism of revivalists over use of funds, Graham formed the Billy Graham Evangelistic Association (BGEA) in 1950 to oversee all the business and organizational arrangements of his growing enterprise. A basic principle in planning a crusade was to garner widespread support from clergy and churches across denominational lines, often including endorsement not only from Protestants but also from Roman Catholics. BGEA quickly found itself overseeing the production and distribution of a wide range of auxiliary materials, ranging from a weekly radio broadcast (and for a time a television program) to Bible study programs and *Decision* magazine mailed to converts, inquirers, and supporters. Subsidiary groups developed religious films and a host of other goods and services to promote Graham's gospel message. In 1955 Graham launched a daily newspaper column, "My Answer," that offered succinct advice and spiritual counsel in response to readers' questions.[8] Graham's willingness to draw on whatever means advancing communications technology provided to carry his message set him apart from those wary of using new media to advance the gospel.

Admirers have praised Graham for his untiring commitment to evangelism and the benefits his crusades brought to the moral and religious tone of host communities. Criticism came from those even more conservative who condemned Graham's willingness to cooperate with persons of many religious affiliations and from those more liberal who regarded his message as simplistic and its results as short-lived. Both adulation and reproach often failed to recognize that Graham and his enterprise did much to sustain popular religiosity. By minimizing denominational distinctions and emphasizing the intensely personal nature of religious commitment, Graham's approach strengthened the individualistic and very private dimension of popular religiosity. By using media that took his message into the home, whether in the form of printed material mailed to individuals, radio and television broadcasts, or even the column in the daily newspaper, Graham further enhanced the understanding of vital religiosity as essentially a personal, private, individual matter. The heart of Graham's message, the ongoing struggle between the forces of good and evil, meshed well with that lively sense of the supernatural endemic to popular religiosity. In this vein, the decision for Christ became an entree to divine power on which one could draw in a personal struggle against Satan, the very personification of evil. While many are intrigued by estimating how many millions might have heard Graham preach and how many may have responded to his invitation to make a decision for Christ, the numbers matter less than the style of personal religiosity implicit in the entire Graham enterprise. Nor does it matter whether the format of a crusade meeting follows a fixed pattern so that the response to the calls for a personal decision for Christ are less spontaneous than they seem.[9] What matters is that the crusade grants public plausibility to what is essentially an intensely personal and private religious experience, the springboard of all popular religiosity.

By his public image and his association with world leaders, Graham granted evangelicalism a renewed plausibility. One cannot overestimate his importance in what by the 1970s and later became called the "age of the evangelical."[10] By 1976 presidential candidate Jimmy Carter actively wooed the evangelical vote through his public affirmation of personal religious faith and his willingness to talk of having been "born again." Four years later, when the Carter administration had not acted on the political agenda advanced by evangelical politicio-religious leaders like Jerry Falwell and Pat Robertson, evangelicals deserted Carter and swarmed to support his opponent, Ronald Reagan.[11] Yet in the political dynamics of public evangelicalism, one can discern some of the recurring elements of popular religiosity. Perhaps two most obvious are seeing the world as the battleground between good and evil, with political choices supporting one or the other, and regarding an evangelical America as having a divine, millennial destiny. For example, abortion is wrong and therefore aligned with the forces of evil; the "pro-life" position is right and therefore aligned with the forces of good. The same construction applies to the public debates from the 1960s on the humanistic cast of public education, gay rights, women's rights, family values, and a host of other public policy issues.[12] The larger implication was that when American public policy endorsed only positions thought reflective of the powers of good, the nation itself would recapture its unique divine destiny. On an individual basis, being able to say one had undergone a "born again" experience became a badge of public acceptability, although precisely how that experience was defined remained as private and personal as it had been in the Great Awakening of the eighteenth century. Yet the evangelicalism stemming from the Graham revivals functioned as had evangelicalism all along; it consigned the ultimate religious experience to the private sphere of personal life, but judged its legitimacy by espousal of certain modes of public behavior.

Graham was not alone in recognizing the potential of television in reaching ordinary Americans with a religious message. Roman Catholic Fulton J. Sheen (1895–1979), who had begun the "Catholic Hour" on NBC radio in 1930, made an extraordinarily successful transition to television in 1952 with his program, "Life Is Worth Living."[13] The program aired on ABC from 1955 to 1957 and was followed from 1961 to 1968 by "The Bishop Sheen Program." A philosophy professor and scholar as well as a church bureaucrat, Sheen possessed the personality and style suited to the early years of television. While his clerical garb endowed him with a sense of authority, his quiet but persuasive voice and his ability to communicate in terms that made sense to ordinary people made his message believable to the estimated twenty million or more Americans who regularly watched his program. At the same time, he wrote more than fifty books, ranging from weighty philosophical tomes to expositions of Roman Catholic doctrine, from theological and devotional works to practical advice for a mass audience on how to appropriate religious faith in daily life. Careful examination of the content of Sheen's program and of many of his books that treat popular rather than doctrinal or philosophical issues reveals little in them that is explicitly Catholic. Sheen did not intend to restrict his audience to those who were part of institutional Roman Catholicism. While he did offer analysis of current issues and events, especially of communism and the malaise it brought to American society, many of his programs dealt with much broader and more basic religious issues that could not be confined to a single religious tradition, issues such as how belief in a supernatural God was basic to human happiness, how vital religious faith would ensure inner triumph over adversity, or how ethical behavior would bring rewards (although not necessarily in a material sense). In dealing with such issues and in minimizing explicitly Catholic content, Sheen transformed both "Life Is Worth Living" and "The Bishop Sheen Program" into vehicles for advancing a highly individualized, very private religiosity. One could follow both the Baptist Graham and the Catholic Sheen, absorb ideas and inspiration from both, combine them together, and fashion that personalized sense of the supernatural that is integral to popular religiosity. And with the increasing use of the media, one did not have to leave the confines of one's home or be part of an explicitly religious group to have this exposure.

Others who have followed Sheen and Graham in capitalizing on advances in communications technology have effected a minor revolution in American religion, helping create what Richard Quebedeaux has called the "rise of personality cults in American Christianity."[14] Robert Schuller, Jerry Falwell, Pat Robertson, Jimmy Swaggart, Norman Vincent Peale, Oral Roberts, Rex Humbard, Jim and Tammy Bakker—the list of those whose names are well known in millions of American households because of their deft use of various media is seemingly endless. By the 1980s students of this phenomenon would be speaking of "televangelism" or the "electronic church" as if it were an entity in its own right, and the studies of who watched which religious television programs and whether viewing religious television was a substitute for active involvement in an organized religious body would multiply.[15] Although the entertainment dimension and appeals for financial support of such programs have increased considerably since Fulton Sheen launched "Life Is Worth Living," religious television has become one of the major buttresses of popular religiosity in late twentieth-century America. As was the case with Sheen, few if any of the religious broadcasters trumpet their denominational affiliations; it seems likely that most who watch religious programming do not know or even care about the connections televangelists might have with formal religious institutions. What does matter is that they all proclaim a message of a God who cares for individuals and their problems. With only minor variation, all proffer a view of the world where the powers of evil are very real and intent on thwarting human happiness. In other words, all support that inchoate understanding basic to popular religiosity of a world where forces of good and evil are constantly engaged in combat for control of human life. All also present exuberant testimonies to the happiness and joy in living that comes from placing ultimate trust in the beneficent power of God who can bring healing of illness and physical ailments as well as healing of psychological unsettledness that might result from divorce or other personal trauma. A simple faith becomes a panacea that brings very specific results and grants individuals a sense that they can muster the power to control their own destiny.

Perhaps this sense of gaining access to a realm of power is most obvious in the television ministry and writings of Robert Schuller (b. 1926). The title of Schuller's weekly program, "The Hour of Power," highlights this emphasis on control over personal destiny. Schuller's message, repeated with only slight change from one sermon to the next, is that through trust in one's self and in God, one can achieve success, happiness, personal fulfillment, and victory over all the forces that would keep life from being what the individual wants it to be. As Schuller put it in the title of one of his numerous books: *You Can Become the Person You Want to Be*.[16] To achieve what Schuller promises, one need not have any formal affiliation with a religious body; the fine points of doctrine and belief associated with denominations are almost encumbrances impeding success. Rather, religion is custom-tailored for the individual.

Schuller's approach builds on the "positive thinking" advanced by Norman Vincent Peale (1898–1993), another voice of popular religiosity who, like Schuller, was affiliated with the Reformed Church in America.[17] Peale, however, was more well known for reaching a mass audience through the printed word than through broadcast media, although he began "The Art of Living" radio program in 1933 and continued it over four decades and for a time had two syndicated television programs, "What's Your Trouble" and "Positive Thinking with Norman Vincent Peale."[18] Peale became a household name in the United States following the publication of his bestselling *The Power of Positive Thinking* in 1952.[19] Other books had preceded that classic, and many more were to follow before Peale went into semiretirement in the mid-1980s. Yet Peale probably reached more people through his monthly inspirational journal *Guideposts*, which had a circulation in excess of three million in the early 1990s. Peale's "positive thinking," while little more than an update of prominent features of New Thought and mind-cure as well as the approach advanced by Russell Conwell and Ralph Waldo Trine half a century earlier, struck a particularly responsive chord in a nation adjusting to the changes in society and culture that swept postwar America.[20] To the millions who felt psychologically "homeless" in the American society that would never be the same as it had been before World War II, Peale proclaimed that self-confidence and trust in God would enable each person to construct a world, a home, where the individual would be in control and where all would promote human happiness.[21] The formula for Peale's positive thinking was a three-step process of mental control: "prayerize," "picturize," then "actualize." In other words, one called on sacred power, created a mental image of how one wanted a situation to develop or work out, and then took appropriate steps, with divine help, to ensure that the desired result was achieved.

By the 1980s the religio-psychological message of Peale and Schuller had helped spawn an explosion of "self-help" books, some explicitly religious, others more secular.[22] Some 25,000 Christian-oriented self-help books were available to the American public by 1985.[23] From diet management and weight loss to gender identity, from family planning to a search for wholeness, guidebooks and manuals pointed Americans to an inner realm of power that would bring control, meaning, and certainty to life.[24] In some cases, self-help led to the formation of support groups, many based on the "twelve-step" principles first developed within Alcoholics Anonymous. From the perspective of established religious traditions, much self-help is ancillary to the religious enterprise, and self-help support groups are peripheral to the religious community. From the vantage of popular religiosity, however, self-help is central, for the very idea of tapping a reservoir of transcendent power latent within the self signals that inchoate, but vital sense of the supernatural central to popular religiosity. Support groups do not necessarily become substitutes for organized religious communities or competitors with them, but part of a personal network of groups and associations upon which individuals draw in creating a meaningful world for themselves.

Those like Robert Schuller, Billy Graham, and Fulton Sheen were not alone in recognizing the possibilities of the visual media explosion in the postwar years. Others turned especially to television to promote yet another strand of popular religiosity. We have already noted deliverance evangelist Kathryn Kuhlman's use of television as she expanded her ministry after the war. Mention must also be made of Oral Roberts (b. 1918), a Pentecostal Holiness faith healer who became a United Methodist in 1968, for Roberts is a key figure in the Neo-Pentecostal and charismatic renewal that spread across the American religious landscape.[25] Roberts began his career as a Pentecostal Holiness pastor, but, following a religious experience as intense as his initial call to the ministry (which had involved his being healed of tuberculosis), in 1947 he became an itinerant faith healer, launched the monthly periodical *Healing Waters*, and began a steady rise to prominence in American religious circles. He began his first television program, "Your Faith Is Power" in 1954 and two years later lent his name to a comic book series, "Oral Roberts' True Stories," which lasted until 1961. By the late 1960s Roberts was at the center of a Pentecostal empire that included a university and hospital complex in Tulsa as well as occasional prime-time television entertainment extravaganzas.

While Roberts the faith healer reaped the routine criticism of skeptics who doubted the authenticity of reported healings, Roberts the Pentecostal has consistently and unabashedly espoused his conviction that with faith in the power of the Holy Spirit, anyone can "expect a miracle." Such miracles in time extended well beyond healing of illness and other physical ailments; miracles represented the infusion of divine power into virtually any aspect of an individual's life. In more recent years, Roberts has also promoted what he calls "seed faith," a brand of religious self-help that offers ready instructions for conquering any of life's problems and for gaining control of one's life through prayer and trust in the Holy Spirit.[26] Oral Roberts's own switching of denominational affiliation demonstrates that his message is not bound to any formal religious tradition or institution, but directed at all persons, regardless of their denominational heritage. At the same time, the center of what Roberts has proclaimed is also the heart of popular religiosity. There is a reservoir of supernatural power—Roberts would call it the power of the Holy Spirit—available to assist all persons in gaining control over their lives and in defeating whatever evil forces they combat, ranging from physical illness to psychological fear. The particular manifestations of evil power are inconsequential; what is important is that total trust in the superior power of the Holy Spirit brings victory and restores control over individual destiny. The impact of Roberts does not revolve around whether purported healings can be authenticated or whether the visions that he has claimed prodded him to ask for millions of dollars in support are empirical. Rather, Roberts helped legitimate trust in supernatural power for postwar American society where the reality of forces of evil was all too apparent in public life given the specter of communism. And if an individual did claim healing, there was something concrete to evidence the superior power of the Spirit.

In traditional Pentecostal form, Oral Roberts has always spoken of both healing and other miracles of divine intervention as "gifts of the Spirit," the same biblical phrase used by those who have been more taken by other presumed manifestations of supernatural power, especially glossolalia or speaking in tongues. While in the 1950s Roberts and other healing evangelists associated with the deliverance revivals may have received more public attention, seeds of a broader Neo-Pentecostal or charismatic movement were planted that were not confined to the denominations that had emerged following the Azusa Street revivals of 1906. One sign that this fresh outburst of interest in direct experience of supernatural power would transcend, if not ignore the formal religious traditions was the formation in 1953 of the Full Gospel Business Men's Fellowship International.[27] This group, organized by Demos Shakarian, was among the first of numerous associations that have been called "parachurch" movements because they disregard traditional denominational boundaries and rely instead on the personal experiences of participants to establish a common ground. In the case of the Full Gospel Business Men's Fellowship International, most have been of a Christian persuasion, but it has mattered not whether one was a Protestant or a Roman Catholic. All that mattered is that individuals believed that the supernatural Spirit could come directly to persons and endow them with power. Shakarian intentionally sought out men who were in business and the professions, for he thought that the prevailing culture viewed intense spirituality as more feminine than masculine and less acceptable among the educated and economically successful. He hoped to shatter those perceptions with a group that would give credence to direct experience of divine power among those who privately believed in it, but had been reluctant to share their personal spirituality with others.

When Dennis Bennett, a Van Nuys, California, Episcopal priest acknowledged in 1960 that the previous year he had spoken in tongues and then when in 1967–68 similar charismatic experience came to Roman Catholics clustered at Duquesne University and the University of Notre Dame as well as at several places in Michigan, affirming direct apprehension of supernatural power became more plausible. Unlike the earlier Pentecostal movement, the later twentieth-century renewal remained denominationally diverse and tended not to lead to the formation of new denominations.[28] Like the earlier manifestation of gifts of the Spirit, the more recent expressions have built on the same premises, namely an abiding belief in the reality of supernatural power and its accessibility to ordinary men and women. Those who are able to tap into this reservoir, whether through ecstatic song, speaking in tongues, or some other means, establish a relationship with the divine in which the supernatural becomes an ally that brings triumph over demonic forces that thwart human happiness. Charismatic experience brings entry into a realm of meaning that supersedes anything empirical. Such has always been at the center of that inchoate spirituality that is popular religiosity.

In the 1950s other events had ramifications for American religion that would be felt for the rest of the century. In 1954 the U.S. Supreme Court's decision in *Brown v. Board of Education*, that providing "separate but equal" facilities based on race was unconstitutional, symbolically launched the civil rights movement that has had enduring consequences for strains of popular religiosity sustaining African Americans. In 1954 as well, the French suffered defeat in then Indo-China that ended their colonial empire on that peninsula and also saw the beginnings of U.S. military involvement in Southeast Asia that grew into full-scale war by the mid-1960s. Controversy over the wisdom of American policy divided the nation, and that division reverberated in the religious institutions even as it brought a fresh interest in various forms of Asian religiosity. Then in 1958, Pope Pius XII died, to be succeeded by the elderly John XXIII. Expected to be something of a caretaker pope because of his age, John XXIII stunned the religious world by calling for a full-scale church council to rethink and refocus the whole of the Roman Catholic tradition. The effects of Vatican II, as the council was called, continued to be felt both within Catholicism as a religious institution and in the popular religiosity shaped by Catholic sensibilities even into the last decade of the century. These three events provide a useful frame to explore currents of popular religiosity as they developed in the 1960s.[29]

The African-American churches and their clergy, most notably Martin Luther King, Jr., provided the leadership for the civil rights movement. The movement drew on the deep conviction in African-American religiosity that through faith in the power of God one could achieve both symbolic and empirical triumph over the forces of oppression. In their monumental study, *The Black Church in the African American Experience*, C. Eric Lincoln and Lawrence Mamiya argue that the historical combination of religious, political, economic, educational, and cultural functions of African-American churches prepared them to be incubators of the civil rights movement. Although expanding educational and vocational opportunities for African Americans have brought challenges to traditional institutions, Lincoln and Mamiya insist that this historical combination of functions remains central to the churches and means that religion continues to be more communal than private. To that extent, Lincoln and Mamiya see the more obvious manifestations of popular religiosity as having little impact on African Americans in the later twentieth century.[30] Yet some have recognized that strains of popular religiosity grounded in the African-American experience may have public as well as private dimensions. There may be intensive experiences of conversion with its attendant development of personal beliefs and practices, but that personal religiosity may more readily have a public focus that calls for change in the social order than other forms of popular religiosity.[31] Even in the shared experience of worship within African-American religious institutions, the sense of supernatural power so basic to popular religiosity looms large. It is there not only in the implicit theology that undergirds worship—for example, in the conviction that God's power will ultimately reverse the injustice of society.[32] But, as William Turner has noted, the style of African-American preaching, with its rhythm and cadence reflecting both the power of God and the force of life that has African roots, is also a kratophany or manifestation of power.[33] Others have called attention to the increase in the number of African Americans, especially in urban areas, who have no formal affiliation with a religious institution and concluded that the same forces that propel privatization elsewhere are operative among African Americans.[34]

The massive changes wrought by the civil rights movement have had an impact on the religious consciousness of African Americans and thus on popular religiosity. The civil rights movement, for example, gave impetus to the development of a distinctive "black theology" that sought to interpret the Christian message from an African-American perspective. Whether in the more radical claims of Albert Cleage (b. 1911) that Jesus was black, since only a black Messiah had relevance for African Americans, or in the more systematic approach of James Cone (b. 1938) that found a model for liberation for all humanity that paralleled the triumph of Christ in the African-American struggle to overcome oppression rooted in slavery, discrimination, and racism, black theology emerged from the lived experience of people.[35] Not bound to particular denominations with which African Americans are affiliated, black theology represents a signal effort to articulate the ongoing belief nurtured by African-American popular religiosity that supernatural power is real and that it has practical consequences for those who appropriate it, in this case in the victory over the oppression of racism. What remains to be seen, though, is the degree to which the formal theological constructs of thinkers like Cone have had a direct influence on the thinking of ordinary men and women who are African American. Lincoln and Mamiya found that nearly two-thirds of the urban African-American clergy they surveyed believed black liberation theology had not influenced their own perspective.[36] One assumes that the percentage of those who are not religious professionals would be even lower. Yet such should not minimize the import of black theology as a form of religious thought emerging more from actual human experience than from abstract musings.

At the same time that the civil rights movement propelled African Americans to become more conscious of their ethnic heritage, other voices emerged that condemned black identification with Christianity precisely because it was the religion of the oppressor. For some, Nation of Islam, whose most conspicuous voice in the early 1960s was Malcolm X, offered an alternative.[37] Adapting tenets of Islam, perceived to be a more authentically African religion than Christianity, the Black Muslims called for separation from the oppressive white culture and rejection of all that was associated with it. While the assassination of Malcolm X in 1965 and the more general apprehension of many forms of black radicalism lowered the public profile for the Nation of Islam, the 1992 release of the film version of *The Autobiography of Malcolm X*, directed by Spike Lee, led to a renewed popular interest in both Malcolm and the Black Muslims. For many, especially younger African-American men and women, wearing attire emblazoned with an "X" became a badge of pride. Many more appropriated some of the ideals of Malcolm X that were based on Islam and fused them with their own personal beliefs to fashion a religious worldview that enabled them to deal with the history of continuing oppression and to be assured of ultimate victory. The result is in part that syncretism that has always shaped currents of popular religiosity.

For others, syncretism involved incorporation of African ways into their personal religiosity. Perhaps the most obvious example is the growing celebration of *Kwanzaa*, based on the African festival of the harvest of the first crops.[38] Introduced to the United States in 1966 by M. Ron Karenga, *Kwanzaa* devotes a day to highlighting each of the seven dimensions of African-American culture that Karenga promoted: unity, self-determination, collective work and responsibility, cooperative economics, purpose, creativity, and faith. Home and community rituals, many grounded in African practice, mark the daily observances that begin on 26 December. It is no coincidence that this celebration coincides with the larger cultural celebration of Christmas, in its origins a major Christian festival, and to some extent represents an African-American alternative to Christmas. Yet thousands of African Americans readily celebrate both Christmas and *Kwanzaa*, fusing dimensions of Christian affirmation with that which is perceived to be distinctively African. In doing so, they reinforce their own private religious worldviews and exemplify the pervasive presence of popular religiosity.

Yet another example of the syncretism basic to popular religiosity that has gained increased currency among African Americans and Hispanic Americans is found in *santeria*.[39] With its name denoting "the way of the saints," *santeria* has its origins in Cuba and other Caribbean areas where

African slaves in the nineteenth century blended together aspects of Roman Catholic spirituality with features of their indigenous African (primarily Yoruba) religious sensibility. The world of the Yoruba spirits, the *orishas*, was easily fused onto the world of the Catholic saints to create a rich realm of the supernatural whose powers could be tapped not only through the rites of the church but even more efficaciously for those properly initiated through the sacrifices, divination, herbalism, and festive dance that retained distinctive African elements. Becoming part of the American religious scene largely through the emigration of Cubans following Castro's rise to power in 1959, for many years *santeria* remained little known outside the circles of Cuban and Puerto Rican communities in the New York metropolitan area and in Florida. On the one hand, practitioners recognized that the larger culture would both condemn and fear some of the rituals basic to *santeria*, especially those involving animal sacrifice. Court cases in the 1980s that sought to outlaw such rituals proved that concern correct. As well, as with many tribal traditions, oral transmission has remained the main vehicle for introducing potential initiates to the realm of power that is *santeria*, making mastery of the world of *santeria* a time-consuming challenge for those who wish full access to its supernatural realm. As shifting immigration patterns brought more persons to the United States from Cuba and other Caribbean areas and as African Americans recognized in *santeria* a religious expression with clear African antecedents, interest in *santeria* likewise increased. By the 1990s thousands of Americans drew at least on aspects of *santeria* in constructing their private religious worlds, even if the number of those fully initiated into its mysteries remained smaller. What has made *santeria* plausible is exactly what has made virtually every expression of popular religious plausible: it offers adherents direct access to a realm of supernatural power in which one can call on spiritual forces to work actively in the empirical sphere on behalf of the faithful. Many who retain some connections with formal religious traditions, both Protestant and Roman Catholic, from time to time consult *santeria* priests, priestesses, and diviners; they participate in cleansing rituals to remove negative influences from their lives; they find the herbal lore helpful in dealing with certain disorders. In other words, they draw on many sources to fashion a way of understanding the world that makes sense to their own experience and grants a sense of control over their destinies.

If the civil rights movement serves as a symbolic marker for looking at various currents of popular religiosity especially among African Americans, the Second Vatican Council (1962–65) provides a similar entree into several strands of popular religiosity shaped by Roman Catholic sensibilities. We cannot detail the transformation that has come to Roman Catholicism worldwide as a result of Vatican II; mention of a few shifts, however, will demonstrate the depth of change that has come to Roman Catholicism as a formal religious tradition. For centuries formal Catholic piety had centered on the mystery of the Mass celebrated by priests who uttered sacred words in a strange language (Latin) while facing the high altar with their backs to the people. After Vatican II, that sacred world collapsed as priests faced the people and spoke in the vernacular, robbing the rite of much of its mystique. As public confession replaced private conversation with priests in the darkness of the confessional booth, as refraining from eating meat on Friday became an optional act of devotion encouraged primarily during Lent, and as more and more of the faithful questioned church teachings on birth control, abortion, and even the value of a celibate priesthood, the foundations of the once-secure world of institutional Catholicism seemed to crumble.[40] The centrality of sacraments and the authority of priests (and by extension the authority of the church itself over all that was sacred) had set institutional Catholicism apart. Now all was up for grabs; some feared the erosion of the Catholic world and the religiosity it once inspired.[41]

Some trends at first glance seem to suggest a degree of erosion. Priests, nuns, and other religious abandoned the cloistered life in unprecedented numbers, their ranks not replenished by a new generation called to religious vocations. Enrollment in parochial schools plummeted in many areas. Polls indicated that despite the reassertion of the traditional taboo regarding use of artificial means of birth control in the 1968 papal encyclical *Humanae vitae*, American Catholics availed themselves of contraceptives in approximately the same proportion as the general population. Attendance at Mass slipped such that Catholic figures approached those of Protestant bodies, although remaining much higher than in most other nations. More and more, persons who regarded themselves as Catholics were refusing to allow the institutional church to define for them what being a Catholic entailed. From the perspective of popular religiosity, however, the purported signs of erosion take on a different character. In part what Vatican II unleashed was not so much a downward spiral in Catholic practice, identity, or even loyalty, but an increased turning inward on the part of those who call themselves Catholic, an increased movement of vital religiosity into the private sphere of popular religion and a corresponding decrease in the import of the public sphere of organized, institutional religion.

Millions of American Catholics have retained a lively sense of the miraculous and the supernatural. How else can one account for the tremendous intrigue with the Shroud of Turin, reportedly the shroud in which the body of Jesus was wrapped after the crucifixion? By the 1970s, when the presumed "crisis" of Catholicism was mushrooming, popular interest in authenticating the shroud was likewise growing apace, leading to the formation in 1978 of the Shroud of Turin Research Project, involving more than thirty American scientists and engineers.[42] If somehow contemporary science could prove that this cloth was indeed the one that covered Christ's body, the sense of the supernatural, of the miraculous, would remain viable. Individuals still claim to see the face of Jesus or the Virgin in billboard designs, natural phenomena, and visions, often to the consternation of the official hierarchy. In ethnic communities around the nation, there remain signs of a vibrant popular religiosity in countless shrines erected in the yards of private homes. As with earlier ethnic expressions of religiosity, the shrines again call attention to the means of access to realm of the sacred, for through patron saints and the Blessed Virgin, in whose honor most shrines are erected, supernatural power comes to the assistance of those who believe. If such shrines were once identified with immigrant communities from Southern and Eastern Europe, they continue among newer immigrant groups. In some areas, they clearly represent the syncretism and privatized piety basic to popular religiosity, for as James Curtis has shown, in the Miami area many of the yard shrines erected by Cuban Americans in honor of Catholic saints and Our Lady of Charity have been built by those who also practice *santeria*.[43]

Perhaps the most judicious judgment is that of Fr. Andrew Greeley. In *The Catholic Myth*, Greeley argued that although challenges have come to the authority structures of formal Catholicism in the years since Vatican II, they cannot all be traced directly to the council itself.[44] Instead, the challenges may be a response to an institutional inertia common to all formal traditions with histories as long as that of the Catholic Church. Greeley also points out that many Catholics who have distanced themselves from the church as an organization still regard and identify themselves as Catholic. Greeley suggested that such folk like the "feeling" of being Catholic. It is precisely this dimension of feeling that draws us into the realm of popular religiosity where formal doctrine and structures of institutional authority make little difference. What does matter is what people feel and whether that feeling gives people a means of making sense out of their experience, of endowing their lives with a layer of meaning.

When Vatican II drew to a close in 1965, discontent was mounting in the United States over governmental policies and military involvement in Southeast Asia. The Vietnam War, as the military action was dubbed although Congress never passed a formal declaration of war, pitted those who feared a communist onslaught should Vietnam fall against those who seriously doubted whether intruding in the domestic affairs of the Vietnamese people was in the nation's interest. American religious institutions found themselves caught up in the turmoil, like the nation divided over whether patriotic loyalty demanded unquestioning support of official policy or prophetic criticism of injustice. For some, debates over the war represented a shift of energy from the civil rights movement that had drawn so much religious support, but had also caused dissent within religious institutions. For a people barely accustomed to seeing clergy participating in interracial marches and protests against discrimination, the sight of priests and nuns ignoring warnings from their religious superiors, sabotaging draft board files, and condemning governmental policies betokened the larger erosion of authority throughout the culture. Those who opposed U.S. policy in Vietnam on the basis of their personal religious views often did so from the vantage of a popular religiosity rather than the doctrine of the formal traditions; it was their inner experience of the sacred that propelled them to act, not dogma.

The Vietnam episode had deeper ramifications for many currents of popular religiosity. For hundreds of thousands of Americans military service brought a sustained exposure to Asian cultures and ways of thinking; thousands returned home with Asian spouses who brought with them a sense of the integrity of their own cultures and ways of being religious. At the same time, emissaries of Asian gurus and religious bodies such as the Divine Light Mission of the Guru Maharaji or the International Society for Krishna Consciousness (often called simply the Hare Krishnas) traveled among the nation's cities and campuses, calling hearers to an alternative spirituality, one rooted in the wisdom of the East rather than in the presumably spiritually bankrupt religious institutions of the West. To many, the Asian alternatives seemed purer than American religious institutions that now were perceived as hopelessly intertwined with a decadent, unjust culture and political order. Little matter that on their home turf, the Asian movements faced similar dilemmas; in the American context they came across as a fresh approach to the supernatural.

As some of these newer Asian-based movements coalesced and organized followers into formal groups, they technically cease to be manifestations of popular religiosity since such defies structure and organization. But forms of Asian spirituality had a wider impact. For example, basic to much formal Asian religious practice is the discipline of meditation in which the individual works diligently to control the body through assuming certain postures, to control breathing through patterned exercises, and to control thought through concentration on specific sounds or words, often taken from Sanskrit, the sacred language of the ancient Hindu religious texts. The surge of interest in Asian religiosity introduced many Americans to various forms of meditation, and in the spirit of the syncretism basic to popular religiosity, millions took up some form of meditation as a means of opening themselves to transcendent, supernatural power, even if they did not abandon other religious practices and formally join an Asian group. Perhaps the most pervasive example of this approach is Transcendental Meditation (TM) as advocated by the Maharishi Mahesh Yogi. Stripped of much of the religious trappings of Asian meditation, TM offered those who adopted its practice a sense of contentment, a release from stress, and a feeling of inner well-being—in other words, a sense of control—if one meditated on one's personal mantra for just fifteen minutes a day. Many became intrigued with TM once the Beatles and other popular entertainers took up its practice. Millions of others were drawn to some form of Asian yoga, the physical posturing that is part of meditation, as a form of physical exercise and practiced yoga even as they continued to identify themselves with any number of the established religious traditions.

The exposure of Asian religiosity reinforced much that is basic to popular religiosity. Through meditation and related practices, one had access to a realm of power, to the arena of the supernatural unencumbered by the links of a religious institution to the larger culture. Individuals were free to pick and choose aspects of Asian practice to add to whatever else they already did in their efforts to construct a world of meaning for themselves. By emphasizing inner experience, most Asian forms of religiosity buttressed the emphasis on personal, private experience fundamental to popular religiosity. For most who gained an appreciation of Asian thought and practice, it was not necessary to join a new religious movement; rather, one simply enhanced one's personal awareness of the sacred in new ways that were perceived as compatible with what one already thought and believed. In another sense, the notion that Asian religiosity offered a wisdom that was rooted in a past more ancient than that of the Western religions and had taken shape in cultures with roots far deeper than those of American culture served as a catalyst for exploration of other forms of religiosity long consigned to the periphery by the established religious institutions. A prime example, one that gained greater currency after the frenzy over things Asian had waned, is the rebirth of interest in magic and the occult. The occult revival has taken shape primarily, but not exclusively in a new concern for wicca and for a religiosity that speaks especially to women's spirituality and also in the fascination with what has been called New Age thinking.[45]

Margot Adler has argued that a sense of spiritual power found in nature lies at the heart of the neopagan revival in its many forms and that the rekindled interest in magic depends less on a specific sense of the supernatural than on an appreciation of the spiritual power that collapses the traditional distinction between the sacred and the secular.[46] Yet J. Gordon Melton is quick to affirm that the neopagan resurgence shares much with the older occult traditions that flourished in the United States as early as the days of European colonial settlement.[47] Critics, of course, have attributed the fascination with the occult to a rejection of the rationalistic base of modern society. Others, like some in times past, have seen the demonic lurking behind all such phenomena, leading to near hysterical opposition in some parts of the country. But such misses the point. The contemporary intrigue with the occult draws on the same sense of the world as a realm of power that has always been part of the occult tradition. Hence, as with earlier forms of religious expression that appeared as a sharp alternative to accepted ways of being religious, they have a basic integrity.[48] Whether one looks to astrology or probes the mysteries of female fertility rituals, whether one arranges crystals and candles in the home or listens to the words of someone who claims to be a channel through whom an ancient mystic communicates eternal wisdom in the present, the occult draws one into a lively arena where supernatural power prevails. Occult and New Age thinking both offer avenues through which individuals may tap that power to give order to life, indeed to transform everyday reality into a sacred sphere.[49] The phenomenon of channeling that marks much New Age thinking is, of course, a means of providing immediate access to supernatural power, but divested of the cultural trappings of the traditional religious institutions. In a way, it is yet another version of "self-help" that has marked occult phenomena for generations and that found more socially acceptable religious manifestation in the message of those of the ilk of Norman Vincent Peale and Robert Schuller. As well, the practice of imaging or creating a mental image of whom one would like to be or of what one would like the world to be is a contemporary version of meditation and the devotional techniques of mysticism, calling on inner power to transform not only the self, but also the empirical world. All these phenomena signal an effort to return to that primal sacred power that has been domesticated and trivialized in religious traditions and institutions. In other words, all draw on the spiritual currents that sustain popular religiosity.

Popular acceptance of the reality of supernatural power may also help account for the intrigue with angels that we noted much earlier, an intrigue fostered by the appearance in 1975 of a widely received book on angels by Billy Graham.[50] Whether perceived as guardian spirits, as forces that offer immediate assistance to those who call upon their help, or as more amorphous supernatural entities, angels represent a means of access to the realm of sacred power that is always available and that requires no mediation through religious professionals or institutions. Angels symbolize those beneficent forces that work on behalf of individuals, but since the sense of the supernatural that fuels popular religiosity includes a strong sense of the power of evil, demons or evil spirits represent the malevolent counterpart of angels. Entertainment media in the 1970s and later exhibited a fascination with demons in films such as *Rosemary's Baby* and the several *Exorcist* presentations. Among ordinary men and women for whom the reality of demons is part of their worldview, the presence of demons may not be as dramatic. Yet the formal religious traditions and occult specialists alike have developed rituals to exorcise demons, rites designed to remove their influence and restore control over life to the supernatural powers of good.[51] Receptiveness to the power of angels or of demons is another form of ecstatic experience, in its operation akin to possession by the Spirit that is part of much Pentecostal experience.

Like earlier manifestations of the occult, the current wave of interest is highly syncretistic. That is, individuals may engage in some occult practices, but combine them with more traditional religious approaches or with a variety of approaches in order to construct a personal religious worldview. This process, along with the sense of the sacred that sustains the occult, take us into the arena of popular religiosity. Even where occult phenomena have taken on the rudiments of organization in, for example, covens of those exploring wicca or circles of women who execute contemporary forms of ancient fertility rituals, the individual and the individual's access to spiritual power remain central. In one of the more institutionalized expressions of the more metaphysical manifestations of this so-called new religiosity, the Spiritual Frontiers Fellowship founded in Evanston, Illinois, in 1956, the aim is for the individual to develop a personal, customized belief system through increased awareness of the inner divine self.[52] Indeed, so central is the individual dimension of the contemporary manifestation of the occult that one scholar, Robert Ellwood, has expressed concern that it could never provide any enduring base for social cohesion.[53] But it is precisely this highly individualized quality in the occult revival that links it to popular religiosity. It should also be no surprise that the current flourishing of the occult has sparked more intense interest among women than men, just as have earlier surges of the occult. *Time* magazine, for example, claimed that by 1991 more than one hundred thousand U.S. women were involved in some form of occult-related spirituality focused on the goddess.[54] Still trapped by religious institutions dominated by male leadership, in many cases excluded from the ranks of religious professionals on the basis of gender, and stung by formal belief systems that rely almost exclusively on male gender-specific language in discussion of the supernatural, once again women have been moving beyond the established religious traditions to probe a realm of power that addresses the specifics of women's experience and to develop rituals and ceremonies that will allow access to that realm of power.[55] Here is a clear expression of popular religiosity, for women are frequently " 'producing a do-it-yourself religion.' . . . once again women are taking control of their own spiritual lives and emotional well-being. They are creating and finding a faith of their own."[56] And they may do so while still affirming aspects of one of the more established religious traditions or while maintaining membership in a religious institution. Of such is the dynamism of popular religiosity and its syncretistic character.

Yet other strains of popular religiosity sought expression, although sometimes in a paradoxical fashion in that their affirmation involved a reassertion of group identity over the more highly individualistic focus on much popular religion. Here the most clear-cut examples come from American Jews and Native American Indians. American Jews entered the postwar era shaken by the devastation of the Holocaust, yet exuberant over the establishment of Israel as an independent nation in 1948. The staunch U.S. government support for Israel combined with the intense support of American Jews for Israel in numerous Arab-Israeli conflicts and wars gave a new focus to Jewish identity. With Jewish religiosity always centered more on private devotion and home-based ritual, promotion of religious institutions of Judaism often seemed less of a concern than support for Israel as a symbol of Jewish identity. Jacob Neusner offered a devastating critique of the perceived decline in overt Jewish religiosity when he condemned "checkbook Judaism," the financial support for Israel or other Jewish causes and agencies without a concomitant commitment to Judaism as a religion.[57] Part of the reason for this ostensible movement away from overt expression of Jewish religiousness was the rapidity of assimilation into the larger culture of the last great wave of Jewish immigrants and the apparent shedding of much "Old World" custom and habit in the process. Assimilation and diffusion throughout the population had also made a high rate of intermarriage inevitable. Given the home orientation of much Jewish religious practice, families with divided religious loyalties were less likely to adhere to the old traditions. Another was the gradual but significant decline in the birth rate among American Jews that meant Jews were accounting for an ever-smaller proportion of the population and sometimes sensing a diminished importance compared with ethnic groups such as Hispanic Americans that were on the increase.[58]

At the same time, however, countercurrents were at work that both kept alive some of the supports for a personal religiosity informed by the Jewish tradition and promoted a fresh appraisal of both private and public identification with Judaism as a religion. While continued support for Jewish religious institutions betokens a modicum of interest in the formal tradition of Judaism, other developments have helped sustain Jewish popular religiosity. For example, theater productions such as the very popular "Fiddler on the Roof" that opened on Broadway in 1964 revitalized some of the notions stemming from the fusion of folk and religious elements among Eastern European Jews in its keen sense of tradition and the prevalence of the supernatural.[59] The routines of a comedian such as Alan Sherman revived awareness of some of the beliefs and practices of popular Judaism, even in making them objects to evoke laughter. In the wake of youth interest in alternative ways of being religious that marked the late 1960s and 1970s, several urban areas saw the formation of Jewish communes whose members were dedicated to recovering the mystique and power of life lived according to Torah. Some of that interest fueled efforts among various rabbinical organizations to urge a more aggressive posture in combatting conversions to other religions or the erosion of an explicit Jewish identity. Then, too, a new generation of American Jews began to seek out their own roots, a quest that has come to many immigrant peoples over the years. Yet given the centrality of home and family to Jewish practice, measuring any increase or decrease in commitment to Judaism as a religious tradition is difficult. There are clues, however, that even in that most private arena, the home, there has been a fresh interest in recapturing the ethos of the traditional Jewish household. How else would one account for the appearance of guidebooks on how to adapt Jewish custom to contemporary times that would include material, for example, on making a dishwasher kosher?[60] Evidence also exists that among some circles of American Jews, old customs, including the use of amulets to bring reassurance of supernatural presence during crises such as sickness and childbirth, remain part of popular religious practice.[61]

What makes these developments paradoxical is that they presume a more obvious interplay of traditional religion and popular religiosity than is often the case. Without a renewal of the formal institutions and traditions of Judaism, there would be little to sustain the personal appropriation of certain practices and customs, even if they are adapted to meet personal circumstances and thus a part of the expression of an individual religiosity. The larger cultural appreciation of ethnic diversity that emerged as one of the offshoots of the civil rights movement has also provided some of the impetus. In other words, the distinctive features of Jewish religiosity, especially elusive because of their locus in the home and family, rely on the existence of the formal traditions that may not receive the same kind of interest and support even from those who are personally and privately religious.

Similar trends mark the story of certain strands of popular religiosity nurtured among Native American Indians in the last half of the twentieth century. The heightened awareness of ethnicity and pride in ethnic origins also brought a renewed interest in traditional tribal culture among many Native Americans.[62] As African Americans had struggled to overcome centuries of oppression, so Native Americans had to combat U.S. government policies that for generations had displaced them from tribal lands, consigned them to reservations where challenges to maintaining a viable tribal identity were nearly insurmountable, and restricted access to and participation in educational, economic, and cultural opportunities.[63] While well-intended representatives of many formal religious bodies operated missions of various sorts on or near the reservations, few saw traditional tribal religious practices as having the same integrity and as offering meaning to life as did the religions they promoted.[64] Where there were attempts to revitalize or adapt tribal religious ways, as in the Native American Church with its ritual use of peyote, advocates frequently encountered hostility and suspicion inside and outside tribal communities, as we have already seen.

Since for tribal cultures religion is not a component that can be isolated from other aspects of the whole, the growing interest among many tribes in seeking legal redress for lands lost to Euro-Americans and regaining access to traditional tribal lands has had profound religious implications. As Robert Michaelsen has reminded us, land itself is sacred to many Native American peoples and not a commodity to be owned or controlled by individuals.[65] By the 1970s, as courts were adjudicating many tribal claims, the U.S. Congress passed the American Indian Religious Freedom Act (1978) that was ostensibly intended to guarantee to Native Americans the same freedom of religious practice and, by implication, of religiosity that the First Amendment guaranteed to all citizens. But the legislation in the end created as many problems as it resolved. If tribes had no claim to sacred lands, how could religious practices be carried out freely? What about practices such as the Sun Dance that had previously been suppressed—not to mention the use of the hallucinogenic peyote? Could tribal shamans freely exercise their roles when they might involve practices that to outsiders might seem to endanger the welfare of participants and hence require regulation under the government's responsibility to protect the general welfare (the same reasoning used to restrict Pentecostal and Holiness groups that engage in snake handling)?[66] When it came to tribal claims that prevailing conditions made "free exercise" of religion impossible, despite the 1978 law, the courts tended to rule against Native Americans, creating an even more complicated situation. Implicit in all the legal hassles remains the Native American conviction that personal religiosity nurtured by tribal ways requires the maintenance of tribal practices, much the way that a good bit of personal religiosity among American Jews plays off the maintenance of the formal traditions of Judaism as a religious institution.

As the twentieth century entered its last decade, then, popular religiosity shaped in part by sensitivity to Native American tribal cultures witnessed some of the same vagaries as Jewish popular religiosity. The larger traditions that sustained a sense of sacred power and access to sacred power confronted obstacles to their own continued vitality. Inroads made by alternative traditions, especially by various strands of Christianity and also by the Church of Jesus Christ of Latter-day Saints, have long generated a syncretism in popular piety, as has the continuing presence of a range of internal movements, ranging from peyotism to the messianism stretching back to Handsome Lake. Sam Gill has captured the dynamics of this syncretism:

An Apache Christian community sings Christian hymns during their worship service; however, they sing in the Apache language, accompanied by music sounding more Apache than European-American . . . . Christian churches are the dominant architectural feature in most Pueblo villages. Not only are these churches attended for the celebration of Mass, but dances and other tribal religious performances may take place in them . . . . A Comanche eagle doctor in Oklahoma uses the Bible to describe her doctoring practice.[67]

Above and beneath it all remains an abiding sense of oneness with sacred land and an appreciation of the divine father in the sky and the divine mother in the earth. For individual Native Americans, a personal religiosity often fuses together remnants of tribal myth and practice, an adopted and adapted version of Christianity, and perhaps some newer alternatives that came from attempts in earlier decades to revitalize tribal integrity. Poverty may yet be rampant among Native Americans, and legislative relief that would recognize the sacred ties of tribes to the land slow in coming. But there remains a popular religiosity that draws individuals into a realm of supernatural power where empirical reality is transformed into a world of meaning.

NOTES

1. On some of the cultural transformations that resulted from World War II, see Philip Gleason, "Americans All: World War II and the Shaping of American Identity," *Review of Politics* 43 (1981): 483–518.

2. On the postwar revival of religion, see Robert T. Handy, *A Christian America: Protestant Hopes and Historical Realities*, 2d ed. (New York: Oxford University Press, 1984), pp. 186–90.

3. Mark A. Noll, *A History of Christianity in the United States and Canada* (Grand Rapids, Mich.: Eerdmans, 1992), p. 437.

4. Quoted in Will Herberg, *Protestant, Catholic, Jew: An Essay in America Religious Sociology*, rev. ed. (Garden City, N.Y.: Doubleday, 1960), p. 95, from the 23 December 1952 *New York Times*.

5. Will Herberg, *Protestant, Catholic, Jew: An Essay in American Religious Sociology* (Garden City, N.Y.: Doubleday, 1955).

6. Robert Bellah's essay, "Civil Religion in America," has been widely reprinted since it appeared in *Daedalus* in 1967. See, for example, Russell E. Richey and Donald G. Jones, eds., *American Civil Religion* (New York: Harper and Row, 1974), pp. 21–44. Mead also advanced his hypothesis about "the religion of the Republic" in a series of essays collected in Sidney E. Mead, *The Nation with the Soul of a Church* (reprinted, Macon, Ga.: Mercer University Press, 1985).

7. The most recent and best full-length study of Graham is William Martin, *A Prophet with Honor: The Billy Graham Story* (New York: Morrow, 1991). But also see Marshall Frady, *Billy Graham: A Parable of American Righteousness* (Boston: Little, Brown, 1979); and William G. McLoughlin, *Billy Graham: Revivalist in a Secular Age* (New York: Ronald Press, 1960). Erling Jorstad, *Popular Religion in America: The Evangelical Voice* (Westport, Conn.: Greenwood, 1993), sees the evangelical surge, in which he includes the renewed interest in fundamentalism, the new charismatic movement, and Neo-Pentecostalism, as encompassing virtually the whole of popular religion in the 1970s and 1980s. My understanding of popular religion is much broader. Douglas Miller, "Popular Religion of the 1950's," *Journal of Popular Culture* 9 (Summer 1975): 66–76, is a brief comparative study.

8. See Charles H. Lippy, "Billy Graham's 'My Answer': Agenda for the Faithful," *Studies in Popular Culture* 5 (1982): 27–34.

9. See Weldon T. Johnson, "The Religious Crusade: Revival or Ritual?" *American Journal of Sociology* 76 (1971): 873–90; and Ronald C. Wimberly et al., "Conversion in a Billy Graham Crusade: Spontaneous Event or Ritual Performance," *Sociological Quarterly* 16 (1975): 162–70.

10. On the larger evangelical movement, see Carol Flake, *Redemptorama: Culture, Politics, and the New Evangelicalism* (Garden City, N.Y.: Doubleday, 1984); and Grant Wacker, "Searching for Norman Rockwell: Popular Evangelicalism in Contemporary America," in *The Evangelical Tradition in America*, edited by Leonard I. Sweet (Macon, Ga.: Mercer University Press, 1984); pp. 289–315.

11. On Falwell, see J. E. Gilbert, "Ballot Salvation," *Journal of Popular Culture* 18 (Summer 1984): 1–8; Mary Murphy, "The Next Billy Graham," *Esquire* 90 (10 October 1978): 25–30; and Dinesh D'Souza, *Falwell: Before the Millennium. A Critical Biography* (Chicago: Regnery Gateway, 1984). On Robertson, see David E. Harrell, Jr., *Pat Robertson: A Personal, Political and Religious Portrait* (San Francisco: Harper and Row, 1987); and Hubert Morken, *Pat Robertson: Religion and Politics in Simple Terms* (Old Tappan, N.J.: Fleming H. Revell, 1987). On the involvement of the religious right in politics, see David G. Bromley and Anson Shupe, eds., *New Christian Politics* (Macon, Ga.: Mercer University Press, 1984); Samuel S. Hill and Dennis E. Owen, *The New Religious Political Right in America* (Nashville: Abingdon, 1982); Erling Jorstad, *Evangelicals in the White House: The Cultural Maturation of Born Again Christianity, 1960–1981* (New York: Mellen, 1981); Erling Jorstad, *The New Christian Right, 1981–1988: Prospects for the Post-Reagan Decade* (Lewiston, N.Y.: Mellen, 1987); John L. Kater, Jr., *Christians on the Right: The Moral Majority in Perspective* (New York: Seabury, 1982); Robert C. Liebman and Robert Wuthnow, *The New Christian Right: Mobilization and Legitimation* (New York: Aldine, 1983); Peggy L. Shriver, *The Bible Vote: Religion and the New Right* (New York: Pilgrim, 1981); Anson Shupe and William A. Stacey, *Born Again Politics and the Moral Majority: What Social Surveys Really Show* (New York: Mellen, 1982); and Robert Zwier, *Born-Again Politics: The New Christian Right in America* (Downers Grove, Ill.: InterVarsity, 1982).

12. See Jorstad, *Popular Religion*, pp. 51–104; and idem, *Holding Fast, Pressing On: Religion in America in the 1980s* (New York: Praeger, 1990), pp. 57–94. For the flavor of evangelicalism in the later twentieth century, see Randall H. Balmer, *Mine Eyes Have Seen the Glory: A Journey into the Evangelical Subculture in America* (New York: Oxford University Press, 1989); and Nancy Tatom Ammerman, *Bible Believers: Fundamentalists in the Modern World.* (New Brunswick, N.J.: Rutgers University Press, 1987). On the formation of independent "Christian" schools as an alternative to secular public education, see Melinda Bollar Wagner, *God's Schools: Choice and Compromise in American Society* (New Brunswick, N.J.: Rutgers University Press, 1990).

13. Given Sheen's eminence as a popular voice for American Catholicism, it is striking that there is virtually no critical literature about him, although he is likely to receive mention in works that deal with Catholic views on social issues and studies that deal with the development of the television industry. See Peter W. Williams, "Fulton J. Sheen," in *Twentieth-Century Shapers of American Popular Religion*, edited by Charles H. Lippy (Westport, Conn.: Greenwood, 1989), pp. 387–93.

14. See Richard Quebedeaux, *By What Authority? The Rise of Personality Cults in American Christianity* (New York: Harper and Row, 1982).

15. The following offers but an introduction to the burgeoning literature on televangelism: Robert Abelman and Kimberly Neuendorf, "How Religious Is Religious Television Programming?" *Journal of Communication* 35 (1985): 98–110; Ben Armstrong, *The Electric Church* (Nashville: Thomas Nelson, 1979); J. Thomas Bisset, "Religious Broadcasting: Assessing the State of the Art," *Christianity Today* 24 (12 December 1980): 28–31; Louise M. Bourgault, "The PTL Club and Protestant Viewers: An Ethnographic Study," *Journal of Communication* 35 (1985): 132–48; Judith M. Buddenbaum, "Characteristics and Media-Related Needs of the

Audience for Religious TV," *Journalism Quarterly* 58 (1981): 266–72; Jerry D. Cardwell, *Mass Media Christianity: Televangelism and the Great Commission* (Lanham, Md.: University Press of America, 1984); William F. Fore, *Television and Religion: The Shaping of Faith, Values, and Culture* (Minneapolis: Augsburg, 1987); Razelle Frankl, *Televangelism: The Marketing of Popular Religion* (Carbondale: Southern Illinois University Press, 1987); Gary D. Gaddy and David Pritchard, "When Watching Religious TV Is Like Attending Church," *Journal of Communication* 35 (1985): 123–31; Jeffrey K. Hadden and Charles E. Swann, *Prime Time Preachers: The Rising Power of Televangelism* (Reading, Mass.: Addison-Wesley, 1981); Jeffrey K. Hadden, "The Rise and Fall of American Televangelism," in *Religion in the Nineties*, edited by Wade Clark Roof, *Annals of the American Academy of Political and Social Science* 527 (Newbury Park, Calif.: Sage Periodicals, 1993), pp. 113–30; idem, "Soul Saving via Video," *Christian Century* 97 (28 May 1980): 609–13; Stewart M. Hoover, *Mass Media Religion: The Social Sources of the Electronic Church* (Newbury Park, Calif.: Sage Publications, 1988); idem, "The Religious Television Audience: A Matter of Significance, or Size?" *Review of Religious Research* 29:2 (Winter 1987): 135–51; Peter G. Horsfield, "Evangelism by Mail: Letters from the Broadcasters," *Journal of Communication* 35 (1985): 89–97; idem, *Religious Television: The American Experience* (New York: Longman, 1984); Martin E. Marty, "The Invisible Religion: A Closer Look at the Theology of the Electric Church," *Presbyterian Survey* 69 (May 1979): 13; Charles Swann, "The Electric Church," *Presbyterian Survey* 69 (May 1979): 9–12, 14–16; Sari Thomas, "The Route to Redemption and Social Class," *Journal of Communication* 35 (1985): 111–22; and Stephen W. Tweedie, "Viewing the Bible Belt," *Journal of Popular Culture* 11 (1978): 865–76.

16. Robert H. Schuller, *You Can Become the Person You Want to Be* (New York: Hawthorn Books, 1973). Parts of this book were distributed through the "Hour of Power" under the title *Become a Possibility Thinker Now*.

17. Only recently has Peale begun to receive sustained scholarly scrutiny, although his theological approach has generated much criticism. The best study is Carol V. R. George, *God's Salesman: Norman Vincent Peale and the Power of Positive Thinking* (New York: Oxford University Press, 1993). See also Richard Weiss, *The American Myth of Success: From Horatio Alger to Norman Vincent Peale* (New York and London: Basic Books, 1969), especially pp. 233–34; Thomas E. Frank, "Norman Vincent Peale," in *Twentieth-Century Shapers of American Popular Religion*, pp. 326–34; and Donald Meyer, *The Positive Thinkers: Popular Religious Psychology from Mary Baker Eddy to Norman Vincent Peale and Ronald Reagan* (Middletown, Conn.: Wesleyan University Press, 1988).

18. On Peale's preference for radio and ambivalence toward television ministry, see Frank, "Norman Vincent Peale," pp. 329–30.

19. Norman Vincent Peale, *The Power of Positive Thinking* (New York: Prentice-Hall, 1952).

20. For the overall story, see Meyer, *The Positive Thinkers*.

21. Following Peter Berger, Richard Quebedeaux in *By What Authority?* argues that the sense of psychological homelessness helps account for the appeal of the likes of Jerry Falwell and his Moral Majority movement of the 1970s and 1980s. I suggest it has broader applicability and is a useful interpretive construct also in understanding the dynamics of an earlier period.

22. See Steven Starker, *Oracle at the Supermarket: The American Preoccupation with Self-Help Books* (New Brunswick, N.J.: Transaction Books, 1989); Patricia Braus, "Selling Self Help," *American Demographics* 14 (March 1992): 48–53; Wendy Kaminer, "Saving Therapy: Exploring the Religious Self-Help Literature," *Theology Today* 48 (Fall 1991): 301–25; and Frank Riesman, "The New Self-Help Backlash," *Social Policy* 20 (Summer 1990): 422–48. Bill Katz and Linda Sternburg Katz, *Self-Help: 1400 Best Books on Personal Growth* (New York: R. R. Bowker, 1985), intentionally excludes explicitly religious titles. For those emerging from within Christianity, a valuable resource is Elise Chase, *Healing Faith: An Annotated Bibliography of Christian Self-Help Books* (Westport, Conn.: Greenwood, 1985). Roy M. Anker, "Popular Religion and Theories of Self-Help," in *Handbook of American Popular Culture*, edited by M. Thomas Inge (Westport, Conn.: Greenwood, 1980), 2:287–316, places contemporary self-help literature in historical context. In addition to Peale and Schuller, Charles L. Allen has been a perennial favorite. See, for example, his *God's Psychiatry* (Old Tappan, N.J.: Fleming H. Revell, 1953), and *Roads to Radiant Living* (Old Tappan, N.J.: Fleming H. Revell, 1968).

23. Chase, p. x. Chase bases her figures on the 1984–85 edition of *Current Christian Books*.

24. Wayne Elzey, "Popular Culture," in *Encyclopedia of the American Religious Experience*, edited by Charles H. Lippy and Peter W. Williams (New York: Scribners, 1988), 3:1727–41, mentions numerous specific titles.

25. The most balanced appraisal of Roberts is David E. Harrell, Jr., *Oral Roberts: An American Life* (Bloomington: Indiana University Press, 1985).

26. A representative example is Oral Roberts, *How To Get through Your Struggles or You Can Walk on the Stormy Waters of Your Life* (Tulsa, Okla.: Oral Roberts Evangelistic Association, 1977). Between November 1977 and September 1978, some 1,350,000 copies of this book were printed.

27. See B. Bird, "The Legacy of Demos Shakarian," *Charisma* 11 (June 1986): 20–25; idem, "FGBMFI: Facing Frustrations and the Future," *Charisma* 11 (June 1986): 25, 26, 28; Demos Shakarian, "FGBMFI Struggles toward the Future," *Charisma* 13 (March 1988): 24.

28. See Richard Quebedeaux, *The New Charismatics: The Origins, Development, and Significance of Neo-Pentecostalism* (Garden City, N.Y.: Doubleday, 1976).

29. Two helpful books look at American religion from the 1960s through the 1980s: Ronald B. Flowers, *Religion in Strange Times: The 1960s and 1970s* (Macon, Ga.: Mercer University Press, 1984); and Erling Jorstad, *Holding Fast, Pressing On: Religion in America in the 1980s*, already noted. Both occasionally touch on matters of popular religiosity, although their overall focus lies elsewhere.

30. C. Eric Lincoln and Lawrence H. Mamiya, *The Black Church in the African American Experience* (Durham, N.C.: Duke University Press, 1990), especially pp. 161–62.

31. William C. Turner Jr., "Black Evangelicalism: Theology, Politics, and Race," *Journal of Religious Thought* 45 (Winter–Spring 1989): 40–56.

32. James M. Washington, "Origins of Black Evangelicalism and the Ethical Function of Evangelical Cosmology," *Union Seminary Quarterly Review* 32 (Winter 1977): 104–16.

33. William C. Turner, "The Musicality of Black Preaching: A Phenomenology," *Journal of Black Sacred Music* 2 (Spring 1988): 21–34.

34. See, for example, Hart M. Nelsen, "Unchurched Black Americans: Patterns of Religiosity and Affiliation," *Review of Religious Research* 29:4 (June 1988): 398–412.

35. Albert Cleage, *The Black Messiah* (New York: Sheed and Ward, 1969). Among James H. Cone's many works, see especially *Black Theology and Black Power* (New York: Seabury, 1969), *A Black Theology of Liberation* (Philadelphia: Lippincott, 1970), *God of the Oppressed* (New York: Seabury, 1975), and *For My People: Black Theology and the Black Church* (Maryknoll, N.Y.: Orbis, 1984). Also helpful is Gayraud S. Wilmore and James H. Cone, eds., *Black Theology: A Documentary History, 1966–1979* (Maryknoll, N.Y.: Orbis, 1979).

36. Lincoln and Mamiya, p. 169.

37. Still helpful, but now dated, is C. Eric Lincoln, *The Black Muslims in America*, rev. ed. (Boston: Beacon, 1973).

38. Most of the literature on *Kwanzaa* is in articles appearing in newspapers and popular periodicals. See, for example, "Kwanzaa: Celebrate in Holiday Style," *Essence* 20 (1989): 50; Eric V. Copage, "The Seven Days of Kwanzaa," *New York Times* 141 (1 December 1991); Janice Simpson, "Tidings of Black Pride and Joy," *Time* 138 (23 December 1991): 81; Martha Southgate, "Merry Kwanzaa to All," *Glamour* 89 (December 1991): 120; Dee Watts-Jones, "The Harvest of Kwanzaa," *Essence* 21 (December 1990): 114.

39. The best introduction to this phenomenon is Joseph M. Murphy, *Santeria: African Spirits in America*, 2d ed. (Boston: Beacon, 1992). Conversations with Professors David Brown and Thee Smith of Emory University have enriched my understanding of *santeria*. See also David H. Brown, "Garden in the Machine: Afro-Cuban Sacred Art in Urban New Jersey and New York" (Ph.D. diss., Yale University, 1989).

40. In the 1950s during the peak of the Cold War, American Catholics whose personal piety was shaped by long-time devotional practices were among the staunchest anti-Communists. See Thomas Kselman and Steven Avella, "Marian Piety and the Cold War in the United States," *Catholic Historical Review* 72 (July 1986): 403–24.

41. The ambiguity that prevailed for many Catholics in the years following Vatican II is brilliantly evoked in Garry Wills, *Bare Ruined Choirs: Doubt, Prophecy, and Radical Religion* (Garden City, N.Y.: Doubleday, 1971).

42. See Patricia C. Click, "High Technology Meets the Spiritual: Objectivity, Popular Opinion, and the Shroud of Turin," *Journal of Popular Culture* 21:4 (1988): 13–23.

43. See, for example, James R. Curtis, "Miami's Little Havana: Yard Shrines, Cultural Religion and Landscape," *Journal of Cultural Geography* 1 (Fall 1980): 1–16; reprinted in *Rituals and Ceremonies in Popular Culture*, edited by Ray B. Browne (Bowling Green, Ohio: Bowling Green University Popular Press, 1980), 105–19.

44. Andrew M. Greeley, *The Catholic Myth: The Behavior and Beliefs of American Catholics* (New York: Scribners, 1990).

45. A helpful collection of essays treating a variety of topics in this area is James R. Lewis and J. Gordon Melton, eds., *Perspectives on the New Age* (Albany: State

University of New York Press, 1992). David Miller, *The New Polytheism: Rebirth of the Gods and Goddesses* (New York: Harper and Row, 1974), analyzes some of the same phenomena from a Jungian perspective. Older, but still useful is Edward F. Heenan, ed., *Mystery, Magic, and Miracle: Religion in a Post-Aquarian Age* (Englewood Cliffs, N.J.: Prentice-Hall, 1973). Catherine L. Albanese, "Fisher Kings and Public Places: The Old New Age in the 1990s," in *Religion in the Nineties*, pp. 131–43, sees the current interest in the occult more as part of the longstanding American involvement in "nature religion" than as part of the heritage of such nineteenth-century phenomena as Theosophy.

46. This is the basic thesis that informs her magisterial study, *Drawing Down the Moon: Witches, Druids, Goddess-Worshippers, and Other Pagans in America Today*, rev. ed. (Boston: Beacon, 1986).

47. J. Gordon Melton, "The Revival of Astrology in the United States," in *Religious Movements: Genesis, Exodus, and Numbers*, edited by Rodney Stark (New York: Paragon House, 1985), pp. 279–99.

48. An analysis that wisely insists on the theological integrity of "new religions" throughout American history is Mary Farrell Bednarowski, *New Religions and the Theological Imagination in America* (Bloomington: Indiana University Press, 1989).

49. This point is emphasized in a more narrow study: Nachman Ben-Yehuda, "The Revival of the Occult and of Science Fiction," *Journal of Popular Culture* 20: 2 (Fall 1986): 1–16.

50. Billy Graham, *Angels: God's Secret Agents* (Garden City, N.Y.: Doubleday, 1975).

51. Perhaps the most insightful analysis of the way belief in demons works in contemporary society is Felicitas D. Goodman, *How about Demons? Possession and Exorcism in the Modern World* (Bloomington: Indiana University Press, 1988).

52. See Melinda Bollar Wagner, "Metaphysics in Midwestern America," *Journal of Popular Culture* 17 (Winter 1983): 131–40, and her expanded study, *Metaphysics in Midwestern America* (Columbus: Ohio State University Press, 1983).

53. Robert S. Ellwood, "Polytheism: Establishment or Liberation Religion?" *Journal of the American Academy of Religion* 42:2 (Winter 1974): 344–49.

54. Richard N. Ostling, "When God Was a Woman: Worshipers of Mother Earth Are Part of a Goddess Resurgence," *Time* 137 (6 May 1991): 73.

55. Representative are Z. (Zsuzsana) Budapest, *The Holy Book of Women's Mysteries* (Oakland, Calif.: Wingbow, 1989); idem, *The Grandmother of Time: A Women's Book of Celebrations, Spells, and Sacred Objects for Every Month of the Year* (San Francisco: HarperSanFrancisco, 1989); idem, *Grandmother Moon* (San Francisco: HarperSanFrancisco, 1991); and Starhawk, *The Spiral Dance* (San Francisco: Harper and Row, 1979).

56. Nancy A. Hardesty, "Seeking the Great Mother: The Goddess for Today," unpublished paper presented to the South Carolina Academy of Religion, February 1993.

57. Jacob Neusner, *American Judaism: Adventure in Modernity* (1973; rev. ed., Englewood Cliffs, N.J.: Prentice-Hall, 1978). Neusner offers much the same argument in "Judaism in Contemporary America," in *Encyclopedia of the American Religious Experience*, 1:311–23.

58. A number of these issues are explored in Nathan Glazer, "Jewish Loyalties," *Wilson Quarterly* 5 (Autumn 1981): 134–45.

59. Marc Lee Raphael, "From Marjorie to Tevya: The Image of the Jews in American Popular Literature, Theatre, and Comedy, 1955–1965," *American Jewish History* 74 (September 1984): 66–72. More generally, also see Norman Friedman, "Jewish Popular Culture in Contemporary America," *Judaism* 24 (Summer 1975): 263–77.

60. See Blu Greenberg, *How to Run a Traditional Jewish Household* (New York: Simon and Schuster, 1983).

61. Marcia Reines-Josephy, "The Use of Amulets in Contemporary Jewish Society," in *Proceedings of the Ninth World Congress of Jewish Studies*, edited by Moshe H. Goshen-Gottstein and David Assaf (Jerusalem: World Union of Jewish Studies, 1986), 7:175–80.

62. See, for example, Vine Deloria, Jr., *God Is Red* (New York: Dell, 1973). Deloria has been a powerful voice in articulating the injustice government policies foisted on tribal life, including religious life. See Vine Deloria, Jr., ed., *American Indian Policy in the Twentieth Century* (Norman: University of Oklahoma Press, 1985); idem, *Behind the Trail of Broken Treaties: An Indian Declaration of Independence* (New York: Delcorte, 1974); idem, *Custer Died for Your Sins: An Indian Manifesto* (New York: Macmillan, 1969); Vine Deloria, Jr., and Clifford M. Lytle, *The Nations Within: The Past and Future of Indian Sovereignty* (New York: Pantheon Books, 1984); and Vine Deloria, Jr., and Sandra L. Cadwalader, eds., *The Aggressions of Civilization: Federal Indian Policy since the 1880s* (Philadelphia: Temple University Press, 1984).

63. For these reasons, Vine Deloria has argued in "Completing the Theological Circle: Civil Religion in America," *Religious Education* 71 (1976): 278–87, Native Americans have never been able to accept the worldview underlying the fusion of religion and patriotism that comprises civil religion.

64. On the ambivalence of attitudes toward Native American culture, see Robert S. Michaelsen, "Red Man's Religion/White Man's Religious History," *Journal of the American Academy of Religion* 51 (1983): 667–84.

65. Robert S. Michaelsen, "Sacred Land in America: What Is It? How Can It Be Protected?" *Religion* 16 (1986): 249–68.

66. Some of these matters and many others are discussed in three essays by Robert S. Michaelsen: " 'We Also Have a Religion': The Free Exercise of Religion among Native Americans," *American Indian Quarterly* 10 (Summer 1983): 111–41; "The Significance of the American Indian Religious Freedom Act of 1978," *Journal of the American Academy of Religion* 52 (1984): 93–115; and "Is the Miner's Canary Silent? Implications of the Supreme Court's Denial of American Indian Free Exercise of Religion Claims," *Journal of Law and Religion* 6 (1988): 97–114.

67. Sam D. Gill, "Native American Religions," in *Encyclopedia of the American Religious Experience*, 1:149–50.

Chapter 9

Toward the Twenty-First Century: The Interplay of Popular Culture and Popular Religiosity

Rather different changes coming to American culture in the decades since the close of World War II have had significant impact on the story of popular religiosity. As leisure time expanded for much of the populace, so, too, did opportunities to fill that time. Tourist attractions were created, including religious theme-parks. Markets for literature geared to the masses expanded to provide not only a popular press targeted toward the ordinary person but also religious, inspirational, and self-help books of the sort found in racks adjacent to supermarket check-out lines. Entertainment media, especially film and television, but also popular music, grew at an unprecedented rate and quickly became major forces in shaping the common values of late twentieth-century Americans. All of these dimensions of popular culture have had important consequences for nurturing and sustaining many strands of popular religiosity. Some have argued that in contemporary American culture, whatever integrative function religion retains is found in such manifestations of popular culture and the mass media, while the salvific dimension remains very personal and private.[1] Most concur with Martin Marty, though, in insisting that distinguishing features of American religion in the 1990s were an emphasis on personal religious experience over the corporate, the continuing relegation of religion to the private sphere (with a concomitant stress on individual autonomy over group authority), and the expectation that religion would provide meaning for personal life.[2]

Religion came to Broadway in the early 1970s quite overtly in the popular musicals "Jesus Christ Superstar," a rock opera by Andrew Lloyd Webber and Tim Rice, and "Godspell," with music and lyrics primarily by Stephen Schwartz. While religious professionals offered both praise and criticism, seeing the Jesus of "Superstar" as overly human and that of "Godspell" as too comical, their appraisals assumed that formal doctrines of the churches should be the norm against which to evaluate such popular presentations.[3] A different angle of vision comes from exploring the broader ways in which rock music affirms the inchoate values of those for whom it is a mechanism to reinforce a personal worldview. The Jesus of "Superstar," for example, is one who appears trapped in a world beyond his control, a world where defeat (crucifixion) appears the likely outcome. But there is also an affirmation of a larger power that maintains ultimate control; in the trial before Pilate, for example, Jesus notes that supernatural power so determines the course of life that humans cannot alter it.[4] A similar understanding of the world as dominated and controlled by supernatural powers has undergirded many strands of popular religiosity.

Less explicitly religious rock music has also attracted the attention of analysts, but often more for possible religious influences on particular singers and composers than for the more subtle ways lyrics and style may buttress a popularly held worldview. There is a considerable body of literature, for example, on the religious background of Elvis Presley that generally emphasizes his Pentecostal roots and fondness for gospel music, even seeing his gyrating style as a manifestation of the ecstatic experience characteristic of much Pentecostal worship.[5] The impact of southern Pentecostalism on other musicians, such as Jerry Lee Lewis and Tammy Wynette, has also been noted.[6] One analysis has found in the lyrics of songs written and sung by Bruce Springsteen an exposition of much religious doctrine; another has seen Springsteen's work mirroring Catholic values.[7] Even the eroticism associated with performers such as Prince, Madonna, Michael Jackson, and Boy George has received a religious construction in which erotic expression becomes an incarnate (bodily) manifestation of transcendence.[8] Here, too, there is a more subtle dimension that is more to the point of popular religiosity. The ambiguity of much rock music, from lyrics to performance, reflects the ambiguity that marks much human experience, perhaps especially for those who are making the transition from adolescence to adulthood. In that context, rock music may well represent a means to step outside of the quandaries that perplex ordinary life in order to gain that sense of power and control fundamental to virtually all popular religiosity. The specific lyrics and the stage machinations of individual performers matter less than the phenomenon of rock itself as a ritualized expression of how certain segments of the population understand their experience and seek to endow it with meaning.[9] As one analyst put it, rock music is "the sacralization of disorder."[10] But it is a sacralization of disorder that is a step along the way to imposing a modicum of meaning on experience, a primary function of popular religiosity.

The more recent fascination with a distinctively "Christian rock" as found, for example, in the music of Amy Grant, Sandi Patti, Andrae

Crouch, and countless others builds even more explicitly on the supposition that music itself becomes a means of gaining access to that realm of power that brings meaning out of disorder.[11] Grant, for example, has produced two albums that reached the top of the charts of best-selling records: "Age to Age" and "Straight Ahead." Especially since 1970, contemporary Christian music has been one of the strongest growth areas of the entire music industry, leading to "how to" workshops and conferences, an awards program ("Dove" awards) comparable to the Grammy awards for secular popular music, the increasing influence of the Gospel Music Association, the expansion of religious radio stations devoted to broadcasting Christian music and related programming, the emergence of a host of itinerant entertainers who work the circuit of receptive local congregations and headline programs at civic centers, and the establishment of several periodicals whose sole focus is contemporary Christian music and even Christian heavy metal music (*Contemporary Christian Music, The Cutting Edge, Heaven's Metal, Gospel Metal*, and others). An offshoot has been the development of a new popular hymnody, particularly as seen in the work of Bill and Gloria Gaither.[12] Virtually all of it centers on wonder and amazement at expressions of divine power in human life and the assurance that such power is accessible to ordinary women and men through prayer and praise. As with most manifestations of popular religion, the denominational background of the hymn writers or performers matters not; most who find support for their own personal religiosity in such music may not even be aware of that formal religious affiliation. Contemporary Christian music's vitality in sustaining popular religiosity stems in part from its presenting a message so simple that its content "may transcend denominational and theological boundaries."[13] In other words, individuals may interpret it as they see fit and incorporate its ideas into their privately held worldviews.

Analysts of popular culture have looked at other entertainment media, from cartoons to film and television, and frequently found in them deep theological and religious dimensions. Much religious scrutiny has approached these popular culture media from the vantage point of formal theology and the doctrines articulated by religious professionals. There has been a tendency, for example, to find Christ-figures in film heroes such as "Cool Hand Luke," or to find parables of the human condition in the films of directors such as Stanley Kubrick and Ingmar Bergman. Cartoon characters such as "Captain America" become redeemer-figures for a way of life, while the several characters in the long-popular cartoon strip "Peanuts" are construed as amateur neo-orthodox theologians in disguise.[14] Archie Bunker of television's "All in the Family" gains new status as a symbol of alienation, while the greed and self-aggrandizement of characters in "Dallas," a favorite prime-time soap opera of the 1970s and 1980s, are transposed into symbols of the eternal conflict between good and evil. Hollywood sustains visions of the coming apocalypse in *Star Wars* and other films of that genre. Religious nuance abounds everywhere.[15] There are also religious voices that condemn many of these same phenomena for their reliance on violence, their flaunting of traditional religious and moral values in some cases, and their minimizing the significance of such phenomena as the apocalypse by viewing them through presumably secular lenses.

Both advocates and critics of the religious dimension in these forms of popular entertainment miss the point from the perspective of popular religiosity. To construe comic book, television, and film characters as theologians or explicit religious figures in disguise or to see film plots as theological exercises is to impose the conceptual coherence endemic to formal religious traditions on what, like popular religiosity, lacks that degree of systematization. Such does not deny that much popular entertainment may reinforce those inchoate ideas that are part of popular religiosity. No doubt millions of Americans did identify with Archie Bunker, who constantly struggled with making sense out of a world that seemed increasingly beyond his control. No doubt, too, the fascination with the apocalyptic found in much science fiction reinforces the perception of an ongoing struggle between good and evil that marks the sense of the supernatural within much popular religiosity, with its millennialist undercurrent looking toward the final triumph of the good. In this more ambiguous sense of sending indirect signals that reinforce privately held perceptions and views entertainment media help sustain popular religiosity, not in their echoing formal religious doctrine.

Mass culture has also responded to the popular urge to make abstract religious feelings and beliefs concrete. Here, too, we are dealing with an indirect mode of reinforcing popular religiosity, for most of the efforts to give visible, concrete form to personal religiosity represent means by which individuals can send a signal to others that they privately hold religious convictions, but they do not have to articulate them in any conceptually coherent fashion. For example, over the past few decades a number of religious theme-parks have become tourist attractions, most of them with a general Christian focus.[16] Among them are Christus Gardens in Gatlinburg, Tennessee, Fields of the Wood near Murphy, North Carolina, and Paradise Gardens, in Rock City, Georgia. A park in Eureka Springs, Arkansas, displays a larger-than-life statue of Jesus and houses an amphitheater known for its version of the passion play. Smaller religious attractions are found at many tourist sites, while the trouble-ridden Heritage Village, once part of the evangelical empire of Jim and Tammy Faye Bakker in Fort Mill, South Carolina, had as its stated intent providing a total resort environment that reflected "Christian values." More recently, news media reported the availability of a two-foot-tall Jesus doll. While the original portrayed Jesus as a blue-eyed white man, other ethnic versions were planned, though the projected God doll called for depicting God as an elderly white male with white hair and a white beard.[17] Those interested may purchase a variety of bumper stickers for motor vehicles that carry a range of ostensibly religious messages. And while religious nuances were once found primarily in sympathy cards because death in formal religious traditions carried so many religious implications, greeting card manufacturers now offer an array of other types of cards and products with religious themes. Rarely, however, are the religious messages doctrinally explicit, but couched in language sufficiently vague to allow both senders and recipients to interpret the messages as bolstering their own personal beliefs.[18]

While the religious professionals may criticize the content of religious theme-parks, the value of Jesus dolls, or the theology implicit in religiously focused greeting cards, they are important in understanding how ordinary people communicate to others that they are religious people, that they have an abiding sense of the supernatural that informs their lives. A pilgrimage to a religious theme-park or a vacation trip to a Christian resort gives visibility to interior, private religiosity. By being at such a site, one is demonstrating that one holds certain unspecified and undefined religious and moral beliefs. The same holds for toys and other similar objects. Regardless of the ethnic identity given to a Jesus doll, its import lies in its being a religious article; it affirms some unarticulated belief in the supernatural in a way that another doll would not. So, too, with greeting cards. The fluidity of the language in them does little more than communicate to the recipient that the sender holds a sense of the supernatural and claims a religious identity. But being able to send indirect indications of one's religiosity is also a way of declaring its legitimacy as a way of being and of buttressing the motley beliefs and values that comprise an individual's personal worldview.

In a different vein, many writers have endowed sports with a religious construction. Rituals that invoke supernatural power to aid in winning are part of most athletic contests. The boom in spectator sports that came when television offered expanded audiences has led fans to identify the team they support with the forces of good and opposing teams with the forces of evil. For some, direct participation in athletic activity takes on a religious cast, bringing an intense inner experience of exhilaration akin to the experience of conversion or an ecstatic encounter with the ultimate.[19] Such an experience is private and personal, since no one else can share exactly what an individual athlete feels. The point is not that sports in and of themselves constitute a formal religion, but that sports become another source on which persons draw in creating and defining a meaningful world for themselves. As other arenas of life, sports for many offer reinforcement for the sense of ultimate good and evil that pervades popular religiosity, though like all popular religiosity that sense never receives systematic articulation, and sports contests become precursors of the final confrontation between the powers of light and the powers of darkness.

In addition to the massive self-help literature, other religious books targeted to a mass audience have also helped sustain popular religiosity. By the early 1980s librarians had noted the growing demand among readers for religious material pitched to ordinary men and women.[20] Much of it has drawn on the sense of millennialism that has long been one current of popular religiosity. A prominent example, published in 1970, is *The Late, Great Planet Earth* by Hal Lindsey (b. 1930), now a commentator for the evangelical Trinity Broadcast Network.[21] Based on the conviction that the world will end within one generation after the founding of Israel as an independent nation, *The Late, Great Planet Earth* offers an interpretation of a host of contemporary events, ranging from the prevalence of skin cancer to the northward movement of killer bees from Brazil. All fit into a pattern of predictions that the end of the world is rapidly approaching and that the advent of the Antichrist, the supernatural personification of evil, is at hand. The message is simple: only those who are identified with the forces of good will survive and prevail. Two years later, Lindsey, again in association with Carole Carlson, released *Satan Is Alive and Well on Planet Earth*.[22] Drawing on popular religiosity's keen sense of the reality of evil, Lindsey discerned signs of increasing satanic presence in the renewed interest in the occult, in the fascination with demons, and even in the glossolalia identified with much Pentecostal religious experience. Both books, written before the dramatic political shifts in the Soviet Union and Eastern Europe, see communism as among the leading indicators of the prevalence of evil and the proximity of the end. *The Late, Great Planet Earth* had sold more than twenty million copies by 1990 and also furnished the basis for a Hollywood film in 1978, reaching millions more with its eschatological message through that medium. Few who read Lindsey's books or saw the film version of *The Late, Great Planet Earth* knew that he was a graduate of the Dallas Theological Seminary, a long-time worker with Campus Crusade for Christ, and then an innovative campus minister in Los Angeles. Lindsey gave no denominational focus to his work; its appeal was to ordinary women and men, regardless of any formal affiliation they might have. It also hit squarely at the profound sense of struggle between good and evil that lies at the center of much popular religiosity. By linking good and evil to current events and contemporary phenomena, Lindsey bolstered the reality of that sense of the powerful presence of evil and the need to have access to the stronger supernatural power of good if one was to survive. To that extent, his work stands not only as a hallmark of popular culture in general, but as a signal of the strength that popular religiosity's awareness of the reality of the supernatural retains in the closing years of the century.

Some have seen the apocalypticism of popular religiosity as present in more subtle ways than in the writings of someone like Hal Lindsey. Ira Chernus, for example, has argued that attitudes of ordinary men and women toward nuclear weapons take on an apocalyptic cast.[23] While the fear of nuclear destruction prompts a desperate desire to become identified with superior supernatural power for redemption, the power inherent in nuclear weapons also becomes a source of redemption. Such holds especially for those who see the United States as a divinely chosen nation. The fear and awe reserved for the sacred in practical terms shift to nuclear weaponry as a more concrete manifestation of brute strength and control. The sense of power fundamental to popular religiosity underlies both the hope and fear attached to nuclear weapons.

Other markers suggest that the diffusion of religion often seen as a concomitant of popular religiosity has become a primary characteristic of American religion in the closing years of the twentieth century. David Poling and George Gallup, whose polling organization has tracked measurable trends in American religion for more than half a century, offer evidence that among Americans reaching adulthood in the 1980s and after, organized religion—the formal religious institutions and traditions—were becoming less important, but that a high degree of personal religiosity still prevailed.[24] Polls in the 1970s showed that although 41 percent of the adult population of the United States did not identify themselves as members of an organized religion, they nevertheless claimed to espouse strong religious beliefs on a personal level.[25] These findings are in keeping with provocative hypotheses advanced by sociologists Robert Wuthnow, Wade Clark Roof, and William McKinney.[26] In one form or another, all of them argue that traditional religious affiliation understood as membership in an organized religious group and maintenance of loyalty to that body had become less important to ordinary Americans over the last half century. While many persons will become involved with a formal religious institution at least while they are rearing children, most assume that no single group captures the whole of religious truth; hence they are more likely to have a practical rather than affective relation to a denomination or similar body. They will remain part of the group while it functions to give some semblance of meaning, provides an experience of community, or offers opportunities for social contact. But they will not retain long-term loyalty once the group ceases to function in these ways. In other words, as long as the group buttresses privately held beliefs and personal moral behavior, as long as it supports what we have called popular religiosity, individuals may remain active. What remains paramount is the constellation of beliefs, values, and practices persons hold individually. James Davison Hunter, who has analyzed contemporary evangelicalism extensively, notes that even among those who claim to hold traditional, orthodox belief, there is an increasing emphasis on private, personal belief and experience.[27]

In this vein, Wuthnow especially has called attention to the proliferation of special interest groups both within established religious groups and independent of any affiliation with a recognized religious institution.[28] Earlier we noted the emergence of some of these "parachurch" bodies such as the Full Gospel Business Men's Fellowship International. But the list of those founded in the twentieth century is virtually endless. It encompasses the older Christian Business Men's Committee International started by Charles E. Fuller in 1937 and more recent groups such Youth for Christ, Inter-Varsity Christian Fellowship, Campus Crusade, the Fellowship of Christian Athletes, the Women's Aglow Fellowship, and outfits like the Esalen Institute and est, which at first glance seem secular in focus.[29] Most established religious groups now have African-American caucuses, women's caucuses, and groups advancing concerns of gays and lesbians, to name a few. Some of these, such as the Daughters of Sarah or the Ecumenical and Evangelical Women's Caucus, cross denominational lines. Add to these the proliferation of support networks based on the twelve-step principles of Alcoholics Anonymous (Narcotics Anonymous, Overeaters Anonymous, and a host of other "recovery" groups), many of which use facilities provided by religious groups.[30] Numerous religious institutions have fashioned their own special interest groups using the twelve-step approach. Many produce newsletters and/or periodicals that reinforce the message offered and keep individuals connected even if they are not always actively participating.[31] All of these are vital to understanding the dynamics of religiosity in the closing years of the twentieth century.

Most of these groups lack identification with particular religious institutions, though many of them have some connection with the formal tradition of Christianity. That means that individuals are able to participate in organizations as diverse as the Fellowship of Christian Athletes and Alcoholics Anonymous while still retaining membership or affiliation with an established religious group. Yet these parachurch bodies obviously contribute to the constellation of beliefs and values that give meaning to participants' lives. Hence they reflect the way that popular religiosity draws on a range of sources in developing a worldview that makes sense to individuals; the syncretism basic to popular religiosity flourishes in this context. Some groups are sufficiently ambiguous in their overt religious content that persons may define terms however they see fit. The numerous twelve-step groups, for example, acknowledge dependence on a "higher power" but do not specify what the term denotes. For some, the higher power may be a vacuous entity. Others, particularly those more readily associated with Christianity, may have a more clear-cut sense of God as that higher power. But what is important about them all is their affirmation of the reality of the supernatural, however defined or not defined. That, too, is a basic element of popular religiosity. Many of these groups see adherents as participating only on a short-term basis and expect that individuals will move on to other groups once their circumstances change. Youth for Christ, for example, primarily targets high school students, while several others find their main constituency among traditional college-age men and women

(Campus Crusade, InterVarsity Christian Fellowship). This short-term dimension is especially compatible with the dynamics of popular religiosity. As individuals mature, as their life situations change, as they confront new circumstances, they naturally make alterations in their worldviews, though they may retain a vital, though not necessarily conceptually coherent, sense of the supernatural throughout their lives.

The idea of the supernatural fostered by these many parachurch groups carries with it a keen understanding of the reality of evil. In one sense, the group becomes a haven from the evil forces that lurk in society at large, a refuge from the dangers inherent in the surrounding culture. Certainly the twelve-step groups function in this way by providing a network of support so that participants will not fall prey to the evil powers that had formerly seized control of their lives (whether those powers be identified with alcohol or substance abuse, overeating, or whatever). Many of the women's groups, such as Women Aglow, consciously offer an alternative to what is perceived as a misdirected materialist culture that distorts the proper role of women. More feminist-inclined groups like Daughters of Sarah would concur, though they would disagree on what the proper role of women should be. Hence all of these groups are concerned with providing members with access to power, another hallmark of popular religiosity, that will endow individuals with control over their lives and bring a sense of order to their existence. In this context, we should also note the emergence of numerous intentional communities that work in much the same way.[32] Groups ranging from Sojourners in Washington, D.C., with its dual commitment to evangelical Christianity and social justice, to the Catholic Pentecostal Community in South Bend, Indiana, demonstrate another dimension of the process of bringing order and organization to personal existence, one of the major tasks of popular religiosity. At first it might seem paradoxical that individuals would seek to gain control over their lives through joining intentional communities, some of which are communitarian in structure. Many of the communities are short-lived, and those that survive have witnessed a heavy turn-over in membership. People are likely to enter such communities to meet an immediate need and then leave once they have succeeded, and many groups disband once they have achieved their initial purpose. That purpose, of course, is to provide individuals with direction in their personal lives, a goal of popular religiosity.

J. Gordon Melton has documented the emergence of more than eight hundred new religions in the United States in the twentieth century.[33] While we have mentioned a few of them, such as *santeria* and the International Society for Krishna Consciousness, we need also to think of the larger significance of this phenomenon. Melton contends that changes in U.S. immigration laws in 1965 and 1990 that increased the numbers of those entering the United States from Asia and the Middle East will bring even greater proliferation. Already Islam is among the fastest growing formal religions in the nation. The pluralism that has marked American religion from the beginning remains robust. What is the import of this new pluralism for our understanding of popular religiosity? Simply put, as more formal religious alternatives become available, beliefs, values, and practices emerging from them will gradually diffuse throughout the larger culture. That process enables individuals who may not have any direct connection with a particular religious group to add to their personal worldview ideas and ways of looking at reality that come from one or more of these alternatives through an unconscious syncretism. The new pluralism increases the range of sources on which individual women and men may draw in constructing a private constellation of beliefs and values through which they will give meaning to their lives.

Nearly a decade ago the agnostic British writer Malise Ruthven set out to travel across the religious landscape of the United States. He was particularly interested in retracing the migration of the Mormons from their upstate New York birthplace to Utah. Ruthven also sought to gain understanding of American evangelicalism and of other religious movements, such as Christian Science, that originated in the United States. While we need not concern ourselves with the details of his journey, the title he gave to the book he wrote about it is suggestive for the pilgrimage we have taken through the historical landscape of popular religiosity in the United States: *The Divine Supermarket: Shopping for God in America*.[34] Popular religiosity is to some extent akin to shopping for God in a divine supermarket, for it involves individuals looking to many sources, picking and choosing beliefs and practices that make sense to them, and ultimately constructing a worldview that enables them to make sense out of their own experience, even if that worldview lacks conceptual coherence. Far from being merely an offshoot of modernization and technological advance, popular religiosity, with its lively, but unsystematic sense of the supernatural and conviction that the empirical world is the arena where forces of good and evil struggle to hold sway, has flourished in America from the very beginning. From Puritans to neopagans, from Cherokees to Christian Scientists, ordinary American men and women have engaged in that human quest for meaning by exploring many ways to gain access to that realm of power, to use that power to benefit themselves in gaining a sense of control over their lives and thus charting their own destiny. Being religious, American style, is to share in that dynamic, but highly personal and ultimately very private enterprise of endowing one's own life with meaning.

NOTES

1. Gregor Goethals, "Religious Communication and Popular Piety," *Journal of Communication* 35 (1985): 149–56.

2. Martin E. Marty, "Where the Energies Go," in *Religion in the Nineties*,

edited by Wade Clark Roof, *Annals of the American Academy of Political and Social Science* 527 (Newbury Park, Calif.: Sage Periodicals, 1993), pp. 11–26. See also W. Widick Schroeder et al., *Suburban Religion: Churches and Synagogues in the American Experience* (Chicago: Center for the Scientific Study of Religion, 1974), which argues that religious institutions basically offer assistance in shaping a private morality and that class and ethnic consciousness have led to a rather different kind of "privatization" of suburban religious institutions in that they have become identified with a particular class or ethnic/racial group (and are therefore "private") rather than reflecting the character of the larger culture.

3. A representative example is H. Elliott Wright, "Jesus on Stage: A Reappraisal," *Christian Century* 89 (19 July 1972): 785–86. See also Richard Hawley, "Some Thoughts on the Pop Jesus," *Anglican Theological Review* 55 (July 1973): 334–46.

4. Andrew Lloyd Webber and Tim Rice, "Trial before Pilate," *Jesus Christ Superstar* (London: Leeds Music, 1969).

5. See, for example, Van K. Brown, "Assemblies of God: Elvis and Pentecostalism," *Bulletin of the Center for the Study of Southern Culture and Religion* 3 (June 1979): 9–15; and Charles M. Wolfe, "Presley and the Gospel Tradition," *Southern Quarterly* 19 (Fall 1979): 135–50.

6. Stephen R. Tucker, "Pentecostalism and Popular Culture in the South: A Study of Four Musicians," *Journal of Popular Culture* 16 (Winter 1982): 68–80. The essay treats James Blackwood, Tammy Wynette, Johnny Cash, and Jerry Lee Lewis, but concentrates primarily on Lewis.

7. Jerry H. Gill, "The Gospel According to Bruce," *Theology Today* 45 (1988): 87–94; Andrew Greeley, "The Catholic Imagination of Bruce Springsteen," *America* 158 (6 February 1988): 110–15.

8. Alton B. Pollard III, "Religion, Rock, and Eroticism," *Journal of Black Sacred Music* 1 (Spring 1987): 47–52.

9. Some of these points are suggested in Benjamin DeMott, "Rock as Salvation," in *Popular Culture in America*, edited by David Manning White (Chicago: Quadrangle Books, 1970), pp. 191–204. This essay originally appeared in the 25 August 1968 Sunday *New York Times Magazine*.

10. Bernice Martin, "The Sacralization of Disorder: Symbolism in Rock Music," *Sociological Analysis* 40 (Summer 1979): 87–124.

11. See William Romanowski, "Contemporary Christian Music: The Business of Music Ministry," in *American Evangelicals and the Mass Media*, edited by Quentin J. Schultze (Grand Rapids, Mich.: Zondervan, 1990); Donald P. Ellsworth, *Christian Music in Contemporary Witness: Historical Antecedents and Contemporary Practice* (Grand Rapids, Mich.: Baker Book House, 1979); Paul Baker, *Contemporary Christian Music*, rev. ed. (Westchester, Ill.: Crossway Books, 1985); Don Cusic, *Sandi Patti: The Voice of Gospel* (New York: Dolphin Books, 1988); Carol Legget, *Amy Grant* (New York: Pocket Books, 1987); and Bob Millard, *Amy Grant: A Biography* (New York: Doubleday, 1986).

12. On the Gaithers, see Stephen R. Graham, "Bill and Gloria Gaither," in *Twentieth-Century Shapers of American Popular Religion*, edited by Charles H. Lippy (Westport, Conn.: Greenwood, 1989), pp. 155–62. Gloria Gaither has also written numerous articles for popular religious magazines.

13. Don Hustad, "The Explosion of Popular Hymnody," *The Hymn* 33 (July 1982): 167.

14. See Robert L. Short, *The Gospel According to Peanuts* (Richmond: John Knox, 1965), and idem, *The Parables of Peanuts* (New York: Harper and Row, 1968).

15. Among the many works that exemplify this analytic approach are: Laurel Arthur Burton, "Close Encounters of a Religious Kind," *Journal of Popular Culture* 17 (Winter 1983): 141–45; Stanley Cohen, "Messianic Motifs, American Popular Culture, and the Judeo-Christian Tradition," *Journal of Religious Studies* 8 (Spring 1980): 24–34; James Eagan, "Sacral Parody in the Fiction of Stephen King," *Journal of Popular Culture* 23 (Winter 1989): 125–41; Gabriel Fackre, "Archie Bunker: Visions and Reality," *Christian Century* 89 (19 July 1972): 772–74; James E. Ford, "*Battlestar Gallactica* and Mormon Theology," *Journal of Popular Culture* 17 (Fall 1983): 83–87; Marlene Goldsmith, "Video Values Education: *Star Trek* as Modern Myth" (Ph.D. diss., University of Minnesota, 1981); Bob Hulteen, "Of Heroic Proportions: Fifty Years of Captain America," *Sojourners* 19 (August–September 1990): 39, 41–43; Neil P. Hurley, "Christ-Transfigurations in Film: Notes on a Meta-Genre," *Journal of Popular Culture* 13 (Spring 1980): 427–33; idem, "Hollywood's New Mythology," *Theology Today* 39 (January 1983): 402–8; G. William Jones, *Sunday Night at the Movies* (Richmond: John Knox, 1967); Frederick A. Kreuziger, *The Religion of Science Fiction* (Bowling Green, Ohio: Bowling Green State University Popular Press, 1986); Mary S. Mander, "*Dallas*: The Mythology of Crime and the Moral Occult," *Journal of Popular Culture* 17 (Fall 1983): 44–50; Spencer Marsh, *God, Man, and Archie Bunker* (New York: Harper and Row, 1975); John R. May and Michael Bird, eds., *Religion in Film* (Knoxville: University of Tennessee Press, 1982); Short, *The Gospel According to Peanuts* and *The Parables of Peanuts*.

16. An R. Trotter, "Paradise Lost: Religious Theme-parks in the Southern United States" (M.A. thesis, New York University, 1991), is one of the few descriptive studies of this phenomenon, although it lacks analytic focus and clarity.

17. See Ken Garfield, "Jesus Doll a New Idea to Toy With," *Charlotte Observer*, 5 December 1992, 1C.

18. On the social and cultural role of sending greeting cards on the occasion of death, see Charles H. Lippy, "Sympathy Cards and Death," *Theology Today* 34 (1977): 167–77; idem, "Sympathy Cards and the Grief Process," *Journal of Popular Culture* 17 (1983): 98–108.

19. A provocative collection of essays exploring these and related topics is Shirl J. Hoffman, ed., *Sport and Religion* (Champaign, Ill.: Human Kinetic Books, 1992). Also see Michael Real, "The Super Bowl: Mythic Spectacle," in *The Popular Culture Reader*, 3d ed., edited by Christopher D. Geist and Jack Nachbar (Bowling Green, Ohio: Bowling Green University Popular Press, 1983), pp. 284–89.

20. Susan Avallone, "Receptivity to Religion," 109 *Library Journal* (15 October 1984): 1891–93.

21. Hal Lindsey (with C. C. Carlson), *The Late, Great Planet Earth* (Grand Rapids, Mich.: Eerdmans, 1970).

22. Hal Lindsey (with C. C. Carlson), *Satan Is Alive and Well on Planet Earth* (Grand Rapids, Mich.: Zondervan, 1972).

23. Ira Chernus, "Nuclear Images in the Popular Press: The Age of Apocalypse,"

in *A Shuddering Dawn: Religious Studies and the Nuclear Age*, edited by Ira Chernus and Edward Linenthal (Albany: State University of New York Press, 1989), pp. 3–19.

24. George Gallup, Jr., and David Poling, *The Search for America's Faith* (Nashville: Abingdon, 1980).

25. Princeton Religious Research Center and the Gallup Organization, Inc., *The Unchurched American* (Princeton, N.J.: Princeton Religious Research Center for the National Council of Churches, 1978).

26. Robert Wuthnow, *The Restructuring of American Religion: Society and Faith since World War II* (Princeton, N.J.: Princeton University Press, 1988), especially chap. 8; Wade Clark Roof and William McKinney, *American Mainline Religion: Its Changing Shape and Future* (New Brunswick, N.J.: Rutgers University Press, 1987); Wade Clark Roof, *A Generation of Seekers: The Spiritual Journeys of the Baby Boom Generation* (San Francisco: HarperSanFrancisco, 1993); and Wade Clark Roof, ed., *Religion in America Today*, Annals of the America Academy of Political and Social Science 480 (Beverly Hills, Calif.: Sage Publications, 1985).

27. See, for example, James Davison Hunter, *American Evangelicalism: Conservative Religion and the Quandary of Modernity* (New Brunswick, N.J.: Rutgers University Press, 1987), especially pp. 120–26.

28. See Wuthnow, especially chaps. 6 and 7.

29. There has been relatively little analytical work done on such groups. But see Richard Quebedeaux, *I Found It! The Story of Bill Bright and Campus Crusade* (San Francisco: Harper and Row, 1979); James W. White and John G. Hallsten, "Campus Crusade Goes Suburban," *Christian Century* 89 (1972): 549–51; Susan M. Setta, "Healing in Suburbia: The Women's Aglow Fellowship," *Journal of Religious Studies* 12:2 (1986): 46–56; Harvey Cox, *The Seduction of the Spirit: The Use and Misuse of People's Religion* (New York: Simon and Schuster, 1973), pp. 197–225; James Hefley, *God Goes to High School* (Waco, Tex.: Word Books, 1970); "Youth for Christ," *Time* 47 (4 February 1946): 46–47; "Wanted: A Miracle of Good Weather and 'Youth for Christ' Rally Got It," *Newsweek* 25 (11 June 1945): 84; David R. Enlow, *Men Aflame: The Story of Christian Business Men's Committee International* (Grand Rapids, Mich.: Zondervan, 1962).

30. See Ernest Kurtz, "Alcoholics Anonymous: A Phenomenon in American Religious History," in *Religion and Philosophy in the United States*, edited by Peter Freese (Essen, Germany: Verlag die Blaue Eule, 1987), 2:447–62; Vernon Bittner, "Taking the Twelve Steps to Church," *Christianity Today* (9 December 1988): 31; Tim Stafford, "The Hidden Gospel of the 12 Steps," *Christianity Today* (22 July 1991): 14–19; Melinda Fish, *When Addiction Comes to the Church* (Old Tappan, N.J.: Fleming H. Revell, 1991); J. Keith Miller, *Hunger for Healing: The Twelve Steps as a Classic Model for Christian Spiritual Growth* (San Francisco: HarperCollins, 1991). A demurring view that is critical of all self-help and recovery approaches is found in Wendy Kaminer, *I'm Dysfunctional, You're Dysfunctional: The Recovery Movement and Other Self-Help Fashions* (Reading, Mass.: Addison-Wesley, 1992), which was widely reviewed in the popular press.

31. See Erling Jorstad, *Popular Religion in America: The Evangelical Voice* (Westport, Conn.: Greenwood, 1993), p. 58.

32. Michael Zeik discusses several of these in his *New Christian Communities: Origins, Style, and Survival* (Williston Park, N.Y.: Roth, 1973). Also see Richard

Quebedeaux, *The Worldly Evangelicals* (New York: Harper and Row, 1978); and idem, *The Young Evangelicals: Revolution in Orthodoxy* (New York: Harper and Row, 1974).

33. See J. Gordon Melton, "Another Look at New Religions," in *Religion in the Nineties*, pp. 97–112.

34. Malise Ruthven, *The Divine Supermarket: Shopping for God in America* (New York: Morrow, 1989).

Select Bibliography

Abelman, Robert, and Kimberly Neuendorf. "How Religious Is Religious Television Programming?" *Journal of Communication* 35 (1985): 98–110.

Aberle, David F. *The Peyote Religion among the Navaho.* Chicago: Aldine, 1956.

Adams, Dickson, W., ed. *Jefferson's Extracts from the Gospels.* Princeton, N.J.: Princeton University Press, 1983.

Adams, George C. S. "Rattlesnake Eye." *Southern Folklore Quarterly* 2 (March 1938): 37–38.

Adler, Margot. *Drawing Down the Moon: Witches, Druids, Goddess-Worshippers, and Other Pagans in America Today.* Rev. ed. Boston: Beacon, 1986.

Ahlstrom, Sydney E. *A Religious History of the American People.* New Haven, Conn.: Yale University Press, 1972.

Albanese, Catherine L. "Fisher Kings and Public Places: The Old New Age in the 1990s." In *Religion in the Nineties.* Edited by Wade Clark Roof. *Annals of the American Academy of Political and Social Science* 527. Newbury Park, Calif.: Sage Periodicals, 1993. 131–43.

———. *Nature Religion in America: From the Algonkian Indians to the New Age.* Chicago: University of Chicago Press, 1990.

———. "The Study of American Popular Religion: Retrospect and Prospect." *Explor* 7 (Fall 1984): 9–15.

Allen, Charles L. *God's Psychiatry.* Old Tappan, N.J.: Fleming H. Revell, 1953.

———. *Roads to Radiant Living.* Old Tappan, N.J.: Fleming H. Revell, 1968.

Allen, Frederick Lewis. *Only Yesterday.* New York: Blue Ribbon Books, 1931.

Allestree, Richard. *The Whole Duty of Man, Laid Down in a Plain and Familiar Way for the Use of All, but Especially the Meanest Reader.* London: For T. Garthwait, 1659. First published as *The Practice of Christian Grace* (1658).

Ames, Nathaniel. *An Astronomical Diary; or Almanacke for the Year of Our Lord 1736.* Boston: J. Draper, 1736.

Ammerman, Nancy Tatom. *Bible Believers: Fundamentalists in the Modern World.* New Brunswick, N.J.: Rutgers University Press, 1987.

Anderson, Robert Mapes. *Vision of the Disinherited: The Making of American Pentecostalism.* New York: Oxford University Press, 1979.

Anker, Roy M. "Popular Religion and Theories of Self-Help." In *Handbook of American Popular Culture.* Edited by Thomas M. Inge. Westport, Conn.: Greenwood, 1980. 2:287–316.

Appleby, R. Scott. "Harry Emerson Fosdick." In *Twentieth-Century Shapers of American Popular Religion.* Edited by Charles H. Lippy. Westport, Conn.: Greenwood, 1989. 141–48.

Ariès, Philippe, and Georges Duby, eds. *A History of Private Life.* 5 vols. Cambridge, Mass.: Belknap Press of Harvard University, 1987–91.

Armstrong, Ben. *The Electric Church.* Nashville: Thomas Nelson, 1979.

Attwater, Donald, ed. *A Catholic Dictionary.* New York: Macmillan, 1942.

Avallone, Susan. "Receptivity to Religion." *Library Journal* 109 (15 October 1984): 1891–93.

Baer, Hans. "Toward a Systematic Theology of Black Folk Healers." *Phylon* 43 (Winter 1982): 327–43.

Bailey, Paul. *Wovoka: The Indian Messiah.* Los Angeles: Westernlore Press, 1957.

Baker, Paul. *Contemporary Christian Music.* Rev. ed. Westchester, Ill.: Crossway Books, 1985.

Baldwin, Lewis V. " 'Deliverance to the Captives': Images of Jesus Christ in the Minds of Afro-American Slaves." *Journal of Religious Studies* 12 (1986): 27–45.

———. " 'A Home in Dat Rock': Afro-American Folk Sources and Slave Visions of Heaven and Hell." *Journal of Religious Thought* 41 (1984): 38–57.

Balmer, Randall H. *Mine Eyes Have Seen the Glory: A Journey into the Evangelical Subculture in America.* New York: Oxford University Press, 1989.

Baranowski, Shelley. *"The Commonweal."* In *Religious Periodicals of the United States: Academic and Scholarly.* Edited by Charles H. Lippy. Westport, Conn.: Greenwood, 1986. 153–58.

Barkowsky, Edward Richard. "The Popular Christian Novel in America, 1918–1953." Ed.D. diss., Ball State University, 1975.

Barnett, James H. *The American Christmas: A Study in National Culture.* New York: Macmillan, 1954.

Barrett, Leonard E. "The African Heritage in Caribbean and North American Religions." In *Encyclopedia of the American Religious Experience.* Edited by Charles H. Lippy and Peter W. Williams. New York: Charles Scribner's Sons, 1988. 1:171–86.

Barry, William J. *The Sacramentals of the Holy Catholic Church, or Flowers for the Garden of the Liturgy.* Cincinnati: John P. Walsh, 1858.

Barton, Andrew. *The Disappointment; or the Force of Credulity.* Philadelphia: Francis Shallus, 1766.

Barton, Bruce. *The Man Nobody Knows.* Indianapolis: Bobbs-Merrill, 1925.

Barton, Josef L. "Religion and Cultural Change in Czech Immigrant Communities, 1850–1920." In *Immigrants and Religion in Urban Culture.* Edited by Randall M. Miller and Thomas D. Marzik. Philadelphia: Temple University Press, 1977. 3–24.

Bayly, Lewis. *The Practice of Piety.* 27th ed. London: [J. Legat for] R. Allot, 1631.

Baym, Nina. *Woman's Fiction: A Guide to Novels by and about Women in America, 1820–1870.* Ithaca, N.Y.: Cornell University Press, 1978.

Beck, H. P. "Herpetological Lore from the Black Ridge." *Midwest Folklore* 2 (1952): 141–50.

Bednarowski, Mary Farrell. *New Religions and the Theological Imagination in America.* Bloomington: Indiana University Press, 1989.

Bellah, Robert. "Civil Religion in America." In *American Civil Religion.* Edited by Russell E. Richey and Donald G. Jones. New York: Harper and Row, 1974. 21–44.

Bellamy, Joseph. *Sermons Upon the Following Subjects, viz. The Divinity of Jesus Christ, The Millenium [sic]. The Wisdom of God, in the Permission of Sin.* Boston: S. Kneeland, 1758.

Ben-Yehuda, Nachman. "The Revival of the Occult and of Science Fiction." *Journal of Popular Culture* 20:2 (Fall 1986): 1–16.

Berkman, Dave. "Long before Falwell: Early Radio and Religion—As Reported by the Nation's Periodical Press." *Journal of Popular Culture* 21:4 (1988): 1–11.

Billman, Carol. "McGuffey's Readers and Alger's Fiction: The Gospel of Virtue According to Popular Children's Literature." *Journal of Popular Culture* 11 (1971): 614–19.

Bird, B. "FGBMFI: Facing Frustrations and the Future." *Charisma* 11 (June 1986): 25, 26, 28.

———. "The Legacy of Demos Shakarian." *Charisma* 11 (June 1986): 20–25.

Bisset, J. Thomas. "Religious Broadcasting: Assessing the State of the Art." *Christianity Today* 24 (12 December 1980): 28–31.

Bittner, Vernon. "Taking the Twelve Steps to Church." *Christianity Today* 32 (9 December 1988): 31.

Bjork, Daniel W. *The Victorian Flight: Russell H. Conwell and the Crisis of American Individualism.* Washington, D.C.: University Press of America, 1979.

Blavatsky, Helena P. *Isis Unveiled.* New York: J. W. Boughton, 1877.

———. *The Secret Doctrine.* New York: William Q. Judge, 1888.

Bloch-Hoell, Nils. *The Pentecostal Movement.* London: Allen and Unwin, 1964.

Block, Ruth H. *Visionary Republic: Millennial Themes in American Thought, 1756–1800.* Cambridge, Eng.: Cambridge University Press, 1985.

Bochen, Christina M. *The Journey to Rome: Conversion Literature by Nineteenth-Century American Catholics.* New York: Garland, 1988.

Bock, E. Wilbur. "Symbols in Conflict: Official versus Folk Religion." *Journal for the Scientific Study of Religion* 5 (1966): 204–12.

Bode, Carl. "Lloyd Douglas: Lost Voice in the Wilderness." *American Quarterly* 2 (1950): 340–58.

Bourgault, Louise M. "The PTL Club and Protestant Viewers: An Ethnographic Study." *Journal of Communication* 35 (1985): 132–48.

Boyer, Paul S. "*In His Steps*: A Reappraisal." *American Quarterly* 13 (1971): 60–71.

Braden, Charles. *Spirits in Rebellion: The Rise and Development of New Thought.* Reprint, Dallas: Southern Methodist University Press, 1987.

Braus, Patricia. "Selling Self Help." *American Demographics* 14 (March 1992): 48–53.

Bredeck, Martin J., S. J. *Imperfect Apostles: The Commonweal and the American Catholic Laity, 1924–1976.* New York: Garland, 1988.

Bromley, David G., and Anson Shupe, eds. *New Christian Politics.* Macon, Ga.: Mercer University Press, 1984.

Brothers, Richard. *Revealed Knowledge of the Prophecies and Times.* Philadelphia: Francis and Robert Bailey, 1795.

Brown, Alexander. *Genesis of the United States.* Boston and New York: Houghton, Mifflin, 1877.

Brown, David H. "Garden in the Machine: Afro-Cuban Sacred Art in Urban New Jersey and New York." Ph.D. diss., Yale University, 1989.

Brown, Richard D. *Knowledge Is Power: The Diffusion of Information in Early America, 1700–1865.* New York: Oxford University Press, 1989.

Brown, Slater. *The Heyday of Spiritualism.* New York: Hawthorne Books, 1970.

Brown, Van K. "Assemblies of God: Elvis and Pentecostalism." *Bulletin for the Center for the Study of Southern Culture and Religion* 3 (June 1979): 9–15.

Budapest, Z [Zsuzsana]. *Grandmother Moon.* San Francisco: HarperSanFrancisco, 1991.

———. *The Grandmother of Time: A Women's Book of Celebrations, Spells, and Sacred Objects for Every Month of the Year.* San Francisco: HarperSanFrancisco, 1989.

———. *The Holy Book of Women's Mysteries.* Oakland, Calif.: Wingbow, 1989.

Buddenbaum, Judith M. "Characteristics and Media-Related Needs of the Audience for Religious TV." *Journalism Quarterly* 58 (1981): 266–72.

Bukowczyk, John. " 'Mary the Messiah': Polish Immigrants, Heresy and the Malleable Ideology of the Roman Catholic Church in America, 1860–1930." In *Disciplines of Faith: Studies in Religion, Politics, and Patriarchy.* Edited by Jim Obelkevich, Lyndal Roper, and Raphael Samuel. New York: Routledge, 1987.

Burgess, Stanley M., and Gary B. McGee, eds. *Dictionary of Pentecostal and Charismatic Movements.* Grand Rapids, Mich.: Zondervan, 1988.

Burkett, Randall K. *Garveyism as a Religious Movement.* Metuchen, N.J.: Scarecrow, 1978.

Burlingame, Roger. *Of Making Many Books: A Hundred Years of Reading, Writing, and Publishing.* New York: Charles Scribner's Sons, 1946.

Burr, George Lincoln, ed. *Narratives of the Witchcraft Cases, 1648–1706.* New York: Barnes and Noble, 1968.

Burton, Laurel Arthur. "Close Encounters of a Religious Kind." *Journal of Popular Culture* 17 (Winter 1983): 141–45.

Bushman, Richard L. *Joseph Smith and the Beginnings of Mormonism.* Urbana: University of Illinois Press, 1984.

Butler, Jon. *Awash in a Sea of Faith: Christianizing the American People.* Cambridge, Mass.: Harvard University Press, 1990.

———. "The Great Awakening as Interpretive Fiction." *Journal of American History* 69 (1982–83): 305–25.

———. "Magic, Astrology, and the Early American Religious Heritage." *American Historical Review* 84 (1979): 317–46.

Cahan, Abraham. *The Rise of David Levinsky.* New York: Harper Colophon, 1960.

Calhoon, Robert M. "The African Heritage, Slavery, and Evangelical Christianity among American Blacks, 1700–1870." *Fides et Historia* 21 (June 1989): 61–66.

Campbell, Bruce F. *Ancient Wisdom Revealed: A History of the Theosophical Movement.* Berkeley: University of California Press, 1980.

Caplow, Theodore, et al. *All Faithful People: Change and Continuity in Middletown's Religion.* Minneapolis: University of Minnesota Press, 1983.

Carden, Maren Lockwood. *Oneida: Utopian Community to Modern Corporation.* Baltimore: Johns Hopkins University Press, 1969.

Cardwell, Jerry D. *Mass Media Christianity: Televangelism and the Great Commission.* Lanham, Md.: University Press of America, 1984.

Carnegie, Dale. *How to Win Friends and Influence People.* New York: Simon and Schuster, 1936.

Carnes, Mark C. *Secret Ritual and Manhood in Victorian America.* New Haven, Conn.: Yale University Press, 1989.

Carpenter, Joel A. "Fundamentalist Institutions and the Growth of Evangelical Protestantism, 1929–1942." *Church History* 49 (1980): 62–75.

————. "The Fundamentalist Leaven and the Rise of an Evangelical United Front." In *The Evangelical Tradition in America.* Edited by Leonard I. Sweet. Macon, Ga.: Mercer University Press, 1984. 257–88.

————. "Revive Us Again: Alienation, Hope and the Resurgence of Fundamentalism, 1930–1950." In *Transforming Faith: The Sacred and Secular in Modern American History.* Edited by M. L. Bradbury and James B. Gilbert. Westport, Conn.: Greenwood, 1989. 105–25.

A Catholic Clergyman of Baltimore. *True Piety or, The Day Well Spent, Being a Catholic Manual of Chosen Prayers, Devout Practices, and Solid Instructions, Adapted to Every State of Life, Taken Partly from the French.* Baltimore: Warner and Hanna, 1809.

Chalmers, Irene, et al. *The Great American Christmas Almanac.* Baltimore: Penguin, 1988.

Chase, Elise. *Healing Faith: An Annotated Bibliography of Christian Self-Help Books.* Westport, Conn.: Greenwood, 1985.

Chauncy, Charles. *Earthquakes a Token of the Righteous Anger of God.* Boston: Edes and Gill, 1755.

————. *The New Creature Describ'd and Consider'd as the Sure Characteristick of a Man's Being in Christ.* Boston: G. Rogers, 1741.

————. *Seasonable Thoughts on the State of Religion in New England.* Boston: Rogers and Fowle, 1743.

Chernus, Ira. "Nuclear Images in the Popular Press: The Age of Apocalypse." In *A Shuddering Dawn: Religious Studies and the Nuclear Age.* Edited by Ira Chernus and Edward Linenthal. Albany: State University of New York Press, 1989. 3–19.

Chinnici, Joseph P. "Organization of the Spiritual Life: American Catholic Devotional Works, 1791–1866." *Theological Studies* 40 (1979): 229–55.

Clarke, Richard. *The Prophetic Numbers of Daniel and John Calculated.* 2d ed. Charleston, S.C.: Peter Timothy, 1759.

Clarke, Samuel. *A True, and Faithful Account of the Four Chiefest Plantations of the English in America.* London: For R. Clavel et al., 1670.

Claudel, Calvin. "Tales from San Francisco." *California Folklore Quarterly* 2 (April 1943): 117–18.

Cleage, Albert. *The Black Messiah*. New York: Sheed and Ward, 1969.

Clemens, Samuel Langhorne. *Adventures of Huckleberry Finn*. Edited by Sculley Bradley, Richmond Groom Beatty, and E. Hudson Long. New York: W. W. Norton, 1961.

Click, Patricia C. "High Technology Meets the Spiritual: Objectivity, Popular Opinion, and the Shroud of Turin." *Journal of Popular Culture* 21:4 (1988): 13–23.

Coakley, Thomas F. "Preaching by Wireless." *Catholic World* 72:5 (January 1922): 516.

Cohen, Naomi W. *Jews in Christian America: The Pursuit of Religious Equality*. New York: Oxford University Press, 1992.

Cohen, Stanley. "Messianic Motifs, American Popular Culture, and the Judeo-Christian Tradition." *Journal of Religious Studies* 8 (Spring 1980): 24–34.

Commager, Henry Steele, intro. *Fifth Eclectic Reader*. New York: Signet Classics, 1962.

Cone, James H. *Black Theology and Black Power*. New York: Seabury, 1969.

———. *A Black Theology of Liberation*. Philadelphia: Lippincott, 1970.

———. *For My People: Black Theology and the Black Church*. Maryknoll, N.Y.: Orbis, 1984.

———. *God of the Oppressed*. New York: Seabury, 1975.

———. *The Spirituals and the Blues*. New York: Seabury, 1972.

Connelly, James T. "William J. Seymour." In *Twentieth-Century Shapers of American Popular Religion*. Edited by Charles H. Lippy. Westport, Conn.: Greenwood, 1989. 381–87.

Conwell, Russell H. *Acres of Diamonds*. New York: J. Y. Huber, 1890.

Cooley, Stephen D. "*Guide to Holiness*." In *Popular Religious Periodicals of the United States*. Edited by Mark Fackler and Charles H. Lippy. Westport, Conn.: Greenwood, forthcoming.

Cooper, Joseph T. *Odd-Fellowship Examined in the Light of Reason and Scripture*. Philadelphia: William S. Young, 1853.

Copage, Eric V. "The Seven Days of Kwanzaa." *New York Times* 141 (1 December 1991).

Corrigan, John. "*The Christian Science Monitor*." In *Religious Periodicals of the United States: Academic and Scholarly*. Edited by Charles H. Lippy. Westport, Conn.: Greenwood, 1986. 124–28.

Cowman, Mrs. Charles E. [Lettie Burd Cowman]. *Streams in the Desert*. Los Angeles: Oriental Missionary Society, 1925.

Cox, Harvey. *The Seduction of the Spirit: The Use and Misuse of People's Religion*. New York: Simon and Schuster, 1973.

Cranston, Sylvia. *H.P.B.: The Extraordinary Life and Influence of Helena Blavatsky, Founder of the Modern Theosophical Movement*. New York: Jeremy P. Tarcher, 1993.

Cross, Robert D. "Origins of the Catholic Parochial Schools in America." *American Benedictine Review* 16 (1965): 194–209.

Cunningham, Raymond. "From Holiness to Healing: The Faith Cure in America, 1872–1892." *Church History* 43 (1974): 499–513.

Curtis, James R. "Miami's Little Havana: Yard Shrines, Cultural Religion and Landscape." *Journal of Cultural Geography* 1 (Fall 1980): 1–16. Reprinted in Ray B. Browne, ed., *Rituals and Ceremonies in Popular Culture*. Bowling Green, Ohio: Bowling Green University Popular Press, 1980. 105–19.

Cusic, Don. *Sandi Patti: The Voice of Gospel*. New York: Dolphin Books, 1988.

[Danforth, Samuel]. *An Almanacke for the Year of Our Lord 1648*. Cambridge, Mass.: [Matthew Daye], 1648.

Davis, David Brion. "Some Themes of Countersubversion: An Analysis of Anti-Masonic, Anti-Catholic, and Anti-Mormon Literature." *Mississippi Valley Historical Review* 47 (1960): 205–24.

Davis, Richard B. *A Colonial Southern Bookshelf: Reading in the Eighteenth Century*. Athens: University of Georgia Press, 1979.

———. *Literature and Society in Early Virginia, 1608–1840*. Baton Rouge: Louisiana State University Press, 1973.

DeBerg, Betty A. *Ungodly Women: Gender and the First Wave of American Fundamentalism*. Minneapolis: Fortress, 1990.

Deloria, Vine, Jr. *Behind the Trail of Broken Treaties: An Indian Declaration of Independence*. New York: Delacorte, 1974.

———. "Completing the Theological Circle: Civil Religion in America." *Religious Education* 71 (1976): 278–87.

———. *Custer Died for Your Sins: An Indian Manifesto*. New York: Macmillan, 1969.

———. *God Is Red*. New York: Dell, 1973.

———, ed. *American Indian Policy in the Twentieth Century*. Norman: University of Oklahoma Press, 1985.

Deloria, Vine, Jr., and Sandra L. Cadwalader, eds. *The Aggressions of Civilization: Federal Indian Policy since the 1880s*. Philadelphia: Temple University Press, 1984.

Deloria, Vine, Jr., and Clifford M. Lytle. *The Nations Within: The Past and Future of Indian Sovereignty*. New York: Pantheon Books, 1984.

Demos, John Putnam. *Entertaining Satan: Witchcraft and the Culture of Early New England*. New York: Oxford University Press, 1982.

DeMott, Benjamin. "Rock as Salvation." In *Popular Culture in America*. Edited by David Manning White. Chicago: Quadrangle Books, 1970. 191–204.

Deshon, George. *Guide for Catholic Young Women*. Reprinted, New York: Arno Press, 1978.

Detter, Raymond Arthur. "A Ministry to Millions: Lloyd C. Douglas, 1877–1951." Ph.D. diss., University of Michigan, 1975.

Dieter, Melvin E. *The Holiness Revival of the Nineteenth Century*. Metuchen, N.J.: Scarecrow, 1980.

Dolan, Jay P. *Catholic Revivalism: The American Experience, 1830–1900*. Notre Dame, Ind.: University of Notre Dame Press, 1978.

Dorsett, Lyle W. *Billy Sunday and the Redemption of Urban America*. Grand Rapids, Mich.: Eerdmans, 1991.

Dorsey, George A. *The Arapaho Sun Dance*. Chicago: Field Museum of Natural History, 1903.

Douglas, Ann. *The Feminization of American Culture*. New York: Knopf, 1978.

Douglas, Lloyd C. *Magnificent Obsession*. Chicago: Willett, Clark, and Colby, 1929.

——. *The Robe*. Boston: Houghton Mifflin, 1942.

Drake, Frederick C. "Witchcraft in the American Colonies, 1647–62." *American Quarterly* 20 (1968): 694–725.

Drake, Milton, comp. *Almanacs of the United States*. New York: Scarecrow, 1962.

Drake, St. Clair, and Horace R. Cayton. *Black Metropolis: A Study of Negro Life in a Northern City*. Rev. ed. 2 vols. New York: Harper and Row, 1962.

Drake, Samuel G. *Annals of Witchcraft in New England and Elsewhere in the United States*. Reprinted, New York: B. Blom, 1967.

——. *The Witchcraft Delusion in New England*. Reprinted, New York: Burt Franklin, 1970.

Dresser, Horatio W. *A History of the New Thought Movement*. New York: Thomas Y. Crowell, 1919.

D'Souza, Dinesh. *Falwell: Before the Millennium. A Critical Biography*. Chicago: Regnery Gateway, 1984.

DuBois, Cora. "The 1870 Ghost Dance." In *Anthropological Records* 3:1. Berkeley: University of California Press, 1939. 1–131.

Dudley, Paul. "An Account of the Rattlesnake." *Philosophical Transactions* 32 (March–April 1723): 292–95.

Eddy, Mary Baker. *No and Yes*. Boston: J. Armstrong, 1891.

——. *Retrospection and Introspection*. Boston: W. G. Nixon, 1891.

——. *Science and Health with Key to the Scriptures*. Boston: Christian Scientist Publishing Co., 1875.

Ede, Alfred J. *The Lay Crusade for a Christian America: A Study of the American Federation of Catholic Societies, 1900–1919*. New York: Garland, 1988.

Edwards, Jonathan. *Some Thoughts Concerning the Present Revival of Religion in New-England*. In *The Great Awakening*. Edited by C. C. Goen. *The Works of Jonathan Edwards* 4. New Haven, Conn.: Yale University Press, 1972.

Egan, James. "Sacral Parody in the Fiction of Stephen King." *Journal of Popular Culture* 23 (Winter 1989): 125–41.

Elizondo, Virgil. "Popular Religion as Support of Identity: A Pastoral-Psychological Case-Study Based on the Mexican-American Experience in the USA." In *Popular Religion*. Edited by Norbert Greinacher and Norbert Mette. Edinburgh: T. and T. Clark, 1986. 36–43.

Ellsworth, Donald P. *Christian Music in Contemporary Witness: Historical Antecedents and Contemporary Practice*. Grand Rapids, Mich.: Baker Book House, 1979.

Ellwood, Robert S. *Alternative Altars: Unconventional and Eastern Spirituality in the United States*. Chicago: University of Chicago Press, 1979.

——. "Occult Movements in America." In *Encyclopedia of the American Religious Experience*. Edited by Charles H. Lippy and Peter W. Williams. New York: Charles Scribner's Sons, 1988. 2:711–22.

——. "Polytheism: Establishment or Liberation Religion?" *Journal of the American Academy of Religion* 42:2 (Winter 1974): 344–49.

Ellwood, Robert S., and Harry Partin. *Religious and Spiritual Groups in Modern America*. 2d ed. Englewood Cliffs, N.J.: Prentice-Hall, 1988.

Elson, Ruth Miller. *Myths and Mores in American Best Sellers, 1865–1965.* New York and London: Garland, 1985.

Elzey, Wayne. "Popular Culture." In *Encyclopedia of the American Religious Experience.* Edited by Charles H. Lippy and Peter W. Williams. New York: Charles Scribner's Sons, 1988. 3:1727–41.

———. " 'What Would Jesus Do?' *In His Steps* and the Moral Codes of the Middle Class." *Soundings* 58 (1975): 463–89.

Engh, Michael E. *Frontier Faiths: Church, Temple, and Synagogue in Los Angeles, 1846–188.* Albuquerque: University of New Mexico Press, 1992.

Enlow, David R. *Men Aflame: The Story of Christian Business Men's Committee International.* Grand Rapids, Mich.: Zondervan, 1962.

Epstein, Daniel M. *Sister Aimee: The Life of Aimee Semple McPherson.* San Diego: Harcourt, Brace, 1993.

Evans, Augusta J. *Beulah.* New York: Derby and Jackson, 1859.

———. *Inez, A Tale of the Alamo.* New York: Harper and Bros., 1855.

———. *St. Elmo.* New York: George W. Carleton, 1867.

Evans, Warren Felt. *The Divine Law of Cure.* Boston: H. H. Carter, 1881.

———. *The Mental Cure.* Boston: H. H. and T. W. Carter, 1869.

———. *Mental Medicine.* Boston: W. White, 1872.

Faber, Frederick William. *All for Jesus: or, The Easy Ways of Divine Love.* 23d ed. Boston: John Murphy, 1854.

Fackre, Gabriel. "Archie Bunker: Visions and Reality." *Christian Century* 89 (19 July 1972): 772–74.

"Father Coughlin (pronounced Kawglin)." *Fortune* 9:2 (February 1934): 34–39, 110, 112.

Ferreira, James. "Only Yesterday and the Two Christs of the Twenties." *South Atlantic Quarterly* 80 (1981): 77–83.

Fidler, William Perry. *Augusta Evans Wilson, 1833–1900: A Biography.* University: University of Alabama Press, 1951.

Findlay, James F., Jr. *Dwight L. Moody: American Evangelist, 1837–1899.* Chicago: University of Chicago Press, 1969.

Finley, Ruth E. *The Lady of Godey's.* Philadelphia: Lippincott, 1931.

Finn, Fr. Francis. *Tom Playfair; or Making a Start.* New York: Benziger Bros., 1892.

Finney, Charles G. *Memoirs.* New York: Fleming H. Revell, 1876.

Fish, Melinda. *When Addiction Comes to Church.* Old Tappan, N.J.: Fleming H. Revell, 1991.

Fishwick, Marshall W. "Father Coughlin Time: The Radio and Redemption." *Journal of Popular Culture* 22:2 (Fall 1988): 33–47.

Flake, Carol. *Redemptorama: Culture, Politics, and the New Evangelicalism.* Garden City, N.Y.: Doubleday, 1984.

Flowers, Ronald B. *Religion in Strange Times: The 1960s and 1970s.* Macon, Ga.: Mercer University Press, 1984.

Ford, James E. "*Battlestar Gallactica* and Mormon Theology." *Journal of Popular Culture* 17 (Fall 1983): 83–87.

Fore, William F. *Television and Religion: The Shaping of Faith, Values, and Culture.* Minneapolis: Augsburg, 1987.

Fornell, Earl W. *Unhappy Medium: Spiritualism and the Life of Margaret Fox.* Austin: University of Texas Press, 1964.

Fosdick, Harry Emerson. *The Hope of the World: Twenty-five Sermons on Christianity Today.* New York: Harper and Brothers, 1933.

Foster, Stephen. "The Godly in Transit: English Popular Protestantism and the Creation of a Puritan Establishment in America." In *Seventeenth-Century New England.* Edited by David D. Hall and David Grayson Allen. *Publications of the Colonial Society of Massachusetts* 63. Boston: Colonial Society of Massachusetts, 1984. 185–238.

Frady, Marshall. *Billy Graham: A Parable of American Righteousness.* Boston: Little, Brown, 1979.

Frank, Douglas W. *Less Than Conquerors: How Evangelicals Entered the Twentieth Century.* Grand Rapids, Mich.: Eerdmans, 1986.

Frank, Thomas E. "Norman Vincent Peale." In *Twentieth-Century Shapers of American Popular Religion.* Edited by Charles H. Lippy. Westport, Conn.: Greenwood, 1989. 326–34.

Frankiel, Sandra Sizer. "California and the Southwest." In *Encyclopedia of the American Religious Experience.* Edited by Charles H. Lippy and Peter W. Williams. New York: Charles Scribner's Sons, 1988. 3:1509–23.

———. *California's Spiritual Frontiers: Religious Alternatives in Anglo-Protestantism, 1850–1910.* Berkeley: University of California Press, 1988.

———. *Gospel Hymns and Social Religion: The Rhetoric of Nineteenth-Century Revivalism.* Philadelphia: Temple University Press, 1978.

———. "Politics and Apolitical Religion: The Great Urban Revivals of the Late Nineteenth Century." *Church History* 48 (1979): 81–98.

Frankl, Razelle. *Televangelism: The Marketing of Popular Religion.* Carbondale: Southern Illinois University Press, 1987.

Franklin, Benjamin. *The Papers of Benjamin Franklin.* Edited by Leonard W. Labaree et al. 29 vols. New Haven, Conn.: Yale University Press, 1960.

Frantz, Clair Gordon. "The Religious Teachings of the German Almanacs Published by the Sauers in Colonial Pennsylvania." Ph.D. diss., Temple University, 1955.

Friedman, Jean E. *The Enclosed Garden: Women and Community in the Evangelical South 1830–1900.* Chapel Hill: University of North Carolina Press, 1985.

Friedman, Norman. "Jewish Popular Culture in Contemporary America." *Judaism* 24 (Summer 1975): 263–77.

Frost, Stanley. *The Challenge of the Klan.* Indianapolis: Bobbs-Merrill, 1923.

Fuller, Mrs. Charles E. *Heavenly Sunshine: Letters to the "Old-Fashioned Revival Hour."* Westwood, N.J.: Fleming H. Revell, 1956.

Fuller, Daniel P. *Give the Winds a Mighty Voice: The Story of Charles E. Fuller.* Waco, Tex.: Word, 1972.

Fuller, Robert C. *Alternative Medicine and American Religious Life.* New York: Oxford University Press, 1989.

———. *Mesmerism and the American Cure of Souls.* Philadelphia: University of Pennsylvania Press, 1982.

Gaddy, Gary D., and David Pritchard. "When Watching Religious TV Is Like Attending Church." *Journal of Communication* 35 (1985): 123–31.

Gallup, George, Jr., and Sarah Jones. *100 Questions and Answers: Religion in America*. Princeton, N.J.: Princeton Religious Research Center, 1989.

Gallup, George, Jr., and David Poling. *The Search for America's Faith*. Nashville: Abingdon, 1980.

Galush, William H. "Faith and Fatherland: Dimensions of Polish-American Ethnoreligion, 1875–1975." In *Immigrants and Religion in Urban Culture*. Edited by Randall M. Miller and Thomas D. Marzik. Philadelphia: Temple University Press, 1977. 84–102.

Garfield, Ken. "Jesus Doll a New Idea to Toy With." *Charlotte Observer*, 5 December 1992, 1C.

———. "People Take Comfort in Wings of Angels." *Charlotte Observer*, 11 October 1993, A1, A10.

Garrett, Clarke. "Popular Religion in the American and French Revolutions." In *Religion, Rebellion, and Revolution*. Edited by Bruce Lincoln. New York: St. Martin's, 1985. 69–88.

Gaustad, Edwin S. *Faith of Our Fathers: Religion and the New Nation*. San Francisco: Harper and Row, 1987.

———. *The Great Awakening in New England*. New York: Harper and Row, 1957.

———, ed. *The Rise of Adventism: Religion and Society in Mid-Nineteenth Century America*. New York: Harper and Row, 1974.

Gehring, Mary Louise. "Russell H. Conwell: American Orator." *Southern Speech Journal* 20 (Winter 1954): 117–24.

Gemmere, Amelia Mott. *Witchcraft and Quakerism*. Philadelphia: Biddle Press, 1908.

George, Carol V. R. *God's Salesman: Norman Vincent Peale and the Power of Positive Thinking*. New York: Oxford University Press, 1993.

Gifford, Carolyn DeSwarte, ed. *The Ideal of "The New Woman" According to the Women's Christian Temperance Union*. New York and London: Garland, 1987.

Gilbert, J. E. "Ballot Salvation." *Journal of Popular Culture* 18 (Summer 1984): 1–8.

Gildrie, Richard. "Visions of Evil: Popular Culture, Puritanism, and the Massachusetts Witchcraft Crisis of 1692." *Journal of American Culture* 8 (Winter 1985): 17–33.

Gill, Jerry H. "The Gospel According to Bruce." *Theology Today* 45 (1988): 87–94.

Gill, Sam D. "Native American Religions." In *Encyclopedia of the American Religious Experience*. Edited by Charles H. Lippy and Peter W. Williams. New York: Charles Scribner's Sons, 1988. 1:137–51.

Gillespie, Joanna B. "Carrie, or the Child in the Rectory: Nineteenth-Century Episcopal Sunday School Prototypes." *Historical Magazine of the Protestant Episcopal Church* 51 (1982): 359–70.

Glazer, Nathan. "Jewish Loyalties." *Wilson Quarterly* 5 (Autumn 1981): 134–45.

Gleason, Philip. "Americans All: World War II and the Shaping of American Identity." *Review of Politics* 43 (1981): 483–518.

Goethals, Gregor. "Religious Communication and Popular Piety." *Journal of Communication* 35 (1985): 149–56.

The Golden Book of the Confraternities. New York: Dunigan, 1854.

Goldsmith, Marlene. "Video Values Education: *Star Trek* as Modern Myth." Ph.D. diss., University of Minnesota, 1981.

Goodman, Felicitas D. *How about Demons? Possession and Exorcism in the Modern World.* Bloomington: Indiana University Press, 1988.

———. *Speaking in Tongues: A Cross-Cultural Study of Glossolalia.* Chicago: University of Chicago Press, 1972.

Gordon, Charles W. [Ralph Connor]. *Black Rock.* New York: Thomas Y. Crowell, 1898.

———. *The Sky Pilot.* New York: Fleming H. Revell, 1899.

Gottschalk, Stephen. "Christian Science and Harmonialism." In *Encyclopedia of the American Religious Experience.* Edited by Charles H. Lippy and Peter W. Williams. New York: Charles Scribner's Sons, 1988. 2:901–16.

———. *The Emergence of Christian Science in American Religious Life.* Berkeley and Los Angeles: University of California Press, 1973.

Graham, Billy. *Angels: God's Secret Agents.* Garden City, N.Y.: Doubleday, 1975.

Graham, Stephen R. "Bill and Gloria Gaither." In *Twentieth-Century Shapers of American Popular Religion.* Edited by Charles H. Lippy. Westport, Conn.: Greenwood, 1989. 155–62.

Greeley, Andrew M. "The Catholic Imagination of Bruce Springsteen." *America* 158 (6 February 1988): 110–15.

———. *The Catholic Myth: The Behavior and Beliefs of American Catholics.* New York: Scribners, 1990.

Greenburg, Blu. *How to Run a Traditional Jewish Household.* New York: Simon and Schuster, 1983.

Greenough, Chester Noyes. "New England Almanacs, 1766–1775, and the American Revolution." *Proceedings of the American Antiquarian Society* 45 (October 1935): 288–316.

Guelzo, Allan C. "God's Designs: The Literature of the Great Awakening." *Evangelical Studies Bulletin* 9 (Spring 1992): 7–10.

Gunderson, Joan R. "The Non-Institutional Church: The Role of Women in Eighteenth-Century Virginia." *Historical Magazine of the Protestant Episcopal Church* 51 (1982): 347–57.

Hackett, Alice Payne. *Seventy Years of Best Sellers, 1895–1965.* New York: R. R. Bowker, 1967.

Hadden, Jeffrey K. "The Rise and Fall of American Televangelism." In *Religion in the Nineties.* Edited by Wade Clark Roof. *Annals of the American Academy of Political and Social Science* 527. Newbury Park, Calif.: Sage Periodicals, 1993. 113–30.

———. "Soul Saving via Video." *Christian Century* 97 (28 May 1980): 609–13.

Hadden, Jeffrey K., and Charles E. Swann. *Prime Time Preachers: The Rising Power of Televangelism.* Reading, Mass.: Addison-Wesley, 1981.

Hale, John. *A Modest Inquiry into the Nature of Witchcraft.* Boston: Kneeland and Adams, 1771. First Published, Boston; B. Green and J. Allen for B. Eliot, 1702.

Halévy, Ludovic. *L'Abbé Constantin.* Translated by Katherine Sullivan. New York: J. W. Lovell, 1892. Translated by Emily H. Hazen. New York: H. P. Putnam's Sons, 1892.

Hall, David D. *The Faithful Shepherd: A History of the New England Ministry in the Seventeenth Century.* Chapel Hill: University of North Carolina Press, 1972.

———. "Toward a History of Popular Religion in Early New England." *William and Mary Quarterly,* 3d ser. 41 (1984): 49–55.

———. "A World of Wonders: The Mentality of the Supernatural in Seventeenth-Century New England." In *Seventeenth-Century New England.* Edited by David D. Hall and David Grayson Allen. *Publications of the Colonial Society of Massachusetts* 63 (Boston: Colonial Society of Massachusetts, 1984): 239–74.

———. *Worlds of Wonder, Days of Judgment: Popular Religious Belief in Early New England.* New York: Knopf, 1989.

———, ed. *The Antinomian Controversy, 1636–1638: A Documentary History.* Middletown, Conn.: Wesleyan University Press, 1968.

———, ed. *Witchcraft in Seventeenth-Century New England: A Documentary History, 1638–1692.* Boston: Northeastern University Press, 1991.

Hall, Michael G. *The Last American Puritan: The Life of Increase Mather, 1639–1723.* Middleton, Conn.: Wesleyan University Press, 1988.

Hambrick-Stowe, Charles E. *The Practice of Piety: Puritan Devotional Disciplines in Seventeenth-Century New England.* Chapel Hill: University of North Carolina Press, 1982.

Hand, Wayland D. "Jewish Popular Beliefs and Customs in Los Angeles." In *Studies in Biblical and Jewish Folklore.* Edited by Raphael Patai, Francis Lee Utley, and Dov Noy. Bloomington: Indiana University Press, 1960. 309–26.

Handy, Robert T. "The American Religious Depression." *Church History* 29 (1960): 3–16.

———. *A Christian America: Protestant Hopes and Historical Realities.* 2d ed. New York: Oxford University Press, 1984.

Hardesty, Nancy A. "Seeking the Great Mother: The Goddess for Today." Paper presented to the South Carolina Academy of Religion, February 1993.

Harrell, David E., Jr. *Oral Roberts: An American Life.* Bloomington: Indiana University Press, 1985.

———. *Pat Robertson: A Personal, Political and Religious Portrait.* San Francisco: Harper and Row, 1987.

Harris, Michael W. *The Rise of Gospel Blues: The Music of Thomas Andrew Dorsey in the Urban Church.* New York: Oxford University Press, 1992.

Hart, James D. *The Popular Book: A History of America's Literary Taste.* New York: Oxford University Press, 1950.

Hatch, Nathan O. "Millennialism and Popular Religion in the Early Republic." In *The Evangelical Tradition in America.* Edited by Leonard I. Sweet. Macon, Ga.: Mercer University Press, 1984. 113–47.

Hawley, John Stratton. *Krishna, the Butter Thief.* Princeton, N.J.: Princeton University Press, 1983.

Hawley, Richard. "Some Thoughts on the Pop Jesus." *Anglican Theological Review* 55 (July 1973): 334–46.

Heenan, Edward F., ed. *Mystery, Magic, and Miracle: Religion in a Post-Aquarian Age.* Englewood Cliffs, N.J.: Prentice-Hall, 1973.

Hefley, James. *God Goes to High School.* Waco, Tex.: Word Books, 1970.

Heilbut, Tony. *The Gospel Sound: Good News and Bad Times.* Garden City, N.Y.: Anchor Books, 1975.

Henau, Ernest. "Popular Religiosity and Christian Faith." In *Popular Religion.* Edited by Norbert Greinacher and Norbert Mette. Edinburgh: T. and T. Clark, 1986. 71–81.

Hennell, Michael. "Evangelicalism and Worldliness, 1770–1870." In *Popular Belief and Practice.* Edited by G. J. Cuming and Derek Baker. *Studies in Church History* 8. Cambridge, Eng.: Cambridge University Press, 1972. 229–36.

Herberg, Will. *Protestant, Catholic, Jew: An Essay in American Religious Sociology.* Garden City, N.Y.: Doubleday, 1960.

Herron, Leonora, and Alice M. Bacon. "Conjuring and Conjure Doctors." *Southern Workman* 24 (November and December 1895).

Herx, Henry. "Religion and Film." In *Encyclopedia of the American Religious Experience.* Edited by Charles H. Lippy and Peter W. Williams. New York: Charles Scribner's Sons, 1988. 3:1341–58.

Hewitt, Nancy A. "The Perimeters of Women's Power in American Religion." In *The Evangelical Tradition in America.* Edited by Leonard I. Sweet. Macon, Ga.: Mercer University Press, 1984. 233–56.

Hill, George H. *Airwaves to the Soul: The Influence and Growth of Religious Broadcasting in America.* Saratoga, Calif.: R & E Publishers, 1983.

Hill, George H., and Lenwood G. Davis. *Religious Broadcasting, 1920–1983: A Selectively Annotated Bibliography.* New York: Garland, 1984.

Hill, Samuel S., and Dennis E. Owen. *The New Religious Political Right in America.* Nashville: Abingdon, 1982.

Hindle, Brooke. *The Pursuit of Science in Revolutionary America, 1735–1789.* Chapel Hill: University of North Carolina Press, 1956.

Hittman, Michael. "Ghost Dance, Disillusionment and Opiate Addiction: An Ethnohistory of Smith and Mason Valley." Ph.D. diss., University of New Mexico, 1973.

Hoffman, Shirl J., ed. *Sport and Religion.* Champaign, Ill.: Human Kinetic Books, 1992.

Hofstadter, Beatrice K. "Popular Culture and the Romantic Heroine." *American Scholar* 30:1 (Winter 1960–61): 98–116.

Hollenweger, W. J. *The Pentecostals: The Charismatic Movement in the Churches.* Minneapolis: Augsburg, 1969.

Holmes, Mary Jane. *Lena Rivers.* New York: Miller, Orton and Co., 1856.

———. *Tempest and Sunshine.* New York: D. Appleton, 1854.

Hoover, Stewart M. *Mass Media Religion: The Social Sources of the Electronic Church.* Newbury Park, Calif.: Sage Publications, 1988.

———. "The Religious Television Audience: A Matter of Significance, or Size?" *Review of Religious Research* 29:2 (Winter 1987): 135–51.

Horsfield, Peter G. "Evangelism by Mail: Letters from the Broadcasters." *Journal of Communication* 35 (1985): 89–97.

———. *Religious Television: The American Experience.* New York: Longman, 1984.

Huber, Richard M. *The American Idea of Success.* New York: McGraw- Hill, 1971.

Hulteen, Bob. "Of Heroic Proportions: Fifty Years of Captain America." *Sojourners* 19 (August–September 1990): 39, 41–43.

Hunter, James Davison. *American Evangelicalism: Conservative Religion and the Quandary of Modernity.* New Brunswick, N.J.: Rutgers University Press, 1987.

Hurley, Neil P. "Christ-Transfiguration in Film: Notes on a Meta-Genre." *Journal of Popular Culture* 13 (Spring 1980): 427–33.

———. "Hollywood's New Mythology." *Theology Today* 39 (January 1983): 402–8.

Hurston, Zora Neale. *The Sanctified Church.* Berkeley, Calif.: Turtle Island, 1981.

Hustad, Don. "The Explosion of Popular Hymnody." *The Hymn* 33 (July 1982): 167.

———. "The Influence of the Religious Novel." *The Nation* 47 (1888): 329–30.

Jackson, Bruce. "The Other Kind of Doctor: Conjure and Magic in Black American Folk Medicine." In *American Folk Medicine: A Symposium.* Edited by Wayland D. Hand. Berkeley: University of California Press, 1976. 259–72.

Jacques-Garvey, Amy, ed. *The Philosophy and Opinions of Marcus Garvey.* 2 vols. London: Frank Cass, 1967.

Johnson, Weldon T. "The Religious Crusade: Revival or Ritual?" *American Journal of Sociology* 76 (1971): 873–90.

Jonas, Thomas J. *The Divided Mind: American Catholic Evangelists in the 1890s.* New York and London: Garland, 1988.

Jones, G. William. *Sunday Night at the Movies.* Richmond: John Knox, 1967.

Jones-Jackson, Patricia. "Oral Tradition of Prayer in Gullah." *Journal of Religious Thought* 39 (1982): 21–33.

Jordan, Winthrop D. *White over Black: American Attitudes toward the Negro, 1550–1812.* Chapel Hill: University of North Carolina Press, 1968.

Jorstad, Erling. *Evangelicals in the White House: The Cultural Maturation of Born Again Christianity, 1960–1981.* New York: Mellen, 1981.

———. *Holding Fast, Pressing On: Religion in America in the 1980s.* New York: Praeger, 1990.

———. *The New Christian Right, 1981–1988: Prospects for the Post-Reagan Decade.* Lewiston, N.Y.: Mellen, 1987.

———. *Popular Religion in America: The Evangelical Voice.* Westport, Conn.: Greenwood, 1993.

Joyner, Charles. *Down by the Riverside: A South Carolina Slave Community.* Urbana: University of Illinois Press, 1984.

Judah, J. Stillson. *The History and Philosophy of the Metaphysical Movements in America.* Philadelphia: Westminster, 1967.

Kaminer, Wendy. *I'm Dysfunctional, You're Dysfunctional: The Recovery Movement and Other Self-Help Fashions.* Reading, Mass.: Addison-Wesley, 1992.

———. "Saving Therapy: Exploring the Religious Self-Help Literature." *Theology Today* 48 (Fall 1991): 301–25.

Karp, Abraham J. "The Emergence of an American Judaism." In *Encyclopedia of the American Religious Experience.* Edited by Charles H. Lippy and Peter W. Williams. New York: Charles Scribner's Sons. 1:273–90.

Karr, Jean. *Grace Livingston Hill, Her Story and Her Writings.* New York: Greenberg, 1948.

Karst, Judith Ward-Steinman. "Newspaper Medicine: A Cultural Study of the Colonial South, 1730–1770." Ph.D. diss., Tulane University, 1971.

Kater, John L., Jr. *Christians on the Right: The Moral Majority in Perspective.* New York: Seabury, 1982.

Katz, Bill, and Linda Sternburg Katz. *Self-Help: 1400 Best Books on Personal Growth.* New York: R. R. Bowker, 1985.

Kerr, Howard. *Mediums, and Spirit-Rappers, and Rearing Radicals: Spiritualism in American Literature, 1850–1900.* Urbana: University of Illinois Press, 1972.

Kidahl, John P. *The Psychology of Speaking in Tongues.* New York: Harper and Row, 1972.

Kimball, Gayle. *The Religious Ideas of Harriet Beecher Stowe.* Lewiston, N.Y.: Mellen, 1974.

Klauber, Laurence M. *Rattlesnakes: Their Habits, Histories, and Influence on Mankind.* 2 vols. Berkeley and Los Angeles: University of California Press for the Zoological Society of San Diego, 1956.

Klein, Christa Ressmeyer. "Literature for America's Roman Catholic Children (1865–1895): An Annotated Bibliography." *American Literary Realism, 1870–1910* 6 (1973): 137–52.

Kloos, John. "*The Upper Room.*" In *Popular Religious Periodicals* [*Magazines*] *of the United States.* Edited by Mark Fackler and Charles H. Lippy. Westport, Conn.: Greenwood, forthcoming.

Koch, Gustav Adolf. *Republican Religion: The American Revolution and the Cult of Reason.* New York: Henry Holt and Co., 1933.

Kreuziger, Frederick A. *The Religion of Science Fiction.* Bowling Green, Ohio: Bowling Green State University Popular Press, 1986.

Kselman, Thomas, and Steven Avella. "Marian Piety and the Cold War in the United States." *Catholic Historical Review* 72 (July 1986): 403–24.

Kurtz, Ernest. "Alcoholics Anonymous: A Phenomenon in American Religious History." In *Religion and Philosophy in the United States.* Edited by Peter Freese. Essen, Germany: Verlag Die Blaue Eule, 1987. 2:447–62.

"Kwanzaa: Celebrate in Holiday Style." *Essence* 20 (1989): 50.

LaBarre, Weston. *The Ghost Dance.* New York: Dell, 1972.

———. *The Peyote Cult.* New York: Schocken, 1969.

Lagerquist, L. DeAne. "Aimee Semple McPherson." In *Twentieth-Century Shapers of American Popular Religion.* Edited by Charles H. Lippy. Westport, Conn.: Greenwood, 1989. 263–70.

Langmuir, Gavin. *History, Religion, and Antisemitism.* Berkeley: University of California Press, 1990.

Lanternari, Vittorio. "La religion populaire: Perspective historique et anthropologique." *Archives de sciences sociales des religions* 53 (1982): 121–43.

———. *The Religions of the Oppressed.* New York: New American Library, 1963.

Lederer, John. *The Discoveries of John Lederer.* Edited by William P. Cumming. Charlottesville: University of Virginia Press, 1958.

Legget, Carol. *Amy Grant.* New York: Pocket Books, 1987.

LeJau, Francis. *The Carolina Chronicle of Dr. Francis LeJau, 1706–1717.* Edited by Frank J. Klingberg. Berkeley and Los Angeles: University of California Press, 1956.

Leventhal, Herbert. *In the Shadow of the Enlightenment: Occultism and Renaissance Science in Eighteenth Century America.* New York: New York University Press, 1976.

Levine, Lawrence. *Black Culture and Black Consciousness: Afro-American Folk Thought from Slavery to Freedom*. New York: Oxford University Press, 1977.

Lewis, James R., and J. Gordon Melton, eds. *Perspectives on the New Age*. Albany: State University of New York Press, 1992.

Lewis, L. David. "Charles E. Fuller." In *Twentieth-Century Shapers of American Popular Religion*. Edited by Charles H. Lippy. Westport, Conn.: Greenwood, 1989. 148–55.

Liebman, Robert C., and Robert Wuthnow. *The New Christian Right: Mobilization and Legitimation*. New York: Aldine, 1983.

Lincoln, C. Eric. *The Black Muslims in America*. Rev. ed. Boston: Beacon, 1973.

Lincoln, C. Eric., and Lawrence H. Mamiya. *The Black Church in the African American Experience*. Durham, N.C.: Duke University Press, 1990.

Lindsey, Hal (with C. C. Carlson). *The Late, Great Planet Earth*. Grand Rapids, Mich.: Eerdmans, 1970.

———. *Satan Is Alive and Well on Planet Earth*. Grand Rapids, Mich.: Zondervan, 1972.

Lippy, Charles H. "Billy Graham's 'My Answer': Agenda for the Faithful." *Studies in Popular Culture* 5 (1982): 27–34.

———. "Social Christianity." In *Encyclopedia of the American Religious Experience*. Edited by Charles H. Lippy and Peter W. Williams. New York: Charles Scribner's Sons, 1988. 2:917–31.

———. "Sympathy Cards and Death." *Theology Today* 34 (1977): 167–77.

———. "Sympathy Cards and the Grief Process." *Journal of Popular Culture* 17 (1983): 98–108.

———. "Waiting for the End: The Social Context of American Apocalyptic Religion." In *The Apocalyptic Vision in America: Interdisciplinary Essays on Myth and Culture*. Edited by Lois P. Zamora. Bowling Green, Ohio: Bowling Green University Popular Press, 1982. 37–63.

———, ed. *Twentieth-Century Shapers of American Popular Religion*. Westport, Conn.: Greenwood, 1989.

Lippy, Charles H., Robert Choquette, and Stafford Poole. *Christianity Comes to the Americas, 1492–1776*. New York: Paragon House, 1992.

Lockridge, Kenneth. *Literacy in Colonial New England: An Inquiry into the Social Context of Literacy in the Early Modern West*. New York: Norton, 1974.

Long, Kathryn. "*Godey's Lady's Book*." In *Popular Religious Periodicals of the United States*. Edited by Mark Fackler and Charles H. Lippy. Westport, Conn.: Greenwood, forthcoming.

Love, Christopher. *The Strange and Wonderful Predictions of Mr. Christopher Love*. Edinburgh: A. Robertson, 1785.

Loveless, Wendell P. *Manual of Gospel Broadcasting*. Chicago: Moody, 1946.

Lovely, N. W. "Notes on the New England Almanacs." *New England Quarterly* 8 (1935): 264–77.

Lovett, Leonard. "The Spiritual Legacy and Role of Black Holiness-Pentecostalism in the Development of American Culture." *One in Christ: A Catholic Ecumenical Review* 23 (1987): 144–56.

Luckmann, Thomas. *The Invisible Religion*. New York: Macmillan, 1967.

Lynd, Robert S., and Helen M. Lynd. *Middletown: A Study in American Culture.* New York: Harcourt and Brace, 1929.

———. *Middletown in Transition: A Study in Cultural Conflicts.* New York: Harcourt and Brace, 1937.

McCauley, Deborah Vansau. "Kathryn Kuhlman." In *Twentieth-Century Shapers of American Popular Religion.* Edited by Charles H. Lippy. Westport, Conn.: Greenwood, 1989. 225–33.

McDannell, Colleen. *The Christian Home in Victorian America, 1840–1900.* Bloomington: Indiana University Press, 1986.

MacDonald, Fergus. *The Catholic Catholic and the Secret Societies in the United States.* Edited by Thomas J. McMahon. United States Catholic Historical Society Monograph Series 22. New York: United States Catholic Historical Society, 1946.

McFadden, Margaret. "The Ironies of Pentecost: Phoebe Palmer, World Evangelism, and Female Networks." *Methodist History* 31 (January 1993): 63–75.

McFarlane, Alan D. J. *Witchcraft in Tudor and Stuart England.* New York: Harper and Row, 1970.

McIllwaine, H. R., ed. *Minutes of the Council and General Court of Colonial Virginia, 1622–1632, 1670–1676.* Richmond: The Colonial Press, Everett Waddey Co., 1924.

[McKever-]Floyd, Preston L. "The Negro Spiritual: Examination of Theological Concepts." *Duke Divinity School Review* 43 (1978): 102–11.

McLoughlin, William G. "Aimee Semple McPherson." In *Notable American Women: A Biographical Dictionary.* Cambridge, Mass.: Harvard University Press, 1971. 2:477–80.

———. "Aimee Semple McPherson: 'Your Sister in the King's Glad Service.' " *Journal of Popular Culture* 1 (Winter 1967): 193–217.

———. *Billy Graham: Revivalist in a Secular Age.* New York: Ronald Press, 1960.

———. *Billy Sunday Was His Real Name.* Chicago: University of Chicago Press, 1955.

———, ed. *The American Evangelicals, 1800–1900.* New York: Harper and Row, 1968.

Mander, Mary S. "*Dallas*: The Mythology of Crime and the Moral Occult." *Journal of Popular Culture* 17 (Fall 1983): 44–50.

Marglin, Frederique. *Wives of the God-King: The Rituals of the Devadasis of Puri.* New York: Oxford University Press, 1985.

Marini, Stephen A. "The Great Awakening." In *Encyclopedia of the American Religious Experience.* Edited by Charles H. Lippy and Peter W. Williams. New York: Charles Scribner's Sons, 1988. 2:775–98.

Marsh, Spencer. *God, Man, and Archie Bunker.* New York: Harper and Row, 1975.

Marshall, Charles C. "An Open Letter to the Honorable Alfred E. Smith." *Atlantic Monthly* 39 (April 1927): 540–49.

Martin, Bernice. "The Sacralization of Disorder: Symbolism in Rock Music." *Sociological Analysis* 40 (Summer 1979): 87–124.

Martin, William C. "The God-Hucksters of Radio." In *Side-Saddle on the Golden Calf: Social Structure and Popular Culture in America.* Edited by George H. Lewis. Pacific Palisades, Calif., Goodyear, 1972. 49–55.

————. *A Prophet with Honor: The Billy Graham Story*. New York: Morrow, 1991.

Marty, Martin E. "The Invisible Religion: A Closer Look at the Theology of the Electric Church." *Presbyterian Survey* 69 (May 1979): 13.

————. *The Noise of Conflict, 1919–1941*. *Modern American Religion* 2. Chicago: University of Chicago Press, 1991.

————. "Where the Energies Go." In *Religion in the Nineties*. Edited by Wade Clark Roof. *Annals of the American Academy of Political and Social Sciences* 527. Newbury Park, Calif.: Sage Periodicals, 1993. 11–26.

Masterson, James R. "Colonial Rattlesnake Lore, 1714." *Zoologica* 23 (July 1938): 213–16.

Mather, Cotton. *Magnalia Christi Americana*. London: T. Parkhurst, 1702.

————. *MDCLXXXIII. The Boston Ephemeris. An Almanac for the (Dionysian) Year of the Christian AEra M.DC.LXXX.III*. Boston: S. Green for S. Sewall, 1683.

————. *Memorable Providences, Relating to Witchcrafts and Possessions*. Boston: [R.P.], 1689.

————. *A Midnight Cry*. Boston: John Allen for Samuel Phillips, 1692.

————. *The Wonders of the Invisible World*. Boston: Benjamin Harris, 1693.

Mather, Increase. *Cases of Conscience Concerning Evil Spirits Personating Men, Witchcrafts, Infallible Proofs of Guilt . . .* Boston: B. Harris, 1693.

————. *Doctrine of Divine Providence Opened and Applyed*. Boston: Richard Pierce, 1684.

————. *An Essay for the Recording of Illustrious Providences*. Boston: Samuel Green, 1684.

————. *Heavens Alarm to the World*. Boston: John Foster, 1681.

————. *Kometographia, Or a Discourse Concerning Comets*. Boston: Samuel Green, 1683.

————. *The Latter Sign Discoursed of*. Boston: For Samuel Sewall, 1682.

Maus, Cynthia Pearl. *The Church and the Fine Arts*. New York: Harper and Bros., 1960.

May, Henry F. *The Enlightenment in America*. New York: Oxford University Press, 1976.

May, John R., and Michael Bird, eds. *Religion in Film*. Knoxville: University of Tennessee Press, 1982.

Mayhew, Jonathan. *A Discourse Concerning Unlimited Submission to the Higher Powers*. Boston: D. Fowle and D. Gookin, 1750.

————. *Seven Sermons*. Boston: Rogers and Fowle, 1749.

————. *Two Discourses Delivered November 23d 1758*. Boston: R. Draper, [1758].

Mbiti, John. *African Religion and Philosophy*. Garden City, N.Y.: Doubleday, 1969.

Mead, Sidney. *The Nation with the Soul of a Church*. Reprinted, Macon, Ga.: Mercer University Press, 1985.

Mecklin, John Moffatt. *The Ku Klux Klan: A Study of the American Mind*. New York: Harcourt and Brace, 1924.

Meldonado, Louis. "Popular Religion: Its Dimensions, Levels, and Types." In *Pop-

ular Religion. Edited by Norbert Greinacher and Norbert Mette. Edinburgh: T. and T. Clark, 1986. 3–11.

Melton, J. Gordon. "Another Look at New Religions." In *Religion in the Nineties.* Edited by Wade Clark Roof. *Annals of the American Academy of Political and Social Science* 527. Newbury Park, Calif.: Sage Periodicals, 1993. 97–112.

———. "The Revival of Astrology in the United States." In *Religious Movements: Genesis, Exodus, and Numbers*. Edited by Rodney Stark. New York: Paragon House, 1985. 279–99.

Mensching, Gustav. "The Masses, Folk Belief, and Universal Religion." In *Religion, Culture, and Society*. Edited by Louis Schneider. New York: Wiley, 1964. 269–73.

Merton, Robert K. "Puritanism, Pietism and Science." In Robert K. Merton, *Social Theory and Social Structure*. New York: Free Press, 1968. 628–60.

Messbarger, Paul R. *Fiction with a Parochial Purpose: Social Uses of American Catholic Literature, 1884–1900*. Boston: Boston University Press, 1971.

Meyer, Donald. *The Positive Thinkers: Popular Religious Psychology from Mary Baker Eddy to Norman Vincent Peale and Ronald Reagan*. Middletown, Conn.: Wesleyan University Press, 1988.

Michaelsen, Robert S. "Is the Miner's Canary Silent? Implications of the Supreme Court's Denial of American Indian Free Exercise of Religion Claims." *Journal of Law and Religion* 6 (1988): 97–114.

———. "Red Man's Religion/White Man's Religious History." *Journal of the American Academy of Religion* 51 (1983): 667–84.

———. "Sacred Land in America: What Is It? How Can It Be Protected?" *Religion* 16 (1986): 249–68.

———. "The Significance of the American Indian Religious Freedom Act of 1978." *Journal of the American Academy of Religion* 52 (1984): 93–115.

———. " 'We Also Have a Religion': The Free Exercise of Religion among Native Americans." *American Indian Quarterly* 10 (Summer 1983): 111–41.

Middlekauff, Robert. *The Mathers: Three Generations of Puritan Intellectuals, 1596–1728*. New York: Oxford University Press, 1971.

Millard, Bob. *Amy Grant: A Biography*. New York: Doubleday, 1986.

Miller, David. *The New Polytheism: Rebirth of the Gods and Goddesses*. New York: Harper and Row, 1974.

Miller, David H. *Ghost Dance*. Reprinted, Lincoln: University of Nebraska Press, 1975.

Miller, Douglas. "Popular Religion of the 1950's." *Journal of Popular Culture* 9 (Summer 1975): 66–76.

Miller, J. Keith. *Hunger for Healing: The Twelve Steps as a Classic Model for Christian Spiritual Growth*. San Francisco: HarperCollins, 1991.

Miller, Robert Moats. *Harry Emerson Fosdick: Preacher, Pastor, Prophet*. New York: Oxford University Press, 1985.

Miller, Timothy. *Following In His Steps: A Biography of Charles M. Sheldon*. Knoxville: University of Tennessee Press, 1987.

Minnick, Harvey C. *William Holmes McGuffey and His Readers*. Cincinnati: American Book Co., 1936.

Mitchell, Brian, ed. *Building the American Catholic City: Parishes and Institutions.* New York: Garland, 1988.

Molson, Francis J. "Francis J. Finn, S.J.: Pioneering Author of Juveniles for Catholic Americans." *Journal of Popular Culture* 11 (1977): 28–41.

Monk, Maria. *Awful Disclosures of the Hotel Dieu Nunnery of Montreal.* New York: Howe and Bates, 1836.

Montgomery, Edrene S. "Bruce Barton and the Twentieth Century Menace of Unreality." Ph.D. diss., University of Arkansas, 1984.

———. "Bruce Barton's *The Man Nobody Knows*: A Popular Advertising Illusion." *Journal of Popular Culture* 19:3 (Winter 1985): 21–34.

Mooney, James. *The Ghost-Dance Religion and the Sioux Outbreak of 1890.* Edited by Anthony F. C. Wallace. Chicago: University of Chicago Press, 1965.

Moore, Deborah Dash. "The Social History of American Judaism." In *Encyclopedia of the American Religious Experience.* Edited by Charles H. Lippy and Peter W. Williams. New York: Charles Scribner's Sons, 1988. 1:291–310.

Moore, R. Laurence. "Religion, Secularization, and the Shaping of the Culture Industry in Antebellum America." *American Quarterly* 41 (June 1989): 216–42.

Morgan, David. "Imaging Protestant Piety: The Icons of Warner Sallman." *Religion and American Culture* 3 (Winter 1993): 29–47.

———. "Sallman's *Head of Christ*: The History of an Image." *Christian Century* 109 (7 October 1992): 868–70.

Morken, Hubert. *Pat Robertson: Religion and Politics in Simple Terms.* Old Tappan, N.J.: Fleming H. Revell, 1987.

Morris, James. *The Preachers.* New York: St. Martin's, 1973.

Mott, Frank Luther. *Golden Multitudes: The Story of Best Sellers in the United States* New York: R. R. Bowker, 1947.

Muchembled, Robert. *Popular Culture and Elite Culture in France, 1400–1750.* Translated by Lydia Cochrane. Baton Rouge: Louisiana State University Press, 1985.

Murphy, Joseph M. *Santéria: African Spirits in America.* 2d ed. Boston: Beacon, 1992.

Murphy, Larry. "Apocalypse and Millennium in America." *Explor* 4 (Spring 1978): 58–65.

Murphy, Mary. "The Next Billy Graham." *Esquire* 90 (10 October 1978): 25–30.

Murray, Robert K. *Red Scare: A Study in National Hysteria, 1919–1920.* Minneapolis: University of Minnesota Press, 1955.

Neill, E. D., ed. "Witchcraft in Virginia." *William and Mary Quarterly*, 1st ser. 2 (July 1893): 58–60.

Nelsen, Hart M. "Unchurched Black Americans: Patterns of Religiosity and Affiliation." *Review of Religious Research* 29:4 (June 1988): 398–412.

Nelson, Clyde K. "Russell H. Conwell and the 'Gospel of Wealth.' " *Foundations* 5 (1962): 39–51.

Nelson, Geoffrey K. *Spiritualism and Society.* New York: Schocken, 1969.

Neuchterlein, James A. "Bruce Barton and the Business Ethos of the 1920's." *South Atlantic Quarterly* 76 (1977): 293–308.

Neusner, Jacob. *American Judaism: Adventure in Modernity.* Rev. ed. Englewood Cliffs, N.J.: Prentice-Hall, 1978.

———. "Judaism in Contemporary America." In *Encyclopedia of the American Religious Experience*. Edited by Charles H. Lippy and Peter W. Williams. New York: Charles Scribner's Sons, 1988. 1:311–23.

Nichol, Francis D. *The Midnight Cry: A Defense of the Character and Conduct of William Miller and the Millerites*. Washington, D.C.: Review and Herald Publishing Association, 1944.

Nichols, Charles L. "Notes on the Almanacs of Massachusetts." *Proceedings of the American Antiquarian Society*, n.s. 22 (1912): 15–134.

Niebuhr, H. Richard. *The Social Sources of Denominationalism*. New York: Henry Holt and Co., 1929. 26–76.

Noll, Mark A. *A History of Christianity in the United States and Canada*. Grand Rapids, Mich.: Eerdmans, 1992.

Norton, Wesley. *Religious Newspapers in the Old Northwest to 1861: A History, Bibliography, and Record of Opinion*. Athens, Ohio: Ohio University Press, 1977.

Noss, David S., and John B. Noss. *A History of the World's Religions*. 8th ed. New York: Macmillan, 1990.

Notestein, Wallace. *A History of Witchcraft in England from 1558 to 1718*. Reprinted, New York: Russell and Russell, 1965; and New York: Thomas Y. Crowell, 1968.

Obelkevich, James, ed. *Religion and the People, 800–1700*. Chapel Hill: University of North Carolina Press, 1979.

O'Flaherty, Wendy Doniger. *Women, Androgynes, and Other Mythical Beasts*. Chicago: University of Chicago Press, 1980.

Oliver, Betty. "Grace Sherwood of Princess Anne: She Was a Witch, They Said." *North Carolina Folklore* 10 (July 1962): 36–39.

Orsi, Robert Anthony. *The Madonna of 115th Street: Faith and Community in Italian Harlem, 1880–1950*. New Haven, Conn.: Yale University Press, 1985.

Osterreich, Shelley Anne. *The American Indian Ghost Dance, 1870 and 1890: An Annotated Bibliography*. Westport, Conn.: Greenwood, 1991.

Ostling, Richard N. "When God Was a Woman: Worshipers of Mother Earth Are Part of a Goddess Resurgence." *Time* 137 (6 May 1991): 73.

Pagels, Elaine. *The Gnostic Gospels*. New York: Random House, 1979.

Palmer, Phoebe. *The Way of Holiness*. New York: Foster and Palmer, [1835].

Parker, Everett C., David W. Barry, and Dallas W. Smythe. *The Television-Radio Audience and Religion*. New York: Harper, 1955.

Parker, Gail Thain. *Mind Cure in New England: From the Civil War to World War I*. Hanover, N.H.: University Press of New England, 1973.

Parsons, Wilfred. "Father Coughlin and Social Justice." *America* 3:6 (18 May 1935): 129–31.

Paz, D. G. "Lloyd Cassell Douglas." In *Twentieth-Century Shapers of American Popular Religion*. Edited by Charles H. Lippy. Westport, Conn.: Greenwood, 1989. 118–25.

Peale, Norman Vincent. *The Power of Positive Thinking*. New York: Prentice-Hall, 1952.

Peck, George. *Early Methodism within the Bounds of the Old Genesee Conference from 1788 to 1838*. New York: Carlton and Porter, 1860.

Phelps, Elizabeth Stuart. *The Gates Ajar*. Edited by Elizabeth Sootin Smith. Cambridge, Mass.: Harvard University Press, 1964.

Phy, Allene. "Retelling the Greatest Story Ever Told: Jesus in Popular Fiction." In *The Bible in American Culture* 2. Edited by Allene Phy. Philadelphia: Fortress, 1985. 42–83.

Pious Guide to Prayer and Devotion, Containing Various Practices of Piety Calculated to Answer the Various Demands of the Different Devout Members of the Roman Catholic Church. Georgetown: James Doyle, 1792.

Pollard, Alton B., III. "Religion, Rock, and Eroticism." *Journal of Black Sacred Music* 1 (Spring 1987): 47–52.

Potter, Richard H. "Popular Religion of the 1930s as Reflected in the Best Sellers of Harry Emerson Fosdick." *Journal of Popular Culture* 3 (1970): 712–28.

Praemonitus Praemunitus. The Protocols of the Wise Men of Zion. New York: Beckwith, 1920.

Price-Mars, Jean. *So Spoke the Uncle*. Translated by Magdalino W. Shannon. Washington, D.C.: Three Continents Press, 1983.

Princeton Religious Research Center and the Gallup Organization, Inc. *The Unchurched American*. [Princeton, N.J.: Princeton Religious Research Center for the National Council of Churches], 1978.

Quebedeaux, Richard. *By What Authority? The Rise of Personality Cults in American Christianity*. New York: Harper and Row, 1982.

———. *I Found It! The Story of Bill Bright and Campus Crusade*. San Francisco: Harper and Row, 1979.

———. *The New Charismatics: The Origins, Development, and Significance of Neo-Pentecostalism*. Garden City, N.Y.: Doubleday, 1976.

———. *The Worldly Evangelicals*. New York: Harper and Row, 1978.

———. *The Young Evangelicals: Revolution in Orthodoxy*. New York: Harper and Row, 1974.

Quinn, D. Michael. *Early Mormonism and the Magic World View*. Salt Lake City, Utah: Signature Books, 1987.

Rabinowitz, Richard. *The Spiritual Self in Everyday Life: The Transformation of Personal Religious Experience in Nineteenth-Century New England*. Boston: Northeastern University Press, 1989.

Raboteau, Albert. "Black Christianity in America." In *Encyclopedia of the American Religious Experience*. Edited by Charles H. Lippy and Peter W. Williams. New York: Charles Scribner's Sons, 1988. 1:635–48.

———. *Slave Religion: The "Invisible Institution" in the Antebellum South*. New York: Oxford University Press, 1977.

Raghavan, V. *The Great Integrators: The Saint Singers of India*. Delhi: Ministry of Education and Broadcasting, 1966.

Ramsbottom, Mary Macmanus. "Religious Society and the Family in Charlestown, Massachusetts, 1630 to 1740." Ph.D. diss., Yale University, 1987.

Raphael, Marc Lee. "From Marjorie to Tevya: The Image of the Jews in American Popular Literature, Theatre, and Comedy, 1955–1965." *American Jewish History* 74 (September 1984): 66–72.

Raser, Harold E. *Phoebe Palmer: Her Life and Thought*. Lewiston, N.Y.: Mellen, 1987.

"The Rattlesnake & Its Congeners." *Harper's New Monthly Magazine* 10 (March 1855): 470–87.

Rauschenbusch, Walter. *Christianity and the Social Crisis.* Edited by Robert D. Cross. New York: Harper and Row, 1964.

———. *For God and the People: Prayers for the Social Awakening.* Boston: Pilgrim, 1910.

Real, Michael. "The Super Bowl: Mythic Spectacle." In *The Popular Culture Reader.* 3d ed. Edited by Christopher D. Geist and Jack Nachbar. Bowling Green, Ohio: Bowling Green University Popular Press, 1983. 284–89.

Redfield, Robert. *Peasant Society and Culture.* Chicago: University of Chicago Press, 1956.

Reid, Christian [Mrs. Frances Tiernen]. *Child of Mary.* Notre Dame, Ind.: Ave Maria Office, 1885.

Reines-Josephy, Marcia. "The Use of Amulets in Contemporary Jewish Society." In *Proceedings of the Ninth World Congress of Jewish Studies.* Edited by Moshe H. Goshen-Gottstein and David Assaf. Jerusalem: World Union of Jewish Studies, 1986. 7:175–80.

Ribuffo, Leo P. "Jesus Christ as Business Statesman: Bruce Barton and the Selling of Corporate Capitalism." *American Quarterly* 33 (1981): 206–231.

———. "Religious Prejudice and Nativism." In *Encyclopedia of the American Religious Experience.* Edited by Charles H. Lippy and Peter W. Williams. New York: Charles Scribner's Sons, 1988. 3:1525–46.

Riesman, Frank. "The New Self-Help Backlash." *Social Policy* 20 (Summer 1990): 422–48.

Roberts, Oral. *How To Get Through Your Struggles or You Can Walk on the Stormy Waters of Your Life.* Tulsa, Okla.: Oral Roberts Evangelistic Association, 1977.

Roebroeck, E.J.M.G. "A Problem for Sociology: Contemporary Developments in the Roman Catholic Church." In *Official and Popular Religion: Analysis of a Theme for Religious Studies.* Edited by Pieter Vrijhof and Jacques Waardenburg. The Hague: Mouton, 1979. 166–99.

Roman Catholic Manual, or Collection of Prayers, Anthems, Hymns, etc. Baltimore: Fielding Lucas, Jr., [1803].

Romanowski, William. "Contemporary Christian Music: The Business of Music Ministry." In *American Evangelicals and the Mass Media.* Edited by Quentin J. Schultze. Grand Rapids, Mich.: Zondervan, 1990.

Roof, Wade Clark. "American Religion in Transition: A Review and Interpretation of Recent Trends." *Social Compass* 31 (1984): 273–89.

———. *A Generation of Seekers: The Spiritual Journeys of the Baby Boom Generation.* San Francisco: HarperSanFrancisco, 1993.

———, ed. *Religion in America Today. Annals of the American Academy of Political and Social Science* 480. Beverly Hills, Calif.: Sage Publications, 1985.

Roof, Wade Clark, and William McKinney. *American Mainline Religion: Its Changing Shape and Future.* New Brunswick, N.J.: Rutgers University Press, 1987.

Ruether, Rosemary Radford. "Women-Church: Emerging Feminist Liturgical Communities." In *Popular Religion.* Edited by Norbert Greinacher and Norbert Mette. Edinburgh: T. and T. Clark, 1986. 52–59.

Ruggles, Alice McGuffey. *The Story of the McGuffeys.* New York: American Book Co., 1950.

Russell, Garth M. "Charles G. Finney: His Place in the Stream." In *The Evangelical Tradition in America.* Edited by Leonard I. Sweet. Macon, Ga.: Mercer University Press, 1984. 131–47.

Russell, Mary Ann Underwood. "Lloyd C. Douglas and His Larger Congregation: The Novels and a Reflection of Some Segments of the American Popular Mind of Two Decades." Ph.D. diss., George Peabody College for Teachers, 1970.

Rutman, Darrett. "The Evolution of Religious Life in Early Virginia." *Lex et Scientia: The Journal of the American Academy of Law and Science* 14 (1978): 190–214.

Sandeen, Ernest R. *The Roots of Fundamentalism.* Grand Rapids, Mich.: Baker Book House, 1970.

Sauer, C. *Die Hoch-Deutsch Americanische Calendar auf das Jahr . . .* Germantown, Pa.: C. Sauer.

———. *Pennsylvania Town and Countrymen's Almanack.* Germantown, Pa.: C. Sauer, 1755– .

Scheinen, Richard. "Do You Believe in Angels?" *Anderson* (S.C.) *Independent-Mail* (27 June 1993): B1, B4.

Schmidt, Jean Miller. "Holiness and Perfection." In *Encyclopedia of the American Religious Experience.* Edited by Charles H. Lippy and Peter W. Williams. New York: Charles Scribner's Sons, 1988. 2:813–29.

Schmitt, Peter. "The Church in the Wildwood: The Nature Cult in Urban America, 1890–1930." *Journal of Popular Culture* 2 (1968): 113–18.

Schneider, Louis, and Sanford M. Dornbusch. *Popular Religion: Inspirational Books in America.* Chicago: University of Chicago Press, 1958.

Schroeder, Widick, et al. *Suburban Religion: Churches and Synagogues in the American Experience.* Chicago: Center for the Scientific Study of Religion, 1974.

Schuller, Robert H. *You Can Become the Person You Want to Be.* New York: Hawthorn Books, 1973.

Schwartz, Hillel. "The End of the Beginning: Millenarian Studies, 1961–1975." *Religious Studies Review* 2 (July 1976): 1–15.

Seguy, Jean. "Images et 'Religion Populaire': Reflexions sur un Colloque." *Archives de sciences sociales des religions* 44 (July–September 1977): 25–43.

Setta, Susan M. "Healing in Suburbia: The Women's Aglow Fellowship." *Journal of Religious Studies* 12:2 (1986): 46–56.

Sevre, Leif. *The Story of the Upper Room.* Nashville, Tenn.: Parthenon Press, 1965.

Shakarian, Demos. "FGBMFI Struggles toward the Future." *Charisma* 13 (March 1988): 24.

Sheldon, Charles M. *In His Steps: What Would Jesus Do?* Chicago: Advance, 1897.

Sherman, John. *An Almanack of Coelestial Motions of the Sun and Planets with Some of Their Principal Aspects.* Cambridge, Mass.: J. Sherman, 1677.

Shils, Edward. "Centre and Periphery." In *The Logic of Personal Knowledge: Essays Presented to Michael Polyani on His Seventieth Birthday.* Edited by Paul Ignotos et al. London: Routledge and Kegan Paul, 1961. 117–30.

Shipps, Jan. *Mormonism: The Story of a New Religion.* Urbana: University of Illinois Press, 1985.

Short, Robert L. *The Gospel According to Peanuts.* Richmond: John Knox, 1965.

———. *The Parables of Peanuts.* New York: Harper and Row, 1968.

Shriver, Peggy L. *The Bible Vote: Religion and the New Right.* New York: Pilgrim, 1981.

Shupe, Anson, and William A. Stacey. *Born Again Politics and the Moral Majority: What Social Surveys Really Show.* New York: Mellen, 1982.

Simpson, Janice. "Tidings of Black Pride and Joy." *Time* 138 (23 December 1991): 81.

Sittser, Gerald L. "Bruce Barton." In *Twentieth-Century Shapers of American Popular Religion.* Edited by Charles H. Lippy. Westport, Conn.: Greenwood, 1989. 20–29.

Slotkin, J. S. *The Peyote Religion: A Study in Indian-White Relations.* Glencoe, Ill.: Free Press, 1956.

Smith, Albert Hatcher. *The Life of Russell H. Conwell.* Boston: Silver, Burdett, 1899.

Smith, Alfred E. "Catholic and Patriot: Governor Smith Replies." *Atlantic Monthly* 139 (May 1927): 721–28.

Smith, David E. "Millenarian Scholarship in America." *American Quarterly* 17 (1965): 535–49.

Smith, Timothy L. "Lay Initiative in the Religious Life of American Immigrants, 1880–1950." In *Anonymous Americans: Explorations in Nineteenth-Century Social History.* Edited by Tamara Hareven. Englewood Cliffs, N.J.: Prentice-Hall, 1971. 214–49.

Smith-Rosenberg, Carroll. "Women and Religious Revivals: Anti-Ritualism, Liminality, and the Emergence of an American Bourgeoisie." In *The Evangelical Tradition in America.* Edited by Leonard I. Sweet. Macon, Ga.: Mercer University Press, 1984. 199–231.

Southgate, Martha. "Merry Kwanzaa to All." *Glamour* 89 (December 1991): 120.

Speck, Frank G. "Reptile Lore of the Northern Indians." *Journal of American Folklore* 36 (1923): 273–80.

Spencer, Jon Michael. "A Theology for the Blues." *Journal of Black Sacred Music* 2 (Spring 1988): 1–20.

Stafford, Joseph. *The Rhode-Island Almanack for the Year . . .* Newport: Joseph Stafford.

———. *The Rhode-Island Almanack . . . for 1738.* Newport: Joseph Stafford, 1738.

Stafford, Tim. "The Hidden Gospel of the 12 Steps." *Christianity Today* 35 (22 July 1991): 14–19.

Stahlman, William D. "Astrology in Colonial America: An Extended Inquiry." *William and Mary Quarterly,* 3d ser. 13 (1956): 551–63.

Staples, P. "Official and Popular Religion in an Ecumenical Perspective." In *Official and Popular Religion: Analysis of a Theme for Religious Studies.* Edited by Pieter Vrijhof and Jacques Waardenburg. The Hague: Mouton, 1979. 244–93.

Starhawk. *The Spiral Dance.* San Francisco: Harper and Row, 1979.

Starker, Steven. *Oracle at the Supermarket: The American Preoccupation with Self-Help Books.* New Brunswick, N.J.: Transaction Books, 1989.

Stein, Judith. *The World of Marcus Garvey: Race and Class in Modern Society.* Baton Rouge: Louisiana State University Press, 1986.

Stein, Stephen J. *The Shaker Experience in America: A History of the United Society of Believers.* New Haven, Conn.: Yale University Press, 1992.

Stevens, Patricia B. *Merry Christmas: A History of the Holiday.* New York: Macmillan, 1979.

Stevenson, Rupert Murrell. "Ira D. Sankey and 'Gospel Hymnody.' " *Religion in Life* 20 (1950–51): 81–88.

Stewart, Omer C. *Peyote Religion.* Norman: University of Oklahoma Press, 1987.

———. *Peyotism in the West: A Historical and Cultural Perspective.* Salt Lake City: University of Utah Press, 1984.

Stiles, Ezra. *The Literary Diary of Ezra Stiles.* Edited by Franklin Bowditch Dexter. 3 vols. New York: Charles Scribner's Sons, 1901.

Stiverson, Gregory A. "Books Both Useful and Entertaining: Reading Habits in Mid-Eighteenth Century Virginia." *Southeastern Librarian* 24:4 (Winter 1975): 52–58.

Stoever, William K. B. *"A Faire and Easie Way to Heaven": Covenant Theology and Antinomianism in Early Massachusetts.* Middletown, Conn.: Wesleyan University Press, 1978.

Stoppe, Richard Leon. "Lloyd C. Douglas." Ph.D. diss., Wayne State University, 1966.

Stowell, Marion Barber. *Early American Almanacs: The Colonial Weekday Bible.* New York: Burt Franklin, 1977.

Suderman, Elmer F. "Elizabeth Stuart Phelps and the Gates Ajar Novels." *Journal of Popular Culture* 3 (1969): 91–106.

Suess, Paulo. "The Creative and Normative Role of Popular Religion in the Church." In *Popular Religion.* Edited by Norbert Greinacher and Norbert Mette. Edinburgh: T. and T. Clark, 1986. 122–31.

Swann, Charles. "The Electric Church." *Presbyterian Survey* 69 (May 1979): 9–12, 14–16.

Swanton, John R. "Religious Beliefs and Medical Practices of the Creek Indians." *U.S. Bureau of Ethnology Annual Report* 42 (1924–25): 473–672.

Sweet, Leonard I. "Millennialism in America: Recent Studies." *Theological Studies* 40 (1979): 510–31.

———. "Nineteenth-Century Evangelicalism." In *Encyclopedia of the American Religious Experience.* Edited by Charles H. Lippy and Peter W. Williams. New York: Scribner, 1988. 2:875–99.

Synan, Vinson. *The Holiness-Pentecostal Movement in the United States.* Grand Rapids, Mich.: Eerdmans, 1971.

Szasz, Ferenc Morton. *The Divided Mind of Protestant America, 1880–1930.* University: University of Alabama Press, 1982.

Taves, Ann. *The Household of Faith: Roman Catholic Devotions in Mid-Nineteenth Century America.* Notre Dame, Ind.: University of Notre Dame Press, 1986.

Teahan, John F. "Warren Felt Evans and Mental Healing: Romantic Idealism and Practical Mysticism in Nineteenth-Century America." *Church History* 48 (1979): 63–80.

Thiesen, Lee Scott. " 'My God, Did I Set All of This in Motion?' General Lew Wallace and *Ben Hur.*" *Journal of Popular Culture* 18:2 (1984): 33–41.

Thomas, Keith. *Religion and the Decline of Magic.* New York: Scribners, 1971.

Thomas, Sari. "The Route to Redemption and Social Class." *Journal of Communication* 35 (1985): 111–22.

Tillotson, Kathleen. *Novels of the Eighteen-Forties.* Oxford: Clarendon Press, 1954.

Tincker, Mary Agnes. *Grapes and Thorns.* New York: Catholic Publication Society, [1874].

———. *House of Yorke.* New York: Catholic Publication Society, 1872.

Tomasi, Silvano M. *Piety and Power: The Role of the Italian American Parishes in the New York Metropolitan Area, 1880–1930.* Staten Island, N.Y.: Center for Migration Studies, 1975.

Towler, Robert. *Homo Religiosus: Sociological Problems in the Study of Religion.* New York: St. Martin's, 1974.

Trachtenberg, Joshua. *Jewish Magic and Superstition: A Study in Folk Religion.* New York: Atheneum, 1974.

Tracy, Joseph. *The Great Awakening: A History of the Revival of Religion in the Time of Edwards and Whitefield.* Boston: Tappan and Sennet, 1842.

Trine, Ralph Waldo. *In Tune with the Infinite.* New York: Thomas Y. Crowell, 1897.

Trobridge, George. *Swedenborg: Life and Teaching.* 4th rev. ed. New York: 1935.

Troeltsch, Ernst. *The Social Teaching of the Christian Churches.* 2 vols. Translated by Olive Wyon. New York: Macmillan, 1931. 1:328–54, 380–83; 2:699–703, 805–7, 993–1000.

Trotter, An R. "Paradise Lost: Religious Theme-parks in the Southern United States." M.A. thesis, New York University, 1991.

Trumbull, J. Hammond, ed. *Public Records of the Colony of Connecticut, 1636–1776.* Hartford, Conn.: Case, Lockwood and Brainard, 1850.

Tucker, Stephen R. "Pentecostalism and Popular Culture in the South: A Study of Four Musicians." *Journal of Popular Culture* 16 (Winter 1982): 68–80.

Tull, Charles J. *Father Coughlin and the New Deal.* Syracuse, N.Y.: Syracuse University Press, 1965.

Turner, William C., Jr. "Black Evangelicalism: Theology, Politics, and Race." *Journal of Religious Thought* 45 (Winter–Spring 1989): 40–56.

———. "The Musicality of Black Preaching." *Journal of Black Sacred Music* 2 (Spring 1988): 21–34.

Tweedie, Stephen W. "Viewing the Bible Belt." *Journal of Popular Culture* 11 (1978): 865–76.

United Methodist Hymnal. Nashville: United Methodist Publishing House, 1989.

Utley, Robert M. *The Last Days of the Sioux Nation.* New Haven: Yale University Press, 1963.

Van Allen, Rodger. *The Commonweal and American Catholicism: The Magazine, the Movement, the Meaning.* Philadelphia: Fortress, 1974.

Vaughn, William Preston. *The Antimasonic Party in the United States, 1826–1843.* Lexington: University Press of Kentucky, 1983.

Vecoli, Rudolph J. "Cult and Occult in Italian-American Culture: The Persistence of a Religious Heritage." In *Immigrants and Religion in Urban Culture.*

Edited by Randall M. Miller and Thomas D. Marzik. Philadelphia: Temple University Press, 1977. 25–47.

———. "Prelates and Peasants: Italian Immigrants and the Catholic Church." *Journal of Social History* 2 (Spring 1969): 217–68.

Veverka, Fayette Breaux. *"For God and Country": Catholic Schooling in the 1920s.* New York: Garland, 1988.

Vrijhof, Pieter. "Official and Popular Religion in Twentieth-Century Western Christianity." In *Official and Popular Religion: Analysis of a Theme for Religious Studies.* Edited by Pieter Vrijhof and Jacques Waardenburg. The Hague: Mouton, 1979. 217–43.

Wacker, Grant. "The Holy Spirit and the Spirit of the Age in American Protestantism, 1880–1920." *Journal of American History* 72 (1985): 45–62.

———. "Pentecostalism." In *Encyclopedia of the American Religious Experience.* Edited by Charles H. Lippy and Peter W. Williams. New York: Charles Scribner's Sons, 1988. 2:933–45.

———. "Searching for Norman Rockwell: Popular Evangelicalism in Contemporary America." In *The Evangelical Tradition in America.* Edited by Leonard I. Sweet. Macon, Ga.: Mercer University Press, 1984. 289–315.

Wagner, Melinda Bollar. *God's Schools: Choice and Compromise in American Society.* New Brunswick, N.J.: Rutgers University Press, 1990.

———. "Metaphysics in Midwestern America." *Journal of Popular Culture* 17 (Winter 1983): 131–40.

———. *Metaphysics in Midwestern America.* Columbus: Ohio State University Press, 1983.

Wallace, Anthony F. C. *The Death and Rebirth of the Seneca.* New York: Knopf, 1970.

"Wanted: A Miracle of Good Weather and 'Youth for Christ' Rally Got It." *Newsweek* 25 (11 June 1945): 84.

Ward, Mrs. Humphrey. *Robert Elsmere.* Chicago: J. S. Ogilvie, 1888.

Ward, Louis B. *Father Charles E. Coughlin: An Authorized Biography.* Detroit: Tower Publications, 1933.

Warner, Susan. *The Wide, Wide World.* New York: G. P. Putnam, 1850.

Washington, James M. "Origins of Black Evangelicalism and the Ethical Function of Evangelical Cosmology." *Union Seminary Quarterly Review* 32 (Winter 1977): 104–16.

Watts-Jones, Dee. "The Harvest of Kwanzaa." *Essence* 21 (December 1990): 114.

Webber, Andrew Lloyd, and Tim Rice. "Trial before Pilate." *Jesus Christ Superstar.* London: Leeds Music, 1969.

Weber, Timothy P. *Living in the Shadow of the Second Coming: American Premillennialism, 1875–1982.* Enl. ed. Grand Rapids, Mich.: Zondervan, 1983.

Weber, Max. "The Protestant Sects and the Spirit of Capitalism." In *From Max Weber: Essays in Sociology.* Translated by Hans H. Gerth and C. Wright Mills. New York: Oxford University Press, 1946. 302–22.

———. *Sociology of Religion.* Translated by Ephraim Fischoff. Boston: Beacon Press, 1963. 95–117.

Weigle, Marta. *Brothers of Light, Brothers of Blood: The Penitentes of the Southwest.* Albuquerque: University of New Mexico, 1976.

Weinrich, Beatrice S. "The Americanization of Passover." In *Studies in Biblical and*

Jewish Folklore. Edited by Raphael Patai, Francis Lee Utley, and Dov Noy. Bloomington: Indiana University Press, 1960. 329–66.

Weisman, Richard. *Witchcraft, Magic, and Religion in Seventeenth Century Massachusetts*. Amherst: University of Massachusetts Press, 1984.

Weiss, Richard. *The American Myth of Success: From Horatio Alger to Norman Vincent Peale*. New York and London: Basic Books, 1969.

Welter, Barbara. "The Cult of True Womanhood, 1820–1860." *American Quarterly* 18 (Summer 1966): 151–74.

———. "The Feminization of American Religion: 1800–1860." In *Clio's Consciousness Raised: New Perspectives on the History of Women*. Edited by Mary S. Hartman and Lois Banner. New York: Harper and Row, 1974. 136–57.

Westerhoff, John H. *McGuffey and His Readers: Piety, Morality, and Education in Nineteenth Century America*. Nashville: Abingdon Press, 1978.

Wheeler, Sir Mortimer. *Civilizations of the Indus Valley and Beyond*. New York: McGraw-Hill, 1966.

———. *The Indus Civilization*. Supplementary volume to the *Cambridge History of India*. Cambridge, Eng.: Cambridge University Press, 1953.

White, Charles E. *The Beauty of Holiness: Phoebe Palmer as Theologian, Revivalist, Feminist, and Humanitarian*. Grand Rapids, Mich.: Zondervan [Francis Asbury Press], 1986.

White, James W., and John G. Hallsten. "Campus Crusade Goes Suburban." *Christian Century* 89 (1972): 549–51.

Whiting, Marvin Yeoman. "Religious Literature in Virginia, 1685–1786: A Preface to a Study in the History of Ideas." M.A. thesis, Emory University, 1975.

Whitmore, William H., ed. *The Colonial Laws of Massachusetts*. Boston: City Council, 1889.

Wigglesworth, Michael. *The Day of Doom; or, a Poetical Description of the Great and Last Judgment*. Cambridge, Mass.: S. Green, 1666.

Wilhoit, Mel R. "Sing Me a Song: Ira D. Sankey and Congregational Singing." *The Hymn* 42 (January 1991): 13–19.

Wilkinson, Ronald Sterne. "The Alchemical Library of John Winthrop, Jr. (1606–1676) and His Descendants in Colonial America." *Ambix* 11 (February 1963): 33–51; 13 (October 1966): 139–86.

———. "New England's Last Alchemists." *Ambix* 10 (October 1972): 128–38.

Willard, Frances. *Women in the Pulpit*. Chicago: Women's Temperance Publishing Association, 1889.

Williams, Michael. *The Shadow of the Pope*. New York: Whittlesey House, 1932.

Williams, Peter W. "Fulton J. Sheen." In *Twentieth-Century Shapers of American Popular Religion*. Edited by Charles H. Lippy. Westport, Conn.: Greenwood, 1989. 387–93.

———. *Popular Religion in America: Symbolic Change and the Modernization Process in Historical Perspective*. Englewood Cliffs, N.J.: Prentice-Hall, 1980.

Williams, Samuel. *The Natural and Civil History of Vermont*. Walpole, N.H.: Isaiah Thomas and David Carlisle, 1794; 2d ed., Burlington, Vt.: Samuel Mills, 1809.

Wills, Garry. *Bare Ruined Choirs: Doubt, Prophecy, and Radical Religion.* Garden City, N.Y.: Doubleday, 1971.

Wilmore, Gayraud S., and James H. Cone, eds. *Black Theology: A Documentary History, 1966–1979.* Maryknoll, N.Y.: Orbis, 1979.

Wilson, Bryan R. *Magic and the Millennium: A Sociological Study of Religious Movements of Protest among Tribal and Third-World Peoples.* London: Heinemann, 1973.

Wilson, Charles Reagan. *Baptized in Blood: The Civil Religion of the Lost Cause, 1865–1920.* Athens: University of Georgia Press, 1980.

Wilson, Elizabeth. *Fifty Years of Association Work among Young Women, 1866–1916.* New York: National Board of the Young Women's Christian Association of the United States of America, 1916. Reprinted, New York and London: Garland, 1987.

Wilson, Thane. "Russell H. Conwell: Who Has Helped 3,000 Young Men to Succeed." *American Magazine* 81 (April 1916): 15.

Wimberly, Robert C., et al. "Conversion in a Billy Graham Crusade: Spontaneous Event or Ritual Performance." *Sociological Quarterly* 16 (1975): 162–70.

Wimmer, John R. "Russell H. Conwell." In *Twentieth-Century Shapers of American Popular Religion.* Edited by Charles H. Lippy. Westport, Conn.: Greenwood, 1989. 80–88.

Winshop, Michael P. "Cotton Mather, Astrologer." *New England Quarterly* 63 (June 1990): 308–14.

Wittenmeyer, Annie Turner. *Women's Work for Jesus.* New York: Nelson and Phillips, 1873. Reprinted, New York: Garland, 1987.

Wolfe, Charles M. "Presley and the Gospel Tradition." *Southern Quarterly* 19 (Fall 1979): 135–50.

Woods, Ralph L., and Henry Woods. *Pilgrim Places in North America.* New York and Toronto: Longman, Green, 1939.

Wright, H. Elliott. "Jesus on Stage: A Reappraisal." *Christian Century* 89 (19 July 1972): 785–86.

Wright, Louis B. *First Gentlemen of Virginia: Intellectual Qualities of the Early Colonial Ruling Class.* San Marino, Calif.: Huntington Library, 1940.

———. "Pious Reading in Colonial Virginia." *Journal of Southern History* 6 (1940): 383–92.

Wuthnow, Robert. *Experimentation in American Religion: The New Mysticisms and Their Implications for the Churches.* Berkeley: University of California Press, 1978.

———. *The Restructuring of American Religion: Society and Faith since World War II.* Princeton, N.J.: Princeton University Press, 1988.

"Youth for Christ." *Time* 47 (4 February 1946): 46–47.

Zeik, Michael. *New Christian Communities: Origins, Style, and Survival.* Williston, N.Y.: Roth, 1973.

Zophy, Angela Marie Howard. "For the Improvement of My Sex: Sarah Josepha Hale's Editorship of Godey's Lady's Book, 1837–1877." Ph.D. diss., Ohio State University, 1978.

Zwier, Robert. *Born-Again Politics: The New Christian Right in America.* Downers Grove, Ill.: InterVarsity, 1982.

Index

About the Author

CHARLES H. LIPPY is Professor of Religion at Clemson University. His previous works include *Seasonable Revolutionary: The Mind of Charles Chauncey* (1981); *Religious Periodicals of the United States* (1986); *The Christadelphians in North America* (1989); and *Christianity Comes to the Americas, 1492–1776* (co-authored, 1992). He is the editor of *Twentieth-Century Shapers of American Popular Religion*, and co-editor of the three-volume *Encyclopedia of the American Religious Experience*. His numerous articles have appeared in *Journal of Religious Studies*, *Journal of Church and State*, *Eighteenth Century Life*, and the *Journal of Popular Culture*.

ISBN 0-313-27895-4

90000>

EAN

9 780313 278952

HARDCOVER BAR CODE